THREE STRIDES
BEFORE THE WIRE

THREE STRIDES BEFORE THE WIRE

THE DARK AND BEAUTIFUL WORLD

OF HORSE RACING

ELIZABETH MITCHELL

HYPERION

NEW YORK

ISBN: 0-7868-6723-X

Hyperion books are available for special promotions and premiums. For details contact
Hyperion Special Markets, 77 West 66th Street, 11th floor, New York, New York, 10023,
or call 212-456-0100.

FIRST EDITION

Designed by Ruth Lee

2 4 6 8 10 9 7 5 3 1

To Eldon, Gypsie, Sally, and the Fulgham family

ACKNOWLEDGMENTS

My deepest gratitude goes to Toby Bryce for his abundant patience, support, and astute editorial advice throughout the writing of this book; I am forever in debt. My agent, Jane Gelfman, went above and beyond the call of duty with good humor and intelligence since the day this book was signed up, and I would like to thank Cathy Gleason and Kelly Gillespie in her office as well. To the team of readers who offered their crucial perspectives at top speed: Michael Klein, René Steinke, Liz Mitchell, Alphonsus Mitchell, Darcey Steinke, Rob Reynolds, Carl Robbins, and Craig Marks. To my friend William Nack, who has been a generous and peerless guide through the world of horse racing. Also Mike Tanner, Anne Marie Mushinsky, Deb Hayes, Jane Carson, and the many turf writers whose reporting over the years formed the spine of this book.

My research editors Priscilla Ryan, Gene Park, Christina Del Valle, and Allison Joyner put in an extra effort when I needed it most. I appreciate the time and effort that so many people I interviewed dedicated to this project, particularly Tom and Robyn Roach, Bob and Beverly Lewis, Kellie and Vladimir Cerin, Greg Roberts, Drew Mollica, and the Antley family.

My thanks to the people at Hyperion who produced this book: Leigh Haber, Cassie Mayer, and Donna Ellis.

And finally to Natalie Standiford, Craig Lively, Chris Mitchell, Ann Mitchell, Hawes Bostic, Bruce Kluger, Austin McKenna, Paul O'Donnell, Jessica Marshall, Mark Woodruff, Ned Martel, Matt Berman, RoseMarie Terenzio, Judy Hottensohn, Collin Wilson, Jerry and Cindy Bryce, Leigh Anne Fitzpatrick, Richard Howorth, Moyra Rondon, Jerry and Kathy at J.R., Kelly Ann Barry, Darnell Powell, Trish Jones, Ed Mitchell, Sam Mitchell, and my favorite reader Will Mitchell, who contributed in their own ways to the creation of this book.

CONTENTS

THREE STRIDES
BEFORE THE WIRE

ONE

DREAM TRIP

The meteorologists of Louisville, Kentucky, could not quite believe how perfectly calibrated the barometric pressure was that first Saturday in May 1999. The skies were as blue as the bottom of a freshly painted pool. The white clapboard steeples of Churchill Downs, which had loomed over thoroughbred races since the turn of the century, were brilliant in the sunshine. That spring, La Niña, the rare weather phenomenon chilling the waters at the equator thirty-five hundred miles away, had communicated its meteorological message north, and now Louisville, and more specifically, the crowds gathering for the last Kentucky Derby of the millennium, were wallowing in heat and happiness. I was there with a man whom I adored. He was tanned, gaining muscle, and proudly cultivating a head of baby-soft hair. It was the first time we had ever been to a thoroughbred track and a perfect day to fall in love with racing.

Only nine weeks earlier, this man—Chuck Fulgham—had emerged from the hospital after a second month of chemotherapy treatments without hair, eyelashes, eyebrows; with fingernails peeling off at the thickened tips. Over those many weeks of his treatment for leukemia at Baylor

Hospital in Dallas, he had dwindled around his bones until he was just a six-foot four-inch wraith who got winded walking across a room. But he had rallied back in that vivid, love-infused spring, and it was for that reason Chuck and I felt our very presence among the drunken, happy hordes of the Churchill Downs infield was a victory, no matter what happened for us at the betting windows.

We had decided to make the trip to Louisville just two days before. Chuck was at the tail end of a five-week stay at my New York home when he saw a brief mention of the upcoming Derby in the newspaper. He was supposed to head back to Dallas, where he had been living in miserable limbo in the hospital and at his father's house ever since the gloomy December day in Mississippi he suddenly learned he had acute myelogenous leukemia.

But the newspaper item sparked a discussion that maybe we should go. Perhaps he should delay his return home and we should go to the Derby, because surely that was the lesson of life: that, within reason, you never regret what you do, but only what you fail to do. Here was the opportunity to be the kind of people we intended to be for the rest of our days—the sort who don't let logistical obstacles or fatigue block them from the thrill of life.

The plan fell into order quickly, with even a place to stay at the home of a man so many steps removed from our acquaintance the situation was almost comic. The rental car buoyed us over thirteen hours of serpentine highway, mainly through West Virginia with its endless broccoli-green forests, and in truth, the marathon drive did leave us in Louisville dizzy and a little grumpy. But we went to bed content, and when we awoke that morning, we were so happy to see each other that Chuck immediately asked, "What did you dream?" as if to account for the time we were apart in sleep.

I did remember my dream. It began with an old lady desperately trying to enroll her greyhound in the Kentucky Derby and segued into a scene in an art gallery at my old college. I was walking through an exhibit when a man hurried up to me. "Do you think the paintings have charisma?" he asked confidentially. I thought the word choice was odd. "I don't know," I said.

The man then led me on through the gallery as other strangers walked up and posed the same question: "Do the paintings have charisma?" "Do they have charisma?" Finally, as I finished the rounds, I paused and declared, "Yes. Yes, they do have charisma. Not enough to be in a museum or art gallery but they definitely have charisma. More than last year." Then I woke up.

That morning Chuck and I headed to Churchill Downs, to the neighborhood of houses where every year people sacrifice their lawns to make some cash parking the cars of spectators. In the infield, more than 150,000 people were just beginning the day's celebration. Emptied julep glasses with mint leaves plastered to the sides piled up around the trash cans. Shirtless college-age boys rang handbells and blew whistles to inspire girls to lift their shirts too. Near the betting windows, handicappers leaned on any surface they could find and calculated their wagers in pencil. Chuck and I bought a program and sat on a curb between the paddock and the grandstand to pick our horses.

And there, as we viewed the list of horses in the big eighth race for the first time—as fate, or coincidence, or the collision of molecules in the universe would have it—was a chestnut colt named Charismatic.

He was a true long shot, at 20 to 1 a horse not likely to even finish in the top four. I would like to say that because of my dream we were so certain of the magical properties of that animal that we did not hedge our bets and that our twenty-dollar vote of confidence went only to him. But we also picked General Challenge, the favorite, who was paired in the betting with another contender, Excellent Meeting; and Aljabr, owned by the sheik of Dubai, paired with Worldly Manner. I suspect Chuck made those choices because both were on split tickets where we thought we would win if either of the two horses crossed the finish line first. In fact, Aljabr had been scratched from the race days before. We were unsophisticated enough not to know that at the time, and optimistic and novice enough as bettors to put our money down only to win, not show or place or woven into a trifecta or other betting option. Those kinds of wagers would become familiar to us in time, but on this, our first visit to a track, they were exotic as unproved theorems. Instead we made a simple prediction of who would come in first.

We spent a happy afternoon wandering through the masses of people, betting occasionally, lying on the last remaining patch of untrampled grass out by the fence. When it came time for the eighth race, the Derby itself, we found a stretch of infield relatively empty of fans and stood there to watch the competition projected on a big screen.

The race went off. The announcer rattled off the names of the horses from the front of the pack to the trailers, but we never heard him mention Charismatic.

But when the horses headed down the homestretch, the announcer suddenly began describing Charismatic's surge, his charge past other horses, and we watched on the big screen as the magic slowly—in a few languorous seconds—transformed into a hard-driving, unchallenged reality that weirdly we watched from the inner circle of the track, our gaze glued to the images racing across the screen, while the actual horses thundered around us. I was screaming. Out of the corner of my eye, I could see Chuck's long limbs flailing and hear his Texas twang engaged in an urgent, ecstatic bark of "C'mon. C'mon." The chestnut colt pounded forward, pulling ahead. I wondered, in the slow motion of shock, if I was in fact watching a premonition come true. And then it seemed the announcer was screaming too, "Charismatic wins the Kentucky Derby! Charismatic wins the Kentucky Derby!" and Chuck and I were jumping and hugging in what seemed to be an otherwise silent field of people who had sent the horse off at the gate with even longer odds than those we thought we bet. They were now 31 to 1—the third longest odds, as it turned out, of any Derby winner in the 125 runnings of the race.

The jockey in his yellow and green silks raised one finger in the sign of victory as he sailed off into the postrace gallop past the clubhouse turn.

*   *   *

Months later, Chuck and I would talk about that moment as being probably the happiest we had yet experienced. It combined everything: the sun,
the drowsy happiness of love, the hope of health after grinding illness, the
dream, reality pouring into the mold of the supernatural in a way that
such particularly beguiling promises of childhood—Santa Claus, flying
carpets—had failed to do. And I was so happy, so blissful as I clung to
Chuck's whirling body, but also suppressing a slight static of sadness because I had dreamt a few months earlier that Chuck told me he had only
eighteen months to live, and I didn't want that dream to come true too.

As it turned out, we won $646, almost exactly matching our bill for
the rental car we had acquired at the last minute and which ate money
with every mile of road it grazed from New York to Louisville and back.
The woman at the payout counter was thrilled for us and our rare bet,
even signing our program next to Charismatic's name. Her friendliness
contrasted touchingly with the sullen looks we got from two men in sport
shirts and chinos in the line behind us who quizzed us about our method
of picking the horse until their necks stiffened.

The newspapers the day after the race expressed their shock that
such a long shot could win and allowed the fluke victory all the fractal
edges deadlines could accommodate. The main protagonists—Charismatic and jockey Chris Antley—were amazing comeback stories. Charismatic, reporters marveled, was a horse said to have had "a problem
with the feed bag," meaning that he overate and should never have lumbered to victory.

Perhaps the bettors should have suspected his potential because he
worked with the right people. His trainer was D. Wayne Lukas, a man
with flash, bravado, and a businessman's interest in the bottom line. His
owners, Bob and Beverly Lewis, had enjoyed more than their share of
triumphs over a decade of buying horses. But few people had guessed
the depth of Charismatic's talents.

He had won only one race as a two-year-old despite seven trips to
the starting gates, and the Lewises were about ready to unload him.

Lukas had tried every variation to inspire victory—running him on the turf course, with blinders to focus his attention, and with a half dozen different jockeys. But Charismatic's three-year-old season, as horse people call a horse's third year of life, began no better. Just three months before Derby day, Lukas ran him in a $62,500 claiming race, a contest in which any of the participating horses can be bought at the price listed by a person putting down a promissory note fifteen minutes before the start. That meant any horseman who had spotted Charismatic's hidden brilliance on that mid-February day in what could be considered the white elephant sale of racing could have paid $62,500, run him in the Derby, and won not only honor but $886,200 on that day alone.

Antley's story was equally remarkable. He had been grateful for the opportunity to ride *any* horse—tubby or not—in the Derby. A year and a half before, he had dropped out of racing after having been brought to the bottom of his career by a severe drug problem and a battle with extra pounds. For months, he watched his days pass from the couch at his father's house in South Carolina. They said he contemplated a career like his dad's with a utility company. Then one day, a horse race appeared on TV and Antley watched, gripped again by his love of the sport. He decided he wanted back in, which meant thinning down to the magic weight that allowed him access to the exclusive throne aboard the backs of thoroughbreds. He began running, often fifteen hours a day; spent so much time zipping along the streets and horizon of his small town that he became known there as Forrest Gump.

He eventually made the qualifying weight. One day, walking through a stable, he ran into Lukas, a trainer he had often worked for back when he was a star. Lukas asked Antley if he would like to ride one of his horses in the Derby. The horse was an extreme long shot, but Antley leapt at the chance because he would be back in the game. Back in the game was good enough for Antley.

The newspapers on the day after the Derby ran pictures of Antley in the winner's circle and stories of his high emotion at the event, how he had wept. "It's too far-fetched," Antley told a reporter, "too far-fetched. . . . I feel like I'm in the midst of a miracle."

And that was how Chuck and I would remember that race: Antley in his lime-green and neon-yellow silks, a man my own age with clear blue eyes, saddled on the sturdy red-brown Charismatic; Antley's tears falling on the blanket of roses draped over Charismatic's neck.

The great thing about horse racing is that once you experience an ecstatic moment at the track, you are granted access to a whole history of rapturous racing experiences anecdote by anecdote—from waitresses and doctors, business executives and children. Everyone wants to tell you their story of an amazing moment betting on thoroughbreds. It seems everyone had a favorite great-uncle who took them to the races in their humid youth, who studied the forms at the kitchen table and on the sly passed out five-dollar bills with which a five-year-old could wager. Or in their memories, they had a cherished horse that had run its shoes off to defeat the big-money competition. And I decided then that I would one day investigate life at the track, and find out why it brightened the eyes of people at New York City cocktail parties who minutes before had been morosely talking shop, or how for some, an interest in racing was tethered to a sore emotion, born from recollections of a father squandering lunch money. For those who worked the tracks, racing was an ordeal, and one with enormous ups and downs, which I recognized, since that was how 1999 seemed to be unfolding. Horse racing encompassed that volatility. "It's not easy," jockey agent Drew Mollica explained to me. "If you want to be on the racetrack, and you have an option to do that or climb Everest . . . climb Everest."

I planned to travel track to track so I could report on the professional life of racing. But on that trail a year later, I realized that everyone who worked the thoroughbred circuit seemed to have a horse story like mine, a story that meant that much to them—not just the soft-hearted track day-trippers like Chuck and me, but the trainers who had risen before dawn for decades and taken the guff of pompous owners, and the guys who worked the stallion barns, and the jockeys. For everyone I inter-viewed, buried in the bare facts of an arduous, sometimes tedious life working the barns was an experience of raw emotion and mystery entan-gled with the enigma of horses.

I wanted to find out if what happened for us that day was truly remarkable. To find out what had made a man back from the brink of fatal illness so happy on that first Saturday of May, a jockey weep on his horse's back. Like a handicapper in reverse, I would go back and trace the facts about Charismatic, about Antley, perhaps to find that nothing incredible had happened that day; that nothing unusual occurred when I dreamed the word *charisma* and then found the name attached to the long-shot horse; that there was nothing unique to the happiest day Chuck and I had experienced up to that point, that nothing special had happened under the La Niña sky. But horse people often took another view. "Always bet the love story," another jockey's agent once advised me. So I did.

TWO

DARK HORSE

Visitors to the racetrack can get seduced by thoroughbreds, watching the daily card of competition and hoping to turn two-dollar bets into dinner money, but the mornings, when the trainers take the horses out for their exercise—to breeze or gallop them—hook anyone who doesn't make their living working with the animals. The air is thick with the sweet smell of hay and oats and the sharp punch of manure. The tractors drive past, furrowing the soft dirt like frosting in a bowl. Usually one of the concessions in the grandstand facing the finish line opens to serve coffee to the clockers who time the horses' workouts. From the commercial kitchen on the backside, across from the grandstand, wafts the scent of more serious food, the smell of bacon and eggs cooked up for the trainers and jockeys. The grooms who tend the horses, "hotwalkers" who cool them down by leading them in slow circles after their gallops, and exercise riders who ride them during training hours eat there too when they can afford it.

The exercise riders look tough and sexy, athletic and responsible, in jeans, sometimes in chaps, in fiberglass caps and impact-absorbing foam vests, plaid flannel shirts, or occasionally a Che Guevara T-shirt. On some tracks, the riders wear helmets with electric lights in front, so in the predawn darkness they can easily be spotted skimming around the oval like fireflies. Occasionally a siren goes off and the riders stop their horses and wait. That wail signals that a horse has thrown his rider and is running wild on the course. One of the pony boys or pony girls goes after him and catches his bridle, and he's brought in. Then all goes back to normal: a river of horses always running that whirlpool.

A few female trainers and jockeys now work the track, and many of the exercise riders are strong ponytailed girls, but for the most part, the track backside is a fraternity. The trainers—mainly middle-aged white men—stand at the fence with their foam coffee cups or ride onto the freshly plowed dirt on docile ponies to give commands and assess the strength of their thoroughbreds. The jockey agents, usually track veterans tagged with nicknames like Doc and Ears, walk through the rows of barns trying, through sweet talk and salesmanship, to convince the trainers to book their jockeys on horses that week.

In the village of stables, the long white leg bandages used to wrap the horses' shins hang on the fences to dry and flutter in the breezes. The grooms slop fat white sponges of soapy water over the horses' backs to bathe them after their workouts, and every newcomer and every horse photographer gets dizzy from the beauty of the steam rising off the horses' hides. In some of the more homey barns, a thoroughbred stands gazing out above the webbing that holds him in his stall, perhaps with his goat beside him. These horses are notoriously high-strung and the constant presence of a goat can calm them down. They share the boredom of almost constant confinement together.

The horses seem perfectly formed for the human gaze—on a scale large enough to intimidate but small enough to be taken in at close range. They stand as if they know how many writers have tried to describe their presence—*noble, majestic*—and know too how words have failed to summarize their mystique, glancing off their hides and piling up around their hooves. The fine thoroughbreds have sculpted haunches, and chests that look like sacks of muscle suspended on stiletto legs. Their heads can look by turns comic and prehistoric.

The silhouette of the horse is crisp, the planes of its body silvery when they catch the light. Part of the awe inspired by the animal comes from the fact that you know, when you stand next to a horse, it could kill you if it chose to. Not that it wants to destroy you or is likely to, but the horse could knock your skull in with one clean shot of its hoof. Something about standing beside a racehorse and recognizing its colossal power, and then watching that same animal amiably accept a rider on its back and sail by, running with its muscles triggering one after another, using those potentially murderous hooves only to launch its tonnage higher and farther in the air, fills one with groveling gratitude.

Riding horses is now anachronistic. For most of human history, everyone from farmers to aristocrats had a working knowledge of and relationship to horses. In the last century, we parted ways and now only specific subcultures—cowboys, polo players, jockeys, urban cops, and fetishistic adolescent girls—continue the bond. Only a small fraction of that group will ever get to climb onto the back of a thoroughbred, a breed so valuable that typically no one over 140 pounds is allowed to mount them.

We as a species have put the horse out to pasture and channeled our obsession into cars. But in the world of the racetrack, that ancient passion flourishes. We invented the car and know its every working part, but the horse, the mode of transportation we used to explore much of the planet from desert to mountain pass, that helped us in our labors and carried us on our journeys, is still a mystery. The scene at the track, therefore, is often sentimental, since it appeals more to emotion than reason. People who work with thoroughbreds for a living—from hotwalkers to owners— admire a good handicapper who rakes in a healthy income every year by judging horseflesh and keeping detailed racing records. They respect a trainer who can diagnose a horse's ailment or run a business with hundreds of employees. But in the hierarchy of racing, those analytic skills pale beside the instinctual ability to connect to a horse.

*   *   *

The relationship between horse and man didn't come easily. We can trace back through the frothy unions of random horses in barns and paddocks, and before that in open fields, and follow that chain to the very first horses. "The history of the horse family," declared G. G. Simpson, the legendary curator of vertebrate paleontology at the American Museum of Natural History in New York, "is still one of the clearest and most convincing for showing that organisms really have evolved, for demonstrating that, so to speak, an onion can turn into a lily."

Imagine the eohippus, the "dawn horse"—a strange creature under a foot high, lifting its delicate snout to the warm wind. There he is in North America or in Europe, on an ordinary day some 54 million years ago, while volcanoes erupt with alarming frequency and a full menagerie of other mammals hunt and fight and mate in the jungle landscape around him. The small beast grazes in the tall grass and scrabbles at the rocks; instead of one hoof on each leg, he has four hooves on each limb up front, splaying out like meaty fingernails, and three hooves on each hind leg. The small fruit of his brain runs a continual chemical loop of reminders to eat, procreate, and sleep.

Then 47 million years pass—a time so long to the small fruit of our human brains we could call it eternity—and, through evolution, the eohippus grows taller. He sheds his useless extra hooves, his muzzle stretches, and his teeth learn to push upward against constant mastication so that the crown never wears out but always is fed by a reservoir of tooth buried deep inside the gum line. Those were the eohippus adaptations that could later be termed evolutionary improvements and not just dead ends. There apparently were many false starts too. The eohippus added features that failed to improve its lot in life or that were adaptations to a world that ceased to exist when the climate changed drastically, whether because a glacier crossed the continent like a colossal zamboni or a meteor plowed into the planet, sending the earth's red dust skyward like an umbrella opening to block the sun. Those eohippus lines died off.

But one eohippus line evolved in a way exactly suited to the development of the rest of the world and its creatures. Through the successful genetic line—from the eohippus, to the mesohippus, to the miohippus, the parahippus, and finally equus—the sculpting and shaving and stretching went on, with those legs unfurling like vines, and the snout lengthening, and the flesh growing less flabby, and the teeth developing a protective coating of cement over the enamel, and the bones finding more hinges and multiplying for quick starts and speed; and the brain, even more remarkably, growing larger, it is believed, to harness the power brewing within this new creature to run and run faster and faster.

Then eight thousand or ten thousand years ago, equus simply vanished from North and South America. The beast that knew this terrain for 54 million years, that evolved with its flora and fauna, and molded its muzzle and bones to this particular continent, disappeared. No one knows exactly why this happened. Some scientists speculate that humans ate too many of the equus or wasted them with the same primitive hunting technique of driving whole herds off of cliffs to their death that almost condemned the American buffalo to extinction. Other experts believe a rare virus swept through and felled the animal in droves. Fifty-one million years earlier, the continents started drifting apart, and the Bering land bridge to Asia, the last tender touch of land between the continents, was washed over. Horses that had journeyed to Asia were cut off from the American continent, and for some seven thousand years, the continent was horseless.

For millennia, humans considered horses to be only food, but gradually other uses for the animals evolved. (Up until the twelfth century, for example, the inauguration of an Irish king included a bath in horse soup. The king climbed into a vat in which a white mare had been boiled and ate the horseflesh and drank the broth.)[1] Around 4000 B.C., humans began to understand equine power more fully. Babylonian soldiers harnessed the animals to draw chariots in battle. In the millennium that followed, people began domesticating horses for labor and the mares for milking, and about that time they also realized horses could be used for sport.

The first horse races are thought to have been held in the Arabian

desert around 3000 B.C., when owners denied their horses water for days
and then set them loose to thunder across the sands to a distant spring.
By 2300 B.C., horse-drawn chariot competitions in India were formally
organized with substantial sums wagered on the outcomes. Early Romans, from the time of the city's founding in 753 B.C., went wild for
chariot racing. Hundreds of thousands of spectators packed the circuses
and screamed themselves hoarse watching up to fifty starts a day
(compared to a typical modern race day of eight or nine). The races
encompassed nearly six miles—much greater distances than the thoroughbred competitions one finds today at Belmont or Churchill Downs;
the chariots stirred the tracks in a whirlpool of dust from dawn to
nightfall. As chariots shattered against the walls and riders were trapped
like bugs in the webs of tangled reins, bettors wagered enormous fortunes
on the outcome. The largest and most spontaneous bets (*audax sponsio*)
were lauded as a sign that the gambler did not care about parting with
money, slaves and concubines, and thus was noble; only lowly people
would mourn the loss of material possessions.[2]

But still humans had not embraced the idea of a union of horse and
human rider, since climbing on board a horse's back seemed too odd and
uncomfortable. In the eighteenth century B.C., King Zimri-Lim of Mari
received a letter telling him he should preserve his dignity by riding in
a chariot or on a mule, but not on a horse, probably since horse sweat
was considered filthy.[3] In the *Iliad*, written around 700 B.C., Homer
describes horseback riding as a "gymnastic display of no practical value."[4]
The first time horse and rider races were held at the Olympics was in
720 B.C., forty-six years after the Games began.

From that point on, mounted horse racing became a widespread and
enduring human passion. Racing came to America by way of Britain,
which inherited racing through the Roman invasion of 55 A.D. Romans
brought Arab horses with them in their conquest, built roads and raced
their imported steeds against Celtic ponies.

Horses returned to America a little over a hundred years before racing got under way here. Seven thousand years had passed from the time

the last horse migrated from the Americas across the Bering land bridge to Asia. In the late fifteenth century, wooden ships bearing Spanish explorers bobbed across the ocean and arrived on the American coast. The Spaniards lowered their planks and the horse, so many generations removed from its North American progenitor, descended on its sinewy legs, plopping its hooves onto ancestral soil once again. The first importer is thought to be Christopher Columbus, who, on his second voyage to America, brought thirty horses on his three ships.[5]

When the first settlers arrived on the eastern seaboard of the New World they imported the racing of their native Britain. In 1665, the first governor of New York, the Englishman Richard Nicholls, commissioned the first racing track in America on Long Island. He hoped that Newmarket, named after the illustrious British track, would forward a serious mission. The track was intended "not so much for the divertissement of youth as for encouraging the betterment of the improvement of the breed of horses, which through great neglect has been impaired."[6] Racing at the track supplemented the competitions in other New York towns, as well as hamlets in Virginia and Kentucky, where a few times a year farmers ran their best stock against neighbors' horses on "race paths."

The Greeks tried to explain how a creature as lovely as the horse could come to be. One story goes that Poseidon, brother of Zeus and ruler of the seas, fell madly, wildly in love with his own sister, the beautiful Demeter, but she showed him no interest. She could not, she said, give herself to him, unless he proved his love by inventing for her the most beautiful being by anyone's measure. Poseidon labored away and concocted the horse. Another version of that myth has Poseidon slaving over his invention, producing one animal after another that missed the mark of unquestionable beauty, until he finally hit upon his equine masterpiece. Demeter was delighted with her final gift. But alas, during Poseidon's long struggles, he lost the kindling of his enchantment with her, and the project ended with no amorous payoff except that the world now was graced with this divine being.

*   *   *

Unquestionable beauty. That's what Tom Roach was after as he sat at his kitchen table nearly four thousand years later dreaming horses, with darkness settling over his farm and the mares rustling in their stalls. He could see the perfect horse. He could run his eyes along the length of its neck, with just the right stretch to balance the thrust of its flanks. He could scan the horizon of its strong back, its long muscular legs. The animal didn't exist yet, but he could imagine its every feature as he sat with the pedigree charts spread in front of him in the big Victorian house at his Parrish Hill Farm in Midway, Kentucky.

In the chilled mornings of October, after the racing season at Keeneland was ended and between the track's auctions, Roach drove to the stallion farms to look over the new talent. The trailers that rolled along the highways spoking out from Lexington and leading to the farm country carried the track stars of the previous year. Now they were shipping to various breeding outfits to be put to work impregnating mares at a cost of anywhere from $2,500 to $400,000 an attempt. They came off the trailers ready to spend the rest of their lives reproducing, heaving themselves onto the backs of broodmares from mid-February to mid-June. Roach began studying them to see which of the Parrish Hill mares could be grafted to them to create a perfect runner. He sat at his computer in the office a hundred yards from the big house and plugged in hypothetical pedigrees, stirring together bloodlines to calculate how much stamina the resulting horse would have, how long its pasterns, giving it spring from the hoof, might be. Four or five studs copulated with each mare in his imaginings and he compared the offspring to see which one was most beautiful.

Each horse Tom Roach crafted was another paving stone in the genetic path of thoroughbred blood that began in the late seventeenth century when British racing enthusiasts realized their equine stock needed improvement and began importing horses from the Middle East for breeding. Three of those stallions were particularly remarkable and now, through the male line, account for every thoroughbred racing today. The Darley Arabian, born in Syria, was said to be the loveliest horse ever seen. A British government official, Thomas Darley, shipped him to his homeland from the port of Aleppo.[7] The Byerly Turk was a military charger captured from a Turkish officer by Captain Byerly in Hungary.[8] And the third horse is said to have entered equine history with a story to rival that of all those Hollywood starlets who were serving up sundaes in backwater ice cream parlors when the talent scouts spotted them: The Godolphin Barb was "discovered" pulling a water cart in Paris. Another account places his origin slightly later in history, saying he was born in Yemen in 1724, then followed a circuitous path from Syria to Tunis to the stables of Louis XV of France, where he was rejected. The earl of Godolphin in Britain bought him, and the Godolphin Barb went on to provide the sire line for the great champion Man o' War.[9]

Those three original stallions will account for all the horses running far into the future, horse by horse through generations—Hastings begetting Fair Play, begetting Man o' War, begetting War Admiral, and on—until that point when the genetic webbing becomes so redundant it describes only fragility. Then foreign spunk will need to be added again to the breed for muscle and bone strength, and the chain continued.

Beginning in 1791, all thoroughbred unions in England were recorded in the *General Stud Book* by a man named James Weatherby to track the genetic lines of every thoroughbred. In the first one hundred years of this controlled mating, breeders increased the potential speed of thoroughbreds by 2 percent. In 1894 the American Jockey Club was founded as the mirror of the British organization. Its main task has been to maintain the *American Stud Book*, a genealogical record of all thoroughbreds for the United States, Canada and Puerto Rico. The first full thoroughbred to arrive in the United States was Bulle Rock in 1730.

The Jockey Club guards procreation in this discrete animal community with the discipline of a Mother Superior standing watch over a convent of young nuns and the mandate of a bordello. The organization ensures all thoroughbreds are conceived by "natural cover," through direct penetration of a thoroughbred mare by a thoroughbred stallion. Each horse then must begin as an act of specific lust. Most horse breeding—for dressage or quarter-horse racing—allows artificial insemination, with the sperm shipped by mail between breeders. But in the thorough-bred community, regulators fear that a wily and amoral breeder could slip lower-tier sperm—the seed of a less important horse pawned off as the seed of a superstar, for example, or even worse, the sperm of a horse outside the thoroughbred line—into one of those vials and with one evil injection contaminate the entire ancestral line that has run unbroken for some three hundred years.

The horses did the deed, but Tom Roach played God, as he liked to say. This was the only profession he could think of where a person got to toy with genetic destiny and then test the results in action—in this case on the track. One of the most commonly applied genetic predictors for how well a horse would run is the dosage theory. This mathematical computation created by Dr. Steven Roman in the 1980s derived from the pedigree studies of Dr. Franco Varolo earlier in that century. The formula worked with five categories of sire, from Brilliant to Professional. Each sire was given a number based on its strength and stamina, and the direct sire counted four times more than the sires going back four generations. Once calculated, a number below 4.0 was considered best since it indicated that the horse possessed as much stamina as speed. Such a horse wouldn't just burn out in five furlongs but could run in the stakes races that were over a mile, particularly the races of the prestigious Triple Crown—the Kentucky Derby, the Preakness, and the Belmont.

But the Dosage Index only took the male line into account, and because of that, Roach thought it was too simple as a mode of prediction. Life was more complicated. And besides, Tom Roach felt quite sure that the mother mattered more than the father. After all, she raised the foal, and fed the foal with her milk. Parrish Hill Farm focused on the mares.

This wasn't a new profession for Roach. He had been imagining perfect horses for thirty-seven years, since he was a boy of about ten. His great-granduncle, Jim Parrish, who founded their farm, would go over the prospects with his nephew, Tom Roach I (Tom's grandfather), who stood to inherit the farm. They would plot their best hopes for the coming breeding season—which stud should impregnate which mare to ignite the biological explosion of a stakes winner; which stallion and mare could be combined to carry genetic inheritances onward, preserving the cellular memory of greatness without introducing too many flaws to a perfect line. And young Tom himself would go through the stud books, draft a wish list, and then pester his grandfather to take one of his choices. He rarely if ever got one of his dream matches approved. As a boy, his tastes were too expensive; he always seemed to pick the stallions whose stud fees hovered out of reach.

Old Jim Parrish had been the area's biggest banker, but he loved the horse track far more than he did the bank. He built the buttermilk-colored brick house with the terra cotta roof in 1910. The rust and light yellow hues became the farm's racing colors. Unlike the larger breeding farms of Claiborne out in Paris, Kentucky, or Lane's End down the road in Versailles, this place looked rumpled—the farm that just got out of bed or went unshaven for the weekend, with tall pin oak, cherry and white pine trees growing where it seemed nature chose, with brambled shrubs, a rabbit hutch, and a bunch of mismatched dogs and cats arriving and departing without a call or whistle as cue. The secret to those strong horse bones lay in the soil, the area breeders believed. Limestone infused the famed bluegrass with minerals, and when the horses grazed in the paddocks, the grass fed the white strength of stone into the white strength of bone.

The farm had bred thirty stakes winners since its beginning, but never a horse that won the Kentucky Derby. A victory in that race meant the most of any horse-racing win to most Americans, and to a Kentuckian meant eternal happiness. Jim Parrish and his good friend Colonel E. R. Bradley from Idle Hour Stock Farm looked over their crops of yearlings each winter and placed bets on which would win which race first. Parrish accumulated a fair amount of pocket change on the wagering, but he never claimed a victory where it really counted for him. He watched Bradley realize the dream of breeding and raising a Derby winner four times. The best Parrish's stock produced was a 1917 third-place finisher, Midway.[10]

From 1875, when the Louisville Jockey Club and Driving Park Association opened—the track that would later be rechristened Churchill

Downs—Kentucky racing weathered a roller coaster of sentiment from local horse lovers and antigambling advocates. By the time Jim Parrish built Parrish Hill Farm, the state's horse-racing business had hit its nadir—undercut continuously by puritan campaigns against wagering—and teetered on the brink of a complete collapse.

What happened up North affected Kentucky. On May 26, 1910, the New York legislature passed the Agnew-Perkins Bill, which held the directors of racing associations criminally responsible for betting at the tracks—whether through bookmakers or through the new pari-mutuel machines, which combined all bets on a race and determined the odds and payout for a win. Five days later, the New York Jockey Club shut down the state's racing for fear their executives would be thrown in jail. New York represented the biggest racing market and soon horse breeders began shipping their horses to South America, France and England in search of racing or breeding opportunities. One after the other, the top racing countries—first Argentina, then England and France—shut their farms to American stock because they didn't want a foreign invasion. Finally American horse breeders started shipping to Australia and Russia.

In 1922, Alben W. Barkley, a U.S. congressman from Paducah, Kentucky, campaigning for governor, crusaded to end horse racing statewide. He hammered on about the evils of the track, but the local horse breeders refused to let their beloved sport go the way of alcohol with Prohibition and rallied to defeat him. Barkley lost, the horse breeders won, and racing was saved in Kentucky. (Barkley was not completely vanquished, however; he later became Harry Truman's running mate, but never again tangled with horse-racing enthusiasts in the political forum.)[11]

Through the ebb and flow of the sport's overall fortunes, the passion of the local breeders never flagged and they passed that obsession on to future generations. As the Depression eased its grip, Lexington businessmen built a track called Keeneland that redistributed its profits to local charities and became a haven of quality racing, and that's where Tom Roach's clan tested their horses first.

Old Jim Parrish died around 1940, and his widow, Lilly, lived in the big house for twenty more years, until she died at age ninety-five. Then

Tom's grandfather and his father, Dr. Ben Roach, took over, and the family moved from the town of Midway out to the farm for good. Dr. Roach maintained a busy practice delivering babies, which financed his racing passion.

From the age of twelve on Tom learned more about the actual needs of horses, from mucking their stables to filling their oat buckets. He planned when he was older to continue the family's horse breeding, but saw how volatile the business could be, and knew firsthand that it was best to have another source of income to back up the interest.

So Tom went off to Duke University for his undergraduate years and then to the University of Kentucky for law school. In the mid-'60s, Dr. Roach became interested in converting Parrish Hill from a family racing farm to a full-time breeding business. He hired additional staff, including a manager, bought more mares and fixed up the buildings. In 1972, when Tom was two years into law school, his father called to tell him the farm manager had made so much money from his percentage take on the breeding that he had gone off and bought his own farm. If Tom harbored any interest in taking over Parrish Hill, his father told him, this was the moment.

Tom was living with his girlfriend, Robyn Pulley, who would soon become his wife and also hailed from Midway; they had known each other since junior high, when they sat across from each other in class, and argued constantly. After college, they ran into each other and the dynamic between them turned out to be romance. After his father's call, Tom and Robyn debated what to do and finally said yes. Robyn had worked with horses and been in the Pony Club as a young girl, so she would prove a savvy business partner.

Roach now tested the theories he worked out for himself in boyhood. He still looked and acted like that old self, with a slight build and brown hair cut like a schoolboy's. He could get that same giddy enthusiasm and talk anybody's ear off if they had the time. But now instead of just advising breeding matches, Roach ran the equine laboratory that stretched over three hundred acres.

In Tom Roach's mind a breeder's job was to guide nature, to train her mysterious forces to head a certain way. Starting in the late winter, Roach and his workers led a teaser—a virile stallion—around each day to the mares on the farm. The teaser sniffed the mare, and if he got excited, Roach knew the mare was in heat. Then it was on to the next mare for the poor frustrated teaser. Roach didn't believe in the hormone injections that the bigger farms used to trick a mare into getting ready sooner in the season. You got a foal earlier, when it was too cold to let it out in the paddock to run and build up muscle, and the mare couldn't gallop off the extra weight after birth. The ground would be too hard for bluegrass. It was better to let nature do her work and simply be ready to help.

As soon as the teaser let Roach know a mare was in heat, Roach called the stallion barns and set up an appointment for the big event. Then the vet came and palpated the mare. He needed to check that she had a good breedable follicle on her ovary. Maybe she had a follicle at one out of four, so you set the breeding appointment for a week out, when you thought she would be ready to release a good-size egg.

The day of the appointment Roach loaded the mare into the trailer and drove her over to a breeding farm to meet her stallion. The procedure basically went the same way each time. A teaser nuzzled the mare again to get her ready. Then one of the stallion men led the prize stud to the breeding barn, and the chain on the stallion's bridle rattled like the fetters of a galley slave as he bowed his neck and threw his head up to the sky. He minced down the path and showed his teeth and whinnied.

Sometimes the men led in a mare teaser to get the stallion worked into a lather. The stallion sniffed her and stiffened, his erection extending halfway up his stomach. He prepared to plow her. Then the stallion men led the teased teaser away. (At many farms, the managers eventually let the male and female teasers have one good go at it, late in the season— like the scullery maid and the gardener tussling in the smokehouse; the offspring would be born into the same class as a teaser or a nurse mare.) If the stud couldn't keep from fooling with himself, the men slipped a cock ring on him.

The stallion men hitched back one of the mare's hind legs so she wouldn't kick. They took a twitch—a loop of nylon rope at the end of a stick—and put it over her muzzle. They twisted the loop so a section of her lip and muzzle bulged out, and all of her attention became focused on that discomfort instead of what was about to happen behind her. A stallion man clucked his tongue and the stud reared up on his hind legs and beached his body on her back. The men guided him in. His front legs scrambled along her sides. He clamped his teeth on her neck. If the first attempt didn't work, he dismounted. The stallion man clucked again, and the stud lunged. ("Not too many candlelight dinners here," a stallion man at another breeding farm once observed to me.)

It used to be that you checked days later to see if the mare was in foal by bringing a stallion around to sniff the mare again. If the stallion became excited, they repeated the process at the breeding shed. If he didn't get aroused, chances were the mare was pregnant. Unfortunately, the stallion's lack of interest also could be caused by the mysteries of mutual attraction, so breeders welcomed a more reliable system. By the late 1990s, ultrasound allowed a breeder to see the foal fetus as early as sixteen days after conception.

There was a strong market by the time Roach got into the business. The Keeneland auctions had been drawing buyers from around the world to Lexington twice a year since 1944, and all the wealthy horse owners or their proxies rolled into town to throw their fortunes at those beautiful animals. Then a year after the Roaches started managing Parrish Hill, the superstar horse Secretariat, bred in Virginia, appeared like a comet on the national racing scene. For twenty-five years, no horse had won the Triple Crown, and racing officials had started talking about changing the lengths of the races, to make the prize more attainable. Then Secretariat arrived, not only winning all three, but winning them easily—triumphing in the final race, the Belmont, by thirty-one lengths. America went horse crazy, and the Roaches benefited from the exuberance. The Roaches bred the stakes winner Cormorant and then Princess Rooney. In 1984, Princess Rooney won the inaugural Breeders' Cup Distaff, which earned her a purse of $450,000. Not too long into the business the Roaches felt like they were doing something right.

*   *   *

Roach bred about forty foals a year. His operation was small compared to what went on over at the two-thousand-acre breeding farm Lane's End, just down the road. From the air, Lane's End looked like the design on some colossal cowboy shirt, with the paddock fences inscribing big loopy shapes across the shamrock-green grass. The farm housed twenty-four first-class stallions that could each impregnate anywhere from fifty to a hundred mares a season. Trailers rolled in and out of the gates all through the spring months bringing the mares to their rendezvous.

In 1996, the owner of Lane's End, Will Farish, offered Roach a deal. He would provide the stud Summer Squall, who won the Preakness in 1990, if Roach would provide a mare. They would then split ownership of the foal. In Roach's estimation, only one mare from Parrish Hill would do. Summer Squall was small and chunky, with short legs. The mare Bali Babe was husky as a draft horse but she had a long leg to counterbalance him. Two years earlier, Farish and Roach had made this match success-fully and sold the comely offspring, Constant Demand, at auction to the California owners Bob and Beverly Lewis. (Constant Demand had the potential to be a great runner, but the horse suffered from foot problems, probably brought on by the hard surface at Santa Anita, a top track near Los Angeles.) The Lewises also had bought another Bali Babe colt, Toss-ofthecoin, for $35,000 at Keeneland; he won a few races for them, then fetched $400,000 at auction. That second buyer went on to enjoy even more stakes victories and sold him for $1 million. So with a potential 150 percent yield on investment, a Bali Babe colt historically pleased powerful owners.

Secretariat genes ran through both sides of the Bali Babe and Sum-mer Squall bloodlines. The strongest connection was that Secretariat was Summer Squall's grandsire. But then Bali Babe had a connection to Sec-retariat too. The parents of Secretariat were the stallion, Bold Ruler, and the mare, Somethingroyal. Somethingroyal was Bali Babe's great-granddam on the stallion side, and Bold Ruler was her great-grandsire on the mare side. The union of Summer Squall and Bali Babe was the most Secretariat blood you could get without the inbreeding getting dangerous.

Roach thought a lot about the temperament of the horses he concocted too. Summer Squall could run like lightning, but he was highstrung, a quality he shared with all the other offspring of the stallion Storm Bird. Even Storm Cat, another Storm Bird progeny and the prime stud of Kentucky at the time, was a little hot. You learned such truths if you hung around the barns and talked to the grooms after the trainers and owners told fairy tales about their strong but sweet-tempered horses and left for the clubhouse boxes. Tom made it a habit to chat with the guys who handled those animals every day—who tugged them to the track and dodged their kicks. Storm Bird foals could run like the wind but they needed a little sweetness and calm bred into them. That's why Roach chose Bali Babe for the mating. That mare was the best mother, short of Roach's own, he had ever come across.

Some mares threw strange surprises. Their foals would be contracted or their tendons so fragile they could never stand. The foals died at birth or had to be put down because chronic deformities eventually would kill them after a brief life of horrible pain. But Bali Babe produced one exquisite foal after another. She had already given birth to nine colts and fillies and each emerged perfect, with straight legs and long backs. She had more than earned back the $7,700 Tom paid for her late one cold, rainy night at the Keeneland auctions in January 1987.

He had watched for days as the breeders, John and Betty Mabee, and Texas oilman Tom Tatham put down hundreds of thousands of dollars for horses, and those price tags were completely out of his league. After the fancy days at the beginning of the week, the big money left town. Roach saw Bali Babe in the walking ring, a powerful, big-boned mare, her belly swollen with a coming foal, and he fell in love. She was sturdy enough to counterbalance all those delicate princes of the Kentucky stud farms and she had such long legs. It happened that the stallion she was in foal to was from New York. Since none of the Kentucky breeders knew him, the price for the mare and baby was low. But Roach saw that Bali Babe's sire was Drone, who'd fathered 609 foals, a remarkable 52 of them stakes winners. Roach respected that horse tremendously and figured Drone's daughter Bali Babe would have potential too.

Just after dinner on March 13, 1996, Garner Kennedy, the Parrish Hill foreman, whom everybody called Slick, telephoned the house to tell the Roaches that Bali Babe seemed ready to give birth. As always, she was right on time with perfect equine gestation—eleven months and ten days. Kennedy noticed all the telltale signs. She was pacing her stall and her waxy teats dripped milk. For centuries at the old family breeding farms, a few mares and stallions gained the status of family members. Those horses had been around so long and provided so much happiness to a family through their offspring that they were like an aunt or uncle, and Bali Babe was that kind of horse. The birth of her foals was always a big event. Tom, Robyn and the two girls—Amanda, eighteen, and Hallie, fourteen—cleaned up the kitchen and went out to the barn to watch. The green stall door was open and the big mare stood inside covered in sweat. Two mares in other stalls could go at any time too, and Kennedy moved from one to the other checking the progress.

Virginia Ballenger was already in the stall with Bali Babe. She was a twenty-one-year-old student in the equine program at Midway College, working a part-time job on the overnight shift at Parrish Hill. She didn't have enough money for a car, so as she did every evening, she had walked the twenty minutes along the country road to the farm.

Bali Babe's water had already broken and, within ten minutes, the foal's forelegs pushed out—white to the cannon bone on one and further up to the knee on the other. That's good, Ballenger thought. The foal will be easier to spot with those white socks when it gets older, breaking out of a pack of horses on the track.[12] Kennedy reached into the mare's birth canal and felt for the foal's nose between its legs. Everything was fine.

The birth proceeded at a normal pace, about ten minutes until the foal was all but out of its mother's womb. At 8:25, the foal of Bali Babe and Summer Squall slid onto the bed of straw. Under the slick of birthing fluid, he was caramel-colored, with the chrome at his ankles and a broad white blaze that looked like the map of North and South America melting down his nose. There was an old horseman's rhyme about those markings, how they were bad luck:

> One white foot, run him for his life;
> Two white feet, keep him for your wife;
> Three white feet, keep him for your man;
> Four white feet, sell him if you can;
> Four white feet and a stripe on his nose,
> Knock him in the head and feed him to the crows.[13]

Tom Roach thought such superstitions were nonsense. He looked at the colt, at its long legs, its back, its markings, and realized its proportions were ideal. This was the perfect horse, the exquisite horse of his dreams lying before him in miniaturized form. He had invented a colt like this and now here the animal was in front of him, in all his unquestionable beauty.

Bali Babe seemed to be cramping and was colicky, so Roach gave her a muscle relaxant. That seemed to soothe her pretty well, so he went back to the house to drink some lemonade and wait for the other foalings.

Ballenger toweled the foal to keep him from getting chilled in the night air. She cleaned the placenta away and, as she always did with new horses, felt like she was opening a Christmas present because each was so different.[14] She left the foal on the straw next to his mother so Bali Babe could finish the job with her tongue. That would help them bond, but was also a key process for encouraging the foal to try to stand. Ballenger went to check on the other mares to see if they were any closer to giving birth.

When Ballenger came back, Bali Babe was on her back in the far corner with her legs pinned against the wall. Even with Ballenger's limited experience working in a foaling barn, she knew that casting, as it was called, was a truly dangerous situation for a horse. If Bali Babe tried to stand, she could smash her legs against the walls and shatter bones that might never heal enough to hold her weight. That could be the end of her life.

Bali Babe's foal still lay a hairbreadth behind his mother's neck. Ballenger wrapped her arms around the newborn and pulled him away so if Bali Babe started thrashing he wouldn't be crushed. Ballenger called Tom, who said he would be right down with Robyn. They brought two thick ropes and tied one to the front legs and the other to the back legs. Tom gave Robyn and Virginia the leads for the front two and took the back ones himself. The mare was jammed into the far wall and so heavy they would be lucky to even rock her.

Pull, he told them.

They leaned their weight and Bali Babe started flailing. Then Virginia lost the grip on the rope. Robyn flew against the back wall.

Years later, Robyn realized that if it weren't for the pain that drove up her spine as she lay crumpled on the ground, she never would have remembered that foaling, from all the hundreds of times she saw the small hooves reaching out of a mare's back haunches. In the years to come, she felt as if fate blessed her with a memorable foaling, because otherwise, if someone had asked her, she would have had to pretend she noticed this birth from all the others. In retrospect, she called the pain a gift to make her remember.

Tom and Virginia rocked Bali Babe some more and she got her legs free. The situation was now stable, but she needed a sedative to calm her. Usually foals stand for the first time between a half hour and an hour after birth. Their mothers lick their flanks to encourage them. But with all the commotion, Bali Babe couldn't turn her attention to her new foal for almost three hours. The colt tried a few times to stand on his own, but immediately collapsed into the straw. Finally, the sedative wore off, and Bali Babe began licking off the afterbirth. Roach gave the foal an enema to get his digestive system moving, and soon the foal locked his legs beneath him and stood.

But there was another problem. The foal couldn't figure out how to nurse. He needed to suckle within an hour or two to get his mother's naturally antibiotic colostrum into his system; for hours Ballenger tried to teach him how, even squirting milk in his face. He seemed to have the hunger, but couldn't figure out how to get it satisfied. Deep in the night, the foal still had not eaten and Ballenger was alone in the silent barn.

Then she heard someone speak behind her. "Let's give him a rest," Tom Roach said. He always walked so softly she didn't hear his comings and goings, and he was up that night worrying over the horses. Ballenger left the foal alone for a bit, then came back and tried again. Finally, after six and a half hours, at 3:00 in the morning, the Bali Babe foal understood and started feeding.

Some thirty-two thousand thoroughbred foals were born in the United States that year, and about forty-five of them entered the world at Parrish Hill. Only twenty would run in the Kentucky Derby, but from the beginning, Tom Roach felt this colt had something special and stated his prediction. "He's going to the Derby," Roach said.[15]

The Bali Babe colt, whom they called Bali until he got his official name, stood out from the beginning. In the spring evenings, the Roaches walked to the paddock after dinner and leaned against the fence to watch the foals challenging each other to playful races. There were about seven foals in each paddock with their mothers, and when they started their light gallops around the perimeter, the Bali Babe foal always won. In the summer months, the Roaches herded in the horses for the mornings to get them out of the heat, and Bali always was the first to the gate for put up. He was the first out in the afternoons. When they let him into the paddock, he ran circles for ten or fifteen minutes. He was well behaved and never mean, but he was a clown, always nipping, bucking and playing, the kind of colt, as Robyn would say, that took the blacksmith's breath away—more mature, stronger than the other foals born that year, with that cinnamon coat.

During the September sales at Keeneland, the Roaches always threw a breakfast to lift the flagging spirits of the out-of-towners weary from days of walking between the shedrows and the sales ring. In 1996, the trainer Ray Bell Jr. was there and asked if he could look at the Bali Babe foal. He had already trained Constant Demand and Tossofthecoin and knew firsthand the potential that ran through that bloodline. Tom Roach walked him and another trainer back to the barns and showed him the newcomer. The trainers took one look at the colt and said they wanted to buy him on the spot. The foal still hadn't been separated from Bali Babe, an event that took place before the end of his first year and transformed him into a weanling, and Roach usually didn't sell foals before they were weanlings. But he talked it over with Will Farish and they agreed to make the exception. They sold the Bali Babe foal for $210,000 to Bell and his partner, the bloodstock agent Tom Moynihan, who were acting as proxies for the California owners Bob and Beverly Lewis.

A few months later, Roach began the weaning process. At some farms, they herded all the mares together and took them away at once, but anyone who witnessed that sort of weaning knew it was hellish. The mares thrashed around and the foals stood at the fence all day crying. Roach preferred weaning one at a time, taking a new mare out each day. Then the foal without a mother could be harbored by another mare. The other foals would see how a foal who lost his mother was not left completely bereft but was befriended by the other mares and foals, then when their mare was taken away, they wouldn't be so traumatized.

Tom left Bali Babe for last. She was not just the star of the farm, but an especially good mother. Her milk bag was always full, and she calmed her colt and the other foals in the paddock. She nuzzled them, stood quietly beside them. She reminded Tom so much of his own mother, how she took in the offspring of others and loved them as her own. Ruth Roach had died two years earlier in a New Year's Eve car accident and no one at the farm seemed quite able to recover from the tragedy. The woman had been like a saint to the people of Midway. She set up food accounts at the Corner Grocery so people who couldn't afford to eat could charge their groceries back to her. She filed the application to get a Head Start grant for the town, and when the local school couldn't find space to hold the classes, she offered her basement. For ten years, fifty children came to the farm every day to study, and she fed them lunch. She held the annual Easter egg hunt for the kids of the area on her front lawn.[16]

On the day that Roach needed to take Bali Babe away, he gave the foals a small dose of tranquilizer to calm them and keep them from jumping the fence and hurting themselves. He led her out. He put her in the trailer and took her down the drive, beneath the pin oaks, onto the road and across Interstate 64 to another farm, far enough away so that her foal could not hear her or catch her scent on the wind. Tom released Bali Babe's foal into the paddock with the others, and the colt handled the event as well as could be hoped.

The Lewises sent the colt over to Charlie and Amy LoPresti to be broken soon after he was weaned, and he became one of the 397,000 horses in training in the United States. He looked so much like his half brother, Tossofthecoin, the Bali Babe colt the LoPrestis also had broken, they called him Little Toss. He didn't have a distinctly masculine head, but a small nose and kind eye. LoPresti grouped him with two other colts born around the same time, and the staff nicknamed them the Three Amigos because they spent every moment together and never bossed each other. For almost six months, Little Toss did nothing but eat, sleep and run in the paddock whenever the spirit moved him. He was a sweet-tempered colt. In late September, LoPresti began breaking him, starting by just circling him in his stall to get him used to motion, then leading him by his halter around her.

She tried him with the bridle, and out in the paddock she threw the line over his back, swishing it across his withers to accustom him to the stimulus. Every new step she took caused Little Toss to start and show her a wild eye. That timid streak must have come from one of his parents, LoPresti thought, probably Bali Babe since all of her colts were that way at first.

Some days later, LoPresti jumped on Little Toss bare back in the stall, trying to get him used to a rider. He never got mean or pushy, but he frequently went skittish on her. LoPresti was careful not to push him too hard, not to cinch his girth too tight, because if she went past the threshold of his anxiety and he bucked out of fear, he would buck for the rest of his life. The goal was to teach him to trust a rider when he entered the chaos of the racetrack, to not panic. For a month, LoPresti and Little Toss worked together every day for forty-five minutes without her actually riding him out of the stall. By the end of the month, Little Toss stood still and let LoPresti get up on his back and ride him to the track.

LoPresti paired him with other yearlings for his first training. They galloped along together and then Little Toss kicked into a long, slightly bumpy stride, falling into a natural lope like the run of a puppy, crossing the finish line far ahead. LoPresti tried him against other pairings. She tried every horse she had and the result was always the same. Little Toss might be a little timid and he might not have the most elegant gait, but he could outrun any horse on the farm. LoPresti took away the competition and clocked Little Toss sprinting on his own. He outpaced any other runner, even when no one was breathing down his neck. Every day she and Little Toss went to the track, he stayed focused on whatever was asked of him. He didn't nip or buck. He got into the bridle and ran as hard as he could. LoPresti tried him at a mile and he roared around the track. She tried him at a mile and a half, at two miles, even at three and he never flagged. The longer she ran him, the stronger he grew and the happier he seemed. Little Toss would do anything to show he could run like a champ.

For Tom Roach, sometimes it felt a little strange to be a breeder. You dreamed these horses up out of thin air. You watched their conception, then witnessed their foaling. You cared for them through their first year and then they were gone, off to a trainer or, maybe down the line, another breeding farm. It was like being a parent and the kids off at school, then leading a new life in another city.

Tom and Robyn Roach heard that the Bali Babe foal wasn't going to Ray Bell Jr. after all. Bob Lewis and Bell had scuffled over a business matter, and the Bali Babe foal was scheduled to ship to the trainer D. Wayne Lukas instead. The Roaches weren't thrilled at that news. They knew Bell liked the horse and would give him unique attention. He recognized how the colt was a latent star and would cultivate that. But to Lukas, the colt would be just another runner in his empire that included entrants at some twenty-four tracks a year and several hundred horses. To most people, a $210,000 horse would be special. To Lukas, that was a second-string piece of horseflesh compared to the multimillion-dollar animals he already trained.

The colt will get lost in the shuffle, Tom Roach thought. The Bali Babe colt would be one talented animal in Lukas's California palace of superstars, brushed and bathed and tended like a little lord, but forced to prove himself from the start or risk being shipped away.

Every six months, the Roaches ran a computer check to see what tracks their colts had shipped to and if they had been named. In the middle of April, when the Bali Babe colt was two, the Roaches saw his name on their screen. *Charismatic.*

What a fantastic thing to call him, they said to each other. The Jockey Club required all thoroughbreds be named by the end of January in their second year. The Club recorded the appellations and checked to make sure they had not been used in the previous fifteen years. The name could be no longer than eighteen letters and with no suggestion of vulgarity. When the Roaches tried to name a horse, they often ran fifteen or twenty names by the Jockey Club before they found a unique one. After all, almost half a million names were unavailable at any given time.

It's unbelievable that Charismatic hasn't been taken already, Robyn thought.

In mid-June, the Roaches saw that Charismatic, or 'Matic, as the girls called him, was slated to run at Hollywood Park. Tom was shocked that the colt was starting so early, only three months after his second birthday. For a stakes contender, a trainer usually waited at least until the autumn for a two-year-old to mature, for its bones to harden. But Lukas must have seen some precocious spark in those mornings when the horse carried an exercise rider around the oval in California.

'Matic's first try was a short race on June 20—five furlongs with jockey David Flores up. The typical racetrack is a mile long, and that mile is divided into eighths, each of which is called a furlong. Races can be as short as a five-furlong sprint, or, on a rare occasion, as long as one mile and a half. Most races are seven furlongs to a mile and one-eighth. The finish line is always constant but the starting gates are moved to accommodate the longer distances.

'Matic's first odds were 12 to 1—that meant he wasn't the favorite, but he wasn't dismissed entirely either. Roach drove to Keeneland to watch Charismatic's debut on simulcast. He saw 'Matic outfitted in the accoutrements of a professional racehorse—saddle, saddle cloth, and Flores in the Lewis's green and yellow silks on his back. In the race, though, 'Matic loped along like he didn't even know he was supposed to fight to get in front. He always had surged to the lead naturally at the LoPrestis, but this time, shy 'Matic had to race right toward the hollering crowds and nothing Flores could do would speed him on.

He's too green, Roach thought.

Every horse in the race thundered by 'Matic and he came in dead last, thirteen lengths behind the winner.

After the debacle of that first race, Roach kept following his colt's path. Even with the loss, he believed the horse was something special but just too young to show his brilliance. Roach noticed then that Lukas was testing the horse at the Del Mar racetrack and was entering him with blinkers to prevent him from getting distracted by the competition heaving along beside him. Blinkers would keep him focused on the path to the finish. Lukas also gave 'Matic a shot of Lasix, a diuretic commonly given to racehorses to lessen the pressure on their lungs so they don't bleed. 'Matic came in third out of eight horses.

Then Lukas started putting the horse in every situation possible to see if he could devise a way to win. Thoroughbred races are run on the outer dirt track or on an inner turf oval. The decision whether a horse runs on turf or dirt primarily has to do with the shape of the horse's hoof, with a wider hoof suited for grass.

There are maiden races, claiming races, allowance races (otherwise known as handicap races), and stakes races. A maiden race is for any colt or filly who has never won a race before. When the horse wins, it is known as "breaking his maiden" and he or she can never enter another maiden race. An allowance race means that the track steward assessed the competing horses by age and gender and assigned a weight each jockey had to carry including his own poundage to even the playing field. A stakes race is any competition where an owner pays a fee to enter. The track management then adds to the money in the purse. The three races of the Triple Crown are stakes races. Between the entrance fees and added funds from the track, they pay out over $1 million apiece to the first finishers, who then disburse various percentages to the trainers and jockeys. All the races of the Breeders' Cup—the richest day of American racing, which falls on the last weekend of October or the first weekend of November—are stakes races.

Lukas told his assistants to try Charismatic on the turf, at longer distances. Nothing seemed to work. 'Matic kept getting beaten badly. The worst debacle came on October 17, when Charismatic ran for one mile on the turf at Santa Anita. He took off like a rocket, right to the lead, then at the top of the stretch slowed to a crawl. The other eight horses pounded by him and he came up over twenty-five lengths behind the winner. In horse racing, a defeat didn't get much worse than that. What could be going on in the horse's head? Roach wondered. 'Matic never would have let that happen in Kentucky.

But still, when Roach saw that Charismatic next would run in a $62,500 claiming race at Hollywood Park in November, he did not interpret that event in the dire way someone else might.

Most races at American tracks are claiming races, which began in the early 1900s in the United States as a variant of the British selling race. The category throws a kind of serendipity into racing that functions like the joker in card games. A $7,500 claiming race, for example, means that each of the horses headed to the starting gate may be purchased for

$7,500 by a licensed buyer who drops off a promissory note for that amount in the steward's office fifteen minutes before the race begins. Win or lose, that horse is then the new purchaser's possession. If the horse wins, the purse money goes to the former owner, but the horse goes to the new owner. If the horse dies on his way to the finish line, the corpse goes to the purchaser. The point of the claiming race is to keep trainers and owners from entering their horses in competitions they are certain they will win. If you owned a great colt, you would naturally want to run him many times against the weakest competition you could find to earn as much money as possible. But then every trainer with lower-tier horses would be bankrupt because they could never triumph and the sport would die. Claiming races are also the best way to keep bettors interested, since they keep the competition tight, and thus raise the total betting pool, or handle.

If you are a trainer and your horse risks being bought for less than his value, you would keep him out of the race. You would not put a million-dollar horse in a $7,500 claiming race. Of course, if you know your horse is only worth $7,500—because of a hidden injury or nasty temperament— you might want to enter him in a $50,000 claiming race. You could be assured he wouldn't win, but maybe someone would be fooled into thinking he was worth the cash. For big-time trainers, claiming races can be a way to unload the dud horses taking up precious barn space.

The serendipitous element lies in the fact that most trainers at some point are forced to enter their horses in claiming races whether they want them bought or not. The trainer needs to test the abilities of the horse before deciding whether or not to shell out the large nomination fees for a stakes race. Or the horse has lost a long series of stakes races and needs to be reminded what it feels like to win. At the track, there are countless stories of heartbreak when a trainer suddenly loses a colt he or she groomed for years and the hotwalker from another barn comes to lead the colt away from the finish line. Bureaucratic snafus can also wreak havoc. I sat in the racing office at Churchill Downs one day as the racing official, David Wedlake, showed me the fine points of filling out a claiming certificate. He ran his finger down a completed form for a race just going off to indicate how this purchaser managed to buy one of the colts running. Then suddenly he stuck on one wrong letter in the horse's name. Anyone would know which horse the purchaser had in mind, but according to the rules of the National Thoroughbred Racing Association, that claiming certificate was null and void. "Oh, boy," said David Wedlake with a Welsh lilt, "he's going to be hot." And the buyer was. He slapped the wall of the racing office and fumed, then took his cell phone outside to delicately try explaining to the owner (who was also probably extremely hot) that somehow the horse had gotten away.

If Roach didn't love Charismatic the way he did, he might have thought that Lukas's entering Charismatic in the six-and-a-half furlong claiming race was a white flag of surrender. The trainer had given up. All he wanted now was to unload a lousy runner. But Roach had faith in 'Matic. He figured that Lukas was trying to build the horse's confidence. There was no way Lukas would accept $62,500 for a horse that the Lewises bought for $210,000. 'Matic was a grandson of Secretariat, for god's sake. Laffit Pincay, a jockey whose name had been inscribed in the horse racing Hall of Fame in 1975, was riding and would surely know how to handle the colt.

Instead of letting 'Matic burn himself out at the start, Pincay kept a firm grip on the reins until the top of the stretch. Although the horse was running without blinkers, he didn't get alarmed by the beasts snorting along beside him. 'Matic started tiring toward the final turn, running off the bit, but he put all his muscle into a sprint that carried him across the finish line first by five lengths. Roach felt pride for his plucky foal. Charismatic had broken his maiden. He won when everyone had soured on him, which was doubly important since he was headed back to the Lukas barn again after not being claimed.

'Matic ran five more times over the next two months, with mixed results. On January 31, 1999, he put in one of his worst performances. The horse that struggled as a newborn to learn how to suckle now could not gorge himself on enough oats. Heavier than ever before, Charismatic lumbered behind the pack for a mile and one-sixteenth, never improving his position, only fading farther back over the course of the race until he came in thirteen-and-a-half lengths behind the winner.

The next race was another $62,500 claimer, and Roach could have again despaired that Lukas wanted to unload the colt, but he chose not to. He thought Lukas was only trying to cultivate the horse's taste for winning.

The race was held on February 11, out at Santa Anita. Now Chris McCarron was up. 'Matic held back all the way around the oval, then as he came up to the eighth pole in mid-stretch, he surged forward and pulled neck and neck with What Say You at the finish line. The stewards issued a query and, when they reviewed the race tape, saw that What Say You clearly bumped 'Matic at that last pole. What Say You was disqualified, and 'Matic moved up to a technical first. Once again, 'Matic pulled off a victory at the moment everyone seemed to be giving up on him and showed he could get jostled and wouldn't fade away.

Lukas then entered 'Matic in the $200,000 El Camino Real Derby at Bay Meadows in San Francisco with local jockey Ron Warren on board.

That's it, Roach thought. *Maybe if 'Matic gets away from Los Angeles, he might be able to do it. . . .* The cool, moist climate up in San Francisco was more like the weather in Kentucky. 'Matic might feel a little bit like he was back home at Parrish Hill where he had been a star. He might remember how he liked to run just for the fun of it back when he was a weanling bucking in the paddock.

Roach watched that March 6 race on television as 'Matic stayed back until the top of the stretch. Then the colt started moving, kicking into a locomotive drive all the way to the finish, the kind of closing that the great horses could pull out of their sinew. Charismatic came in second, beaten only by a head.

He's starting to show what he's made of, Roach thought excitedly.

In the early spring, Bali Babe suffered a severe colic attack and Roach rushed her to Hagyard-Davidson-McGee veterinary hospital in Lexington. Dr. Michael Spirito sliced down her belly and removed growths in her twisted intestine. Roach thought they saved her, but two weeks later,

Bali Babe began bobbing her head in pain. On March 15, 1999, Roach took her back for another operation. She was eighteen years old and pregnant. She had recently gotten in foal to the sire Cryptoclearance. Dr. Bob Hunt asked Roach to come into the operating room when Bali Babe was sliced open. He showed Roach the intestinal infections, the way the disease was eating away at her insides.

There's really no way to keep her alive, he told Roach. We need to put her down. Otherwise she will have a slow death over the next three weeks.

It was devastating news. Bali Babe was like a family member, the Roaches' number-one mare. Ever since that rainy night Tom Roach picked her up at Keeneland for a song, she had delivered one beautiful foal after another. The horses were a miracle and the family marveled at their perfect conformation, but the bottom line was that Bali Babe also was their number-one moneymaker. The foal in her womb was too new to be saved. The Roaches would lose her whole bloodline. There were no Bali Babe offspring still on the farm.

Go ahead and put her down, Roach told the vet.

It was two days after Charismatic's third birthday.

Roach went home. He usually didn't show his emotions to his employees. Sometimes he was a little happier, then he hit his blue moods or showed a burr in his temper, but he did not talk about what provoked him. Ballenger saw Roach the day after he went to the veterinary hospital with Bali Babe. She asked how the mare was doing. "She isn't," Roach said and kept filling an oat bucket.

A few weeks later, Roach took out a full-page ad in his industry's magazine, *The Blood-Horse*. The ad was a tribute to great mothers and included two pictures: one of his own mother and another of Bali Babe with one of her foals, Millennium Wind, at her flank. When the ad ran, Roach tore the page from the magazine and hung it on the wall of his office so he could look at it every day.

A few weeks later, Tom Roach heard Lukas was sending 'Matic to Keeneland for the 1999 Coolmore Lexington Stakes on April 18. Lukas's assistant trainer, Randy Bradshaw, had said in the first days of April that the horse would run either in the Coolmore *or* the Derby,[17] not both, so in a way, the decision could have been a disappointment. The horse would not be running in the Derby. But Tom Roach only wanted him to do well and he thought a Kentucky race was exactly what the horse needed.

Good, Tom thought. *Bring him home. That horse likes it back home.*

Lukas hired Jerry Bailey, a Hall of Fame jockey since 1995, to ride 'Matic for the mile-and-one-sixteenth competition. If you looked at the bottom line, 'Matic didn't seem to have a chance. He hadn't grabbed a clean win for seven races, going back to November of his two-year-old season. But even the fact that Bailey agreed to ride him in one of the prep races for the Derby looked like a hopeful sign that he might at least have a shot in the Coolmore.

Of course, if Lukas or the Lewises harbored even a weak dream of getting 'Matic into the Derby, he needed to dazzle in the Coolmore. Over the long history of the Kentucky Derby, there had been as few as three horses competing, back in 1892; and as many as twenty-three in 1974, the year after Secretariat blazed across the public imagination. Starting in 1980, the racing authorities started limiting the possible number of runners to twenty, because with more, the track became too dangerous.

For the first time since 1984, more horses were likely to be entered than could compete. If the officials needed to winnow the field, they would look at the nominated horses' earnings and pick those with the highest totals. Going into the race, Charismatic showed purse earnings of only $157,070 in all of his thirteen races.[18] If he surprised everyone and won the Coolmore, he would make another $234,794. If he ran second, he would make just $75,740, or third, $37,870. In this race, they even paid out down to fifth place at $11,361, and the money would be welcome, but the Derby would never happen for him.

The whole Roach family would go to Keeneland for the Coolmore. That was a given; the family needed an occasion to celebrate. Bali Babe's death had been just a final trial in a difficult year. In October, eighteen-year-old Amanda nearly died when she crashed into a big tree by Lane's End Farm on her way back from Keeneland. She was now fully recovered, but the accident churned up the pain of Tom's mother's death.

Then Tom started feeling sick, low on energy. He dropped almost fifty pounds in a few months and looked pale as frost. On Breeders' Cup Day, those health problems peaked, which couldn't have been worse timing. The event rotated tracks each year and in 1998 the Breeders' Cup was held at Churchill Downs, an hour's drive away from Parrish Hill Farm. The Roaches traditionally held a Breeders' Cup eve party at which the neighboring horse people could handicap the competition and debate the merits of their picks. The next day, the guests watched the races on television, and whooped and hollered for their selections. This year the Roaches would throw the party and then the guests could caravan to Churchill in the morning to watch the events live.

Tom Roach wrote down his wagers at the celebration, but felt weaker than ever before. On the morning of the race, he told Robyn to escort their guests to the track without him. "I'll get dressed and meet you later," he said, then got down on his hands and knees and crawled up the stairs to their bedroom. He lay in bed, facing away from the door. Robyn rushed in to change clothes. She was talking to him, but couldn't see his face and didn't realize how ill he was. She went downstairs to organize the departures.

Tom's father, Dr. Ben Roach, stopped by to pick up a gate pass. He had a car full of visitors, including his friend Bill DeVries, a horse-racing fan and, coincidentally, the world-famous surgeon who performed the first artificial heart transplant in 1982. The farm manager, Brad Murrey, saw Dr. Roach and told him that his son didn't look too good that morning. Maybe Dr. Roach ought to go upstairs and take a look.

Dr. Roach walked into his son's bedroom and saw immediately how weak he was. *Go get Bill DeVries*, he told Murrey.

DeVries came in. Dr. Roach told his friend that he was considering calling an ambulance and having his son taken to the hospital.

DeVries took one look at Tom. He turned to Dr. Roach. "If you wait for an ambulance," DeVries said, "he will be dead." They loaded Tom onto a chair because he was too weak to stand and carried him downstairs and out to the car.

As it turned out, Tom Roach had massive internal bleeding from a previously undetected ulcer and a white count down to almost zero. Hours later, in the hospital, DeVries told Robyn, "I've done heart transplants and seen many sick people. He's the sickest live man I have ever seen." A racing fan even in times of darkest struggle, Tom insisted that he watch the Breeders' Cup on television as the nurses pumped him with transfusions. It annoyed him that he picked the exacta but hadn't been able to get his wager to the betting windows.

Still, how could he not feel lucky? If events had unfolded differently, Robyn could have come home from the track to find her husband dead. If a passenger in Dr. Roach's car hadn't been a world-famous heart surgeon, Tom Roach could have expired waiting for the Midway ambulance to race along the perimeters of those enormous Kentucky farms. After such a close brush with mortality, every celebratory moment was an even bigger reason for the Roaches to relish the joy of being. The year that 'Matic turned three was the last year Amanda was still at home before going off to college. This was the last Triple Crown season they would have together as a family and they had only one equine prospect to watch head toward the roses. It was the caramel-colored colt they helped into the world on that March night. The Roaches couldn't help but feel sentimental about 'Matic, not only because of what he could do as an athlete, but because of his gentleness. He was fun to be around, Robyn would say. She thought how, even counting all the great horses she had seen in her life, it was remarkable how magnetic 'Matic's personality was. Tom and Robyn would remark again and again how spectacular it was to share the excitement of this last family-reared horse together.

The day of the Coolmore Lexington Stakes, April 18, 1999, was a dreary one in Lexington with a cold wind gusting and clouds dumping showers from time to time. The horses cantering back to the finish line after the races were coated with mud that traced the veins on their necks and bellies like chocolate syrup. After the races, the grooms made their way across the track, slick as caramel taffy, and undid the buckles of the saddles; the horses exhaled and everything within a few feet was enveloped in a cloud of steam and oaty scent.

The trees in the paddock dripped rain, and only a few stragglers hung around the fence to watch the horses saddle up for the 4:27 P.M. start. George "Bucky" Sallee walked onto the dirt track, raised the bugle to his lips and blew the call to the races. Sallee had the broad face and stout build of an innkeeper from old England, a comparison further encouraged by the green jacket and black knickers he wore tucked into tall boots. Sallee made that walk in front of the grandstand and played those bars at least ten times a day for thirty-five years of racing. He won the gig when he was a young man playing saxophone and trumpet in the band at a local country club. One day a man from the track approached him to see if he was interested in playing the bugle at Keeneland since they were having trouble with their regular bugle guys getting too deep into gambling. Sallee agreed and got his break soon thereafter when one of the buglers cut out at midday with a wad of winnings. He worked the job ever since and liked being around horses because the scene felt familiar. His uncle had been a trainer and his father worked with polo ponies. But every race looked the same to Sallee now. It didn't matter who was running. He didn't bet when he was working. Perhaps he learned his lesson thirty-five years ago, understanding that his boat came in when the other buglers lost their way at the betting windows.

Sallee liked meeting people, but something in his pale blue eyes suggested that he didn't meet enough people to make his world feel truly cozy. He reported to work each day, to his small closet off the First Aid station underneath the grandstand. His bugle sat on the shelf, his green jacket hung on a hook, and if he left the closet door open he felt comfortable standing and chatting with a passerby. There was no room for a chair. It wouldn't be until the following year, his thirty-sixth on the job, that the Keeneland race program for the Bluegrass Stakes would include George "Bucky" Sallee's name for the very first time, and he would point it out with true pride.[19] But on this day, Sallee put the bugle to his lips, and in the paddock, the horses came around.

The Roaches—Tom, Robyn and the girls all bundled up in raincoats and hats—had come to witness their beloved horse running. They had watched every one of his races, either on television or on tapes that friends sent, but this was the first time he had been back with them and they had seen him again in flesh and blood.

'Matic was no longer the precocious foal that the Roaches remembered cantering around his paddock, but a twelve-hundred-pound colt who stood about sixteen hands high—five feet four inches to the withers at the base of his neck.[20] He was still colored like a collie with a bright rust-colored coat and snowy markings, but he had grown so much bigger that the blaze that once covered his nose was now a delicate trail of white. The groom began to walk 'Matic toward the tunnel, leading through the center of the grandstand onto the track. As Charismatic took his first steps forward, Jerry Bailey leapt onto his back.

He loves Churchill Downs, D. Wayne Lukas told the Roaches in the paddock. *You watch out. This colt is getting better and better.*[21]

Much as Tom Roach loved 'Matic, he thought the trainer was just pumping up his horse the way the trainer was famous for. Everyone knew that Lukas might not think much of a horse during the horse's regular workout, but he knew how to promote his animals on a race day. At showtime, he could take a penny and make a person think it was a million dollars.

Lukas told them he thought Charismatic could win one of the Triple Crown races. *I think the Belmont*, he told them.

The gates opened and 'Matic ran back in the crowded pack of eleven horses, but he kept pushing forward, closer and closer to the lead, until at the six-furlong mark he was in fourth place. At the top of the stretch, he took third, and then he romped past Texas Glitter with only Yankee Victor ahead of him at the eighth pole. The Roaches shouted him on, their screams ricocheting through the nearly empty grandstand. Then 'Matic pushed forward and crossed the finish line first a full two-and-a-half lengths ahead of Yankee Victor.

He had won. And not only had he won, he had set the stakes record on one of the dreariest days anyone at Keeneland could remember. The $234,794 purse pushed him over the edge to qualify for the Derby. In the winner's circle, it was the Roaches, Bailey, Lukas, and Charismatic. "I've got Worldly Manner in the Derby," Bailey told the trainer, "but if something happens, keep me in mind. If there's an opening, I'd like to ride your colt."[22]

Lukas called the Lewises out in California. "Bob, I'd like to put Charismatic in the Derby," Lukas said. Bob Lewis, ever the optimist, agreed.

The next day even the experts conceded that 'Matic had impressed. Andrew Beyer of the *Washington Post* had devised a rating system for the speed of thoroughbreds back in 1975. *The Daily Racing Form* included those numbers as a clue to how a horse might fare in future competition. Before the Coolmore, Charismatic never got above a 95, which he earned at the El Camino Derby. But this time his speed rating was 108—as good as any horse going into the Derby.[23]

Still, despite the Roaches' hopes, a claimer had not won the Derby in twenty-nine years, since Dust Commander shot across the finish line first. There hadn't been such an underdog headed to Churchill in all the Roaches' years in racing.

THREE

BUG BOY

Elloree, South Carolina, is a town of 939 souls an hour south of Columbia and to the west of Lake Marion. Driving toward Elloree, the radio
stations drop away into static one by one until just two country stations
beam out, on either end of a field of buzzing drone. On both sides of
Route 6, cotton fields and soybean fields stretch into a wall of woods far
in the distance, and the road glides through these, past a gas station,
through more woods and cotton fields, past the brick church, a couple
of small clapboard houses, and stops for one red light in Elloree at the
crossing of Old Route 6 and Cleveland Street. Not much ever rattles
Elloree. A few years back, a couple of hoodlums, who it is thought were
just rolling through town on a straightaway to a more fascinating city,
paused at the pharmacy with its fluorescent lights already glowing at
dawn, tied up the clerk and held a gun to his head while they robbed
him of cash and pills. The people of Elloree never did get the full story
of why the culprits picked Elloree over any other town in that land of
open spaces, because within an hour, cops in another town down the line
shot one culprit dead and the other died in custody not long after. That

kind of excitement rarely came to Elloree, which remained true to its name, the Santee Indian word for "the home I love."

The biggest event by far in Elloree each year is the Elloree Trials, the day of horse racing held at the thoroughbred training center owned by Franklin "Goree" Smith. The Trials give the horses that he boards for folks up North a chance to show what they learned under his stewardship and provides a competitive venue for area horse breeders and trainers.

Back in the 1930s, the Elloree Training Center was the Palmetto Racing Park, which put on a program of monthly contests. The oval nestled in a gently sloped basin, and pleasure seekers found seats on the hillsides all the way up to the forest. Bookies set up stands and the gentlemen in suits and ties clustered around placing bets while their fashionable wives applauded the winning jockeys. Then in 1946, Strom Thurmond, who later served as U.S. senator for more than forty-six years, ran for governor on an antigambling platform. He won, laws were passed, and the track closed. The oval flooded over. Trees and weeds grew up in the patches of dry infield. In the 1960s, Phil Utman, an avid pigeon racer, bought the place and tried to shave the land back to working condition for horses.

Mayor R. Vernon Shirer, Reverend Irvin Shuler, and the Jaycees approached him about holding one day of racing each year with no official gambling.[1] The trainers could test the strength and agility of their animals at the Elloree Trials before shipping them for a season to the official tracks around the country where betting paid the bills. To put the sheen of wagering back into the event, the real horsemen gathered the night before the Trials for the Calcutta, an auction where anyone could "buy" a horse for the next day's races and pick up the purse at the winner's circle if they "owned" the winner. For hours in the night, when the only illumination came from the moon and the pavilion in the dark field, the auctioneer rattled through the names of the horses like a wind-up alarm clock, while below his podium the proprietors of the town's coffee shop sold ham sandwiches, brownies, beer and sweet tea. On the day of the races, good old boys quietly functioned as small-scale bookies, collecting bets at the nearby tailgate parties, as if time had been pushed back to British racing of the sixteenth century when everyone simply bet the people sitting near them.

In August 1976, Goree Smith, a wiry thirty-three-year-old man with a narrow face and ready smile whose voice had the same surprise and sweep as a horse tail shooing flies, bought the place. He kept the Trials going, because to him the sight of horses running was a miracle. Gambling or no gambling, racing stirred the blood. He never could figure why a man felt he needed to gamble to justify being with horses.[2]

One day around 1980, Smith met a kid who he thought understood that sentiment better than most anyone he had ever met. He looked out from the office porch that afternoon and saw a boy pedaling a bike up the dirt road by the paddock, a little sportster leaning back in his seat, his arms folded across his chest. Smith could tell what Chris Antley wanted even before he asked. He had come to see if somebody could teach him how to ride the thoroughbreds. He pedaled right up to the brick office, and when he took the turn, he pulled it fast and never put his hands down on the bars.

He was only thirteen or so, and small for his age, with blond hair, freckles, and blue eyes that looked lit from behind. Antley had been fishing with his friend for bream and large-mouth bass over at Shirer's pond. Through the trees, he had seen the horses at the center, wandering the paddocks and stalking the fence. His mother had told him that her friend who worked as an exercise rider at the training center recently lost his job because he got too heavy. Maybe Smith would have work for him, she said.

Antley had gotten up on a horse once before, when he was around eight. He climbed onto his aunt's colt while the animal was boarding at their small farm in Sumter. The horse took off, ducking under trees, racing across to the edge of their eleven acres. Antley clung to anything he could—the mane, the neck, the rippling sides—screaming, "Mama, Mama, help me!" She raced out of the house with her sister and they corraled the horse, and when she pulled her son off he was sore and terrified. "I will never get on a horse again," he said.[3]

But five years is a long time in the life of a kid, and Antley wasn't afraid of much anymore. Challenges and competition made him happy. When he was around eleven, he talked one of the Fogel girls, whose father ran the funeral home in town, into lending him her bike for the big fund-raising race that went through Elloree, and Wimpy, the deaf television repairman in town, sponsored him. Antley hadn't trained and the bike wasn't the best out there that day, but he tore away from the pack and won. He liked anything fast and those horses at the training center clearly were. He had always loved animals too; he had fought his father to keep their few hogs from the slaughter.

Smith could tell that Chris Antley understood animals, and when he put him to work the first day, Smith saw Antley knew the meaning of labor too. He raked the stable area or "shedrow," and mucked the stalls. He wasn't paid officially, but Smith gave him some money for doing extra chores. Antley made twenty dollars that first weekend, and the money thrilled him because he could buy an Izod shirt like the other kids at school wore.[4]

Will and Cindy Gomes, an old Mexican couple who put out the feed, took Antley under their wing at the training center. They looked the boy over, saw how small and athletic he was and told him he could be a jock one day. At his height, he could never really dominate in any sport, but at the track, the standards turned upside down; lightness was what he needed to race. From that point on, all Antley wanted was to ride. He followed the Gomeses around all morning long, pestering them while he helped fill oat buckets. After a few weeks, they finally put him up on a pony, Buck, to see how he liked it.

There Antley was, stalking down the shedrow, when he ran into Gorce Smith. Antley looked nervous because he knew Smith usually waited a long time before he let the kids ride. But Smith saw how easily Antley fell into the pony's rhythm, how he seemed completely comfortable up there, bright-eyed and awestruck. From then on, he let Antley ride the pony to escort the high-strung thoroughbreds and quarter horses to the tracks in the mornings. A few weeks after Antley first got up on Buck, Smith let him ride one of the more easygoing racehorses bareback in the paddock to feel the horse's power. Smith checked Antley's balance, saw how he handled the reins, how he communicated with the horse. Smith only needed to show Antley how to do something with a horse once; pretty soon Antley was breaking yearlings.

Antley went to the training center in the mornings before school, then returned after the last bell to help until dark. If for some reason the grooms were already leading the horses out of the paddock, Antley would sit on his bike with his arms crossed, leaning on the paddock railing, and Goree could see he was disappointed as hell.[5]

A kid who graduated to riding in just a few short weeks could have gotten high-handed with the rest of the workers, but Antley never did. He pitched in on the dirty work along with them. He was all boy, Smith thought, optimistic about everything, never fussing or arguing. Smith showed Antley tapes of races and pointed out the riders' errors or moments of genius. Then Antley watched videos of himself riding and demonstrated how quickly the lessons took when he showed Smith where he saw he needed to improve.

Antley had wandered onto that farm like he was trying to crawl out of his other life and pull the hatch closed after him. His parents' marriage had dissolved about a year before, and the chaos at home hit Antley hard. He always had been a little too sensitive for his own good. "He had a lot on him," Smith said, "but he never cried about it. He hooked onto this thing with horses and that was his avenue to focus his mind."[6]

Once Chris Antley became a star in the racing world, the media reported that he had moved thirty times in his youth, suggesting that his home life was inherently unstable, but that wasn't true.[7] The family made only one significant move, to South Carolina from Fort Lauderdale, Florida. That's where Chris's mother, Michelle, or Shelly, had been raised, and where at age nineteen, when she went into labor, she drove to the hospital in borrowed shoes because she couldn't find her own. She named her eldest son Christopher Wiley Antley. His first name was one Shelly had picked out when she was twelve, and the middle name was his paternal grandfather's—a Cherokee name. On January 6, 1966, twenty-four-year-old Lester looked into his son's bright blue eyes. "He's a special person," Lester said. "But I don't know what he's going to be special for."[8] It could have been the new-father syndrome, but then that feeling stayed as Chris grew up. Les couldn't pinpoint exactly what the magical quality was. There was something in Chris's actions, the way he did things that other kids couldn't. He showed a stubborn streak, as if he were insisting on a way of life that he knew Shelly and Les didn't yet understand.

In those early years, Shelly wanted to be the perfect mother. She was tiny, blonde and pretty, with blue-green eyes. As a little girl pirouetting in oversized toe shoes in her carport, she dreamed of being a dancer, but then she met Les and went along with her other dream— being a wife and mother. When she first got married she was so young and inexperienced she didn't even know how to drive. She rode her bike everywhere with her girlfriends and charged the dime-store candy back to her father-in-law. She played the maternal role to an extreme, insisting her baby Chris always wear clean white tennis shoes, so she bought him six pairs. He never wore rubber pants because then she might not know when he wet himself. If something dropped off the line it had to be rewashed. The floors gleamed.

All the rules were clear. Shelly and Les insisted that Chris finish everything on his plate, but he refused. He shook his head and smiled and it went on like that for hours with Shelly pleading, trying to out-stubborn him. But he wouldn't eat normally. He gazed at his parents while he put every forkful into his mouth and never swallowed. Shelly asked the pharmacist what she could do. "My son doesn't eat much," she said. "I want him to eat more. I'm scared he's going to get sick."

"You're going to make him a nervous wreck," he told her. "He's not perfect. He will never be perfect."

"I know that," she said, cowed. But she kept feeding him by hand until he was four years old. "Of course, I'd already ruined him," she joked decades later. "Because your first three years are the most important."⁹

When Chris was five and his little brother, Brian, was two, the family moved to Sumter, about thirty miles from Elloree, where Les's family went back several generations. Les's grandfather had owned the seed and feed in town. Then Les's father served as postmaster while his mother taught high school business classes. Les moved his own family back to South Carolina because he and his brother thought real money could be made if they started a fertilizer business. For a year, Les ran a cotton gin, then they bought the eleven-acre farm with a nice brick house near the end of a dirt road. They built a treehouse for the kids. The boys and the baby, Leslie, who was born about a year into their time in Sumter, ran around buck naked, free, happy kids surrounded by the smell of earth.

The kids could be lighthearted but they also had dark moods and, as the eldest, Chris seemed most aware of it. He once told his mother that he was her clone and not just because he looked so much like her. "Sorry for you," she said, "because that means you're going to feel everything I have ever felt. And that's not an easy life to feel it because you run up against a lot of sadness. But also a lot of joy. You're either up or you're down."

Shelly tried to get him off his moods by encouraging him to draw. She called it his "venting." Draw a dog, she would say, or draw that chair against the wall. His brother would draw three lines on a page and tell him to make a picture out of it and he would come up with an elegant solution. The Piggly Wiggly supermarket hired him when he was around eleven to draw their signs. He would sketch a pork chop then write the price per pound in handwriting that was so nice it was like calligraphy.

The Antleys lived out on that dirt road, entertaining each other by playing piano and coming up with games, and they attracted all the area kids to their house. One day Shelly and the kids were coming home from the grocery store and they saw a huge plume of smoke coming from somewhere up the road. The house must be on fire, Shelly said. But then, toward the head of the road, they saw the inferno. It was the broken-down house of a black family that lived toward the head of the road. All six children were standing outside, with no parents around, looking confused and frightened. No firemen had come, no neighbors. The littlest one, who was Leslie's age—around eighteen months at the time—kept trying to go back into the blaze for a toy or something she had left behind. Eventually, the Antleys coaxed them to abandon the inferno and brought them to their home. They bathed them and fed them. The kids wandered around the Antleys' house amazed. They didn't even have a bathroom in their shack.

"Mama, they're looking in your drawers," Chris and Brian told Shelly.

"Let them look," she said. "We might not have as much as we like, but there are people who don't have anything. Let them see what it is to take care of things, to put clothes in your closets."

That began one of Chris's closest friendships. The family eventually found a place to live, but all six kids showed up at the Antleys every morning to play. The oldest, Eugene, and Chris talked constantly and camped out in the back. When Chris was eleven, he spent the summer working in the tobacco fields because Eugene did. He was the one little white kid among all the black workers arriving at five in the morning for a day of heavy labor. He came home completely worn out, his small body covered in dirt. Eugene labored in those fields because it was expected of him, but Chris did it because he couldn't spend the whole day apart from his best buddy. He made fifty-two dollars at the end of each week.

One day Chris asked his mother if Eugene could go with them to church. Of course, she told him. But then she started wondering how the First Baptist Church, with its all-white congregation, would treat Eugene. She pulled Chris aside one day. "Honey," she said, "of course you can take Eugene to church. I'd be delighted for him to go with us. But I do want you to understand something. There may be a lot of staring and a lot of looks. There may be remarks, I do not know. But if you can handle it, then it will help Eugene handle it. He is your best friend in this world. That's who you are sharing your beliefs with."

Chris thought about it all weekend. Then he went to her crying. "Mama," he said, "I can't do it. I can't hurt Eugene."

"Babe," she said, "you don't have to cry for him because this is something he's going to have to deal with all his life. This is the way the world is. But having friendships like yours is what helps people go through what they have to go through." Eugene didn't go with them to church, and Chris stopped caring about the congregation and its activities.

When Chris was twelve, Les and Shelly separated, and Chris was devastated. Les drifted away from his children as he tried to put his life back together, so his boys rarely saw him.

Chris had idolized his mother. Later he would say she was, at the time, the love of his life.[10] But now, barely into her thirties and beautiful, she went on a wild tear. In a small town, everyone knew how wild she could get. "I didn't do a lot of things people do until I got divorced," Shelly said. "And then I did them. I was a typical mommy who stayed at home for the longest time. I didn't have a childhood. So when I hit thirty-two, I got a grip. Or I thought I got a grip but I didn't. I was a little crazy. So when Chris first started to see me take a drink, he was like, 'My mother's having a drink?' It really affected him because he had me way up there. And I guess it's also because I was very strict with him."

At age fourteen, Chris Antley began dreaming of his future, and it would all take place on the racetrack. He liked earning money, to buy things his parents couldn't afford, and he heard racing could be lucrative. He knew he had talent, that he had an easy way with horses. He loved the charge he got from coming so close to injury and danger, then passing it by.[11] Brian had started working with the thoroughbreds too, and in the dawn, they jogged together from their mother's house to the training center. The movie *Rocky* had just come out with its story of the boxer from modest means training for the championship in the bleak streets of working-class Philadelphia. The wordless soundtrack obsessed Chris. When he and Brian turned the corner by the First Baptist Church, Chris would start his monologue. He would tell his eleven-year-old brother what a big star he was going to be. They ran by the open fields and the grove of long-needle fir, and he would say how he was going to get to the Kentucky Derby one day. They would pass Shirer's pond with the mist hanging above the glassy surface and Chris would describe the way he would win the Triple Crown. And Brian running along next to him in that silence punctuated only by bird calls and this rambling vision would roll his eyes and think, *My brother is stupid. He's the biggest bullshitter I ever knew. My brother is actually stupid.*[12]

Then they would see the end of the road and the gate of the training center and the long dirt drive carved out between the paddocks, and Chris would run right to the stables. "One day you'll get to the Kentucky Derby," Goree Smith told Chris. "And I'll be there to cheer you on."[13]

When Chris was fourteen, he stopped by his grandmother Eugenia's house a few blocks from the downtown shops. Things had become more chaotic at his mother's house and there had been a fire because of the woodburning stove, their only source of heat. The place was now nearly unlivable. Chris Antley stood there in his grandmother's living room with its thick rugs and the silence and dusted knickknacks and asked if he could move in with her for a while.

Eugenia was even tinier than Chris—put together with delicate sparrow bones but stronger than probably anyone in the family. She came from that kind of stock. The pastor at her church, Reverend McCrary, recalled how in 1981 he started serving a community up in the hills of Chesterfield county. On his rounds, McCrary stopped by the home of Eugenia's mother, eighty-four-year-old Ethel Griffith, to check on her. As he approached the house, he saw two spindly legs jutting out from under the magnolia tree.

"Oh, no," he thought. "Granny's dead." He paused for a moment in confusion, wondering whom he should call.

Then he heard a sharp squawk. "Get down here," Granny snapped, "and help me pick up these cones."

Eugenia's mother lived to be 101. When Chris went to stay with Eugenia, she was in her mid-sixties and spry; two decades later, she went to step aerobics three times a week. She believed in God and sang in the choir at the First Baptist Church. Chris lived with her for two years. He rode his bike to the training center every morning, bused out to Clarendon Hall School, a private Christian school, then came back to his grandmother's house in the evenings after finishing the chores for Smith.

The girls at school liked him because he was sweet and had those intense blue eyes, which when he looked at you made you feel like there was no one else in the world. But they also babied him and felt sorry for him that he was so small. He went to the prom in a light blue tuxedo and carrying a cane like Fred Astaire.

Chris played pool with a bunch of boys, but one time one of them said something smart about his mother and he had to take a pool stick to him. At the training center, everyone left you alone. It was just you and the horses and the workers—mostly good guys who were white, black, and Hispanic, who based their loyalty on their mutual love of horses and didn't pay attention to social standing.

He was fifteen and had been riding for a couple of years. The other kids at school were flirting at the pizza parlor but Antley preferred to spend his afternoons with a horse. The sign on the stall door read PARADE OF STARS.

In the mornings, Antley exercised the big brown colt, and if Antley asked him to go, Parade of Stars answered quickly. When they walked back to the barn, Antley didn't even hold his shank. The colt followed him like a dog. In the afternoon, Antley visited in the stall. If the colt lay down on the straw, Antley lay across his belly. He talked constantly about the horse, until Brian couldn't help but laugh. Antley drew a wreath of stars on the stall door and ordered his own riding helmet, gold with six large stars circling the sides.[14]

Smith understood how Antley felt. Sometimes you spotted an animal—the fastest, smartest, easiest of them all—and you couldn't help but admire the horse completely. Horses' behavior was consistent with how you treated them. They could sense your calm and go quiet themselves. They let you know when they were bothered and gave you a chance to understand. You cared for them like babies, and in those chores you forgot yourself, loving them in that selfless way that a parent could love a child. But the horse was also your superior—stronger, bigger, faster, and it handed over all those gifts to you as a rider. It was one thing to be talented at a sport, but to have the respect of a horse was to be sanctified. Everything could be chaotic at home, at school, but when Antley walked up to the stall that held Parade of Stars, he knew the colt would hear his call and look out. Antley extended his hand and the horse pressed against it, and out on the track—while at sixteen Antley was just five feet one—he sat eight feet high, and flew by all the other riders.

In the spring of 1982, Smith asked Antley to ride at the Trials. Antley wanted to ride Parade of Stars in his first real race more than anything. At that time, he discovered that Parade of Stars was actually the name of the colt's sire. A horse officially holds the name of its mare or sire until it is two. The horse that Antley had fallen in love with was now Surviving the Life. Smith had named him after a Neil Diamond song.

The day of the Trials, the fence posts leading to the training center entrance were decorated with small American flags. The cars and trucks started arriving around 9:00 in the morning and parked in the fields. Spectators set up their fried chicken dinners and coolers of beer on the backs. Smith booked Antley to ride two races, including one on Surviving the Life, and before the day ended, Antley picked up two more mounts. He came in second in his first race, then won the other three. He took home two trophies, and the coveted Elloree Cup for his victory on the back of Vernon Shirer's horse Cristy Key. He was sixteen and had $620 in purse money to take home. A picture of the local hero ran in the newspaper—so young and small at the time he looked like a cricket on the horse's back.

Two months after the Elloree Trials, Surviving the Life was scheduled to ship to the racetracks up North with the other two-year-olds. Antley had galloped that horse most every morning, and most afternoons he sat beside him in his stall. The first time they went to the winner's circle, they were together. They knew each other. They understood each other.

The day Surviving the Life was set to depart, Antley crouched beside him and carefully wound the bandages around his legs for the last time. Then he led him onto the van.

Antley started crying. The van's ignition caught and the trailer began moving away, down the dirt lane toward the road. Antley watched the van go, and then he couldn't take it anymore. He got in his Ford Escort and started following. He later said he drove through most of North Carolina, trailing the horse he loved. "It was killing me," he remembered. But then he realized he should turn back. He went home and began packing an old army trunk.[15]

He ended up needing the help of Goree Smith to go to the track, but that didn't prove to be a problem. Smith could see Antley had everything it took to be a jockey, but felt he needed that last itch to get possessed with the sport and then spend one more year riding in Elloree to hone his skills. Goree Smith asked the Antleys if Chris could go to Atlantic City that summer, where his brother, Hamilton Smith, or "Hammy," had transported Surviving the Life, and Antley's parents said he could.

Goree Smith made Antley take summer-school classes at night. In the mornings at the track, Antley exercised the horses and schooled them in the paddock. He was so full of life he was almost hyperactive. He asked questions constantly and stood all day by the starting gate to watch the technique of the other riders and the intoxicating blast of power at the start. Most of the riders were male, usually Hispanic or white boys from rural areas. Before the Civil War, most star American jockeys were black—slaves or sons of slaves. But anti-gambling laws shut down tracks in the early part of the century, and, a decade or two later, when the tracks reopened, the black riders didn't come back. Edward Hotaling, the preeminent historian on the subject, theorized that trainers decided white jockeys would have it easier with the owners than the black riders and started booking accordingly.[16] In the early 1980s, there were only a few black jockeys riding in the United States.

The top jock that season was Julie Krone out of John Forbes's stable. She had just lost her apprentice allowance that spring. Once jockeys become established, they operate as independents, riding for whichever trainer will book them. But when a jock starts out, he or she is an apprentice, brought along on contract by one trainer. The apprentice, or bug boy, as he is called, can ride for other trainers, but only after he fulfills his day's commitments to the trainer who holds the contract. If an apprentice wins a stakes race, he doesn't get paid part of the purse, just his riding fee. For his first five wins, an apprentice can carry ten pounds more than the pros. The program notes the weight allowance with three asterisks, and that's why apprentice riders got the nickname bug rider or bug boy, because the mark looks like a bug. After five wins, the weight allowance shifts down to seven pounds up to forty wins. After an apprentice wins forty times, he can only ride at five pounds over weight until the year anniversary of his first five wins. If he still is on contract when he hits the anniversary, he can sometimes get another waiver for three pounds during the time he has left on the contract. But otherwise his handicap for extra weight vanishes once he turns pro. For many jocks, the grueling battle with starvation and diuretics begins then.

Krone was two years older than Antley and he greatly admired her. She had grown up on horses in Michigan, standing on their backs barefoot like Pippi Longstocking while they trotted. Krone and Antley would stalk out to the gates on their horses for their morning breezes and Krone would tell Antley what she knew about the life of a jockey. Even more exciting, Antley watched when Surviving the Life raced in Atlantic City and won, proving he had been worthy of Antley's admiration all along. Antley stood at the rail when Willie Shoemaker, then the winningest jockey ever, sped around the oval. Antley asked for his autograph and liked how Shoemaker's valet wore a shirt that said "The Shoe." Antley wrote down "The Ant" on a piece of paper and hoped one day people would call him that.[17]

Antley went back to Elloree for school in the fall. When his mother unpacked his bags, she found a stolen bottle of her diuretic pills stashed among his clothes. To work consistently, a jock needs to stay around 105 pounds and certainly under 116 pounds. Colts in the Triple Crown races are assigned 126 pounds, including the four pounds taken up by the clothing, boots, saddle, girth and saddle pad. The clerk of scales directs each jock to add a certain number of lead weight pads to the pockets of his or her saddle to get up to the 126 for the race. But most races limit a jockey to 120 pounds or less all the way down to 105. Antley was only sixteen years old when he was working in Atlantic City and naturally light enough, but the fear of weight gain already gripped him.

At the end of Antley's junior year of high school, he told his father his plans to go to Maryland to ride professionally. He wanted to drop out of school, but his father begged him to stay until he graduated. Chris insisted. If he didn't go then, he said, he might never get the chance. His weight was fine, but who knew what would happen down the line. If everything worked out riding, he said, he could make ten thousand to twenty thousand dollars a year.[18]

"I don't believe you," Les told him, "but if you think you can make that much money, go on and do it." His father thought the whole thing was a pipe dream, but he allowed that he couldn't stop his son. "I know if you make up your mind about something, you're going to do it," Les said. He gave Chris one hundred dollars to start out.

"If you will let me take you up there, I will be glad to," Shelly told Chris when he gave her the news. "In my heart, I can not see you pull out of this driveway by yourself at seventeen, not knowing what this world has to offer."

So he and his mother headed to the track in Jersey, where the meet started before shifting down to Maryland. They stopped in Salisbury, Maryland, where Shelly was born, to have a doughnut at the shop where she went as a child. Chris hadn't been nervous at the start of the trip, but now he sat there, shoveling down doughnut after doughnut. He went through a dozen and kept going. "Chris, you're going to be ill," Shelly warned him.

And then he was. He vomited for the next three and a half hours, while she drove. They pulled up to the track in New Jersey at 4:30 in the morning and slept in the car outside the gate until the grooms started walking through the shedrows.

Antley eventually moved into Hammy Smith's house in Maryland. His licensing paperwork was completed, but the notary at the track refused to certify the documents because the pages didn't have both parents' signatures. If Antley wanted to race, he would have to wait for everything to ship down to South Carolina and come back, which meant he'd be sitting on the sidelines for at least another week. Antley literally spent most of that week in tears, in desperation to ride. But one day Smith noticed a notary sign at a liquor store of all places, and got the proprietor, who didn't pay attention to the fine print, to authorize the documents. The pay amount on the contract was blank when Antley signed, because Ham Smith didn't want to take a cut of Antley's earnings. All he wanted was to help the kid ride, and his only stipulation was that Antley couldn't ride against one of Smith's horses.

One day Smith and Antley were in the racing secretary's office at the Pimlico Race Course in Maryland, and they ran into the jockey agent Lou Rosenthal. "Antley had instant dollar signs written all over him," Rosenthal purred, remembering the moment. "He was the perfect size, small but muscular. He glowed with personality."

"Ham," Rosenthal said, looking the kid over. "What's this?"

"Take it easy, Lou," Smith said. "He's not ready yet." He didn't want the kid to get sucked into the rough-and-tumble of the business so soon.

One winter morning at Bowie racecourse, Rosenthal stopped by Smith's barn with the list of horses scratched from the card that day. "Do you want to try it with Chris Antley?" Smith asked out of the blue.

"Do I? Sure," Rosenthal said. "Ham, if I don't think I'm doing the job right or I'm doing him an injustice, you won't have to fire me, I'll come to you myself."

"I ain't worried about that," Smith said, "just don't try to put him on too many too soon. Start him on Monday, put him on a couple, go easy."

Chris Antley's first race was June 1, 1983, at Pimlico. The season at that track had started in April and ran for a few months, then the Maryland action shifted to Bowie through the end of July and then on to Timonium, then Laurel, and back to Bowie for February and March.

Riding in a real race was different from competing at the Elloree Trials. In the Trials, the horses were all levels of talent, and when they raced they would string out across a whole furlong. In the pros, the horses were better matched, and ran clustered together. The noise was deafening. You could hear the horses with breathing problems working like old steam radiators. You could hear other jocks kissing or clucking or cursing at their horses. A horse would jump a lane and a jock would scream as he got pinched against another mount. In the stretch, the jocks barked "Hah! Hah!" as they whipped their horses home. When the track was dry and hard, the hooves sounded like thunder beneath the jocks and their hearts would be drilling fast. When the track was wet, the mud sprayed in their faces all the way around the course. Their goggles kept going dark and they would peel one set away and let it hang from their necks; in seconds, the new set would go black, and they would strip it away, all the way to the finish. The jocks might go through five or six sets of goggles and would be covered with mud from head to toe except for the clean circles around their eyes where the goggles had been.

Ten days after Chris Antley started racing at Pimlico, the seventeen-year-old rode his first winner, Vaya Con Dinero, which meant *Go with the money*.

Antley won another that day, hitting the double, and that victory felt as big as winning a stakes race. He hit a hot streak right from the beginning. Hammy Smith would walk over to the Laurel Park track in the afternoons. "How's Antley doing?" he would ask one of the hot-walkers.

"He's winning," the hotwalker would say. "In fact, he's won all of them." Smith looked at the card and Antley would be three for three, going for four. Already Antley hoped to attain the title of leading rider for a season at one of the tracks he rode, meaning winning the most races of any jockey in the meet.

Antley was so athletic, he could recover from any snafu. Once his saddle slid down at the start and he nearly went off the horse, but he pulled himself up and kept riding. Another time his foot came out of the iron and he tucked it under him, and his form was so clean no one could tell.[19]

Antley earned big money right from the start and piled it in a cigar box under his bed. In that first year, the jock won the most races of any apprentice nationally, and was second in purse money earned with $1,851,865, of which his share was a little less than 10 percent. But the wealth couldn't buy him adult maturity. He was still too young to get a credit card and he had to get one of the horse owners, Fred Green, to open a bank account for him.

The meet moved over to Bowie, an austere old track with a glassed-in grandstand named after the founding horse-racing enthusiast Governor Oden Bowie. Rosenthal liked to say Indians named the track in the late 1800s, when they crossed the center field in January. A big wind hit them square on, five below zero. "*Booooooooweeeeee*," they said, "it's cold."[20]

On January 2, 1984, only six months after Antley started riding professionally and while still an apprentice, he shaved a second off the Bowie record time for a mile and a sixteenth riding Count My Love in the $55,700 Resolution Handicap. The largest crowd in the history of the race turned out and cheered for the track's new natural.

It could have been the most wonderful, exciting time any young apprentice could imagine, any kid who spent years dreaming and training for that moment among the pros. But in mid-January, Antley and two other riders, Greg Hutton and Donald Miller, were fined fifty dollars each for failure to ride their horses out in a race,[21] meaning the stewards suspected they held the horses back to fix the race.

Race fixing was not that uncommon at that time. Farther north, the New Jersey State Police Race Track Unit started working undercover in 1981 to investigate illegal activities in the horse-racing industry, including race fixing. The key informant was a man named Anthony Ciulla, who claimed to have fixed two thousand races over a fifteen-year period, primarily in the late '70s. It wasn't difficult, he testified, to get the jockeys

to cooperate with the finish-line outcome he chose. Through interme-
diaries, Ciulla would approach all the jockeys except one and pay them
to hold back their horses while giving the impression they were riding
them hard to the wire. If a jockey won a twenty-thousand-dollar race
legitimately, he would only take home around six hundred dollars of the
purse. But if the jock held his horse back, Ciulla would pay him five
thousand dollars because Ciulla could make so much more by placing
well-informed bets.[22] Ciulla's evidence convicted over fifty jockeys and
trainers nationwide, and he lived out his life under the witness protection
program. Even the New York racing authorities wished Ciulla would
stop squealing and tried to destroy his credibility, because if people believed what he said, racing's reputation would be demolished.

In one darkly comic piece of testimony, Ciulla claimed to have tried
to bribe the jockey Mike Hole to pull back his horse at a race in Saratoga
in 1974. The New York racing authorities argued that Ciulla couldn't
be believed because a different witness claimed Hole had pointed out
Jacinto Vasquez, the jockey who won the Kentucky Derby with Foolish
Pleasure in 1975 and Genuine Risk in 1980, as the man who tried to
bribe him to fix that Saratoga race. Ciulla insisted there was no contra-
diction to his testimony.

He had tried to bribe Hole. Vasquez could have tried to bribe Hole.
Everyone had tried to bribe Hole over the years, but Hole never caved.
"I don't understand why people won't believe the plain fact that jockeys
were operating all the time, fixing races from Maine to Spain and in New
York. Yeah, they're the greatest riders in the world and pound for pound
they're also the biggest crooks," Ciulla said. "These guys were so good
at holding horses, they could hold an elephant away from a bale of pea-
nuts."[23] Unfortunately, Hole himself couldn't testify to Ciulla's credibility. In 1976, he was found dead of asphyxiation in his car at a Jones
Beach parking lot, an apparent but mysterious suicide.

Track authorities believed that most of the corruption was purged
with the race fixing trials, but no one believed the tracks were squeaky
clean. The best way to keep yourself out of trouble was to go public as

someone pursuing track records for wins, and the thing Antley cared about more than money was track records.

On March 7, 1984, Antley rode a horse at Bowie that stumbled in the stretch and threw him. Antley broke his collarbone and was laid up for six weeks. He kept trying to persuade the doctors to let him ride again, but they insisted he recuperate. He exercised to keep his weight down and passed the time at Hammy Smith's house drawing sketches of horses and crafting subtle little portraits of the people who stopped by. Even with that layoff, Antley came in second in wins for the meet going up against even the veteran riders.

By the time Antley could go back to racing in late April, the game had shifted to Monmouth Park, a resort track in Oceanport, New Jersey. The venue started as a five-day meet in 1870 to boost tourism along the Jersey Shore and evolved into a full summer season of racing that attracted presidents Grover Cleveland, James A. Garfield, and Ulysses S. Grant, the gangster Diamond Jim Brady, actress Lillie Langtry, and many wealthy socialites of New York. In 1893, the New Jersey legislature banned horse racing because smaller tracks with few controls had begun cropping up, and Monmouth stayed closed for more than fifty years.

Just prior to World War II, Armory L. Haskell, the former General Motors executive and founder of Triplex Safety Glass, lobbied the state legislature to make an exception to the gambling ban for thoroughbred and standardbred racing.[24] With the beginning of the war, the state was desperate for funds so they agreed to the waiver to gain a percentage from the pari-mutuel pool. Haskell built his new Monmouth track in 1946.

Monmouth looked like other American tracks, with an airplane hangar of a grandstand, potted petunias and geraniums lining the walkways, and manicured infield, but it also felt like a cabana, with green-and-white-striped awnings on the clubhouse patios taking the full summer sun. Low beech trees shaded the walking ring, which was posted with the playful sign ALIBI ZONE, in honor of all the excuses that would be made by horsemen for their losses within its boundaries. The breezes blowing through the cavern below the grandstand wafted the concession stand aromas, steamed hot dogs and crab cakes, chocolate sauce and caramel. A small stand by the stairs up to the clubhouse sold souvenirs and horse toys for children, while behind glass, a few paces away, a barbershop offered quick trims and manicures. Park benches filled the apron, and past the final turn was a grove of umbrella-shaded picnic tables.

For a jockey, the place was luxurious, with a sparkling six-lane swimming pool in the fenced yard right off the jocks' room and a well-stocked game room. Philip Iselin made those improvements in the 1960s and '70s as a way to attract the best riders, and the lures worked. There were about sixty jockeys there that season, and a dozen apprentices. Vince Bracciale Jr., who rode the great filly Ruffian a few times in the mid-'70s, was one of the big guns. Jimmy Edwards was nine years into a career that began with him breaking a Monmouth season record for wins when he was an apprentice in 1975. And there was Craig Perret, a grand old man of thirty-three from New Orleans. Herb McCauley, the year before, was offered such outstanding mounts for the Derby he had retreated to a cathedral to pray on the decision. They were the top clique, king of kings, and then the little bug boy, Chris Antley, flopped in—a nice baby-faced kid, but one of the shyest, quietest new riders they had ever seen, barely speaking even when spoken to.[25]

Perret liked the kid's talent right away. He and Bracciale watched Antley on the track, then took him aside in the jocks' room to give pointers. Antley asked a lot of questions, which endeared him to those older guys. Clearly, he wanted to learn from the pros. He wasn't one of those cocky kids who came in thinking they knew everything and were washed out within a year or two.

Antley still didn't understand strategy, the idea that he should be looking for the gaps between horses so he could shoot through to the lead. He would get on a horse and ride him gung-ho to the finish line. "Hey, child, mellow out," Perret told him. "You're doing fine. Just settle down. You're shooting at a hole you can't get to. You're shooting at it from five lengths back and when you get there, it closes up. The whole length there, you seen it, but you ain't there. That means it *ain't* there." Antley would drift up against the other horse's rump and then have to slow his horse to steady him, so he wouldn't clip hooves. "You sneak," Perret and Bracciale would tell him. "You *sneak*. When it opens, *boom*! Then you go for it. Then you *belong*. But you don't belong five lengths back." Antley kept making the same mistake.

Every morning at 11:00 the track stewards handed the jockeys what was called a movie list. If a jock's name appeared, he was required to report to a special room with television monitors where the stewards convened. The jock then had to answer to any infraction that might have occurred on the track the day before. On the racetrack, each furlong, as well as the halfway point within furlongs, is marked by a pole, adding up to sixteen poles. The poles structure the mile so that a horse's running time can be measured every four poles counting from the highest number down from the start to the finish. The racing order at each of those four poles is displayed on the totalisor, the electric board across from the grandstand where the betting odds and track conditions are posted.

The quarter poles give the announcer a point of reference for calling the race, and when the times are posted later, inform the handicappers so they can better predict the outcome of a future competition with specific data showing whether a horse starts fast or closes strong. The Monmouth stewards would roll tape showing the turn into the final stretch in race five, for example, from all angles—a bird's-eye view panning around the whole oval, the turn into the backstretch from the third turn to the final turn, and head-on through the stretch and finish line. The stewards would say to the jock who bumped the rider next to him, "What do you have to say for yourself?"

And the jock did his best to explain his efforts to ride clean. "Well, my horse ducked in and I tried to grab him," the rider explained. He couldn't lie because the moment was on tape. If a horse veered for no reason, and a rider tried to straighten him, then the stewards wouldn't penalize the jock. They might take the purse from the trainer, but a rider wasn't held responsible for the strange behavior of an animal. If the jock bumped another rider, out of competitiveness, then he would get hit with a suspension.

"Go take five days, son," the steward would say. "Take a vacation."

Perret told Antley to go to the movies every day, to study racing from all of those angles. "Chris, watch this," Perret said, pointing to the video of himself riding from the day before. Perret was about five lengths behind the lead, riding at the flank of another horse.

Antley watched Perret trailing. "Why did you get in there?" Antley whispered.

"Now watch this," Perret said, still staring at the screen. "See that horse? He's trying to drift a little bit. I sat behind him." The horses on the monitor streamed toward the turn. "When he hit the elbow," Perret said, "you *know* he's going to drift a little more. *Boom!* There's my spot. I'm *gone*." They watched as Perret moved to the whip and let the horse run on its full power. "But make sure you've got the horse to do it," he cautioned Antley. If a horse didn't have enough strength to accelerate and hit his mark, horse and rider could get crushed.

One day on the track, Perret saw Antley sprinting up and trailing behind another horse. The horse ahead shifted toward the outer rail, and Antley threaded through the opening onto clear track. "There you go," Perret said to himself proudly. "That's the move."

Antley was at Monmouth for about a month, learning how to ride from the pros, but then the work ground to a halt. The Jockeys' Guild called a strike. The guild had started in 1940 to protect the interests of riders, and one of the main reasons for a jock to join the guild in the 1980s was to secure health insurance. A rider paid eight dollars a mount to the guild. Three dollars of that went into their pension and the rest paid for disability and health insurance coverage for themselves and their families. In New Jersey, the trainers had recently won a 5 percent pay raise on all second- and third-place finishers, but the jockeys hadn't had an increase for twenty-five years. The jockey pay rate then was 10 percent of the purse for a win. For second and third, the jock received nothing more than his mount rate, which was thirty-five dollars. The riders wanted the mount rate to increase to fifty dollars, and to get 5 percent for second and third too.

One night in early May, about forty riders gathered in the jocks' room and barred anyone else from entering. Bracciale, McCauley and Perret served as Jockeys' Guild officers. They asked how many riders wanted a pay raise. All forty hands went up.

"Okay let me tell you," Perret announced to the group, "it may cause a strike." The jocks winced and started shifting in their seats. "Here's the deal, guys," he said. He motioned to himself and the other officers. "We're the ones who are going to lose the mounts because we got all the business," he said. "But if we stick, you got to stick too. That's the only way we'll get the raise done."

All the jocks agreed to stop riding for as long as it took. For two days, none of the Monmouth jockeys rode. They went fishing or crabbing with their kids to pass the time. The trainers and owners started hiring exercise boys to ride the races. They hustled in hack jockeys from other tracks.

The Monmouth riders got word that the races were going off. For three days, they didn't compete. That third day, Antley paid a visit to Perret at his home. "I got to ride," Antley told Perret.

"If you ride," Perret said, "you're not in the guild."

Antley looked desperate. "I got to ride," he said.

"What's your problem?"

Antley told him that Hamilton Smith refused to let him out of his contract.

"Well, ride his horses," Perret said. "Don't ride the rest."

"Mister Craig," Antley pleaded, "I'm trying to get started."

Perret looked at him. "Chris, do what your heart tells you to do," he said. "If that's what you got to do, you do it. But if you're out of the guild, you're out of the guild. That's all I can tell you, pardner."

The jockey Joe Rocco could see how much the problem was eating at Antley. Rocco's agent was making him ride for any trainer who would volunteer to pay the 5 percent for second and third. Antley was greener, and wouldn't get those kinds of concessions. If a jock didn't do well at the beginning of a meet, he was doomed for the rest of that season. A winner got the pick of the best equine talent running, and so kept winning through a meet. A loser only got to ride the broken down horses. Rocco could see Antley didn't want to go up against the guys he admired, but he was hungry to make something of himself.

Antley started riding for Hamilton Smith again. Then in the minds of some of the jocks, he crossed the line even further. Word got around that Antley was taking mounts from other trainers too. Perret went to him. "Chris," he said, "this ain't the right thing."

"I got no choice," Antley said.

"Ride Mr. Hamilton's because you're under contract. Don't ride the others."

"Mister Craig," he said, "it's a chance for me to get off."

Perret had had enough. "Do what you want to do," he said.

Suddenly, Antley started winning consistently. For three days, then four, he was a star. He was the only real rider out there going up against a bunch of exercise boys. The strike went on for seven days. The scab riders were whipping the horses to death because they were so bent on winning. Finally, the owners came around to the jocks and said they would pay them to come back. "Otherwise, I ain't running," one trainer lamented, "because my horses are coming back crippled."

When the jocks came back to the track, Perret approached Antley. "Let me tell you something now, son," Perret said. "You're a friend of mine, but you was wrong."

"Mister Craig," Antley said, "I had no choice. They all wanted me. I just wanted to get going."

"Well, we're going to let it fly by," Perret said. "But you was wrong." Eventually the jocks let all of the riders who broke the strike back in the guild. "Where were they going to go?" Perret said. "Most had lots of kids and no health insurance." Perret was seriously disappointed in Antley, but he couldn't help forgiving the jockey. "He had a lot of energy," Perret recalled. "If you were sitting and talking to him for two minutes, you'd like him. Only because he kind of lights your fire a little bit."

As it turned out, Antley had never even asked Hamilton Smith if he could be excused from his contract.[26]

Antley won only one graded stakes races that year, but by the end of the 1984 summer season, he shattered the Monmouth Park record of wins during a meet. He not only had made the goal of leading rider he set himself when he was just an apprentice, he had beaten all the other leading riders in Monmouth history.[27] The year before, the swaggering jockey Tony Vega stunned the racing fans by winning 134 times in 110 days. But Antley rode a total of 849 races through that late spring and summer, and went to the winner's circle 171 times in 110 days. That record of 171 wins still stood seventeen years later.

The average jockey wins 7 percent of his races and Antley had won over 20 percent. The average jockey places second or third around eight percent of the time, and Antley had made 30 percent.

On July 30, Antley rode six winners—the first six races of the day—which tied him for the track record.[28] Lou Rosenthal told the girls who pestered him to pass their numbers to Antley, "Look, I handle his afternoon business, sweetheart, I don't do nothing with his evenings."

In homage to Antley's nickname—the Ant—Rosenthal made white hats with a cartoon of a blue ant wearing a jockey skullcap and carrying a whip. Rosenthal walked through the shedrow each day slapping backs and shaking hands, reciting in dramatic tones his ode to his star:

> He flies like a butterfly,
> And he stings like a bee,
> Look out, everybody,
> Here comes Ant-leeee.

The track's official 1984 summary reads: "The season will long be remembered for the riding heroics of eighteen-year-old apprentice jockey Chris Antley, who shattered the record for most wins in a season in an awesome display of riding ability. . . . Antley was so popular that

Monmouth decided to honor him with a special day on Saturday, August 26. Free color pictures of Antley were distributed to the large crowd on hand."[29]

Lost in the early part of that summer, amid all those victories, was Antley's apprentice bug, vanished from the program after the year anniversary of his first five victories. Now, he was required to ride at weight like the other professionals. The summer Chris Antley was eighteen years old, he weighed in at only 114 with his equipment, so no achievement seemed very far out of reach. He was making between sixteen thousand and twenty thousand dollars a week. "Hey, Louie, you know what's strange?" Antley asked Rosenthal.

"What's that, Chris?"

"They pay me all this money and I'm out there having fun every day."

FOUR

LUCKY FELLOW

Who knew the reasons why, if a person had the financial means, they bought thoroughbreds instead of sports cars, why they preferred to see their silks crossing the finish line first to watching their sailboat cut through the water, why they liked gambling on horseflesh more than oil rigs. Late into his seventies, the thoroughbred owner Bob Lewis could still remember how the colors flashed—canary yellow, scarlet, royal blue—and how the crowds of people cackled and shouted. He recalled an ornate building, which he later guessed was the casino. But he couldn't remember much more. He was only four years old in 1928, when his parents drove from their home in Pasadena, California, to the new Agua Caliente racetrack in Tijuana, the Mexican town that absorbed America's wilder impulses during Prohibition. Those kaleidoscopic memories of Bob Lewis's first race settled in his mind, and in the alchemy of the years that followed, his passion for thoroughbreds intensified until he became one of the nearly 30,000 owners who shelled out tens of millions of dollars a year on the sport.

Since 1909, when the state government passed the Anti-Racetrack

Gambling bill, California had been without its racetracks. Until then, tracks at the county fairs had flourished, perhaps because the California settlers who attended them embodied everything a person needed to enjoy racing: Western horse sense, a Gold-Rush love of quick money, and a spirit of adventure. One of the fair courses, the Pleasanton oval, was said to have been constructed in 1858 by a Spanish Don, Augustin Bernal, and claimed the distinction of being the oldest American track.

The Santa Anita track started almost a half century later. In 1875, an Ohio native named Elias Jackson "Lucky" Baldwin arrived at the foot of the San Gabriel Mountains northeast of Los Angeles and declared, "This is paradise, the spot I've been looking for all my life."[1] In five years, he made a fortune on gold mine investments and purchased an eight-thousand-acre tract at a cost of $200,000, naming the place for his daughter, Anita. East of Pasadena, Lucky planted Rancho Santa Anita with grape arbors and groves of lemon, orange and walnut trees, eventually commanding sixty-three thousand acres stretching over more than five counties. He raised thoroughbreds and shipped them to tracks around the country, but he dreamed of starting a world-class track of his own right there in California. In December 1907, that fantasy became a reality when he opened Santa Anita racetrack off Huntington Drive.

Two years later, in 1909, the Anti-Racetrack Gambling law went into effect, the Santa Anita track closed, and, not surprisingly, Lucky promptly died. Three years after his death, the grandstand burned down, Anita sold the property to Los Angeles during World War I, and the city leased the land to the War Department to use for the U.S. Army Balloon School. Racing remained illegal in the state for more than two decades.

Ironically the Depression resurrected the tracks. With California stretched on an economic rack, statewide initiatives were introduced three times to legalize gambling since the government would get a percentage of track revenues to fill their coffers. In 1933, the initiative passed, the stated purpose being the "encouragement of agriculture and breeding of horses." Immediately, Anita, her daddy's girl, began building a new track on a portion of the estate she retained. About a year into the project she fell into financial difficulties, and Hal Roach, the producer of Laurel and Hardy movies, bought her out. He and his partner Dr. Charles Strub, a San Francisco dentist, hired Gordon Kaufman, architect of the Hoover Dam, to design the grandstand. On Christmas Day 1934, the track opened, full to capacity and decorated with movie stars—Al Jolson, Clark Gable, and Will Rogers, among others. Fred Astaire started spending time at Santa Anita, and later in life married a jockey he met there, Robyn Smith.

Bob Lewis's parents took young Bob to the track almost every Saturday. The gates opened at ten and Bob's job was to sprint ahead of the spectators in their fedoras and plumed hats to secure seats for his parents and their friends as they strolled, all dressed up and happy, past the manicured paddock and the wrought-iron palm-tree pillars of the balconies. After the crash of 1929, Bob had seen anxiety etch his parents' faces as they struggled to keep a lumber-supply business afloat amid a building bust. The reopening of the track represented the first bud of a welcome frivolity.

Other tracks soon followed. Bing Crosby built the Del Mar track near San Diego in 1937. Then the next year, Hollywood Park opened in Inglewood, with a glittering roster of shareholders, including Crosby, Al Jolson, Walt Disney, Sam Goldwyn, and Darryl Zanuck. Racing in California was reborn.

The lighthearted pleasure ended, however, on December 7, 1941, when the Japanese bombed Pearl Harbor. With the United States' entry into World War II, the government banned horse racing nationally for fear that large gatherings made easy enemy targets and because racing seemed an unjustifiable luxury in a time of extreme rationing. The government decided to put the empty racetracks to other uses. On February 19, 1942, President Franklin Roosevelt issued an executive order, commanding that all West Coast residents of Japanese descent be interned. The Western Defense Command chose Santa Anita as the site of one of the larger camps.

Within a month, the army built five hundred shelters at the track to house twenty thousand Japanese Americans. Even the shedrows were whitewashed and put to use. The detainees bathed in the horse showers and slept on mattresses stuffed with straw. In the summer, the stalls grew so hot the cot legs sank into the asphalt. Guards patrolled the perimeter with machine guns, and searchlights swept over the camp through the night. "Everyone who was in a stable area claimed they were housed in the stall that housed the great Seabiscuit," one detainee recalled, referring to the ungainly horse that rallied to dominate the sport and newspaper headlines in 1938.[2] In October 1942 the detainees were shipped to desert camps in California, Arizona, and Utah, after which the track was converted to a weapons training center.

Soon after the end of the war, the ban on horse racing was lifted, and the tracks reopened one or two at a time across the country. Santa Anita welcomed spectators again on May 15, 1945, refurbished with two thousand flowering plants and a sweeping new ramp leading to the grandstand, as if these cosmetic improvements might wash away the uncomfortable memories of the war.

Bob Lewis had served stateside and was released from the service around the time Santa Anita reopened. For a few months he and another veteran buddy put off adult responsibilities and enjoyed themselves. Every day the tracks opened for business, Bob Lewis and his buddy drove to Santa Anita or Hollywood Park, with betting money to burn and the radio tuned to whatever station was playing Nat King Cole.

Bob Lewis noticed the girl the minute he walked into the College Side Inn that September day in 1946. Students at the University of Oregon filled every booth, drinking Olympia beer and playing bridge between classes, and Bob could almost imagine the war had never happened. She sat in the front booth with her friends, drinking a Coke and playing a hand of cards, a sandy-haired nineteen-year-old who looked as sweet as could be. Bob turned to his Delta Tau Delta brothers. "Guys," he said in his thrumming baritone, "I'm going to meet that young lady." Shyness got the best of him that day, however, and he decided to wait for another chance.

As luck would have it, Bob found an opportunity within days. As one of the three Yell Leaders for the cheerleading squad, Bob helped interview the girls trying out for the Rally Squad. He saw her waiting in the hall on the morning of the interviews, and, coincidentally, his job was to collect the names, phone numbers and addresses of all the young hopefuls. *Beverly Deichler.*

Beverly would always remember his blond crewcut, starched white shirt, rust-colored V-neck cashmere sweater and clean jeans. When Bob called her at her sorority that afternoon, she was surprised to hear from him, but she knew immediately who he was. Of course she would see him.

Bob Lewis picked Beverly up in his 1941 green Buick Sedanet at 2:00 P.M. and knew exactly where he was going—out into the countryside, whizzing along the tangle of turns to Tiny's Tavern, a spotless place with a big fireplace, where Mr. and Mrs. Johnson served a good bowl of chili and a nice cold beer and were particularly friendly to veterans. Bob and Beverly began dating steadily from that point on. They were the Yell Leader and the Rally Squad beauty, and they always remembered those years as probably the happiest of their lives, being young and spirited, dancing together down by the river in Willamette Park, driving the Green Hornet on outings all around Eugene. Bob escorted the mascot Puddles the Duck to football games, and helped Beverly run for Betty Coed (although at her victory celebration, he stood on the sidelines fuming with jealousy as she danced with Joe College, Willie Straub).[3]

Bob invited Beverly to Pasadena that Christmas to meet his parents and took her to the track for the first time. Santa Anita gripped her. She was nineteen years old and the closest she had ever been to racing was watching her uncle, who roomed with her family for a while in San Francisco, going over the racing form each morning at the breakfast table before heading off to work as a court reporter. Bob proved himself terribly lucky that day at the track, and they decided the source of their good fortune was the brown leather gloves Beverly wore to match her suit. Back at school the next semester, they went to the local track, Portland Meadows, and Beverly always made sure to wear the lucky gloves. Once on a visit to her family, she lost the gloves somewhere between an underground San Francisco streetcar and the bus going home. A few days later, she found herself at that stop again and there they were, tucked into the top of the floor-selection panel inside the elevator. She kept wearing them to races for years.

Bob asked Beverly to marry him many times from the moment they met in September through the spring of 1947. In late April, she accepted. Beverly had so much confidence in her fiancé. At the age of nine, he had worked a magazine route so he never needed to ask his parents to buy him anything. At thirteen, he purchased his first car, a Model A Ford, so he could drive to his job stocking shelves and selling ties at a men's clothing store. Beverly Deichler knew that Bob Lewis would be a hard worker. Even better, he was a lucky man at the track. "I think she thought she had found the great messiah," he joked.[4]

Bob got a job after graduation driving a truck for Acme brewery. Payday came on the first of every month, so Bob and Beverly got married Saturday, August 2, 1947, to have some extra cash to enjoy themselves. True to form, they went to the Del Mar racetrack the evening of their wedding. On Sunday, they traveled down to Agua Caliente in Tijuana. They were back at Del Mar on Monday. The money they won at the tracks that weekend paid for their honeymoon.

Their first child, Jeff, arrived on August 13, 1949. Bob and Beverly had an inkling that Beverly might deliver that day, but they didn't tell Bob's parents because it was Saturday and they didn't want to ruin the Lewises' weekly pilgrimage to the racetrack. Bob paced the waiting room until the doctor, who rode horses on the weekends, strolled out in his cowboy boots. "Go have lunch," he told Bob. "Your baby's coming around the clubhouse turn." That showed how well known the Lewises were for their love of horse racing.[5]

Eventually Bob worked his way up to a management position at a San Francisco brewery. He and Beverly and three-year-old Jeff moved into a small house in San Mateo. It all made for a fine, stable life, but people who loved the thrill of the track couldn't stay content with such uneventful comfort forever. One fateful night, Bob and Beverly went to dinner with friends who had started a beer distributorship. The Lewises sat listening as their friends regaled them with marvelous stories of a recent vacation to Europe. The friends told Bob and Beverly that they planned to take another three-week frolic to Hawaii soon.

Driving home, Bob got to thinking how their friends lived the American Dream while he and Beverly lived safely but struggled to keep their heads above water. "Honey," Bob Lewis said, "either we have to own a brewery or own a distributorship." Beverly agreed.

As luck would have it, in 1954, Anheuser-Busch opened a $25 million plant in Van Nuys, California. The brewery had never cracked the Western market before, so the Van Nuys plant served as their beachhead. Bob Lewis gave up his salary and expense-account lunches at the Brown Derby, and he and a buddy opened their own distribution business, Foothill Beverage Company, to move the Anheuser-Busch brew through Southern California. Bob and Beverly didn't have two nickels to rub together to finance the venture, so they borrowed twenty thousand dollars from the partner's father-in-law. Beverly kept the books and Bob drove the delivery trucks. When the Lewises made any money, they immediately owed it to someone else. Anheuser-Busch rode rough herd on Bob to make sure the bills were paid on time, but Bob enjoyed the pressure and the pleasure of being his own boss.

Bob and Beverly did a little better all the time, and so did their neighbors in the San Diego valley. All around them, the new developments grew like topsy. When Bob started, 250,000 people lived in the area he serviced. Within the next decades, that number grew nearly eightfold, and Anheuser-Busch blanketed the market with advertising. The new home owners of Southern California were out on a Saturday mowing their new lawns, and when they got thirsty, what did they do? They cracked open an ice-cold Budweiser beer. Life got more comfortable for Bob and Beverly Lewis. They felt lucky.

*   *   *

Then Bob Lewis almost died.

In 1972, at forty-eight years of age, Bob Lewis endured a massive heart attack. If someone had cut off his arms he would have kissed them for relieving the agony in his limbs.[6] Bob survived the attack, but he thought he would be lucky to make it to his fifty-fifth year. A couple of years later, he underwent bypass surgery. Death would surely come for him soon, he thought. But Bob Lewis refused to give in to pessimism. He saw what had happened to his father after he retired at age sixty-five. The doctors asked Bun Lewis what he planned to do with his newly freed time. "I'm going to go home, watch TV, and read the paper," Bun said.[7] He sat down and never got up again. Four years later, Bun Lewis died. Bob Lewis sure as hell didn't want to give up like that and let death take him before he lived all his dreams.

And his dreams were driven by the hypnosis of that memory when he was four years old, and saw the colors flash at Agua Caliente. He never forgot the intoxication of seeing his parents' happy faces at the Santa Anita track. In the years right after Bob Lewis's brush with death, in the late 1970s, O. "Bud" Straub, who started a large wholesale beer business in Southern California, bought a foal, which he named Brewery Boy. The horse fared well on the tracks and Straub put together an ownership franchise for other beer wholesalers. Bob Lewis was among those who invested, but none of the horses performed.

One day in 1989, Bob Lewis ran into an acquaintance enjoying a day with his son out at Santa Anita. The son, Frank Vega, told him that he worked with the trainer D. Wayne Lukas and planned to put together his own training business. Bob Lewis now had extra cash to play with. Foothill Beverage Company had grown substantially over the years, with 175 trucks now on the road and hundreds of employees on the payroll. The Lewises also owned Antelope Valley Distributing Company in Lancaster.

By the end of the year, Bob and Beverly found themselves sitting next to Frank Vega at the inaugural Barrett sale for two-year-olds in training at the Hinds Pavilion at the Los Angeles fairgrounds, ready to buy horses. The fact that the horses were two years old and in training meant they could compete right away; a horse had to be two years old to run. And the horses weren't too old to enter the glamorous Triple Crown; that series of races allowed only three-year-olds to compete. New buyers thrilled at the prospect of owning an instant Triple Crown competitor and the Lewises were among them.

The Lewises were typical of thoroughbred owners in the United States at the end of the twentieth century. Up until the early part of the seventeenth century, formal racing truly was the "sport of kings," and maintaining racehorses made sense in a world organized around equine power—for transportation, hunting, labor and war. Every castle, manor and estate had its own stable. The first British ruler to transform racing into a popular pastime was James I, who built stables and worked mightily to entice spectators to the tracks. In England, debates sparked over the centuries about who should be allowed to participate and who should be content to watch. Only the upper class was allowed to actually run animals. The lower classes might occasionally be needed as spectators, but were discouraged from competing. In 1674, a British tailor was punished for racing against a planter, "it being contrary to Law for Labourer to make a race, being a sport only for Gentleman."[8]

At the end of the twentieth century, the average American horse owner in racing, showing, or breeding had an annual income of sixty thousand dollars, but most highly successful owners were old money aristocracy or wealthy businesspeople—the founders of oil companies and McDonald's franchises; the owner of Big Bear Grocery; or the manufacturer of Jif peanut butter—looking for excitement.

In 1940, the Santa Anita racetrack introduced the first six-figure contest, the $100,000 Santa Anita Handicap. Once that ceiling broke, tracks around the country started hosting six-figure races, and owners flocked to the sport in pursuit of the big-money prizes. In 1950, winning owners divvied up $50 million nationally. A decade later, the total purse across the country was $93.7 million.

The U.S. owner with the highest earnings for twelve years (eleven of them consecutive) was Calumet Farm, located in Lexington, Kentucky, run during its heydey of the 1940s and '50s by Warren Wright Sr. In 1996, Allen E. Paulson, the founder of Gulfstream Aerospace Corp., set the record for most money earned by an owner in one year with $9 million. In 1990, when the Lewises entered the Hinds Pavilion for the auction, such figures seemed like far-off fantasies.

That day Bob and Beverly watched the horses parade into the ring with the hip numbers stuck to their flanks. Beverly shook with nerves. Before the night ended, Bob and Beverly bought a good-looking filly for $200,000 and a Damascus colt for $225,000. The first time buying their own horses, the Lewises were leaving the Hinds Pavilion almost half a million dollars lighter.

The Lewises named the filly Destiny's Divine, and the colt, Deduction. They sent the horses to a farm before shipping them to Vega for training. About six weeks after the purchase, the Lewises got a call from the farm that the filly's back legs shimmied when she walked. She suffered from Wobbler's Syndrome, an often incurable and fatal spinal cord disease, and had to be put down, which was both tragic and a loss of $200,000.

Deduction, as it turned out, couldn't run for the life of him. He failed to make it to the track for years and when he finally did, he ran eleven times before he broke his maiden at the Pleasanton oval. He was claimed in that race, so his name turned out to be appropriate, as he had done nothing but accumulate losses for them.

Despite those initial setbacks, Bob and Beverly Lewis persisted in buying horses. Long before they ever owned a horse, they agreed that their silks should be yellow and green—the colors of the University of Oregon. On June 2, 1990, just months after they started in the business and already with about a dozen horses in their stable, the Lewises made their inaugural trip to the gate for a stakes race at Hollywood Park. Laffit Pincay, who would in future years top the all-time win record, wore their yellow and green silks on board the horse Sunshine Machine. The Lewises were such novices in ownership they had never met a jockey before, and yet they won that first time out on the track, earning a purse of around $28,000. They felt unbelievably lucky and the good fortune swept them along quickly. Within the first year and a half of ownership, Bob Lewis sat in top hat and tails in the Queen's stand at the Irish Derby in Curragh, watching another of their horses run.

Then, as luck would have it, the Lewises discovered that their daughter Nancy's sorority sister, Melissa Baffert, was the cousin of the trainer Bob Baffert. He had cleaned up on the quarter-horse circuit and was now having a winning season in stakes races. One day Bob Lewis approached Baffert at Clocker's Corner, the grill and coffee bar on the apron at Santa Anita, and told the trainer if he ever saw an interesting horse, he should go ahead and buy it for the Lewises. In September of that year, Baffert was training a horse that he purchased for another owner for $14,000. The owner wanted to sell the horse for $100,000, an uptick he felt was justified by the horse's stunning performances. Lewis liked the horse, bought him, and immediately won a $100,000 race with him. Lewis told Baffert after that victory he was willing to spend $2 million on horses at the Keeneland July sales, but Baffert pushed him off to the September sales, thinking it was a better time to buy. By the time the September sales rolled around, Lewis had found other trainers ready to spend his money.

One of the most aggressive new hires for the Lewises was D. Wayne Lukas, another quarter-horse champion who had moved over to thoroughbreds in the late 1970s and had been winning Triple Crown races for over a decade. At Baffert's suggestion, Lukas approached the Lewises with a tightly crafted program. He laid the future out for them—how many horses to acquire, the races the horses would run, and the budgets. Bob Lewis liked Lukas's businessman style and signed on.

One day Lukas called Bob and Beverly to ask them if they were interested in a filly for $150,000. They gave the go-ahead and Serena's Song started winning. She ran thirty-eight times, and thirty-two times she ran in the money. The National Thoroughbred Association classifies stakes races by grade—one through three—to match the European system so that transatlantic competitions can be arranged more easily. Serena's Song had eighteen graded wins, of which eleven were grade-one wins, the most prestigious. She retired in 1996 as the third top-earning filly in history with $3,283,388. (This was far from the earning power of the top male earner, Cigar, who won $9,999,815 in his career, but Serena's Song was still astounding.[9])

One night in 1996, around dinnertime, Bob Lewis got a call from Bob Baffert. "I've got this horse . . ." Baffert told Lewis. "You've got to buy it. I just saw a tape." He had purchased the two-year-old gray at auction in Ocala, Florida, for $85,000, because he loved his graceful stride. Baffert had actually picked up the horse for another owner, but the owner's accountant told him he couldn't take the risk at that time. Baffert tried other buyers, without success.[10] With a horse on his hands and no extra cash to spare, Baffert finally called Bob Lewis, and as luck would have it, Lewis was home.

Bob Lewis never set a limit on how many horses he bought in a given year, just as, in the years he and Beverly held to a tight budget, he never imposed an artificial betting cap. A horse-racing fan should never play with scared dollars, Bob Lewis thought, nor should he or she limit bets to five dollars on a day when great horses were running. Lewis did not mind adding another horse to his team.

He didn't usually buy two-year-olds since it meant he forfeited control of their early training, but he also believed that a good businessman selects the right people to do a job and then gets out of their way. In this case, Lewis had selected Baffert, and Baffert was over the moon about the horse from the Ocala sale.

"Okay, I'll buy him," Lewis told Baffert.

Years later, Baffert would say that fate guided this business decision, because he believed that Bob Lewis was destined to own that horse.[11]

The horse, rechristened Silver Charm, ran well from the beginning. By September of his two-year-old year, another owner, Michael Tabor, offered Lewis $500,000 for him, but Baffert advised Lewis not to sell. By November, the offer surged to $1.7 million, and Baffert and Lewis agreed they could not refuse. Before the deal was finalized, David Lambert, who worked for Tabor, phoned to say he wanted to come by to see Silver Charm's morning workout one last time.

Baffert called Lewis. He now regretted selling their one Derby hope from beneath them and wished they could renege, but he knew he couldn't officially pull out of the deal at that point. He came up with a plan. The morning of Lambert's arrival, Baffert told his exercise rider, Larry Damore, how he wanted him to handle Silver Charm.

When Lambert arrived, they walked over to the fence to watch the work. Silver Charm stepped onto the dirt and Damore warmed the colt up a little, then ran him stiff-backed around the oval. Damore trotted back to the gate. "So, Larry, he went good?" Baffert asked Damore.

"Yeah, like usual," Damore said. "It took him about a mile to warm up. He wasn't like he was at Del Mar. Maybe it's the track." Lambert listened. A couple of days later Bob Lewis received a fax that the deal was off.[12]

The Lewises went to the festivities leading up to the 1997 Kentucky Derby with the other owners competing. The partners Trudy Mc-Caffery and John Toffan, who had made their money in gold exploration, flew in from Canada. There was the Team Valor partnership headed by longtime pals and former turf reporters Jeff Siegel and Barry Irwin from California. Cot Campbell, the head of the syndicate Dogwood Stables in Aiken, South Carolina, a former show rider and long-time born-again Christian, wandered the backside shaking hands and providing colorful quotes for the press. There was W. Cal Partee, an eighty-seven-year-old oil, banking and lumber tycoon based in Magnolia, Arkansas, and last but not least, the British visitors, Mrs. John Magnier, the wife of an Irish breeding farm owner, and Michael Tabor, second in the world for thoroughbred buying power after the Maktoum family of Dubai. Tabor made his initial fortune owning a chain of betting shops in England and now enjoyed that fortune at his home in Monaco.

On Kentucky Derby Day, May 3, 1997, Silver Charm was the handicapper's second choice in the running. With Gary Stevens on board, the colt held toward the front all the way around the oval and won by a head. In the winner's circle, the scent from the winner's blanket of roses overwhelmed Beverly, and she marveled at the number of people crowding around them. Not only did Silver Charm win the Derby, he won the Preakness too, again by a head. With the Belmont coming in the first week of June, Silver Charm was poised to win the Triple Crown, the achievement that had eluded every horse since 1978.

Bob and Beverly would mark their fiftieth anniversary in August, and Bob started thinking about what they could do to celebrate. "Let's get a plane and take some of our friends to the Belmont," he suggested to Beverly. Bob believed the secret to their marriage was that he was crazy enough to devise adventures for them and she was crazy enough to go along. Beverly thought ferrying their friends to New York sounded like a wonderful idea.[13]

So the Lewises chartered a 727. Within a few days, they found so many more pals who wanted to go, they decided to book an L-1011, one of those airplanes that could take you full around the world. They painted a silver charm on the side and, on the Friday before the Belmont, 109 friends and family members boarded. A stand-up bar offered mixed cocktails and thirteen waiters served a magnificent sit-down gourmet meal. The Lewises put their guests up for three days at the Garden City hotel, a few miles from the track. They hired enough limousines for each group of eight to go wherever they wanted, whenever they wanted, for the whole stay. The only glitch along the way was that Bob picked up a bad case of bronchitis, but he wasn't one to complain about something so minor.

On Belmont Day, Silver Charm was the odds-on favorite, paying only $1.05 on a $1 bet if he won. The colt hit second place by the mile mark and started gaining, taking the lead a quarter of a mile from the finish. Then, at the wire Touch Gold surged ahead and crossed the finish three-quarters of a length before Silver Charm.

Beverly blanked out.

*   *   *

We lost the Triple Crown, Bob Lewis thought. The idea was almost too much for him. They had gotten so close to the ultimate dream of racing and now the dream vanished. He felt the eyes of his 109 friends and loved ones on the back of his neck, looking at him for a way to handle this defeat, and he didn't have a clue what to say.

Then his mind started working. He looked around. Over eighty thousand people were in the grandstand that day, and Bob Lewis could have heard a pin drop. He could picture the doldrums that lay ahead. He could not live the balance of that day and evening, going home tomorrow to California, in that atmosphere of gloom.

He turned around. He spoke to the group, all those people who had been wined and dined for days and whipped into a frenzy of anticipation. "This is not the end of the world," he said, his voice croaking from illness. People around him were crying.

"Hey," Bob Lewis said, summoning all his experience as Yell Leader from the days back in Oregon. "Let's get ahold of ourselves and recognize that we too can get beat. And we get beat in good style and by a magnificent horse who did a better job on this particular day. But let's not let it bring an atmosphere of gloom over the whole party. Please. Buck up and get your spirits together, and we'll move on from here. Who knows, maybe we'll be back next year."

He felt the despair and disappointment of losing for two or three minutes. Then Bob accepted the loss. The Lewises' horse would go into the record book as the runner-up in the 1997 Belmont, and that information became fact. Then Bob Lewis began living with that fact. The secret to life was seeing how good things really were.

The next year, the Lewises took Silver Charm to the Dubai World Cup, the richest day of racing anywhere in the world, held in the tiny United Arab Emirate country. Sheikh Mohammed bin Rashid al-Maktoum, the crown prince of Dubai and the minister of defense, had created the Godolphin Stable there in 1994 to satisfy his personal passion for thoroughbreds. He built a $27 million facility, with a track that exactly simulated the shape and conditions of Churchill Downs, close enough to the palace and at such an angle that the sheikh could peer at his thoroughbreds through his binoculars as they ran. He constructed his own feed mill, air-conditioned stables, and equine hospital. He trained his horses there until the last possible moment, then shipped them to races around the world. For the Dubai World Cup, introduced in 1996, gambling was forbidden by national law, in accordance with the strictures of Islam. But the government paid fifteen thousand dollars to anyone who picked the seven winners of the whole slate of races that day. Bob and Beverly had a marvelous time at the race and ended up winning the $4 million Dubai World Cup when Silver Charm crossed the finish line first by inches in the big race.

A great horse is like a Faberge egg, a Mercedes Gullwing Coupe, or a blue diamond. An owner takes pride in possessing something magically beautiful and powerful, and the hunt for that enchanted object provides a daily challenge and entertainment. Of all the great thoroughbreds to stride the earth, the colt Man o' War was deemed by the experts to be the most amazing. He arrived on the racetrack in 1919, with a dazzling combination of strength and speed, "the mostest horse that ever was," as his groom, Will Harbut, declared. In full gallop, Man o' War had a stride of twenty-six feet, compared to an average horse's twenty-foot reach. During his two-year-old year, he won nine out of ten races, most of them with a hefty weight handicap of 130 pounds.[14] Man o' War never had a chance to be a Triple Crown winner, however. His owner, Sam Riddle, did not book him for the Kentucky Derby, choosing instead to run him for the first time as a three-year-old in the Preakness. The choice of that race, held at the Pimlico Race Course in Baltimore, Maryland, for the great horse's three-year-old debut, burnished the event's reputation for decades to come.

Man o' War flew to victory in the Preakness and then in the Belmont. Ten days later, he entered the Lawrence Realization Handicap at Belmont Park, a race of one and five-eighths miles. Despite his clear superiority to other horses, Man o' War usually submitted to such normal racing strategies as having the jockey hold him back for the first furlongs so he did not tire out early, and then running him at the limits of his power only for the last sprint. But when the day of the Lawrence Realization Handicap came, Mrs. Riddle said to her husband, "Why not let him run all the way. If he can set a new record, let him do it. The public deserves to see him show what he is and not just canter around the course and sprint the last quarter."

Her husband conceded. "Let him run," he told the jockey, Clarence Kummer.[15] Let him do what he can do.

For the full one and five-eighths miles, Man o' War ran as fast as he wanted. By the finish, he was one hundred lengths ahead of the next horse, and had turned in a record time of 2:40 4/5. As a three-year-old he ran eleven races and took first place in every one of them. In his entire career of twenty-one races, he lost only one. Over time, the potential competitors for Man o' War dropped away because no owners felt justified exhausting their own horses in a losing cause. Man o' War's odds in the Jockey Club stakes were said to have been an amazing 1 to 100, meaning that a winning bet of one dollar on the horse would pay one extra penny against his sole competitor, Damask, 80 to 1.

Man o' War died on November 1, 1947. The announcement came from Faraway Farm in Kentucky, where he stood as stud, and the Associated Press relayed the mournful news. "Our big horse just died," was the simple statement.[16] Five hundred mourners gathered around Man o' War's casket and radio stations carried the ceremony to fans across the country.[17]

Perhaps surprisingly, a horse so perfect in conformation and talent did not bring a simple joy to his owner, Sam Riddle, because he sensed the responsibility that possessing such an animal entailed and the possibility for disappointment. Riddle understood that, because of Man o' War's unique greatness, the horse was not only his, but the world's. He felt melancholy that the colt's effervescence spoke of its own end since nothing perfect could last in this world. "Even in the case of so great a horse as Man o' War," Riddle wrote, "there is a difference in degree only. You may know he is pounds better than any other horse in training . . . but you know that a misstep at a racetrack, a seemingly insignificant accident in the stable, a bad ship, a cold caught by chance, any one of a thousand trivial things may ruin his career. There are also unprincipled persons that must be guarded against, that will not hesitate at anything dastardly. Some of the most famous horses here and abroad have been their victims.

"That it is not a wonderful thing to own a Man o' War I am not trying to assert," said Riddle, "for there is no other feeling in the world to compare with it if one loves a great horse. It gives a thrill that nothing else ever can. It cannot be put into words, because words cannot express it."[18] Bob Lewis was one of 30,000 owners in the country who searched breeding farms and auctions for the horse that would bring that feeling.

In November 1996, Bob Lewis got a call from the California trainer Ray Bell Jr. and bloodstock agent Tom Moynihan. By that time, the Lewises' stable included about a hundred horses. Bell told Lewis that he and Moynihan had been over to Parrish Hill Farm in Midway, Kentucky, and had seen an athletic-looking weanling. It was a Summer Squall colt out of Bali Babe, the same stock as another of the Lewises' colts, Constant Demand, who had run well until a hoof injury acted up. Bell said he could probably get the new weanling for about $200,000. Lewis gave them the okay and the deal was done.

Because Bell brought the Bali Babe colt to Lewis, Bell ordinarily would have trained him. But Bob Lewis started hearing funny stuff about Ray's father, Tom Bell, a bloodstock agent, who was selling another one of Lewis's horses for him for $25,000. A trainer told Lewis that the price he heard for the colt was $50,000.[19]

Bob Lewis told Ray Bell he could either train the colt or stay in partnership with his father, but not both. Bell said he had to choose his own father, and Bob understood. The two trainers who handled most of the Lewises' horses were Bob Baffert and D. Wayne Lukas. Bob Lewis liked to give an equal number of horses to both men since it kept feelings from being hurt and nurtured healthy competition. Lewis looked at his list of horses and realized Lukas was down a couple of horses and sent the Bali Babe colt to him.

According to the rules of the Jockey Club, the Bali Babe colt needed a name by the end of January in its two-year-old year. That was Beverly's job—she had christened over two hundred horses—but in 1998, she was procrastinating in naming that year's crop. Usually owners make passing reference to the horse's parentage in the designation of a new colt or filly. A filly by Moscow Ballet out of Teach You, for example, becomes Ballet Lesson. The offspring of Lear Fan out of Hypochondriac becomes Fan of Pain. But Beverly didn't often make that link with the parents, preferring inspiration to tradition.

She was up late one January night, around two or three in the morning, at their home along the canal in Newport Beach with her dictionary beside her, looking for a spark.

Charisma, she suddenly thought. That was a lovely name. *Charisma*. It sounded magical, but strong. It said right from the start that this horse was a star. But then Beverly thought maybe the name sounded a little too feminine. *Charismatic*. That was better.

The next day Beverly called Bob's secretary to have her check Equibase, the online site run by the Jockey Club and the Thoroughbred Racing Association, to see if the name was taken, and to her surprise there was no other Charismatic. Charismatic it was.

The Silver Charm defeat in the Belmont had been difficult for the Lewises, but by the end of 1998, they were in second place for owner earnings nationally with almost $6 million. On top of that, 1999 looked to be their year for a potential Triple Crown winner. The oddsmakers thought the Lewises would be back to win the Kentucky Derby and probably more, because they owned a brilliant colt that burned up the track, and no competition seemed strong enough to beat him. The Lewis horse all the handicappers loved was a Storm Cat offspring named Exploit, trained by Bob Baffert, which had won all six of his starts.

Meanwhile, Charismatic only drew Bob Lewis's attention because he drained Lewis's finances. Once a week, Lukas called Bob Lewis at his office to give his progress report on their 40 thoroughbreds, and with Charismatic, the report always went the same. Another losing run. Yet the bills rolled in, around a hundred dollars a day for upkeep, thousands of dollars in fees and nothing coming in on the income side except the third-, fourth-, and fifth-place finishes since July, adding up to only $30,660 for the year. With his dismal record, Charismatic wouldn't even garner a high stud fee, since he appeared to be the rare offspring of Summer Squall and Bali Babe not to inherit talent.

When Lukas called Lewis in early February to say he wanted to put Charismatic in a claiming race, Lewis signed on without hesitation. He had paid $210,000 for him, and then the colt cost over $9,000 in upkeep alone since he started racing. Maybe if someone claimed the horse, Lewis could recoup some losses and end the useless feed bills. Beverly might be emotional about horse racing, but Bob went into the sport as a business, and he hadn't become a successful businessman by letting losing situations go on forever. He might like a horse a great deal, but if the animal wasn't performing, they had to put the horse in a claiming race or sell him. Horse racing was a bottom-line enterprise ultimately, and by keeping this in mind, he had made a lot of money. He suspected other owners hated him and Beverly for waltzing into racing in the 1990s and cleaning up, but he felt proud of what they had achieved.

Lewis joined Lukas in the stands to watch the Santa Anita claiming race. Charismatic held in sixth all the way around the oval, then started making up ground going into the far turn. His put his head down and thumped along, pulling toward the head of the pack. As the horses sped toward the eighth pole, he surged forward and came neck and neck with What Say You. After the finish, the stewards issued the query and reviewed the tape that revealed What Say You had bumped Charismatic at the last pole. Charismatic moved up to first.

"Whew," Lukas said. "I don't think we'll be risking this again." Charismatic might have talent that they overlooked. Perhaps he could start earning his keep, beginning with the $28,200 he made with that win.

Later that month, Lukas called Lewis again. "Bob," he said, "we had Charismatic out this morning and he is so laid back and lazy I felt it was time to try a different tack with him." So Lukas had worked him longer and harder. "The horse seemed to perform well," Lukas said. "I'd like to, with your approval, send the horse up to Bay Meadows. The El Camino Real Derby is coming up and I'd like to run him there."[20]

Bob agreed and paid $2,200 to enter Charismatic in the race. Charismatic looked like a different horse in the paddock on the day of competition, with a shiny coat and bouncing step. At the start he broke slowly and faded into sixth, but he kept a steady pace and, turning toward home, took off, steamrolling past the leaders to finish second by a nose to Cliquot. He won $40,000 for the Lewises, with 10 percent each to Lukas and the jockey Ron Warren Jr.

Two weeks later, the Lewises paid $18,000 to enter him in the Santa Anita Derby. In the paddock, Randy Bradshaw, who helped run Lukas's California stables, and Lukas's son, Jeff, helped saddle the colt. Laffit Pincay was riding. "I think Charismatic can win the Triple Crown," Lukas told the group confidentially. Lewis wanted to believe Lukas but he was hard pressed to. The bettors sent Charismatic off at extremely long odds of 44 to 1. The colt didn't run in the money that day, finishing fourth. He didn't necessarily look like a Triple Crown contender, the Lewises thought, but he did show some fight in the stretch against tough competition.

Meanwhile, their three-year-old, Exploit, kept proving his excellence. On March 13, Baffert entered Exploit, still the handicappers' favorite for the Derby, in the San Felipe at Santa Anita. He held a steady second through most of the race, but faded slightly in the stretch and for the first time lost a race. Sensing trouble, the veterinarians immediately took him to be x-rayed and found a chip in his knee bone. The Lewises were forced to retire him a few days later. They started pinning their Derby hopes on another horse trained by Baffert, Straight Man, but he showed poorly in his last prep race, the Gallery Furniture.com Stakes, on March 27.

They had nothing, no horse to bring to the most magical day in racing on May 1, nothing to show for their investment. But then, out of nowhere, Lukas started calling the Lewises and telling them how well Charismatic was doing, how his spirit had changed. The day Exploit

suffered his career-ending injury, Charismatic turned three by the calendar and was coming into his own. When Lukas told the exercise girl
to gallop him for two miles, he lasted the distance at full speed. How
odd it was, Bob Lewis thought, that he and Beverly had been so down,
so depressed after losing their two Derby hopes—Exploit and Straight
Man—and now hope emerged from the clear blue. It was like something
looked out for them, cheered them when they felt down.

Lukas put Charismatic in the Coolmore Lexington Stakes at Keeneland, and the Lewises watched on television from California as Charismatic took command nearing the final turn and roared down the
homestretch to his record-setting victory. The phone rang and Lukas
was on the line to congratulate them on their $234,794 win. Charismatic
had just paid off his bills.

"Bob, I want to enter him in the Derby," Lukas said. He needed to
know if Lewis would sign off on the $40,000 entry fee.

Bob gave the go-ahead and felt a surge of confidence. Lukas held up
possibility—a horse that could win the Derby—even if he was nothing
but a claimer, and Lewis, the optimist, happily caught the lure. "I'll tell
you one thing," Bob Lewis told a reporter. "I think we've got a Belmont
horse. I may be putting the onus on Wayne, and I apologize, but this
horse will run all day long."[21]

The Lewises hoped Laffit Pincay would ride Charismatic in the
Derby, but he told them another owner had booked him to ride at Hollywood Park that first Saturday of May. Jockeys usually didn't like to sit
out the Derby, so Pincay's refusal wasn't a great sign for Charismatic.
Lukas had hired Jerry Bailey to ride the Lexington Stakes, but in the
winner's circle that day, Bailey told Lukas he had the Sheikh Maktoum
mount, Worldly Manner, for the Derby and couldn't ride Charismatic.

Lukas told the Lewises he wanted to use the jockey Chris Antley,
who rode for them a few times before. Lukas explained that Derby experience counted a great deal and Antley had not only ridden in that
race seven times before, he had won the race with Strike the Gold in
1991. Over the years, the Lewises had heard a great deal about Antley's
problems with drugs and depression, but, Bob Lewis thought, one of our

responsibilities as human beings is to help people with problems. If Wayne Lukas, a man who cared about winning above all else, wanted to give Antley a chance, why shouldn't they.

The way this Derby possibility came together out of the ether underscored to Bob Lewis an element of his life that always caused him to marvel. He felt he exerted some measure of control over his horse-racing success, even if the control was to cede management to someone more expert in the ways of thoroughbreds. At the end of the day, that's what being an executive was all about. But Bob Lewis sometimes wondered too about a mystery humming beneath the surface of his life, a power that swept through and bestowed enormous gifts. To really understand that force, one needed to look back, far back, to a time remembered in black and white, and walking across that grainy screen was a twenty-year-old Bob Lewis eager to fight in World War II and prove himself a hero. He would be haunted by this story for his entire life.

When Bob Lewis enlisted in 1943, he wanted to serve in the Air Force. He was bound and determined to train at Fort Sill, Oklahoma, receive his instruction and ship out to the most brutal battle zones. He went into basic training, and as that phase neared completion, he planned to head to Air Force commissioning. But his battalion went on alert to ship overseas. By military rules, you could not transfer to another division after you got that call, so Bob Lewis was unable to switch to the Air Force, and shipped with his battalion to Louisiana to await the next order.

But the command to go overseas was revoked and Lewis worked again to requalify for the Air Force. As he neared completion of his training yet again, the battalion went on alert and this time shipped to Hawaii. Lewis waited in Hawaii and went through training one more time. Finally, after ninety-one days, he thought he would have the opportunity to be a real hero, in the action, in the Air Force. He was almost finished with Air Force training when he was awakened in the night. "Sergeant, pack your bag," an officer told him, "you're shipping back to the States."

Lewis returned to California to await his next assignment when, without any warning, the War Department issued a new order: Even if a serviceman was in sound health, if he had been out of the continental United States for ninety days, he would no longer be subject to or eligible for foreign or overseas duty. That meant that Lewis's stint in Hawaii, by only one day, disqualified him from the active combat he so actively sought. Now he would never be a pilot. He was reassigned to a recruit training center at Camp Roberts, California, where he ate three full meals a day and taught grunts how to crawl on their bellies with machine guns. His assignment, Bob thought disgustedly, was not heroic. He wanted to go fight for his country, and instead he found himself stuck right back in California living the easy life while his peers proved their courage on the front lines.

But then Bob Lewis watched over the months, the years, as so many young men came back from the war scarred, physically and mentally. He saw parents and wives waiting for soldiers who would never return. His buddy from childhood never made it out of the Doolittle Raid over Japan, perishing within a week or so of enlisting. And over the years, Bob began to believe a streak of good fortune ran through his life. When he went into horse racing, he could see the luck more vividly, like a river running through the years.

Bob had been blessed with a fifty-three-year marriage, three great sons and a wonderful daughter. He had a business association throughout his life with the brewing industry, which he loved dearly. "It had been a fun existence," he liked to say. He had learned a few things along the way. You live for today.[22] Don't worry about tomorrow. If you had problems yesterday, forget them because you can't do anything about them. Do something positive today, and in the end, it would all work out. He and Beverly had endured their tragedies, a child lost at birth, the death of their parents, and many other things, but they also had experienced many joys. Bob Lewis wondered time and again why he was especially blessed. Whatever the reason, he was thankful.

Providence and good fortune played a role in virtually every part of life, he thought. A person couldn't have so many good things happen without attributing some portion to luck. If it turned out that the soul headed to reincarnation after death, if it happened that Bob Lewis got another life to live, he would ask the good Lord to direct him back to the brewing industry as he knew it and give him some exposure to the thoroughbred racing industry. He wanted the life he had just lived exactly. He felt fortunate, and that worked well for him, because a person needed a larger share of luck when he or she played in thoroughbred racing, a game on the edge of riskiness.

FIVE

THE ANT

At the end of August 1984, the jockey agent Lou Rosenthal held a coming-out party to introduce his eighteen-year-old prodigy to the New York press. Chris Antley had moved from the Monmouth track, where in two and a half months he won 171 races, 37 more than the track record, to the autumn meet at the Meadowlands—known as "the Big M" to the horse-racing crowd. The New York turf writers, the reporters who covered racing, wanted to see what miracles he could pull off next at the track only eight miles from the city.

Rosenthal, wearing a beige three-piece suit, tinted shades and gold medallion, held court while his star sat beside him, wordlessly ravaging a plate of cold pasta with smoked salmon. Rosenthal told the press how he knew from first glance that Antley was a gold mine. The reporters started asking questions about the risks for a young rider in the big time. "A lot of 'em get spoiled," Rosenthal said. "Fame, money, girls, all that stuff comes quickly, and they think it won't stop. When it does, they don't know what hit them." He looked over at his star. "This kid's just unbelievable, though," he said. "Nothing fazes him. He wins six races in a day—did it twice at Monmouth—and the next morning he's out at six A.M. calling people 'mister' and asking for rides."[1]

Steven Crist, the racing reporter for the *New York Times*, commented on the odd scene the next day.

> These are funny-looking gold mines, these young and even younger-looking teenagers, one of whom usually arrives in or around New York every year or two with a riding helmet and a reputation. When dressed up and taken out in public, they look like the young gentlemen in children's clothing ads, not like ambitious athletes who dream of slashing and driving from the backs of huge and dangerous animals. . . . Antley says all the things a wide-eyed apprentice should, about "what an honor it will be just to ride against" Cordero and Company, and that "I hope to learn from the experience." But he also shows a little more spunk and character than most of the Wunderkind apprentices, who try to live up to their choirboyish appearances when anyone is watching. When asked about riding against [Wesley] Ward, the top apprentice in the country, Antley remarked that Ward had been to Monmouth several times and "went away empty" [meaning he couldn't win against Antley and his crew].

At the end of that year, Ward received the Eclipse Award for outstanding apprentice jockey and Antley came in second. But a few years later, Ward dropped out of the game because of weight issues, while Antley kept winning.

Antley's success fed his cockiness. He took the riding title at Monmouth in 1984, as well as for the next two years. The hot jocks could pick and choose their races, and geography was no obstacle. Jockey Craig Perret, who had mentored Antley in his first weeks in New Jersey, remembered the glamour of life then. "Me and him used to jump in a helicopter from Monmouth," Perret recalled about Antley, who was fifteen years his junior. "We'd go to Atlantic City at night. Eighteen minutes. *Boom*. We go over there, go ride. *Boom*. Helicopter would take us back. Go out and eat dinner. *Boom*. Go home. We did that constantly. Tomorrow, we ride in the third, fourth and fifth race in New Jersey. I'm in New York in the eighth race, the feature. Chris is too. *Boom*. We got a helicopter. Fly right over. Right in our silks. They drop us off and we run to the jocks' room, then jump in a helicopter and come back in fifteen minutes. We did some awesome stuff."[2] They rented limousines stocked with liquor so after the race day they could drive to the Atlantic City casinos with other jockey friends.

The jockeys rode hard against each other, got mad, showered off, then drove to whichever party one of the jockeys was throwing that night. They put together barbecues, beach picnics, and hard-fought baseball games between the jockeys and the backside workers. When Monmouth was dark on Mondays, with no racing, management would open the jock-room swimming pool for the riders and their families. Antley always was the first person there, pacing behind the chaise lounges. "Come on, come on," he would holler, "let's get in the pool." Then Antley and all the children cannonballed in.

"When he was on, he was just a beautiful kid," the trainer Nick Zito recalled. "Whatever demons go on in these poor people's lives that get them off the beaten path. . . . when he was on, he was such a joy to be around. I used to see him, after we'd win a race, I'd actually see him skipping back to the jocks' room. *Skipping* back to the jocks' room."[3]

The riders often played practical jokes on each other, a long-standing tradition in the jockey community at Monmouth, going back to one classic prank remembered lovingly from the 1950s involving a valet (a word which, at the track, rhymes with mallet), a track worker responsible for laying out the right silks and equipment for a jockey between races. This valet had a glass eye, and one day he plucked the orb from his socket and put it in a jock's ice bucket, under a towel.[4] When the jock went to wash up after a race, he nearly passed out.

Perret and Antley kept up the tradition. They shared a valet, who also worked for another rider. One day Perret and Antley saw the other rider's stuff sitting on the bench in the jocks' room.

"Oh, boy," Perret said to Antley. "Take this shaving cream. Fill up his goggles and put the goggles on his helmet."

"That would be neat," Antley agreed.

"Just fill it up and wipe it off," Perret said. "Then when he gets in the gate and pulls his goggles down, he's gonna see all shaving cream."

Antley filled the goggles. The riders came in and suited up, then headed to the paddock to saddle their horses, all serious. The unsuspecting rider walked out in his helmet and found his horse. He had no idea what was coming. Antley and Perret stifled their snickering. They chatted with the trainers who had booked them and got their directions, then mounted. They rode out to the starting gate. Perret loaded into the second post and Antley walked his horse into the fourth slot. The guy they booby-trapped sat right between them in the three slot.

Perret saw that only one rider down the line waited now to be loaded in the gate. The start was seconds away. "Hey, man," Perret said to the other jock. "Get your goggles down, get your goggles down."

"Aw, yeah, yeah," the rider said.

Perret and Antley heard him screeching. "Hold the start, hold the start," he yelled to the official.

"Pull us, man," Perret yelled to the starter. "Let's go!"

The jocks were young and having fun. Antley and jockey Joe Rocco drove most days between tracks in Philadelphia and New Jersey with the heat on high to sweat off pounds so they could ride the best races. They became so close that Rocco and his wife, Debra, wanted to name their third baby after Chris if it was a boy; but they had a girl and made Antley the godfather. He ended up bringing Debra and the baby home from the hospital because Rocco was stuck riding a mount. Antley led them in adventures. One winter day, he convinced Rocco to get off his mounts so Antley could teach him how to ski. They drove northwest to the Pocono mountains and found a low incline called Shawnee. Antley sent Rocco down the slope.

"Man, you're real good, Due," Antley said. "Now try this one."

Rocco went down a steeper incline. He headed right toward a tree and stuck his ski pole out to protect himself, then slammed into both. He came down hours later on a stretcher and with a black eye, while Antley and Debra waited at the bottom. They all went back to their lodge and slept in the same bed like kids. The next morning at 6:00, Antley woke. "Come on, Due, you ready to go again?" he said.

"Are you crazy?" Rocco asked. He looked at Antley through his swollen eye and laughed.[5]

Drew Mollica sat on the edge of his seat at Yonkers Raceway, gazing through the plate-glass window of the jockeys' viewing booth at the empty track. The cars on the Major Deegan Expressway roared behind the clubhouse turn toward the Bronx. The high January winds rattling the jocks' quarters had shut down the harness meet, but outside the oval a few brave souls took their horses and chariots for a grim trot across the frozen mud. There is nothing sadder than an empty track on a gray day. "Are you ready for me yet?" Mollica called huskily to a couple of guys wearing headphones on the other side of the room. They were broadcasting for Thoroughbred Central, on which Mollica would handicap the area races.

"Not yet," the producer yelled back.

Mollica settled in. He was a big man, forty-two years of age, who talked like a Jersey toughie and looked like he would triumph in a barroom brawl. There was something soft about him though too: the ripe cherubic features of a Caravaggio boy aged into a man and a vocabulary of Eastern philosophies and self-help books. He was thinking more than a decade back to the go-go years of the late '80s and early '90s. "I fell in love with him," he said of the client he agented then. "He had the eyes of an angel, the face of an angel. . . . For all his bravado, once you scratched the surface he was a teddy bear. He was just a kid."

Mollica and Chris Antley didn't hit it off right away. "The first time I knew of him, the first cognition I had of him, I was at the Meadowlands," Mollica recalled. One of Mollica's trainer friends booked the new ten-pound bug boy from the Maryland tracks to ride, and Mollica watched the kid win the race. Right away, the seventeen-year-old jock's skill impressed Mollica, the way he could maneuver the horse, the way his strength didn't flag coming down the stretch. In 1984, in the dead heat of summer, Mollica was working at Monmouth Park as a paddock judge. His job was to get the procession of horses from the paddock to the gate—the post parade—out on time. Antley rode nine or ten races a day, which meant that, after he galloped a horse out after the finish line, he trotted him back, handed the horse over to the trainer, hustled through the tunnel to the jocks' room, changed into a new owner's silks and ran to get on the next horse. For whatever reason, Antley always showed up late in the paddock to mount up that summer. All the horses would be out and the riders waiting with the trainers. Only Antley would be missing.

One day the riders were up on their mounts and killing time until Antley showed, and, with nothing else to do, a filly and a colt fell in love right there in the paddock. All hell broke loose. Mollica reported the problem to the stewards and they fined Antley one hundred dollars.

After the race, Antley walked up to Mollica with a roll of bills. "Hey, big boy," the teenager drawled. "I'll smack you with these hundreds."

"Typical little asshole," Mollica snarled.

"Typical big asshole," Antley said.

A little later, Lou Rosenthal ran into troubles and had to stop agent-ing. ("Long story," Rosenthal said. "Not Chris's fault. My fault."[6])

Mollica was working as an agent, but his jock, Doug Thomas, got injured. Mollica was flat busted, driving a 1978 orange Cutlass Supreme with white bucket seats, living in his father's basement. A trainer friend of Mollica's, Mel Grossman, suggested Mollica and Antley work together since they both needed a partnership and were up-and-comers in their own ways. Mollica listened to Grossman boost Antley.

"Well, he hates me," Mollica said, "and I ain't real fond of him."

"Don't be an idiot," Grossman said.

One day at the track, Grossman walked Mollica over to Antley. "You better take this guy, he's the best agent on the East Coast," Grossman told Antley.

"Aww, he's a jerk," the jock said.

"He may be a jerk . . ." Grossman said. Mollica interrupted. Bills needed to be paid.

"How about this, jock," he said. "I'll work for you for a week for free and by that time your agent will be out of trouble. We'll take it from there." Antley accepted and never went back to Rosenthal.

Mollica and Antley were the track odd couple—the big fast-talking Italian-American from the city and the small, blue-eyed rider from the southern sticks. "Our first meetings, I might as well have been from Mars and he might as well have been from Venus," recalled Mollica. "I'm a kid from New York, grew up in northern New Jersey. He's a kid from Elloree, South Carolina, which is not as big as this half-mile oval," he said, gesturing to the track, "but we had success from the moment I got with him. Our affair, if you will, or our *relationship* grew from then." Antley would tell Mollica about working at the Piggly Wiggly grocery store, and Mollica told ragged tales about the apartment houses in the Bronx.

Antley valued Mollica's loyalty above all else. Once Antley was booked to ride the Lukas horse Bordeaux Bob in the Iselin Invitational at Monmouth, but the day he went to the airport in Saratoga to catch a private plane down to New Jersey a storm raged. Mollica, dressed in his barn clothes, arrived at the airport to see him off, but his jock refused to get on the plane in that bad weather unless Mollica went with him. Mollica pointed out he wasn't dressed or ready for such a trip, and they fought on the tarmac until Mollica relented and got on the plane. They bounced all the way down the East Coast, and when they landed in New Jersey, Mollica descended the steps and kissed the ground. Antley rode Bordeaux Bob, the longest shot in the race, to win by a nose. When he walked out of the winner's circle and through the tunnel, he saw Mollica standing waiting for him. Antley hugged Mollica and kissed him. "This is why I love you so much, Drewsky," Antley said.[7]

"We were truly as polarized as two people could be," Mollica said, "yet I think he needed, in retrospect, somebody to look out for him, and I needed the opportunity to get a career. It was just magic. He and I were magic from the first day we got together."

*   *   *

Nowadays, on a normal day of wagering, urban American racetracks can feel a little like the *Titanic* lolling on the ocean floor, haunted by the ghost of reveling crowds. Whereas many Kentuckians stake their livelihoods on horses and pack the tracks to see the animals run, northern city people only know horses from the patrols at parades. At the urban tracks there is always a seat in the grandstand and never a wait at the betting windows. The jockey Billy Passmore, who rode with Chris Antley at the Bowie racetrack in Maryland, remembered the crowds thinning out almost suddenly in the mid-1980s. The IRS decided horse owners needed to prove their endeavor had quickly turned into a business and wasn't just a hobby to get a write-off. Then the oil crisis depleted any excess wealth that might be spent on racing. The extended racing calendars instituted in the 1970s had diluted fans' enthusiasm, transforming racing from a seasonal sport like football or baseball to a ubiquitous entertainment, and the years were ticking by without a Triple Crown winner.

Before then, when a jock paraded to the post or came back from riding the horse out past the finish line, he would see the apron by the rail packed with people. The fans loved him and shouted praise, or hated him for losing and told him what a bum he was. To a jock, it didn't matter which way the commentary went. The fans and the rider had a relationship, through thick and thin, for better or worse, which was one of the best things about being a jockey. Then one day the apron was nearly empty. When the jock rode back to the finish line after the race, he saw only a handful of people, mainly old men, standing there, staring at him. He didn't get the catcalls or the love, and it felt sad.

In New York, the dining rooms on a regular race day are lined with empty white-clothed tables surveyed constantly by waiters in black tie, but Jacqueline Bouvier and Fred Astaire are long gone, and so are the hordes of people who followed them to those cathedrals of chance. Now only a big-stakes day exudes some of the glamour that daily racing possessed even a decade ago—before online gambling and fresh-scrubbed casino towns sucked away all the greedy people and the dreamers. Then there was a dark enchantment in knowing that an instant exchange of fortunes took place there ten or more times a day—decided by equine muscle and the wily daring of the small, sculpted jockeys. The tracks had a place for everyone and everyone in his class—from the froufrou types in the skyboxes, who financed the adventures of the businessmen trainers, to the trainers who paid the unofficial clockers to get the exercise times of their competitors, to the clockers who sold the totality of their records to the professional gamblers at a price. New York—which included the Belmont, Aqueduct, and, in the summer, the Saratoga track—was called "the Show," and in the mid-'80s, all the great jockeys rode there—the young Turks like Gary Stevens and Jose Santos. There were the veterans, Jorge Velasquez and Richard Migliore. But in that era, no one compared to forty-three-year-old Angel Cordero Jr.

Cordero was a Puerto Rican immigrant with a sweet smile, a fiery competitiveness, and a subterranean voice that rumbled through the phonetics of his native Spanish. Racing fans knew Cordero for his victories in six Triple Crown races (although the Triple Crown itself eluded him). Trainers and owners counted on him to drive every horse to its limit and earn them big purse money. The other riders worshipped him because he looked magnificent in the saddle—flat, fluid, in rhythm with the horse. In the heat of the race, with the horse rumbling beneath him, he could flip his whip from his left hand to his right like a samurai and never lose the reins. He made the most aggressive moves on the track and paid often with injuries. Almost every joint of his body was broken—both knees, both ankles, both elbows and nine fingers. He shattered his collarbone, vertebrae, and the ribs on one side of his body, among other calamities. All that on the way to an amazing 7,057 career victories by the time of his retirement in 1993.

On the track and off, the other jockeys mentally crumbled around him. In 1979, Ronnie Franklin was headed to the Triple Crown on board Spectacular Bid, but Cordero kept fanning the flames of their grudge match through that spring by taking him wide in the Preakness and almost upsetting Spectacular Bid's win there. In the week before the Belmont, they bumped horses in a regular race and had to be pried apart, wrestling on the jock room floor. That blast of anger robbed Franklin of his concentration. At the far turn, headed toward the final victory he needed to secure the most prestigious prize in racing, Franklin saw Cordero coming up next to him and hesitated. The dream for Franklin disappeared before Spectacular Bid hit the finish line, as two horses ran past him and he came in third.

In November of 1984, when most top jocks were spending the winter season riding the balmy Florida circuit, Chris Antley made his debut in the Show. Racetrack legend has it that the eighteen-year-old Antley walked up to Angel Cordero and declared, "There's a new sheriff in town." That was the kind of story that explained track dynamics to horse fans for decades, but in fact, wasn't true. When Antley arrived in New York, Cordero was riding down in Florida with all the other top jocks. A local paper reported that the young star from South Carolina said something to the effect that Cordero was getting old, so there would be a place for Antley at the New York tracks. When the article ran, Antley was mortified. Drew Mollica called Cordero and told him Antley didn't mean the jock was over the hill and that Cordero was in fact his hero.[8]

When Cordero returned to New York, he and Antley embarked on a friendly rivalry and mentorship. Cordero could see a young version of himself in Antley. The way Antley was with Cordero was the way Cordero had been with the greatest jockey of all time, Eddie Arcaro. Back in 1959, Cordero, then only a seventeen-year-old apprentice, walked up to Arcaro at the El Commandante track in San Juan. "I want to be just like you," he told the champ, and then spent years emulating his technique.[9]

Everyone could see Antley was trying to copy Cordero's riding style, from the fast whip, to the aggressive riding, to the way he pumped his elbows as he rode to make it look like he was working a horse hard when he was really saving him up. It was all within the rules but not by much. Cordero and Antley each leaned their half ton of horse against the other as they took the turns at thirty-five miles an hour, trying to heave the other to the outside. Antley learned to navigate the legal edge. He studied camera positions, so if he accidentally bumped another rider, he knew the spots the judges wouldn't see and call an infraction that might lead to a suspension. He pressed his weight on one side of the horse and whipped the other so a judge would understand he was trying to get out of the way when really he was moving deeper inside. It took magnificent skill and every top rider wanted to get to that point, to ride right on the line, where he could be aggressive without earning a suspension or fine.

A jockey's world is claustrophobic. Most riders compete at least three times a day and up to ten against the exact same people. Between races, they retire to a single shared locker room to change shirts before they are at it again. Cordero's and Antley's riding styles ran the risk of creating lasting enemies. But off the track, they both knew how to charm, even after they pushed another rider too far.

They came back to the jocks' room and saw the rider they had boxed in. "Poppy, I'm sorry. I didn't do that on purpose," they said sweetly. A few minutes earlier, the other jock was ready to explode. But when he was on the receiving end of an Antley or Cordero charm offensive, he gave in. He knew Cordero and Antley understood exactly what they were doing on the track, but the other jock had to brush off the infraction. No one could be upset with nice guys like them for very long. "Okay, I'll let it go this time," the jock said. Then he waited for the next time.[10]

Cordero and Antley kept their own scorecards of how many times they bumped each other. They stood next to each other, arms crossed, staring at the monitor in the jocks' room where the race replayed. "Okay, Poppa, you got me twice," Antley would say, smiling. "Let's mark it down. I'll get you back." And he was always true to his word.

Despite the competition, and apart from a few jockey room scuffles, all the riders were basically friends in those days in New York. In the early dawn, they hung out in the backside kitchen drinking coffee while they waited to work their horses. They went back in the jocks' room around 10:00 A.M. to sit in the hotbox for hours, talking and listening to the radio, while they sweated off the last pounds to get to legal weight.

Between races, the jocks sat down for a game of cards. They congratulated each other on a string of multiple wins or passed the hat for each other if there was a costly injury or a funeral in the family. At night, they gathered at each other's houses and played a dice game with cardboard horses on a portable track. On the track's dark days, they played golf. And in the beautiful Saratoga season, at night with the summer breezes rolling through the maple leaves, the lucky jockeys that got to go up there met at the same karaoke bar and celebrated the best riding of the year.

Although the general mood was light and friendly, Antley was a serious scientist of the track, some might say a fortune-teller. He calculated ahead of time how each race would end. Before a workday, he drew out the drama, using the fractional times in the racing form to plot how each horse would move, including too the psychological complexes lightly sketched in the brief notes on the right hand of the racing form stats, such as "failed to menace" or "retreated." When he was done, the race with its five to a dozen horses would exist in a dream state—an informed prognostication onto which he only needed to lay his horse to complete the story. He could calculate what flick of the whip or pacing he needed to come out the winner.[11] He sketched the scenario on a race form and showed it to Cordero. Certain times he saw he had no hope. He marked a point on the turn or backstretch and said, "That's where you're going to screw me," and laughed.

"Chris was exceptional at breaking down the way a race was going to come up," recalled Ron Anderson, an agent who worked with him later in California. "He did it on his racing form mostly. All the great ones do it. It's another dimension to their greatness. They are not only in sync with the horse and what the horse will do and feel, but the great jocks have this feel for the way everything is going to unfold. 'This guy's going to be here and that guy's going to be there, and this guy's going at one point to try to do this.' Chris was a mental kid, he was an *extremely* intelligent person. For somebody who never went through high school or college, the guy was brilliant in his own way."

Antley won—on 20 percent of the horses he rode compared to the average jockey's 7 percent—through that combination of analysis, theatrics and guts. His methods of prediction helped him on the track, but his instincts with the animals he rode magnified that intelligence. "He truly had a gift. God gave him a gift and he communicated with the horse," Mollica said. "And of course, he had no fear, and of course, he was athletic and all of that. But he was unbelievable on horseback. It was surreal.

"He was," Mollica concluded, "part horse."

A trainer would tell Antley out in the paddock, "Look, this horse is tough. You'll have a tough time reining him back." But Antley would shake his head and smile. "Naw," he'd say. "No problem." (He told Mollica by the time he and the horse got to the gate, in the ten minutes it would take, "Him and me are friends.") Sure enough, the horse would come back minding Antley like a little pony. Or the trainer would tell him, "This one's lazy, you're going to have to ask him."

"Naw," Antley would say, and he would simply cluck to the colt on the homestretch and the horse would take off.

And if he rode an old sore horse that a trainer warned needed special care, Antley turned the equation around. He would say: "Oh, that old guy knows nothing bad's going to happen to him when I'm riding him."

"He made the horse believe that he was going to be okay," said Mollica. "I think he was cocky enough to know he was great and smart enough to know he was lucky, and he was loyal enough to know it was a team effort. But he knew he was gifted. He carried himself like that. Everything he did exuded confidence. When he was tuned in, everybody else was second best."

Antley's friends always seemed to struggle to get enough work, but finding mounts never proved a problem for Antley. Many of the jocks were immigrants from Peru, Chile, Puerto Rico, and might have difficulty even speaking English with the trainers. As soon as Antley walked into the barns and shook hands with the trainers, he got bookings. He had those choirboy looks, with his blond hair, blue eyes and freckles. He joked with the trainers in his soft Carolina drawl, and gave them the "yes, sir," always looking them straight in the eye. Then when Antley got on the horses, he seemed to win with ease. If there was a track record, he could break it, even though he was just starting out. The big time, the elusive pinnacle that seemed a challenge to last a lifetime when Antley was a kid planning and training down in Elloree, turned out to be easily surmounted. At least it was for Chris Antley.

Back when Mollica and Antley met that day in the Monmouth Park paddock in the summer of 1984, the jockey was eighteen. He never drank alcohol or used drugs through the time he was in Maryland. But now, in New Jersey, he started to drink a little at parties and smoke pot from time to time. The crowd at the Meadowlands for the fall season was wilder.[12] Antley drank more, although never around his closest friends. His acquaintances sometimes talked about snorting coke, but Antley didn't try the drug. He thought it sounded disgusting.

By 1985, drug use hit epidemic proportions at the track, following the same pattern as in the rest of the country. That year, the New Jersey Racing Commission adopted a random drug-testing policy like one New York racing started in 1983. Before then, the track employed a "fitness" rule. If a rider seemed inebriated, he or she was ejected from the race because of the threat to other riders.[13] But picking out a rider who used drugs was more difficult than noticing one who reeked of alcohol. At that time, few industries wanted to ferret out substance abusers because of the stigma that clung to a business after violators were discovered.

The ensuing protest about the new rules said a great deal about the self-esteem problems riders suffered. In early September, five jockeys connected to the Jockeys' Guild—president Bill Shoemaker, Herb McCauley, Angel Cordero Jr., Philip Grove, and Vince Bracciale Jr.— filed suit in U.S. District Court against the New Jersey Commission arguing that random drug testing was unconstitutional. "Reasonable cause" ought to be the criteria for testing, they argued. If someone looked drunk or stoned, an official could ask them to take a drug test, but a person shouldn't have to supply a urine sample simply because his or her number was drawn out of a hat. The jockeys' opposition to the testing, they wrote in their appeal, "reflects their lifelong struggle to maintain their basic dignity against the barbs brought upon them by their short stature and their often humble background. Thus, the tests tend to un- dermine the element of self-respect, which is the greatest deterrent to the use of drugs and alcohol."[14] The court rejected the appeal a year later, and random testing became policy.

Meanwhile Antley rode so well in 1985 he drove home 422 winners by the third week in November, accounting for more than $5.4 million in purse money. The nineteen-year-old wanted 500 wins to be the first jock in eleven years to hit that mark. He rode up to nineteen races a day, getting on horses at Philadelphia Park in Pennsylvania, then driving up to the Meadowlands for the night card. He thought he had a shot at the more prestigious Eclipse Award for the best jockey of the year, decided by the *Daily Racing Form*, National Thoroughbred Racing Association and the National Turf Writers Association. Veteran riders Jorge Velasquez and Laffit Pincay were favored, but Antley, only two years into the game, believed he had a chance.

On November 26, 1985, Antley was named the national leading rider for wins with 435 but a kind of mania had seized him. "I didn't ride this afternoon because Philadelphia Park was dark," he told a reporter covering that achievement. "I went crazy. I tried to sleep as much as I could, but I ended up calling my parents, Michelle and Les Antley, and doing my laundry. Your body gets used to this kind of schedule."[15] Not long after, Antley was passed by for the Eclipse Award and the prize went to Laffit Pincay.

For a while, Craig Perret had watched Cordero and Antley engaging in their light-hearted rivalry, but Perret started noticing that Antley took the Cordero act a little too far. Coming into the final turn, Antley gawked over his shoulder, to his right, to his left, more interested in blocking another rider than riding out his horse. Now Perret saw him standing under the monitors with that season's apprentices. "Look how I screwed this guy," Antley said, pointing at the screen.

One day, Perret walked up to him and grabbed him by the neck. "Get over here," he said. He pulled Antley away from the group. "What, are you feeling like a big hero," Perret said, "telling everybody how much you can screw people? Is that making you feel big?"

"Well, he played with me," Antley said. "I was just telling them, 'Look how I did him.'"

"Remember this game, Chris," Perret warned him. "Silence is golden. That's the ticket of this game. Shut up. You watch, you listen, and you learn."

That year was the stormiest in U.S. history. In September, hurricane winds whipped up torrents that hammered the Jersey Shore. The jocks in their street clothes looked blankly out from the grandstand at the tracks that had gone from fast, to sloppy, to unridable overnight. The paddocks had flooded. Every day, the riders checked to see if maybe some miracle had occurred and the tracks had started to drain, but the season was shortened. At the end of the year, Chris Antley, at age nineteen, was 31 wins from his goal of 500 victories for the year. His 469 wins made him the nation's leading rider, he drilled home eight races in one day, and his total purse earnings that year were $6 million. But for Antley to fulfill his dream of making 500 wins in a year, he would have to start over again in January, beginning with a first victory and then the next, riding nineteen races a day again, starting from scratch.

Around that time, nineteen-year-old Chris Antley invited a group of track people to his house in Lodi, New Jersey, to check out the races on TV. He sat on the couch watching the horses while some of his guests sat around the table doing something he couldn't see. He got up and walked by them and noticed a rock of cocaine. He felt uneasy and went back to watching TV, but he kept wondering what effect the drug had on them.

The crowd eventually thinned out and Antley sat alone in the room, the races playing on TV, and the cocaine on the table. He went over and ran his finger over the rock, then put his finger to his tongue. His tongue went numb. He tried snorting a line, but he didn't feel anything.[16] Unfortunately, there are always more chances to fall in love with trouble. In the early part of 1986, four or five months after Antley first tried cocaine, he tried the drug again and liked it.

At the time, Antley made weight pretty easily, but a jockey never wanted to risk gaining pounds with a binge on anything, food or alcohol. For a jockey, snorting coke was better than drinking alcohol. You could get high and not add one calorie to your daily intake. Coke was better than pot because the drug suppressed your appetite. Antley had plenty of money to spend on drugs. As the second leading rider in New York, he earned around $600,000 a year, with Mollica taking 25 percent of that.[17] Antley took home about $20,000 to $30,000 a week when he was riding—more in a week than he told his father he could make in a year back when he first left for the track. Antley told a reporter he was saving. "I put most of it in the bank. It's going to stay there until I'm thirty," he said. "I don't know how long I'm going to ride, but it will only be as long as I enjoy it."[18]

Antley bought an $80,000 white Mercedes 560SEC with gold trim, by far the flashiest car owned by anyone at the track.[19] It was part of his image now: the handsome racing star trailed by swooning teenage girls at Monmouth Park. He owned a house in Floral Park. "When you go, go first class," Antley and Mollica said to each other.[20] But Mollica started seeing signs of moodiness in Antley. The usually easygoing Antley got in jockey-room brawls. He was getting physically weak.

Craig Perret tried to counsel Antley that the best thing for him would be to get married and settle down. "Chris, you know what you need in your life?" he'd say. "Find you a girl and get married. Raise a baby."

Antley would tell him about all the girls he was seeing. "All he had, he never had nothing," Perret said years later. "All he talked about was, 'Oh, I met this one. This one's so pretty and I was with her.' He never had none of it. To me, I think it was a fantasy, because if he'd had it, I think he would have latched. It had to be like an ego buildup. 'Oh, man, I was with the prettiest little girl last night,' and this and that, he'd say. I'd say, 'Well, how come nobody ever seen you? Why didn't you show up at the party?'

" 'Oh, man she was so nice,' Antley would say, 'but she's shy.' "

On Saturday, October 18, 1986, Antley went to a Rutgers-Florida football game at Giants Stadium and drank too much beer. He was riding at the Meadowlands that day, and the track required that all jocks take a Breathalyzer test to make sure the alcohol level in their blood was below .05 of 1 percent. Antley walked into the jocks' room at 6:15 P.M., took the test, then went to the steam room. The stewards came to him there and told him he had failed. He assured them he felt fine. The problem, he said, was that he only ate a bacon-and-egg sandwich in the morning before drinking four beers over the course of the afternoon. He bought milk and half a sandwich and ate it, then took the test again. He failed a second time. The officials took him off his mounts for the day and fined him $250.[21] "I'm sorry this happened," Antley told a reporter. "I want to apologize to any owner and trainer or fan I inconvenienced. It's not the way I do things, and it won't happen again." Away from the press, Antley decided the problem was that alcohol could be easily detected, so he stopped drinking.

To the press, that failed test could have looked like Antley was just behaving like a twenty-year-old fraternity brother, a kid who got caught up in the moment and forgot that he wasn't like most twenty-year-olds and actually had to go to the track later that day and drive a ton of horse through a potentially fatal stampede. But after the penalty at the Meadowlands, Mollica began hearing whispers that the problem with his jock was not too much beer on a Saturday afternoon, but a real drug problem. "At the beginning he was still very country," said Mollica. "But he got city real fast, I'm afraid. He was a very quick read." Antley, it turned out, was doing coke two out of three days. Mollica began trying to occupy every spare moment of Antley's time to keep him out of trouble. For five months, it worked and Antley stayed sober. Then, in early 1987, he started smoking pot again.[22]

Up in Saratoga that summer, Antley rode the D. Wayne Lukas horse Without Feathers in the Alabama Stakes. Another horse, Up the Apalachee, held the lead from the starting gate, but then on the last stretch, Antley started gaining on the horse. He pulled to Up the Apalachee's neck. Then, at the quarter pole, Antley dropped his whip. He slapped the horse's neck to the finish line but lost by a head. The crowd booed and Lukas fired him on the spot.[23]

A couple of weeks later, on opening day at Belmont, Antley rode Single Blade in the Gazelle Handicap. The horse was the biggest long shot in the race, with odds of 70 to 1. But coming down the homestretch, Single Blade exploded with energy and pulled up to the front-runner, Without Feathers. Antley blew by Without Feathers to win. "She made my day," Antley told the press about Single Blade. He said he had nothing against Lukas, but marveled at the change of fortunes that allowed him to get even with the trainer for firing him. This "goes to show how things can turn around in this business," he said.[24] It seemed that nothing Antley ever did went wrong for long.

Throughout that year of 1987, Antley rode remarkably well, and his mounts earned more than $8 million but he was driving back and forth frantically between tracks to achieve those numbers. On the way home from the Meadowlands on the night of October 30, a *Daily News* delivery truck smashed into Antley's Mercedes with Mollica driving. Antley and Mollica got out unscathed but the car was demolished.[25] The next day, Antley went to the track to ride.

It was October 31, 1987, Halloween day, that Antley's name entered the *Guiness Book of World Records* for winning the most races of any rider in one day in any country—a total of nine winners. He won four races at Aqueduct, then he and Mollica drove to the Meadowlands, where he won the first five in a row, then capped off the record with a win in the eighth race on a horse named Prince Lyph. The record of eight had been set back in 1886 by the British rider, Fred Archer, then five more jockeys matched the figure but never surpassed it. Even fourteen years later Antley's record of nine still stood.

"It's almost like a dream," Antley told the press then. "Believe it or not, I didn't know what the record was until they announced it. I've been having bad luck. My car got hit last night, but everything sure turned around Saturday. After I won four in New York, I was flying at an all-time high," he said, referring to the fact that he had matched the world record. "This is even better," he went on, about surpassing their achievement. "I just can't believe it. I just want to thank all these horsemen that put me on horses tonight."[26]

At the end of that day, Antley and Mollica drove toward the George Washington Bridge from the Meadowlands on their way home to Floral Park. Antley looked over at Mollica. "You know," he said, "I did good today." For all Antley's swagger, that was the first time Mollica felt the jock believed he deserved his successes. On that rare occasion, Mollica thought Antley really believed he was all right.[27]

That record-breaking achievement in itself described the frenzy Antley's life had become. He made big money, but given how often he won, the press noted, his earnings were surprisingly low. With a schedule where he often rode nineteen races a day, divided between the Meadowlands and Aqueduct, a lot of Antley's wins came in the prevalent claiming races, which had purses as little as $10,000 divided among the owners of the top finishers.

He rented an apartment out in Bayside, but rarely spent time there. He shuttled between the two tracks, sleeping in the passenger seat of Mollica's car. It seemed like Mollica and he worked double time to get the trainers to put him, still a young kid, on horses with the same frequency they used the veteran jockeys. The whole thing was getting to be a grind with no ordinary life or relaxation. Nothing but the jocks' room, the track, and the passenger seat, watching New York melt into New Jersey and then New Jersey give way to New York again.[28] Less than a week after Antley set that world record, he went to Aqueduct and won two races. He was supposed to ride four horses at the Meadowlands that evening, but the stewards announced that he was scratched off all of them. There was no explanation given officially, but a sudden change of plans like that smelled of trouble.

In 1988, the New York State Racing and Wagering Board conducted 360 drug tests, of which 91 came up positive. In February, Antley tested positive for marijuana. According to track rules, his suspension would be voluntary and private, but he was required to go through a drug-evaluation program. He promised never to take drugs again and the officials let him back in the sport.

Because Antley couldn't smoke pot, he went back to drinking. And when he was drinking, he couldn't resist cocaine. On May 30, he rode at Belmont on a horse named Imanair. Turning toward home, he let

Imanair charge too fast and clipped hoofs with the horse ahead. Antley and Imanair crashed to the ground. Jockey Robert Migliore came hard behind on Madame Alydar and had to vault them, but Imanair panicked and tried to stand. Migliore slammed right into the horse, got thrown and was nearly paralyzed. Antley suffered a concussion. When Antley was in the hospital, his friends brought him cocaine.[29]

In Antley's calculation, it wasn't hard to start using the drug again. He didn't blame the drug for the accident, since he hadn't used for a week before the race.[30] The only problem with using was getting caught when tested, Antley thought. Since he wouldn't be tested while he was recuperating, he thought he might as well use again. He figured the coke would be out of his system by the time he went back.

But once Antley started, he couldn't stop. He began doing coke again, once every three weeks, once every week, and then more often. The trainer Nick Zito remembered staring into Antley's eyes when giving riding instructions. "Do you understand? Do you understand?" he would say and Antley would look at him vacantly.[31] Zito never asked Antley directly if he was on drugs. For a while, Antley seemed zonked but his performances didn't suffer. Then Antley stopped showing up to exercise horses in the morning. He missed races. "It was quite obvious for a while," Mollica said. "You can't hide these things. He fell into the normal pattern. . . . There were times when you wanted to hit him with a bat, but basically you wanted to hug him."[32] Mollica searched for him and found him in hotel rooms with the curtains drawn or in rundown apartments where his drug buddies hung out.

In July, Antley dropped out of racing for a week because, he said, he had walking pneumonia.[33] That explanation raised eyebrows at the track that perhaps pneumonia was a cover story for something else. He went to Saratoga for the summer meet, and on August 24 was listed on a mount named Drachma in the sixth race on turf. The horse was a four-year-old gelding, a castrated horse, solid but not superior, with a five-for-twenty-five lifetime record and $240,098 in purses.

Antley rode Drachma hard right up to the top of the homestretch.

Then the horse buckled. Antley pulled him up sharply and the horse stopped by the eighth pole. Antley jumped off his back and it seemed at first he was doing the compassionate thing for the horse and was ready to help him get the care he needed. But then, inexplicably, Antley let the reins go. Drachma kept running, flailing along on his shattered foreleg all the way down the stretch. Antley sauntered behind, strolled down the grass course after the horse. Drachma hobbled across the finish line, then stopped. The silent crowd in the grandstands watched in horror as the horse turned and looked their way, appearing almost baffled by the pain. Drachma's assistant trainer ran to him and held his bridle. His trainer, Bruce Johnstone, sprinted across the track to the turf blinded by tears. They began wrapping Drachma's front leg. Antley strolled up. He flipped his whip to his valet, then patted Johnstone's back and headed off to the jocks' room. Drachma was carted away by ambulance and put down.

Even the veteran racing spectators, who over the years saw so many mishaps with horse and rider, were horrified. "A race rider, a person with even the faintest hint of compassion for thoroughbreds, would have stayed with the horse," wrote Paul Moran of The (Bergen) Record the next day. "He would have dismounted, held him still to avoid further damage to the leg, and waited for help. Not Antley."

He went on. "Sometimes, and thankfully, these times are infrequent," he wrote, "a grandstand full of people is reminded that while quality in a game this violent is defined as guts, class, and heart, not everyone has them."[34]

That year, on October 13, 1988, a race went off at Belmont that did not include Antley, but which, because of its horrific outcome, Mollica hoped might shake his client up enough to arrest the downward spiral. The jockey Jose Santos remembered coming up alongside jockey Mike Venezia well before the far turn at Belmont and then passing him. Santos heard Venezia's horse stumble and knew the animal veered out. "When I come back to the room that day," Santos recalled years later, "I told my valet, who was Cliff, I told him, 'Mike is going to lose his confidence, because when he was falling down, I hear this scream, like a very scared scream.' " Santos shook his head. "Then when I find out Mike was pronounced dead, I found out the scream was because the horse behind him stepped on his face."[35]

That death pulled every jockey at Belmont down too. It wasn't a drug-related accident, but Mollica hoped Antley would finally see how dangerous racing was—how he was risking his own life, not to mention the lives of other jockeys with his addiction. "This business is hard enough without having to worry about so many ancillary things," Mollica told the *Thoroughbred Record* not long after the accident. "I was a basket case. Where is he? What is he doing? Where is his car parked? It was a hell ride."[36]

Toward the end of October that year, the jockeys went on strike in New York for the same type of pay schedule they had fought for in New Jersey. A rider in New York usually got around $50 for a race, but if he was in the money in a $25,000 race, he got $250 for second and $100 for third. The problem was that in a race of more than $100,000, he got only $400 for second, and $250 for third. The purse money could be as high as $1 million in a race, and the jockeys didn't see any significant increase for place or show. This time, Chris Antley joined the picket line. Aqueduct started bringing in scab riders and tensions heated. One of the riders crossing the line was a guild member named Billy Fox. One day, in the tunnel leading to the track, Antley and Fox started throwing punches. Fox popped Antley in the face. The other jocks watched to see if Antley would clock him. But Antley put his hands down.

Perret saw the incident. *That ain't Antley*, he thought. No jock liked fighting for its own sake, but if someone, and a scab rider at that, cold-cocked you, there was no choice but to fight back.

Antley went up to one of the officials to complain. "Look here, judge," he said. "He hit me."

Perret went over to him. "What's going on, Chris?" he asked.

"He hit me," Antley said over and over. "He hit me. I got five stitches."

Perret told Antley to forget about the incident. A few days later, after the strike was settled, Perret watched Antley in a race at Belmont. He was riding everyone nasty. Taking a rider out. Shutting another one off. He came back into the jocks' room. "Look how I screwed this guy," he said to Perret, while he watched the replay on monitors.

Perret looked at him. "Who are you?" he said incredulously. "This ain't *you*, Chris."

The competition between Antley and Jerry Bailey heated up. They both were going for the top clients. One day, Perret was riding behind both of them in a race and saw Antley whipping Bailey across the back. The riders got back to the jocks' room and Bailey looked ready to fight. Antley walked in and pulled down his pants. "Here," he said, mooning Bailey. "Kiss my ass."

He's a *monster*, Perret thought. What's going on?

He went up to Antley, and the jock wouldn't stop ranting. "Chris," Perret said. "Chill. Out."

"Well, he can kiss my ass," Antley said.

"Okay," Perret said, "you made your point. Forget about it."[37]

Friends would drop by Antley's house now in Garden City, Long Island, at night and see the lights on, the car in the driveway, but no one answered the phone or the door.

Antley flew to Japan in mid November 1988 to ride Salem Drive in the Fuji International Stakes. His seventeen-year-old sister, Leslie, was living with him and he took her along. He won the race and planned to bring his father with him to Japan when he returned two weeks later for the Japan Cup, on November 27, since he thought his father would like how polite and friendly the people were. On the flight back, as his sister slept in the seat next to him, Antley watched the movie *Big*, which had come out that year. Tom Hanks starred as a twelve-year-old boy turned into a thirty-year-old man by a video arcade swami. He makes his way in the world, huddling in his first apartment, a rundown hovel, crying into his pillow while the neighbors fight, being scared of girls and missing his mother. Antley began to cry. He never wrote letters, but he got out paper and a pen there on the plane.

"Dear God," he wrote. "Since being young, I've come a long way so very fast and I'm not complaining about my success. But is this all, and should I live the rest of my life the way it is now? I've pulled away from living and enjoying every minute of my life. When I am old, will I sit and think about the things that just flew by unnoticed and the things I passed not doing and the people that sometimes feel imaginary? God, you've given me so much talent, opportunity, money, friends, and people who really care for me. And now do I really push all of this to its right fulfillment? And am I truly happy?"[38]

It could have been a breakthrough for Antley, but the next day, he bought cocaine. He was asked to take a urine test the following day, November 24, at Aqueduct. Under track rules, he knew a jock could fail a test and avoid public humiliation and professional disgrace if he temporarily left racing to seek treatment. The only unforgivable sin was to ride again before the treatment was complete. Knowing he likely failed the test, Antley boarded a plane to ride in the Japan Cup. The whole time he was there he feared that the news would break. He would be pulled off the horse. His father would be publicly humiliated. The newspapers would scream his shame.

But nothing happened. As the days ticked by, he wondered if maybe he hadn't tested positive after all.

When Antley got back, Mollica called him. "Get over here," Mollica said. At his apartment, Mollica sat Antley down and told him they were ruled off the horses indefinitely. The suspension was official as of November 28, 1988. Antley lowered his head. Five minutes went by without a word. Then he stood and left.

For four or five days, Antley stayed in his room, staring at the ceiling. The media probably was devouring this story, he thought. He was twenty-two and had burned through his dream of being a great rider in five years. How had his story become this one? He called one of his dealers for cocaine. He thought, *If I use this until I die, then they won't feel sorry for me.*[39]

For three days, Antley snorted coke until he was crazed. He tried to kill himself with the stuff, but couldn't. His nose tissues broke down, but his heart still wouldn't stop.[40] He could hear Leslie come home from school and he felt so bad for her, but he didn't know what to do. He lay on the floor and screamed, "What's the difference?" At times, he thought maybe he could go to rehab and move back to South Carolina and the world would leave him alone.

But the track provided a way to earn back forgiveness. Antley checked into the Smithers Institute, part of St. Luke's–Roosevelt Hospital, in New York, on December 4 for a twenty-eight-day program, and the racing authorities supported him. "They laid my life on a map," he told a reporter around that time. "People from all walks of life were there, and they all found something to blame their addiction on. Some blame no money. Some blame having too much money. Some blame their families.[41]

"In the program, they made us look at ourselves. It was scary how screwed up I was. . . ." he said. "They make you look at a lot of different things, like friends and who you have—what's important in life. My whole life was working and people-pleasing. They had my whole life down. They could have written it down in one page, and it just made me see things a lot different."

Antley's biggest fear was that Mollica would leave him, but Mollica waited for his rider to get through the program. When everyone in rehab was told to call the person who meant the most to them in the world, Antley phoned Mollica. "I'm getting closer to my family now," Antley told the reporter, "I call my dad almost every day—but Drew also is my family. He's my best friend in the world. Without Drew I wouldn't have made it."

Antley graduated from Smithers on January 4, 1989, two days before his twenty-third birthday. He kept going to support group meetings three times a week, he said, including Alcoholics Anonymous, Cocaine Anonymous and Narcotics Anonymous. He gave up nightlife. He replaced the Mercedes with a sturdy Blazer 4×4 to change his image.[42] He got engaged to his girlfriend, Kathy Hoveling. He publicly disavowed drugs. "I have no temptation whatsoever to use cocaine," he told the press. "I have a hatred for what it caused me. I look down on it now." He knew if he tested positive again, he would lose his license for at least a year.[43] But he wasn't worried. He thought he was only a recreational user who got caught and the problem was solved.[44]

On January 25, the New York Racing Association gave Antley back his license. He hadn't raced for two months and was terrified to return to the track. Walking out of the jockeys' room at Aqueduct to saddle up in the paddock, he felt more nervous than he had been even on his first Derby day. But the fans and jocks came through. No one said anything negative.[45] They accepted him back without criticizing him for his frailty.

A few weeks later, the magic started again for Antley. On February 8, he won a race on Lady Seaul. Then he continued to drive home first-place finishes through that whole week. He piled up purse money sometimes on five or six winning mounts a day, on and on. There wasn't a racing day that Chris Antley didn't go into the winner's circle through all of February and March. The streak was unprecedented, and everyone began to take notice.

The winning streak continued through April. To keep the luck going, Mollica stopped cutting his hair. Antley told reporters he didn't feel pressure—that the streak was like a bonus.[46] But every day when he woke up, he thought, *I've got to get a winner*. He was suspended for rough riding in April, but decided to take the days in June so he could keep pursuing the streak.[47] "I've never seen anything like it," Sam Renick, an esteemed ex-jockey and broadcast commentator, told the *Chicago Tribune*. "The closest thing to it I can remember is Steve Cauthen going thirty-some days in a row when he was here in the mid-1970s."[48] It was like Joe DiMaggio and his 56-game hitting streak. Craig Perret worried that huge success was coming too quickly for Antley after rehabilitation for him to keep his wits about him. If such a feat was this easy for Antley, he might forget that just staying sober wasn't so simple.

On day fifty-three, Antley rode seven horses and none came up winners. There was one race on turf—the eighth—where a mount still didn't have a jock. Mollica drove by the trainer Joe Canto on his way to the

Aqueduct barns. Canto flagged him down. "Hey, genius," he said. "You wanna ride a winner?" Antley came up the fence in first place to continue the streak.

Antley put together eleven more winning days. On May 1, day sixty-five, Antley rode one of Willard Thompson's horses—a four-to-five shot—in a New York maiden race and lost. The streak ended with sixty-four days. Mollica was relieved, and Antley seemed to accept the end of the run gracefully too. He went on to win twenty out of the next twenty-three days.[49]

The streak was over, but the feat was unbelievable, unprecedented. "That sixty-four-days-in-a-row streak will never be broken by anyone, anywhere," Mollica declared.

In June, Antley took the days of his postponed suspension and spent them in Atlantic City, where friends said he might have gotten back into coke.[50]

In 1989, Antley's record for the full year ended up totalling a staggering 23 percent victory rate on the 1,057 mounts he rode. The average win rate is 7 percent. But those kinds of highs could be stopped dead by an injury. On August 25, 1989, Antley rode a colt named Cousteau at Saratoga. As he was galloping Cousteau after the finish line, he was thrown. He tore the ligaments in his knee and underwent arthroscopic surgery but the injury did not heal quickly.

A few days off was all it took. Antley never seemed to know what to do with his downtime. His engagement had been broken off. He started smoking pot and doing coke again.[51] On Saturday, September 23, Antley was scheduled to ride two horses at Belmont. He hadn't been on a horse since the accident. Mollica waited for him at the track that morning, but Antley didn't show. Mollica called Antley's house. The jock picked up.

"I overslept," Antley told him. "I'll be right over."

Mollica waited. The first race was coming up. Antley still didn't appear. Mollica called again.

"The car ran out of gas, Drewsky," Antley told him.

Mollica called the track stewards at 10:45 and took Antley off all his mounts.[52] The race day ended and Antley never got there. Mollica went and found him.

"I was at the tanning salon," Antley explained to Mollica.

After all the counseling they went through together, Mollica couldn't accommodate this behavior even if he wanted to. That would make him, in the word of the counselors, an enabler. Mollica let the stewards at the New York Racing Association know he made a decision he never wanted to make before—all those times chasing Antley around, keeping him busy, sitting through session after session at the Smithers Institute. He quit as Chris Antley's agent and told the stewards that the jock was not fit to ride.[53] The next day, Mollica's mother died.[54]

The New York State Racing and Wagering Board asked Antley to take another test, but he refused. If he tested positive, he would lose his license for life.[55] He met with them early that next week, and on September 27, 1989, the Board put out a statement. Antley "had acknowledged that he has a substance abuse problem" and voluntarily surrendered his license.[56] Until New York approved him again, he could not ride in any state.

With the high winds whistling, Mollica leaned back in the theater seat at Yonkers Raceway and looked out at the empty track. "After countless rehabs and fighting and tough love," he said, "we just went our separate ways. I didn't turn him in. Our psychiatrist said I was his 'enabler'— language that, on the racetrack, is . . . you know, crazy. Bottom line is I loved him very much, he loved me very much, but he loved his addiction more. And I was married, had a kid on the way. We split, he went into rehab, he came back, and truth be told, professionally, he kicked my ass. I had Cordero and did very well, but Antley was the Man. But I don't regret one moment of leaving him, if I thought it would get him straight . . . I feared for his life, and I took a lot of grief from people who were uninformed about it—saying it was no big deal, saying that I abandoned him. It wasn't any of that. . . . I adored him, I loved him, and for his part, he loved me, but he was not well, he was sick and we couldn't coexist anymore. So on the advice of the people at Smithers and some other people, it was time to move on and maybe he would bottom out.

"The thing that I didn't see then that I see now was that I was very replaceable," Mollica added. "I mean, I really thought that my quitting would shock him into some sort of . . . like in the movies. But this ain't the movies. I was under the impression he'd come to his senses the next day and you know, James Garner would drive him over and this would all be better now. But this was a mistake. Because he just found someone he could pay enough money to enable him. I mean, I really miscalculated it. Not that it was a calculated thing.

"I lied for him as much as anybody. I didn't want to be his pimp, I wanted to be his agent. I wanted to be his friend. I took a lot of shit about it. It was a very bad spot to be in, and I was a little young to be in it, but I was there." He looked out at the Yonkers racetrack and shrugged. "As Maya Angelou likes to say, 'We did then what we knew then. Now that we know better, we'll do better.' "

SIX

MORNING GLORY

When Darrell Wayne Lukas drove up to Santa Anita track each morning before dawn and pulled his GMC SUV into the lot beneath the San Gabriel mountains, there was nothing but silence because he was one of the first ones there, first of the trainers. When he walked up to his barn, he gazed through the dark lenses of his gold-framed aviator shades and saw nothing but order, the shedrow raked in a herringbone pattern and the forest-green-and-white barns as immaculate as a tennis club.

At age sixty-three, Lukas had the face of a cowboy, with thin lips, a strong jaw and capped teeth so white and straight they seemed chiseled of one bone. His voice was the drawl of a movieland sheriff, a Western twang coated with syrup and dragged through fine sand. The years had styled him, making him look even more like a man who knew how to handle horses than he did as a young man. His wiry black hair gave in, through the eighties and nineties, to a cloud of thick silver. Now he favored navy-blue suits for race days, and cowboy hats and buttery suede chaps for the morning works with his horses. His colleagues in the early

1960s, back when he was a high school basketball coach, had called him Luke, but for several decades now, he had gone by the horseman's name of initial and middle name: *Deee-wane*.

For most people who spend their lives working the tracks, horse racing is a land of disorder—a cauldron of skittish horses swirling at breakneck speed, broken bones for jockeys and animals; for grooms and hotwalkers, there are hundreds of miles dozing in the backs of horse trailers on the way to another track, with straw whipping down their necks. For jockeys, there are lost wagers and wages lost when an injury slows them down, and dust and dirt and shouting. Rain pours down on the shedrow roofs, turning everything into moats of mud, and there is bitter loneliness, heavy drinking and stolen girlfriends, and a life traveling town to town like circus performers. But Lukas entered that thorough-bred world as a forty-two-year-old man and decided he would change it, or at least, by force of will, would create a small corner of order in that chaos.

At the end of the millennium, Lukas strode through his barns like a cowboy colossus. He could hear every slight shift of a horse in its stall because he had banned radios and loud talk. His own day started when he rose at 3:00 A.M. By 4:20 A.M. he was at an all-night doughnut shop going over the daily plan with his son, Jeff, his assistant trainer at Santa Anita then.[1] By 4:45, he was at the track.[2] If Lukas got tired in the afternoon, he took a six-minute nap, and if he felt really whipped, he extended the rest to seven.[3] At the earliest stages of his career, he banned women from the barns to avoid the distraction, but then he realized he couldn't find enough talent pulling only from the ranks of available males and changed his policy.[4] The 23 staffers at Lukas's Santa Anita barn arrived at the track each morning fifteen minutes before their boss. There was no chitchat since Lukas had barred that magnet of workplace fri-volity—the coffee urn—from the premises long ago.[5] His own D. Wayne Lukas trailers drove up to deliver some of his horses from another track, and the sides of the vehicles were clean chrome in that world of mud and dust. "A shedrow is a hospital," Hall of Fame trainer John Nerud once told a reporter, "and Wayne has the best of everything—feed, hay, wraps. Even when he didn't have much he always acted like the first-class horseman that he is."[6]

Lukas looked at his Triple Crown watch with the first eleven hours marked by the silk colors of history's eleven Triple Crown winners. Fourteen years ago, Lukas found the watch in a shop and bought it on the spot. From the black and orange of Sir Barton's winning silks in 1919, to the black and flamingo hues of Affirmed in 1978, they were all there. But the twelve at the top was blank, waiting for the next victor.[7] Lukas had been wearing that watch for fourteen years, watching the hands sweep past that empty space, waiting for his time to come.

Historically, horse training was part of a kingdom's war machine, and the trainer readied the royal horses for long battles in faraway lands. The first trainer to leave a historical trace was a man named Kikkulis from Mesopotamia, horsemaster to King Suppiluliumas of the Hittites, who recorded his seven-month-interval training regime on stone tablets around 1350 B.C.[8] The horses needed stamina to make their way to the front lines, a four-week journey away, and speed and agility to carry a soldier in and out of battle safely. Kikkulis devoted his talents to developing these attributes in the horses of the Hittite king, but in so doing betrayed his own Mitannian people, because his powerful steeds carried Hittites through a successful Mitannian genocide. He left no useful legacy for the conquerors, though, after his own death. The instructions, written in Hittite, frequently include words from Kikkulis's native tongue when he was at a loss for the correct word. The Hittite horsemen were confused for generations.

Kikkulis focused first on developing a horse's leg muscles, then his cardiovascular system, and third, the animal's neuromuscular functions. Three to five times a day, he raced the horses to their hearts' peak capacity, then cooled them down. "2½ DANNA he trots," wrote Kikkulis, "and canters at the 71KU marker. Then he drives again. And at the 10 IKU marker he canters." He specified four daily feedings in liters. He indicated that on days eleven through twenty, a horse should be tested for physical defects by blocking all gaps in the stall walls and checking if the increased levels of dust, fungus, and ammonia caused the horse to wheeze.

Horse training for racing evolved from such war efforts. The best way to keep horses fit for battle was to prime them in competition against each other. Before long, people began enjoying racing for its own sake, and trainers were retained to look after the stable. For centuries, trainers seemed to be divided into two categories. There were the lower-tier trainers considered just this side of pickpockets, who spent more time scheming to win through cheating, than they did actually training their animals to run well. They stuffed sponges in their horses' noses to keep them from running strong, thereby raising their odds the next time out. They pumped them with stimulants, or calmed them with half a grain of heroin on the tongue. Testing for illegal substances began around 1946, when, after the war, track officials hoped to scour racing's image for a larger audience. The next year, the National Racing Association introduced horse-lip tattooing to stop trainers from sending unannounced ringers into races.

The other type of trainer was the gentleman horseman—like Charlie Whittingham or Jimmy Jones—who earned fortunes but trained horses like they were restoring Rembrandts, treating them with such meticulous patience and care that the horses spent more time ripening in the barns than they did running on the track. In the late twentieth century, there were hundreds of thoroughbred trainers in the United States, making an average $45,000. D. Wayne Lukas was by no means average.

The hands now showed that it was 6:00 sharp, so D. Wayne Lukas told his exercise riders to mount the horses to take them to the track for their morning works. Lukas believed in discipline and order, but he adhered to those virtues when they etched a clear line, a straight directive to win.

There was one thing that drove Lukas crazy: Say a trainer sent a horse out to have the exercise rider breeze him in the morning, maybe gallop him a few times around the oval. When the exercise rider finished, the trainer would ask him to walk the horse over to the grandstand, to the entrance to the tunnel that led to the paddock, where on race day the horse would be saddled. The rider would face the horse in toward the track with his back end to the tunnel. Then the exercise rider and the horse would just stand there—the theory being that if the horse could fight the impulse to turn around and walk into the tunnel toward the paddock, then he would stand calm during saddling on a race day. He would be quiet in the trailer when he was being shipped track to track. The trainer was trying to make a horse calm enough to withstand any temptation.

But the situation always went the same way. After a few seconds, the horse started shifting a little, picking his hooves up. Then the rider got impatient with the fidgeting. "Whoa, come here," the exercise rider said and kicked the horse in the belly. The horse quieted down, but a few seconds later, he started mincing again. Then the trainer got involved. And this was the problem. Trainers were always trying to set up situations where they could be the trainer, the disciplinarian, when it didn't make sense. That horse didn't need to learn to stand in the middle of the tunnel. The trainer was just creating a situation that made the horse mad for no good reason.

One day at Santa Anita, Lukas put the question to the trainer Noble Threewitt, who had worked with horses some fifty-five years. "Noble," Lukas said, "have you ever in all these years seen a horse run down through here in the afternoon and duck out that gap?"[9]

"Are you crazy?" Threewitt said.

Lukas asked the question to get the answer he knew was coming. "Have you ever seen a horse try to duck out that gap?" he demanded.

"No, never," Threewitt told him.

That was all Lukas wanted. If a horse didn't by natural instinct duck out the tunnel in the middle of the race, there was no point in teaching him not to do it during his morning exercise. A trainer didn't need to teach a horse how to fight its *every* natural impulse—just the ones that kept it from winning races. A horse *did* need to be schooled in the paddock—that is, taught to stay calm while he was being saddled and waiting for a race, and he had to be taught how to load into the starting gate without panicking. And how to run. That was it. All he needed to learn was what he needed to win. That simple.

But everywhere you went, people were trying to teach things that didn't need to be learned, just so they could set up the dynamic of discipline—spouses, parents, you name it. There were so many useless lessons being muscled into human beings and animals.

What horses wanted was for you to handle them every day in a clear, calm manner. Then they would be quiet to their core and trust you.

Lukas liked to remind himself of the wisdom of Aristotle: Man is a goal-seeking animal, the philosopher said. You set a goal for horse and man and they would be happy. Or what his hero, Vince Lombardi, the great Green Bay Packers coach from his home state of Wisconsin believed, that the quality of a person's life is in direct proportion to his commitment to excellence regardless of chosen endeavor. Having the shedrow raked in a herringbone pattern was not an unrelated task in Lukas's book. It was a way to boost the morale of the workers. Lukas told a reporter once that his demand for the task was a gift to the night man; that it "made him mentally finish off the day in a positive way."[10] Everyone on the team needed to feel they were the best, that from the very get-go they stood out as winners. Lukas did not drink, golf, or go to movies.[11] He did not want to be a drunk, a golfer, or a movie buff. He wanted to win horse races. The key was to set the goal, demand the result, and not interfere with the path. It was the only way to get anything good out of life. The Lukas family would repeat Lincoln's observation, "A man becomes what he thinks about all day long."[12] Lukas thought about winning races, and he believed he could exert real control over whether or not a horse came in first. He did not believe in luck. If a person had to depend on luck in horse racing, Lukas thought, he would get beaten a lot.[13]

Lukas brought that kind of motivational thinking into the thoroughbred racing world when he first got serious about the sport in 1978. Even horse racing, he believed, the world of chance, could operate as a well-oiled business. He ran barns around the country, starting horses at up to twenty-four different tracks to ensure he had a horse entered in every big stakes race. Most tracks limited the number of horses a trainer could house on the backside at any given time. But if a trainer diversified his holdings—if he had horses all over the country—he could ship the right animal to a specific race and increase his opportunities to win. Upping your chances of winning by upping the number of times you played was the Lukas way.

He branded his operation. All of the Lukas barns bore his distinctive marks—the green and white painted sign that said "D. Wayne Lukas, Riding Stables," the crisply manicured yards with potted geraniums hanging from the beams of the shedrows, the stall webbing embossed with his monogram, and brass plating on the halters polished to a Rodeo Drive sheen. He gave his assistant trainers Lukas Jeeps and cell phones. Lukas horses wore white bridles so they stood out from the pack. All the bettors and spectators would know in an instant when a Lukas horse crossed the finish line first. That underscored to owners that the Lukas brand was synonymous with success. When owners began shopping for a trainer of their thoroughbreds, they would want to give their horses to him, a CEO they could trust.

Lukas insisted on unflagging professionalism from his staff. Early in assistant trainer Mark Hennig's tenure with Lukas, he called his boss to report the results of a day's racing at Aqueduct. Hennig's brother-in-law Kiarnan McLaughlin had worked for Lukas for years and told him how much Lukas liked to hear about victory. Hennig proudly told his boss that two of the Lukas horses had won. "The horses ran good," Hennig reported.

There was a split-second silence on the other end, then the explosion. "I give you quality horses to train," Lukas said. "I supply you with owners that have spent millions of dollars in this industry. The one thing you and that hillbilly brother-in-law of yours need to do is learn how to communicate with them: Horses do not run good, they run well."[14] Lukas didn't mind hurling an insult to make a point.

With professionalism as a mandate and large numbers of horses running at any time, Lukas shattered the annual earnings record of Charlie

Whittingham, the king of all trainers, by pulling in a total of $5.8 million in 1984. He nearly doubled that the following year with $11.1 million. By 1999, Lukas had won nearly $235 million for his horse owners, and that had convinced those owners to let him spend an equal amount to buy horses.[15] He had trained nineteen Eclipse Award–winning horses and won more than five hundred stakes races. He had met the Queen of England and saddled thoroughbreds in front of four presidents. When he delivered motivational speeches, they paid him $7,500 a pop. His empire expanded to a 1,000-acre training facility in Summerfield, Florida, and an 184-acre training center in Santa Ynez, California. He had achieved glamour and wealth—even driving a Rolls Royce to the track for a time[16]—by setting goals and sticking to them.

Lukas's motivation was to win stakes races with high purses, particularly the Triple Crown races, which owners doubly loved for their prestige. As the great Kentucky basketball coach Adolph Rupp said, "If winning isn't important, why do they keep score?" A person might assume that all trainers liked having horses in the Derby at any cost, but this was not so. Whittingham ran his first horse in the Derby in 1958 and came in eighth. He ran his second two years later and came in ninth. He was so embarrassed with those weak finishes he vowed not to enter the Derby again until he had a horse that he thought could win.[17] He kept his promise, waiting twenty-seven years until 1986 when the colt Ferdinand came to his barn. He was seventy-three at the time, and Whittingham asked his good friend, then the winningest jockey of all time, Willie Shoemaker, to come out of retirement to ride the colt. Shoemaker, at age fifty-four, agreed, and he and Whittingham made history as the oldest trainer and rider ever to win the Derby. Whittingham broke his own record three years later at age seventy-six with Sunday Silence.

But for Whittingham, those were only two Derby wins in a whole lifetime of training. Going into 1999, Lukas already had come up with three winners—Winning Colors, Thunder Gulch, and Grindstone—tying him for third place for the most Derby wins. Of course, he had taken thirty-three shots at the prize to get those. Critics grumbled that Lukas's method was like using a sawed-off shotgun to hit a dove. Of the thirty-three runners Lukas sent to the Derby, twenty-six horses hadn't placed, meaning they hadn't come in first, second or third. That gave Lukas the trainer record for most unplaced Derby entrants, which to some would be an embarrassment. H. J. "Dick" Thompson had the second most with seventeen. By comparison, Ben Jones, who held the record for Derby wins with six, only had two unplaced horses in his career.

But Lukas thought it was silly to wait until you had the perfect horse to run in the Derby. Cot Campbell, who put together the first ownership franchise, Dogwood Stables, expressed the Derby issue succinctly. "I don't believe in waiting," Campbell said. "A lot of people say wait. You'll have a better horse in the fall. Well, we might all be dead in the fall."[18]

That was Lukas's sentiment exactly. "Wayne has a motto," trainer Bob Baffert once said, speaking of his archrival. "When they're hot, they're hot. You better run 'em. Tomorrow they might be dead."[19] Lukas felt jealous of young trainers like Elliot Walden from Kentucky, who at age thirty-six had already sent two horses to the Derby. Lukas was a grand old man of forty-five when he took his first horse to Churchill Downs on that first Saturday in May. He was now sixty-three. How many shots would he have left?

Vince Lombardi once said, "The dictionary is the only place that success comes before work." Darrell Wayne Lukas, born September 2, 1935, understood the value of labor from the first, growing up in Antigo, Wisconsin, population eight thousand. Most of the kids who attended the one-room schoolhouse run by Miss Caulson dropped out as soon as they were old enough to work on their families' farms, but Wayne's father, Ted, the son of Czechoslovakian immigrants, believed in education.[20] He was a farmer of ten acres, an owner of twenty cows, a milk-truck driver, construction worker and strict disciplinarian. He drilled into his children—Dauna, the oldest, Wayne, and Lowell, eighteen months Wayne's junior—the need for both schooling and labor. "Do a day's work for a day's pay," he told them, "and then do a little more."[21]

Wayne didn't need his father's punishments and warnings to drive him. Every weekday he and Lowell worked the milk route with their father, and every Sunday they delivered newspapers. Even as a boy, Wayne Lukas wanted to buy horses and make money, to be successful, and from the age of six, he would wake at 3:30 each morning to further his goal. He raised animals—bunnies at Easter, chickens for the area farms—so he could sell or trade them up, always aiming for another, better horse. At the local sales, eight-year-old Wayne would sit next to his father and raise his hand to show his buying interest, but the auctioneer would look right past him because he was so small. "Take the kid's bid," his father would say.[22]

At age eleven, Wayne heard that the town's string bean cannery would give free seed if you planted it, harvested it, then sold the crop back to the cannery. Wayne thought that sounded like a fine way to make good money, so he recruited Lowell to work the deal with him. They asked their uncle for two acres to plant themselves. Up in that country, the farmers grew wheat, and the seed scattered in the wind and rained down everywhere. The wheat and weeds started twining up among the rows of string beans, and there was nothing Wayne and Lowell could do but hoe the string bean field by hand. One night, Wayne and Lowell came in exhausted from their work and sat down at the table with their sister, Dauna, and mother, Bea.[23] Their father started yelling.

"Get your feet on the floor," Ted Lukas barked. "Sit straight."

He looked at his oldest son. "Wayne, how many rows did you hoe today?" he asked.

"I don't know," Wayne said, "forty-two, forty-three."

"That's not good enough," said his father.

"What do you mean not good enough?"

"That's not good enough. That's not good enough," his father said. "Do better." Then, he softened. "I'll tell you what I'm going to do," he told Wayne. "I'm gonna come out tomorrow and help you."

Wayne thought that was a great idea. He could use the extra hands.

Early the next morning, Wayne and his brother set off for hoeing, fully expecting their father to join them. At around nine or ten, they saw their father's pickup driving along the road near the field and pulling to a stop under a big oak tree at the far end. They saw their neighbor come to join their father. Their mother had fixed their father and the neighbor iced tea in a big fruit jar, and his father and the neighbor sat there under the tree drinking iced tea all day.

At dinnertime, Wayne and his brother headed back to the house. They sat down at the table. "How many rows did you get today?" his father asked Wayne.

"Oh, we did a lot better," Wayne said. "Lowell got about fifty, and I got about sixty-five."

"That's great," his father said. He didn't add anything further.

"Hey, Dad," Wayne said. "Let me ask you something. You told me you were going to help us, and all you did was go drive under that tree and drink iced tea with the neighbor."

His father looked at him. "Son," Ted Lukas said, "when you counted your rows today, mine were in there."

What Wayne got from that exchange over the dinner table was the lesson that he found worthy of recounting later in life: You have to be present. His father might have been half taunting them by enjoying himself under the shady tree while his sons worked, but his being there spurred them on. In Wayne's book, that gift of being present for a person more than compensated for any harshness that might be doled out when you were there.

When Lukas was still in grade school, he bought his first horse, Queenie, by agreeing to pay a local kid two dollars a week for two years. He earned the money by selling newspapers. He took Queenie on long rides through the Menominee reservation with a satchel packed with Spam and eggs.[24] He rode Queenie to the racing competitions at the Antigo County Fairgrounds and chatted up the trainers to pick up tips on how to get horses to run. The fairground trainers were only small-time but Lukas treated them like gods of the track. He traveled to the fairs at Rhinelander and Eagle River, almost at the border of Canada, to learn more.

Eventually, Lukas and his buddy Clyde Rice got the itch to train horses themselves. Lukas knew how to make a horse mind him well enough to trick ride, swinging under a horse's neck and up around again, and doing handsprings off the horse's back. Now, Lukas and Rice started testing what they learned about racing from the trainers. In high school, Lukas and Rice drove to the nearby mink ranches and sat watching horses from the Dakotas being unloaded to be ground into mink feed. They picked out the best-looking ones, then offered the ranchers slightly more per pound for the horse than the ranchers had paid.[25] Lukas and Rice then either raced the horses or resold them. Their mission in life was to trade up, constantly. Trading up was how you got places in the world. When Lukas wanted a pickup truck, he financed the purchase by selling a horse.

Lukas was always industrious and responsible, but in 1952, more weight fell on his seventeen-year-old shoulders. His father went off to Missouri in search of construction work and left the farm to be worked by Bea and his two sons. But the Lukases believed in education and doing good in the world above all else. Dauna was studying at the University of Wisconsin at Madison.[26] A year after Ted Lukas's departure, Wayne enrolled there too. Bea and Lowell sold the farm and joined Ted in Missouri, and Lukas paid his college tuition with his horse trading and racing. While the rest of his fraternity brothers at Kappa Sigma drank beer and chased girls, Lukas loaded his saddle into the back of his pickup truck and went to work horses through Iowa and Nebraska.[27]

Lukas graduated from the University of Wisconsin with a degree in physical education. He married his girlfriend, Janet, and moved them to Blair, Wisconsin, with a population under a thousand, for the first step in a coaching career, albeit into the small-time. Lukas's heroes were John Wooden, the gentleman coach of the University of California at Los Angeles, and Adolph Rupp, the hard-bitten leader of the University of Kentucky, who led his teams to four NCAA championships and 876 wins. Lukas tried to apply their sophisticated techniques to his coaching, but unfortunately, the teenagers of Blair couldn't attain college heights, and he was forced to scale back expectations.[28]

Lukas needed better material to work with, to test his ideas, and an advanced degree to get access to the best players. In 1959, he returned to the University of Wisconsin for a master's in education, and coach Johnny Erickson hired him as an assistant basketball coach. Never content to let good enough alone, Lukas invented a basketball training shoe weighted in the sole with BBs. A player plodded along in the sneakers during practice, then when he took the shoe off for a game, he felt feather light. Converse ended up marketing the shoe as the All Star Trainer.[29]

Lukas finished his master's and took a job at a high school in La Crosse, Wisconsin. He taught American Problems, a course combining economics, civics and sociology, but that was secondary to his task of whipping the school's basketball team into shape. Presentation, Lukas decided, was critical to success. He outfitted the whole team in matching blazers from a downtown clothing store. He hired Greyhound buses to take the students to games. Each player's locker was neatly painted with his name,[30] and every boy was required to shine his shoes and keep his tie straight when traveling. Lukas hired a woman from the local Y to teach manners. His constant refrain, according to one of his former players, Terry Erickson, was, "Just because you win doesn't make you a winner, just because you lose doesn't make you a poor person. It's how you prepare and dedicate yourself, how much you improve."[31] And to get his boys to improve, he would yell and berate them. They feared him, but they respected him. Despite Lukas's exhortations, however, the team still couldn't get past a two-and-sixteen record.[32] While Lukas taught and coached, he also trained horses. Every morning he rose at 4:00 A.M. and drove sixty miles to Rochester, Minnesota, to tend to his quarter horses.

The breed originated in the eighteenth century as a cross between British and Spanish horses. When racing began in the United States, these were the runners brought to the tracks, and since most tracks were then a quarter of a mile long, the quarter horse got its name. Mustang and thoroughbred blood was later added to the mix to make the horses faster still. The quarter horse could sprint five furlongs at higher speed than a thoroughbred, but it would be hard-pressed to maintain that velocity for a mile, which a thoroughbred could regularly do. For a trainer just starting out, the quarter horse was easier to train, however, and the price tag on these mild-tempered animals was lower on average than that of thoroughbreds. The stakes money, however, was lower too. The top quarter horse trainer could dream of pulling in $1.5 million in purse money a year, compared to the apex income of $15 million for training thoroughbreds.

But a dream of $1.5 million looked good enough to Lukas at that point. He took the animals through their workouts each morning, then drove back to La Crosse, showered, changed clothes and was at the school ready to drill his students through another day before the first bell rang.[33] In 1966, he earned over four thousand dollars from his horses, which constituted a sizeable percentage of his income.[34] Lukas could see that he had more hope of achieving significant success at the track than working his way up the coaching ladder. He quit teaching that year and moved to Claremore, Oklahoma, to a track named Thundering Downs.

Lukas started at Thundering Downs with about seven two-year-old horses. He took them onto the frozen track in the bitter gales and tried to teach them the right way to run and the correct moment to burst from the gate. An elderly trainer named O. Woodson used to sit in a rocking chair out by the track and watch Lukas go through his meticulous lessons, four horses at a time. Finally, one day Woodson yelled to Lukas. "Wayne, come over here," he said.[35]

Lukas went to him. "Why are you spending all that time on these horses?" Woodson asked.

"Well," said Lukas, "I want them to have a good headset and get their alignment right and have them go to the bit—do it all right, the way I think it's proper."

Woodson listened to Lukas then offered his own view. "Well, there's a lot simpler way to do that," he said. "I'll tell you what we'll do. . . . I got an old cattle truck out there. Let's load up those horses. I got a farm out here eight or ten miles. We'll take them and walk them up the fence and we'll get in the car and we'll honk the horn a couple times and chase them up that lane that's probably half a mile. The first two that get there, those are the two we'll break. We'll get rid of those others."

It was true what Woodson said. You could spend a lot of time teaching, but if you didn't have the right talent to work with, it all came to nothing. You couldn't get anywhere as a basketball coach unless you had the right players. And you couldn't get anywhere as a trainer unless you had the right horses. For Lukas that became a goal: Be a person whom owners give the best horses to.

Lukas worked at Thundering Downs, for two months, but the track never thawed, so he pulled up stakes and moved to Texas. He settled into El Paso, conveniently situated within driving distance of other Sunbelt tracks such as Ruidoso Downs and Sunland Park in New Mexico. Lukas immediately hit it off with the oil men of the area, who were back-slapping good old boys with a taste for flash and a strict business sense.[36]

Lukas worked the quarter-horse trade with single-minded devotion. In 1970, he won seventy-three quarter-horse races—more than anyone else in the business—and earned hundreds of thousands of dollars. A year later, Wayne and Janet Lukas divorced and she moved back to Wisconsin with their thirteen-year-old son, Jeff. Lukas loaded seven horses into trailers and moved to California to try a new life.[37] There he teamed up with Mel Hatley, a banker and real estate developer. He ran the horses while Hatley kept the books and oversaw finances.

Lukas found his first "big horse" among the crop he brought from Texas. In 1973, Native Empress won with such regularity that Lukas was able to sell her eight different times to different owners he worked with. Her price went from $3,500 to $250,000, but she always stayed in Lukas's barn and he took a percentage of the sale, customarily 10 percent, each time.[38]

By the mid-'70s, Lukas had won almost every major competition in quarter-horse racing—breaking records and filling his bank account. In 1975, he won 150 races, double the number of victories any quarter-horse trainer had previously gotten in a year. He ran multiple leaders in every race. Lukas understood the extent of his own dominance. He told *New Yorker* writer Carol Flake about another quarter-horse owner who became fed up with Lukas's power. "Someday, it'll be like this," Lukas said this woman told a friend. "He'll just come out on the track and clap his hands, and the lights will go on. He'll run all the races. Then he'll clap his hands, and the lights will go off. And it will be over."[39]

In April 1977, one of Lukas's quarter horses, Moving Moon, tested positive for a morphinelike drug called numorphan and Lukas was suspended for sixty days and given probation through the end of the year. When Lukas went into thoroughbred racing full-time a few months after the ruling, with a whole new community of trainers and owners, it seemed he might be trying to erase the imperfection in his reputation by pursuing a new lease on life.[40]

In 1982, L. R. French and Barry Beal gave Lukas a thoroughbred filly named Landaluce to train. She was the daughter of Seattle Slew, a beauty with a black coat stretched over delicate legs, muscular flanks, and the neck of a princess. Usually, the trainer's task was to get a horse strong enough to run, but with Landaluce, the job was different. Lukas just needed to keep her healthy and happy, remove all obstacles to the excellence that was bred into her every molecule. She ran five times and five times she won, by a total of forty-six and a half lengths.

At the California tracks, she developed a fan club. People came to the track to see her run and gambling took a backseat. "You search and you look, and then, all of a sudden, it comes," Lukas told a reporter, "that star, and you know you have been blessed with something special. It happened to Lucien Laurin with Secretariat. You know you will go down in the history books."[41]

Lukas entered Landaluce to run in the Hollywood Starlet on Sunday, November 28, 1982. But on the Monday before the race, she completely ignored her 10:00 A.M. feeding.[42] By afternoon her temperature hit 103 degrees. Lukas called the veterinarian, Roy Bishop, to run tests, but he kept coming up blank and her condition worsened. They pumped her with antibiotics but the fever held steady. Lukas stayed with her the whole week, trying every technique he knew to defeat the illness, but her lungs filled. At 5:30 in the morning on the day of the Hollywood Starlet, Landaluce collapsed onto the straw and died with her head in Lukas's lap.[43]

A few months later, Landaluce posthumously received the Eclipse Award for best two-year-old filly, beating her main rival, Princess Rooney, who was bred by Tom and Robyn Roach. Lukas sat down and wrote the Roaches a letter. This prize is an honor, he wrote, but I would rather have Landaluce in the barn than this prize in my hand.[44] What Lukas got from that experience was this lesson: Never get too close to one horse. It was one of the hardest things he ever had to get over. After that, he seemed even more businesslike in his handling of his equine athletes.

By 1983, Lukas was the leading trainer in purse earnings, bringing in a whopping $4,267,261 for his owners.[45] His clients, high on success, went right back to the horse auctions to buy more talent, to keep the euphoria going. Lukas and his clients spent $17,850,000 at the Keeneland auctions in those years—nothing compared to the $124,015,000 that the Maktoum family of Dubai put down—but it was the most spent by any American purchaser. Lukas trained 250 horses around the country and started running multiple horses in all the big stakes races.

Lukas sent his first horse, Partez, to the Derby in 1981 and he came in third. For the next six years, Lukas sent a total of eleven horses to the Derby starting gate. At age fifty-two, he won the blanket of roses in 1988 with Winning Colors, the third filly ever to finish first in the Derby. Seven years later, Lukas won the Derby again with Thunder Gulch, a 24 to 1 shot. The next year, he arrived at the Kentucky Derby winner's circle with Grindstone, who had gone through three knee operations between his two-year-old and three-year-old years, and still won the blanket of roses.

In 1985, Lukas won two Breeders' Cup races, and kept winning the races' big purses over the next ten years. He ruled the sport, while the middle-class trainers who couldn't convince owners to go with them instead of brand Lukas began to disappear, off to work construction, or farm, or paint signs to make a buck. In 1987, Lukas was the first trainer to amass more purses than that year's winningest jockey. The next year, he won $17,842,358 in a single season, the most he had ever earned.

From 1985 through 1990, Lukas owners bought 337 yearlings at a cost of $104.6 million, and those yearlings all went to Lukas eventually for training. The owners provided the capital and Lukas gave his life to winning from 3:00 in the morning on. Racing was like a ham-and-egg breakfast, Lukas liked to say. The chicken is involved; she lays the eggs. But the pig has made a real commitment. Thoroughbred racing needed the trainers; it needed the pigs.[46]

"The thing about racing," Lukas liked to say, "is they don't let you enjoy it very long." The money rolled in so fast, it seemed as if Lukas had opened a pipeline to the Federal Reserve, but without warning, the torrent slowed, and suddenly Lukas's hold on the prestigious races ended. He won the Breeders' Cup Mile in 1989, and then not another one for four years. He won a grade-one stakes race on October 1, but then not another for two long years. Calumet Farm, by far the country's most prestigious breeding operation for decades, and where Lukas had invested, went bankrupt in 1991 when an investigation revealed that the farm owed $118,050,732 to banks around the country.[47] Lukas lost $3.1 million of his own money in the ensuing debacle and was deep in debt.

In 1993, he ran a horse named Union City in the Derby and finished fifteenth. Then he brought the horse back for the Preakness. Coming to the four-and-a-half-furlong marker, Union City stumbled and shattered the sesamoid bone in his front ankle in front of the crowd of nearly 85,000. Later, Union City had to be destroyed by lethal injection. The press wrote stories saying Lukas ran a lame horse just because he was trying to pay the bills, and he became infuriated. It was like the first two of coach John Wooden's "Six of Life's Puzzlers": Why is it easier to criticize than compliment? Why is it easier to give others blame than to give them credit?

Lukas stopped talking to people, refused to see anyone. His depression worsened until finally his son, Jeff, realized he needed to intervene. He brought Lukas's old friends together. For seven hours, the friends told Lukas what he meant to them, how much they loved him, and Lukas told them he thought he had made mistakes in his life. Later he said he didn't think he was depressed, but he admitted they helped him.[48]

But then the misery deepened after a freak accident at Lukas's barn. On December 15, 1993, one of Lukas's star horses, Tabasco Cat, got loose from his stall at Santa Anita, charged down the shedrow, and knocked thirty-six-year-old Jeff to the ground. Jeff suffered multiple skull fractures and a herniated brain stem and immediately slipped into a coma. His brain swelled.[49] For thirty-three days, he never regained consciousness. When Jeff finally did recover, he needed to spend many months in rehab, and his father's client, Bob Lewis, directed him to the center at Casa Colinas, which he and his wife Beverly had helped finance.

Nothing ever brought Lukas as low as that incident. Ultimately, he realized that to get over the tragedy, he needed to forgive the horse.[50] He personally took over the training of Tabasco Cat, and that spring the horse ended up winning the Preakness and Belmont.

Injuries to Lukas's high-profile horses kept coming though, including Tabasco Cat, who had to retire at four. Flanders, Timber Country, Thunder Gulch, and Grindstone also left racing because of injuries over the next few years. The press began compiling the string of misfortunes and wondered in print if Lukas wasn't running his horses too hard in order to save himself financially.

Lukas couldn't stand the second-guessing. He ran more horses than other trainers, he said, so the number of injuries to his horses looked high as a total number, but not as a percentage. His business was geared for the high-priced stakes races, he said, so all eyes were on him.[51]

He watched as Bobby Frankel, Jimmy Croll, and Phil Johnson were inducted into the Hall of Fame in Saratoga Springs, and the selection committee kept passing him by. They said it was because a trainer needed to have worked continuously with thoroughbreds for twenty-five years, and they considered Lukas's career as starting from 1974, even though he had run some thoroughbreds in the 1960s. Lukas announced to the press that were he ever to be inducted, he wouldn't attend the ceremony in protest at his mistreatment.[52]

Sometimes he banned reporters, or "cockroaches" as he called them, from his barn outright. "The nature of the game will cause you to doubt yourself," Lukas told journalist Carol Flake in 1988. "You're making snap judgments, dealing with flesh, nerve endings, heart, bones. It will eat you up if you don't believe in yourself. Horses are suicidal by nature. The thing is, you can't live at the temple of regret in this game. You must always dwell on the positives. Or the negatives will eat you alive."[53]

Just as Lukas hit his losing streak, Bob Baffert, a thirty-eight-year-old trainer from New Mexico, started having big years. Like Lukas, Baffert began as a trick rider, and became a quarter-horse trainer. When he was getting started with quarter horses as a teenager, he had called Lukas to see if he could get a job as a gallop boy in Lukas's stable. The year was 1971 and Lukas ruled the track in Sonoita, Arizona, so even though Lukas turned him down, Baffert was thrilled. He had just talked to the sport's greatest practitioner.[54]

Years later, when Lukas departed the quarter-horse business to go into thoroughbred racing full-time, Baffert enjoyed his own gilded seasons in quarter horses. When Baffert moved to thoroughbreds full-time too, he and Lukas struck up a friendship based on their mutual interest, speaking every day.

While both were upper-tier trainers, their personal styles could not have been more different. While Lukas's workday began well before dawn, Baffert rolled into his barn around 9:00 to watch his horses work in the last hour before the track closed for training and the maintenance crews began readying it for regular racing. Lukas showed up in his barns neatly pressed and coiffed, while Baffert looked like an overgrown kid, with prematurely white hair flopping in his eyes and round hippie sunglasses. Baffert admitted he spent some high school years smoking pot and dropping acid, but he gave that up when he realized falling into trouble would keep him from realizing his dream at the track.[55] He had been married to the same woman, Sherry, since 1984, while Lukas already had wed three times by 1991.

Baffert and Lukas both trained horses for Bob and Beverly Lewis, and they traded off moments of pleasing their clients. Baffert fanned the rivalry. He called Bob Lewis once when the Lukas-trained Gold Tribute was going up against Silver Charm at Saratoga. "Bob, your horse is in," Baffert said, "but he's up against your real expensive horse, Gold Tribute. I hate to do it to you, but I'm gonna kick your $725,000 horse's ass with my $80,000 horse." And he did.[56]

The ugly side of the rivalry sparked in 1990. That year the turf writers fell in love with Baffert when he made a joke at Lukas's expense on ESPN. Baffert was running a superb colt, Thirty Slews, and the cable station interviewed him about his prospects for the big races. The interviewer commented approvingly that Baffert was the next Wayne Lukas.

"I don't think so," Baffert said.

"How long have you known Wayne Lukas?" the interviewer asked, knowing the two trainers had both worked with quarter horses.

"Hell," said Baffert, "I knew Wayne when he had bad teeth." Everyone in the studio howled with laughter and Baffert understood, at that moment, his star was born.[57]

In 1995, Lukas won a Triple Crown of sorts, with two of his horses taking first in the three races. In 1996, he decided to run five horses in the Derby, the largest number of entrants for any one trainer, which looked almost too ostentatious to be believed. The press liked to provoke the Baffert-Lukas rivalry, and when they came to Baffert asking questions, he was only too happy to oblige. Leading up to that Derby, he made fun of Lukas all week long, saying his cowboy hat was so big it would get caught in elevator doors.

"Why do you think Lukas is running five horses?" Rick Bozich of the *Louisville Courier-Journal* asked. "The Derby is all about ego," Baffert explained. He meant the ego of the owners, but the newspapers cut the quote there, and it was read as a slur against Lukas.

That week, Baffert was in the President's Room at Churchill, toasting his win with Criollito in the Churchill Downs Handicap. Lukas walked in and glared at him. "Why did you take that shot at me in the paper?" he asked. "You want to go toe-to-toe with me in the press, I'll go toe-to-toe with you."[58] Lukas's fury seemed out of place in that setting, and Baffert wasn't sure what he was talking about until he read the article later. Lukas got his revenge on Derby Day, when his Grindstone beat Baffert's Cavonnier by a nose at the wire.[59]

At the Preakness, Baffert confronted Lukas. "Why are you so worried about me?" he asked. "I'm no threat to you. You just won the Derby and I'm here with this damn Cal-bred, and you'll probably never see me back here again."[60] Grindstone had to be retired before that race because of an injury, but Lukas ran three other horses and placed third with one.

The next year, Lukas entered Deeds Not Words in the Derby at the last minute and came in an embarrassing last, beaten by more than twenty-five lengths. Baffert, on the other hand, was on a roll. In 1997 and 1998, he became the first trainer to win the Kentucky Derby and the Preakness in consecutive years. In 1998, Lukas won only $7,248,532 in purses, his lowest total since his slump.

Lukas needed a big horse, an animal so talented he or she would win the larger purses and attract media interest again, make owners choose him over Baffert and have them come swarming back to his barn. His best prospects were two colts by Mr. Prospector, a superior stud. Satish Sanan bought Sasha's Prospect for $2.3 million at the 1997 Keeneland yearling sale. The other, Cape Canaveral, had a little Seattle Slew in him on the mare's side. Lukas also had a Storm Cat colt named Cat Thief.

Bob Lewis sent two horses over to Lukas in the early spring of 1998. One of them was Charismatic, a pretty red chestnut colt with white chrome on the ankles and a star, stripe, and snip down his nose. Lukas started him in the same program that all the two-year-olds received. Amy LoPresti had already worked Charismatic to increase his stamina from an eighth to a quarter mile. Now Lukas took him out in the mornings to build his strength, jogging for a mile then galloping. He taught him to run against other horses in the barn and break from the gate. Charismatic was an amiable horse but a heavy eater and a plodder in sprints.

But Lukas needed runners. You couldn't win races without taking a shot, and not every horse could go to the track early in its two-year-old year. Until the 1950s, two-year-old horses rarely raced. They were considered too fragile for heavy competition. But then Garden State Park in New Jersey started the first six-figure race for two-year-olds and all the other tracks followed suit. Within a short time, the two-year-old year became a lucrative one for trainers. Smart trainers held the best-bred horses out of contention as late as possible to keep them sound for the Triple Crown season. Yet somebody had to go to the starting gate, and Charismatic would be one of those regular competitors for Lukas.

Lukas first ran Charismatic in June 1998 to test his abilities. The colt came in dead last. That meant back to the drawing board with Lasix and blinkers, then trying different distances, even turf. Occasionally, Charismatic, who looked like a child's version of a pretty horse, rang in a little purse money for third or fourth. But a trainer could not pay the salaries of twenty-three California employees on his 10 percent of third- and fourth-place purses.

On October 17, Charismatic dragged in a full twenty-five lengths behind the winner Lexington Beach at Santa Anita and Lukas turned to his assistant, Mike Marlow. "What can we try to get this colt going?"[61] Marlow didn't have an answer. In the morning, the colt breezed well enough and seemed determined to get his head out in front, but then in the afternoon, at the track, he labored to the finish line. Charismatic was what they called on the backside a "morning glory," good in the works at dawn and a mysterious disaster in afternoon competition.

Lukas didn't have much time for morning glories. He had thirty-two horses in his California barns competing for his attention. Cat Thief, after a disappointing finish in his first race all the way back in April, was running first and second every time. Gold Market had run in the money his two times out. Satish Sanan's other horses Yes It's True and Time Bandit looked like they might tear up the track. At some point you had to look at life the way the old trainer Woodson did back at Thundering Downs. Put the horses out there. The ones that get to the finish first you work with, the rest get unloaded. With Charismatic's maintenance bills hovering around $21,000 since his debut four months earlier, and his earnings at just $10,860, Lukas had to start worrying about burning the limits of Bob Lewis's patience. It was time to cut losses.

On November 21, Charismatic went to Hollywood Park for the $62,500 claiming race. If Lukas and Lewis were lucky, the walk with the colt to the paddock would be the last time a D. Wayne Lukas employee handled Charismatic.

Vladimir Cerin, who came to the United States by way of Bosnia and to horse training after conditioning human athletes such as the New York Knicks, considered claiming Charismatic. Cerin had watched the colt's morning works and liked his muscle. He filled out a claim ticket, then went to the paddock for one last look.

Watching Charismatic arrive, Cerin had second thoughts. There had to be something seriously wrong with that colt, he suspected as he took a look at Charismatic's circling the ring, for Lukas to let go of him at that price. If you watched carefully, the colt did seem to walk a little awkwardly. At the deadline fifteen minutes before post, Cerin still held the claiming slip.[62]

Seventeen minutes later, Charismatic won and Cerin cursed his luck. But despite a better than expected showing in that race, Charismatic didn't suddenly blossom into a superstar. Winding up 1998, he had earned $30,660, only slightly more than his maintenance fees. He wasn't pulling his weight and that was just one of the reasons that Lukas, formerly the king of the track, took third place in trainer earnings in 1998, trailing Bob Baffert by a full $5 million.

Lukas sent Sasha's Prospect and Cape Canaveral to the starting gate for the first time December 26, and both broke their maidens handily, earning $27,000 each. They could be trusted to rate whenever they competed. Lukas didn't want to run them ragged, however.[63] "There's no better bred horse in the country than this horse," Lukas said of Sasha's Prospect. "His pedigree is unbelievable." Cape Canaveral, son of perhaps the greatest sire, Mr. Prospector, had "a beautiful mind and a great stride," Lukas said.

Charismatic didn't register in the trainer's press commentary. Amy LoPresti, who broke the colt as a yearling, called Lukas from time to time offering advice on what would make Charismatic a first-string player too. "I sure would like to see that horse run long," she told him, remembering what had sparked the colt's brilliance in his youth. She wasn't sure Lukas heard her.[64]

Despite Charismatic's weak one-win record and that in a claiming race, Lukas slugged him in as a possible starter for the Golden Gate Derby on January 16, the first major West Coast prep race for the Kentucky Derby.[65] Lukas needed horses in the gate. But then he thought better of it and put the colt in a one and one-sixteenth mile allowance race in pursuit of $54,000 at Santa Anita on the same day. Charismatic ran seventh out of ten for most of the race and finished fifth, winning only $1,080. Baffert won $10,800 in the same race with Brilliantly, a horse just beginning to show promise.

Two weeks later, on January 31, Lukas put Charismatic in the grade-three Santa Catalina Stakes at Santa Anita running at one and one-sixteenth for $100,000. Charismatic was so fat at that point, he practically waddled into the paddock. Baffert was saddling Brilliantly and General Challenge, a tall colt owned by John and Betty Mabee, the proprietors of one of the best breeding businesses in the country. Of General Challenge's four most recent starts, he had finished first all but once. Unfortunately for Baffert, the talented colt was neurotic. His head was so small, his bridle constantly slipped off and startled him. He couldn't handle crowded fields since, when a pack kicked dirt in his face, he went berserk.

Lukas looked at Charismatic, who stood serenely in the paddock waiting to be saddled, with his curved flanks and thick neck, and wondered if the grooms were feeding him extra oats at night.[66] A trainer usually liked when a horse ate heartily, since maintaining a horse's weight was one of the hardest tasks of keeping an animal in shape for competition. A horse burned off about fifteen pounds in a race, and if you worked them too hard, they backed off their feed. But Charismatic never seemed to shed the weight. He just got fatter and plodded around the track.

The fat horse lost to everyone that day, and Baffert's General Challenge won, beating Charismatic by a full thirteen lengths. Charismatic picked up $2,130, but that was pity money, fifth place in a five-horse race, compared to Baffert's total take of nearly $77,000.

For twenty-one years, Lukas hadn't missed a Santa Anita Derby, the most prestigious West Coast race. Four times he had won, with Codex in 1980, Muttering in 1982, Marfa in 1983 and Winning Colors in 1988. In early February, Lukas nominated Sasha's Prospect, Cape Canaveral, and Charismatic for the Santa Anita Derby to be run in early April, with the hope of continuing his attendance streak and adding another title to his roster.

The first two horses were obvious nominees, but in a way, Lukas just included Charismatic's name in the field to keep his options open. *We're leading with our hearts here*, Lukas thought. *He's a big, pretty chestnut horse.*[67] Keeping Charismatic in the program was getting to be nuts. But Lukas had one last strategy.

He decided Charismatic needed to be reminded how it felt to win, to be at the front of the pack. Lukas called Lewis and asked if he could put Charismatic in another $62,500 claiming race on February 11 at six and a half furlongs, this time for a purse of $47,000. "I want to give this horse the opportunity to see the front ends of horses, because he's been seeing their butts all the time," Lukas told Lewis.[68] He knew Bob Lewis would be relieved if he sold the horse that day.

On February 11, Vladimir Cerin again filled out a claiming slip for Charismatic. But again, the deadline for dropping the form in the racing office's locked box came and went and Cerin still had the paper in his pocket. The trainer Mike Mitchell, who built his business claiming horses, thought about picking up Charismatic too. But just a few days before, Bob Lewis had given Mitchell tickets to the Pomona drag races and Mitchell didn't want to buy a horse from under Lewis if he wasn't exactly sure that's what Lewis wanted.[69] Later Ray Bell Jr. said he wanted to take Charismatic off Lukas's hands before the race and offered $80,000 for him, but never heard back. Bell was shocked when he saw Charismatic was running at a price $17,000 less than the offer he made off the track.

Bell didn't try to claim the colt, however, because he didn't want to further test his relationship with Bob Lewis.[70]

When the stewards lit Charismatic's number on the totalisor that afternoon, moving him to a technical first, Lukas exhaled. "Whew," he said to Bob Lewis. "We're not going to do this again."[71] Devil's Judge, a horse owned by Wesley Ward, was claimed out of that race for $62,500. Lukas wasn't going to give anyone another opportunity to pluck Charismatic away.

And what if someone had claimed Charismatic that day? Within a little more than a week, Lukas's team fell apart. On February 13, Lukas's horse Gold Market ran in an eight and a half furlong race at Gulfstream Park after just a two-week break and finished second. But he shattered his ankle stampeding toward the finish. The veterinarians put three screws in the bone and Lukas tried to prep him to race again, but the colt never could get strong enough to compete. Three years later, Lukas couldn't recall ever training a horse named Gold Market; the horse had moved on to be a favorite stud out on an Ohio farm. By February 19, Lukas knew that Cape Canaveral had suffered a stress fracture in his right foreleg and needed to take the rest of the year off.[72] John Asher, the director of news and information at Churchill heard the rumors and checked with the horse's owners at Overbrook Farm to see if Cape Canaveral really was hurt. When he discovered the truth, he pulled him out of the early betting for the Derby. Yes It's True turned out to be a sprinter, worthless at the longer distances, and Time Bandit could only perform on grass.

Who could run the stakes races? Only Cat Thief and Charismatic. Lukas started paying more attention to Charismatic. He dictated the distances he would run each morning. He let him stretch out, then told the exercise riders to push him, to work him hard. Charismatic responded. He focused on grinding around the oval and delivered blistering times. Lukas would get the fractions from the clocker and nod. The colt's pace was picking up. With this specialized attention to his workouts, Charismatic even started to look different. When his adrenaline kicked in, his coat changed, gleaming in the sun. He showed more pride around the barn.[73]

Sasha's Prospect hadn't run since January and his next matchup was an allowance race on March 10. Months earlier, Lukas had nominated Charismatic and Gold Market to run in the El Camino Real Derby on March 6 at Bay Meadows in San Francisco.[74] The hard reality was he now had only one horse to count on when race day rolled around. Charismatic, his fat mild marathon runner whose only victories came in claiming races, would have to try to run with the big boys. Lukas sat in a box with Lewis to watch.

Just before the final turn, Charismatic locked into gear and dashed past Tobycapote, Brave Gun, and No Cal Bread. He finished second, beaten only by a head and won $40,000. Lukas would later say that was the first time he really understood the horse.

Lukas saw in the way Charismatic negotiated the El Camino what he was capable of: He warmed up a little slowly, but when all the other horses tired, he churned hard through a final sprint. The opposite of the quarter horse, who sped through short distances with ease and flagged with distance, Charismatic was a true thoroughbred with stamina bred into his bone. All those times Lukas told the jocks to keep him back early meant he crossed the finish line with a full tank of gas. Charismatic taught Lukas something.

"I think this might be our Belmont horse," Lukas told Bob Lewis.

The racing press, the "cockroaches," of course loved Baffert for the Derby because with two consecutive Derby wins, and with Exploit in his barn, he was primed for victory. But then on March 13, cruel fate visited Baffert too. The favorite Exploit got injured and had to be retired. Baffert's talent pool was deep however. He still had General Challenge, Finder's Gold, Prime Timber, and the fillies Silverbulletday and Excellent Meeting in his barn.

The day of the Santa Anita approached. Lukas's assistant, Mike Marlow, had told the press at the beginning of April that Charismatic only had a fifty-fifty possibility of running in the Santa Anita. Cat Thief was booked in another stakes. As race day grew near, Lukas needed to enter

Charismatic or sit out the fight for the $750,000 purse. A year without a horse running meant his twenty-one-year streak of entering horses would be broken.

On April 3, Charismatic stood ready in the Santa Anita paddock to perpetuate the streak. The handicappers gave Charismatic odds of 15 to 1 the day before the race. By post time he was down to a brutal 44 to 1, the second longest shot. The worst odds of 70 to 1 went to Walk that Walk with Chris Antley on board. Bill Finley of the New York *Daily News* summarized the talents of the field. "Charismatic and Walk That Walk don't belong," he wrote.[75]

Lukas kept plugging Charismatic in the paddock. "I think Charismatic can win the Triple Crown," he told the Lewises, his son, Jeff, and assistant, Randy Bradshaw. Everyone rolled their eyes.[76]

A few stalls down, Baffert prepared his competitors Prime Timber, recently recovered from a bruised foot, and General Challenge, with blinkers on to calm the nervous star.

Within seconds of the race's start, General Challenge took the lead and ended up winning by three lengths, Prime Timber came in second, and Charismatic came in fourth. Walk That Walk pulled in right behind him in fifth.

That gave Baffert the one-two finish at Santa Anita and $600,000 for his owners. That same day, at Oaklawn Park in Hot Springs, Arkansas, Excellent Meeting won the Fantasy Stakes, and one hour before the Santa Anita Derby, Baffert's filly Silverbulletday romped to a seven-length victory in the Ashland Stakes at Keeneland. That was three stakes winners for Baffert in one day.

Baffert's dominance in the 1999 spring season was obvious, but Lukas refused to follow the Derby script. "We're not down to two or three [Derby] favorites by any means," Lukas told the press the next day. "I think if you talked to any twenty Derby gurus, you'd get eighteen opinions. This could be a Ferdinand or Gato Del Sol kind of year," he said, referring to past winners with long odds.[77]

Lukas wanted to send Charismatic and Cat Thief to the Wood Memorial at Aqueduct on April 16, but the best three-year-olds in the country were entering there, and the Lukas horses needed to boost their purse money if they wanted to qualify for the Derby.[78] By April 17, Charismatic had only accumulated $157,070. On April 5, Randy Bradshaw said that Charismatic would run in either the Kentucky Derby or the $325,000 Coolmore at Keeneland, but he was ignoring the fact that Charismatic probably had to run in the Coolmore as a bridge to the Derby.[79]

On April 18, Charismatic ran in the Coolmore and won. Lukas told the press, "This horse can be my Villanova," referring to the unsung team that knocked off seemingly invincible Georgetown in the 1985 college basketball final. "I made up my mind to burn the fat off him and see if there was anything there. The more I drilled him, the better he got," Lukas told the press.[80]

Who knew what miraculous things might happen at the Derby, Lukas thought. Either one of his horses could claim victory. "If you want to win the Derby," the trainer Woody Stephens once said, "you better not show up wearing short pants."[81] But with that philosophy Stephens only entered the Derby fourteen times in forty years and won just twice. Lukas had already pulled off three. Lukas might not have the most talented beasts out there that year, but you had to take a shot if you coveted the Triple Crown the way he did. D. Wayne Lukas was determined that the twelve on his watch would not be blank when he died.

SEVEN

THE HOTBOX

Racing legend has it that the greatest British rider of all time, Fred Archer, shot himself on November 8, 1886, at age twenty-nine, after he gained too much weight to compete. Archer had had an astounding career; he was famous for being the first jockey to win eight races in one day—one shy of Antley's *Guinness Book* achievement. The real story of Archer's misery was a little more complicated, however, than just a few extra pounds. One year and two days earlier, his beloved wife, Nellie, at age twenty-three, gave birth to their daughter and died immediately from complications. Archer had been depressive and irritable before this tragedy, a state attributed to living under the constant tension of keeping his five-feet-ten-inch frame light enough for his chosen profession. Archer gained weight in the year after the tragedy and trainers began abandoning him. "Archer had been wasting very hard to reduce himself before the Cambridgeshire week," the *Newmarket Journal* reported on November 13, 1886. "He must have wasted considerably to ride 8 stone, 7 pounds [119 pounds]."[1]

The death came as a complete surprise to his fans throughout London. A few days before, after riding Lucretius and Tommy Tittlemouse at the Newmarket track, he seemed despondent and complained of feeling unwell. He informed the trainers he needed to go home to rest and was soon beset by fevers and chills. His doctor, John Rowland Wright, diagnosed him with typhoid fever. "He had a delusion that a dinner he had eaten three days before was still in his stomach, although he suffered from diarrhoea all night," Wright told the coroner later. "He told me the medicine I was giving him would do him no good, a dose of his wasting mixture would cure him." Because of Archer's popularity as an athlete, worry about his ailment spread quickly throughout London. The Prince of Wales sent a note inquiring after his health and wishing him a speedy recovery. The next day Archer reclaimed some mental reasoning. "He talked sensibly and quietly," Wright explained, "but always on the subject of death."

A few days later, his sister, who was tending him, was looking the other way when she heard her brother speak. "Are they coming?" he asked. She turned to see a revolver in his hand and lunged for the gun, but it was too late. "I thought he did too much to ride St. Mirin," she later told the coroner, mournfully. "He seemed very anxious, he has seldom ridden so light as 8 stone, 7 pounds."[2]

The most relevant aspect of the story is that horse-racing people pass that bit of history along as simply, "Fred Archer gained weight and shot himself." To people at the track, that sentence needs no further explication because everyone knows the devastating consequences of added pounds.

Picture, if you will, another famous bit of jockey lore: the great rider Laffit Pincay boarding a plane for a flight across the United States. Imagine among all those passengers shoveling down their chicken pilaf and sugary desserts—eating without distinct pleasure but with caloric abandon—this small, muscled man taking just one peanut from his complimentary packet and delicately carving it into fourths. Each hour and a half or so, he pinched a tiny section of nut between his finger and thumb and placed it on his tongue, allowing the shard to loll there. Then he let the peanut fragment slip back down his throat and disappear into the canyon of his stomach. He did this four times to sustain himself across the country because he only allowed himself to consume 700 calories a day. If he were to "go off" for one night—that is, eat a normal dinner— he would gain about seven pounds and have to drop out of racing for a month to get back to legal weight, he said.[3]

Imagine how different was Pincay's struggle—or any jockey's labor to maintain themselves at the ideal 105 pounds—from that of other athletes in training. Other athletes endure the same rigorous toning and muscle building, and yet they are allowed, and often urged, to gorge on certain foods, such as protein shakes and plates of pasta. Jockeys' lives resemble only those of gymnasts, who starve and purge to be feather light. Consider how culturally odd it is to be a man pursuing this path of diminution, to be a man trying, even on a transcontinental flight, to shrink.

Chris Antley stood around five feet one, a frame that normally carried 130 pounds or more. After a few years of riding, he never ate dairy or meat. He cooked his vegetables precisely so no vitamins were lost or calories added. He drank rice milk, and his biggest binge was a box of cereal on very rare occasions. Since he was never very good at inducing himself to vomit—what jockeys call flipping—he usually starved himself and took laxatives to purge his body quickly before the food could be absorbed. He sat on the highest step of the hotbox for hours, which often causes jockeys' skin to crack and their hearts to weaken. He drove his car with the heat on full blast even in summer to try to sweat off water weight. Chris Antley was known as an extremely athletic jockey. From a young age, he lifted weights for strength; his friends believed it was to make up in power what he lacked in size. His healthy interest in building muscle made his struggle to stay under 113 pounds even harder and led to a cruel endless cycle of building up for self-esteem and then starving out of self-hatred.

By the fall of 1989, Antley had lost the battle. There was no other way to see his story. The guys on the racing beat used to love his saga. A country boy with nothing but talent and natural instinct for thoroughbreds shoots to the top of the sport of kings. The kid with humble beginnings makes it big, like *Rocky* on horses. Now the story had turned sour. A country boy rockets to stardom then plunges to the depths. His friend jockey Craig Perret once saw how dark the fairy tale could get if Antley weren't careful. He laid it all out in the papers during one of Antley's clean periods. "Chris is another rider," Perret said. "There is no one rider. If he's a man in a man's game, he's got to make his own way. I hope he does for himself. And if he doesn't, the game's going to pass him by, go right by him, and there will just be somebody in his spot. And that will be a shame, because he's got a lot of talent."[4]

Within hours of Antley's resigning his license in 1989, he knew the other jockey agents were circling his mounts, slotting their riders in. The races were going off at tracks around the world, without Antley, without the wonderboy.

Antley put himself back in rehab. Seven months later, the racing association allowed him to get his license again, and the trainers began hiring their superstar immediately. His first day back at Aqueduct on Saturday, March 17, 1990, Antley had bookings for all but one race. He worried about the fans' reaction, but they applauded him in the paddock. In the fourth race, he finished first on board Affy with a substantial eight-and-a-half-length lead. He looked up into the stands and everyone was on their feet, cheering. All the way back to the jocks' room, people stopped him to give him hugs. He got so choked up, he could barely talk. He won three that day, finishing in the money in seven of his eight races.[5]

That summer, he went up to Saratoga. For an astounding eleven consecutive years, Cordero had won the Saratoga title, which in a jock's world was like winning an Oscar eleven times in a row. Saratoga was the oldest official track in the country and the best horses were shipped in for the brief August season. That meant the best jockeys insisted on booking there too. Jose Santos broke Cordero's streak in 1987, but Cordero took the title back in 1988 and 1989. That summer of 1990, Antley and Cordero chased each other in the standings through the whole four weeks. Antley wrested the crown from Cordero by only three wins.[6] It was an incredible comeback from the depths he suffered less than a year before.

But good news has a short shelf life. Eleven days later, on September 8, the jocks were back riding at Belmont. Antley might have won Saratoga, but Cordero ruled Belmont. Cordero blocked Antley's horse, and Antley fell and lacerated his right elbow. Antley was sidelined, and Cordero got almost a week's suspension.[7]

Two months later, fifty thousand fans gathered at Belmont to watch the seventh meet of the Breeders' Cup, the richest day in American racing. Antley was on Mr. Nickerson, a four-year-old colt in the $1 million Sprint, the horse's last race before retirement. As Mr. Nickerson approached the first turn, he unexpectedly reared up and collapsed, throwing Antley. Jose Santos, riding on Shaker Knit, collided with them. Antley regained consciousness in the hospital with a broken clavicle. He learned that Shaker Knit had been taken away by ambulance too, and Mr. Nickerson had died on the spot.[8] That Breeders' Cup turned out to be the most brutal in the event's history. Two races down the docket, a filly named Go for Wand shattered her leg in the last hundred yards of the $1 million Distaff. Officials set up screens around her and euthanized her while the weeping crowd waited.

At age twenty-five, Antley already had ridden in two Derbies, on Private Terms and Shy Tom. Neither time did he think he had a chance of winning, and he was right; he had come in ninth and tenth, respectively.[9] But to win a Derby meant everything to a jockey. "If you're going to be in racing and say that you accomplished something," jockey Angel Cordero Jr. said, "you better win a Kentucky Derby. You may win a lot of races, but if you go out on the street, people say, 'You're a jockey? Have you won the Kentucky Derby?' "[10]

In 1991, Nick Zito, a young, husky-voiced New York trainer had a colt named Strike the Gold in his barn, who he thought could go all the way to the Triple Crown. Strike the Gold's sire, Alydar, was a brilliant runner, famous for turning three in the wrong year. In 1978, he chased

Affirmed through the Derby, Preakness, and Belmont, battling to the wire each time and always finishing second to Affirmed, the last horse to win the Triple Crown.

Strike the Gold hadn't shown much sign of his father's brilliance in his two-year-old year. He was beaten by a total of thirty-two and three-quarter lengths in his first two races. But then on November 15, with Mike Smith on board, he broke his maiden in spectacular style, coming in first by eight and a half lengths. Coincidentally, the day of his victory was also the day his sire, Alydar, died. Zito found such coincidences meaningful, but he didn't like to talk about such controversial theories too much at the track.[11]

Zito took the horse down to Florida and ran him in an allowance race. Mike Smith stayed up in New York, so Zito used Jerry Bailey and they came in third. Zito felt good about the horse's performance because of the high-level competition in Florida for the winter meet and began harboring Derby aspirations.

Zito next put Strike the Gold in an allowance race at Gulfstream on February 23 with Pat Day up. Strike the Gold came in second. Zito ran down to the track, excited to get Day's reaction to the colt's improvement.

"Pat," Zito said, "what do you think?"

"Aw," Day said, "he's got to run better than that."

"What do you mean?" Zito said. "He'll run good the first Saturday in May." That was the magic date of the Kentucky Derby.

Day laughed. "I doubt it," he said.

Zito disregarded Day's pessimism and enrolled Strike the Gold in the Florida Derby. He booked Craig Perret to ride, and Strike the Gold came in second again, but this time against even more formidable competition. Based on that performance, the son of Alydar definitely was going to the Derby, but Perret wouldn't be in the saddle since he already had found a Derby horse with Cahill Road.

By early April, Zito didn't have many options among the top riders for Strike the Gold. Chris Antley occurred to him as a possibility since they had been friends from when the jock first started riding in New York seven years earlier. Zito admired the kid's talent and charisma. Zito's father always used to say, "You know who's the worst person in the world? A boring person." And Chris Antley was definitely not boring.

Zito put Antley on Strike the Gold in the Bluegrass Stakes at Keeneland, a prep race for the Derby, and they charged down the stretch to win by three lengths. That was enough to convince Zito, who stabbed the air with his index finger, screaming to the man upstairs all the way down the stretch, that Antley was his man. Antley was going to the Derby for the third time.

Antley had an almost eerie feeling that Strike the Gold would win and told his father ahead of time.[12] The experts agreed the horse had a chance and gave him third pick in the odds at 9 to 2.

The jock flew down to Louisville the last week of April to work the horse for Zito and hung around the barn most of the day, jawing with the grooms and hotwalkers. He napped on bales of hay. The Zito barn felt like family, like a team,[13] even a little like Elloree. Antley heard Zito plugging him to the reporters all day long. "He's a young Angel Cordero," Zito kept saying.

But then on Wednesday, four days before the Derby, Antley showed up late for a 6:20 A.M. appointment to exercise the horse. He told Zito he was talking to his girlfriend and Zito immediately informed the reporters how much that annoyed him. Everybody started gossiping.[14] Another day a pack of journalists came by the barn to watch Strike the Gold's morning breeze. Before they escorted the horse to the track, Zito looked at Antley. "Where's your helmet?" he asked.[15]

"Shit," said Antley. The whole procession waited while he ran back to his hotel to get it. Zito knew there was a problem, but he didn't say anything to Antley directly.

Days before the Derby, the *Lexington-Herald Leader* ran an article by the turf writer Billy Reed arguing that Zito ought to dump Antley for the Derby and get Day back on Strike the Gold. "Even the most veteran of riders can make a mistake under pressure," Reed wrote, "but the chances are less with Day than with Antley." He noted that Antley had a reckless riding suspension pending in California, implying that Antley couldn't control himself on the tracks as well as Day could.[16] But Zito refused to let the column influence him and stayed loyal to Antley, who had turned his horse into a winner in the Bluegrass.

Sixteen horses went to the starting gate that muggy Saturday, May 4, 1991, for the momentous eighth race. "My Old Kentucky Home" played over the loudspeakers, and the crowd roared as the horses promenaded to their post positions. Antley wore sky-blue silks with a pink star on his chest, the colors of the horse's ownership team. Cordero on Quintana sported stripes of purple, white and blue. Jerry Bailey, on the favorite Best Pal, rode out in a yellow and lime-green checkerboard shirt.

Walking to the gate, Strike the Gold showed some spirit, rearing up and limping around. Antley hoped that might mean the horse would lay a little closer in the race, stay at the front of the pack. An assistant starter grabbed Strike the Gold's bridle, led him into post five, and pushed the padded doors closed. The horse backed up, slamming himself in the gate like a bronco waiting to be released. Quintana, the last horse, loaded down the line and the final set of padded gates shut behind him. "All in line," the starter shouted.

With the start, the horses dug deep, kicking up dirt, and the sand flew into Strike the Gold's face. He started jumping and Antley tried to settle him. They ran a few paces, then Strike the Gold fell into his stride, joining the pack streaming down the straightaway.[17]

Antley worked him, nudging him along. Along the backside, they were laying tenth. Antley had Cordero hammering along on Quintana to his right.

Antley and Strike the Gold hit the five-eighths pole and Antley was right up next to Cordero. Cash Asmussen in bright orange silks on Happy Jazz Band prowled along the rail and Mane Minister was hanging out in the six path. There was an opening only big enough for one horse just in front of them, and Cordero and Antley were neck and neck, inching toward the gap. Only one of them would get to ride into that pocket. If they both went, Cordero probably would shove Antley further inside and then Antley would be facing a wall of horses—seven or eight across—with no way of threading into the clear. Antley would stand a good shot at breaking his neck, too, since his horse would probably clip hooves with the horse in front. He knew there was no way to truly control Strike the Gold. He couldn't count on that horse to get smart and start listening. If Strike the Gold felt like slowing he would. If he preferred to run full on, he would, even if it killed them both.

"You got any horse?" Antley heard Cordero shout. He had been talking to Antley the whole way up the backstretch and now he was checking how much power Antley still had beneath him.

"Yeah, I got some horse, Poppy," Antley yelled back.

They were edging closer to that horse in the six slot. Antley knew he was going to get squeezed. He made a move. He shoved Cordero out, and Cordero got caught against the horse coming up the outside. Antley angled out, way out. He was still in twelfth from the lead, but he was running so far outside, no other horse stood in his way. Strike the Gold started passing his competitors, steaming by them like all those other horses were in a leisurely gallop. Then Antley found himself in a show-girl line with the leaders, but with nothing but beautiful empty track ahead.

Antley knew there was no winning the Derby on a horse closing from the final turn. You needed momentum before that, at the quarter pole. He could feel Strike the Gold quickening beneath him and he started to smile.[18] He began whipping the colt on the left and pulling lightly on the right rein but the horse refused to shift to his right lead to angle back in toward the rail. Strike the Gold started drifting. He was roaring toward the grandstands. Antley could see the security guards, usually planted like statues on that outer rail, hustling away. The horse hit untrammeled track on the outer edge. Then he switched leads and his stride ratcheted up a few notches. Antley and Strike the Gold were ahead. Gary Stevens on Best Pal was almost two lengths back.

Antley hit the wire then. He raised his stick in the air. He never wanted to put it down again.[19] He later said he blacked out, but the spectators didn't notice anything unusual beyond the scene of a Kentucky Derby winner galloping his horse out after the finish line.

The next moment Antley remembered, he was getting close to the outrider and realized he should sit down. The outrider galloped to him and Antley remembered that he should pull up the horse. Strike the Gold had run the Derby in 2:03.

Antley was in shock during the ceremony. He kept thinking, *Did this really happen?*[20] Lee Iacocca, the president of Chrysler, presented him with the keys to a red LeBaron convertible, and General Norman Schwarzkopf, newly minted as a celebrity in the Gulf War, stood next to him amiably answering questions about his day at the track, using military metaphors.

Nothing compared to the feeling of winning a Derby. All the jocks slapped Antley on the back and the crowd cheered him. Antley's father had come up from South Carolina to watch the competition and was so happy for his son when he stood in the Derby winner's circle. Antley retreated to the jocks' room after the ceremony and the whole time he was showering and changing he was thinking about what it was to be a Derby winner. He wanted to watch the replay over and over. But as soon as the excitement of the race subsided, the reality hit him, as it had every other Derby winner before him. Fun's over. Time to start thinking about the next point of the Triple Crown, the Preakness.

Antley and Strike the Gold went on to the Preakness. But the stubborn Alydar gene came out in Strike the Gold, and Antley couldn't get him to finish better than sixth. Hansel won that race, and then in June, Antley and Strike the Gold lost by a head to Hansel in the Belmont.

After the Derby, fans and interviewers used to ask Antley who his favorite horse was, and Strike the Gold never made the list. Antley felt harsh saying it, but that horse was an ass. He didn't listen, he didn't pay attention. He did exactly what he wanted when he wanted.[21]

For Antley, it was bad enough to lose the Belmont, but then an ugly court fight broke out over the colt's ownership. In August, the owners took Antley off the horse for the Travers at Saratoga because they thought he hadn't been riding the horse hard enough.[22] They put Cordero on Strike the Gold for that race and the horse came in fourth. Still, in 1991, with Antley's earnings for the year anchored by his Derby win, he won the most purse money he had yet in his career: $8 million.

*   *   *

That August, syndicated turf reporter Paul Moran wrote a scathing piece about how badly Angel Cordero Jr. was aging in the saddle. At Saratoga, where Cordero once led every season, the gates opened and Cordero immediately began whipping his mount. The jockey's once elegant urging had deteriorated into desperate thrashing. The big owners stopped using him regularly,[23] an ignominy for a man who had won nearly seven thousand races by that point.

On January 12, 1992, Cordero was flying around the far turn at Aqueduct on a colt named Grey Tailwind. He and Jorge Valesquez, Jorge Chavez and Jean-Luc Samyn collided. Cordero went up in the air, heels above his head. Below him was a metal fence post. He slammed down on the pole, his body curling like a tossed horseshoe rattling to the ground. "Doctor," he yelled over and over to whomever would listen. "Give me something for the pain."[24]

Cordero didn't remember shouting that, or much else of the next nine days in intensive care or ten days after in his hospital room. But he never forgot his image of that day: bright orange horses racing under the stark tangerine sky in front of bright orange grandstands filled with those brilliant peach-colored fans. That's how he relived that accident night after horrifying night, the whole world colored the same hue as the glaring orange silks he wore the day he broke his right elbow, four ribs, ripped through his small intestines and kidneys, destroyed his spleen forever, and ended his racing career.[25]

Later his wife, Margie, told him that Chris Antley came to the hospital during his month-long stay and sat with him for hours crying. "He hugged me and told me he loved me," Cordero remembered from a fleeting moment of consciousness.

Cordero dwindled from 114 pounds to 98 and creaked around his Greenvale, Long Island, house for months in a robe and slippers, looking out at the squirrels running up the bare trees in the backyard.[26] Antley went by the house once in a while. "Are you okay?" he would ask. "Do you need anything? What can people do for you, for what we lost?"[27]

Their friendship took on more depth. "Me and my wife were very close," said Cordero. He watched how Antley looked at them almost wistfully. "You need a wife to give you a hug," Cordero told Antley, "to hold you tight."

"Aww, not me," Antley said.

"You need somebody who will tell you they love you every day," Cordero told him, "who will make you feel the way you are important. You know, you don't realize that you're important because you don't have anybody next to you telling you this. Just people from the outside that you don't pay any attention to.

"I didn't realize that I was important until I married my wife," Cordero said. "I thought I was just another lucky guy. People say, 'Good job. How are you doing?' That's about it. That's not being important."

Antley preferred the company of children to that of adults, and he would go to Cordero's and play with his kids all the time. "Do you want kids?" Cordero asked.

"No, if I did I'd come rent them from you," Antley said.

"That might work," Cordero said. "Spend a day with them and then you'll know."

Jockeys always fear an accident—fatal or simply catastrophic—but those mishaps could be expected. Antley had rallied back from injuries several times in his career. But in 1992, a horror befell him that he could never have anticipated so many years into the game. At age twenty-six, Antley began a growth spurt. Over the next six years, he added another inch and a half to his frame, taking him from a little over five feet one to five feet three. That meant one thing: more weight. It guaranteed more weight.[28] The average weight for his height increased by about fifteen pounds.

Antley began running fifteen to twenty miles a day. He climbed on a stationary bicycle and rode another twenty-six miles. He tried to flip as often as he could. He starved himself and even took the Lasix that the trainers used on the horses as a diuretic.[29] He sat in the 130-degree hotbox in the jockeys' room for hours with a radio playing behind his head and sweat pouring off his body. Most days he tried to pull five or seven pounds off in the morning before the race day began.

Every morning the alarm broke him from sleep, and the first thought of the day sizzled across his mind: *How much lighter do I need to be by noon?* Noon was when he would step on the scale in the jocks' room before his first race of the day. Antley knew that thinking this way was the death zone. He would get on a scale at home and know how awful the next hours were going to be. On a good day, maybe he could get away with just fasting and driving with the car heater on full blast, and then spend some time on the treadmill and a couple of hours in the hotbox. If it were a bad day, he needed to pull out some superhuman trick, some way to peel the fat and water weight off like a rubber suit. And the worst part was, he knew how heavy he was when he went to work the horses around 5:30 in the morning and saw the trainers. What they wanted was blue eyes and charisma. They wanted confidence and energy and jokes. But inside he knew that if the trainers didn't let him finish up the morning works quickly and let him get to the hotbox, he would never make weight by noon. And the trainers were fair-weather friends to the jockeys. If Antley won three races the day before, the trainer would ask him where his agent was to book him for more horses. If he didn't do so well, the trainer punched him on the shoulder and said, "Next time," and he would have no work to count on. Inside, he felt like he had been run over by a truck, but he was terrified to let anyone know.[30] Nobody wanted a pessimist riding their lucky horse.

In the summer of 1993, Antley got suspended in New York for rough riding so he went out to Del Mar to ride. Within days, he got suspended there too. But he hung around for almost a week because there was nowhere for him to work. He ended up enjoying the feel of the place.[31] He had threatened to move out there a few years before, when his car skidded off the road as he was leaving the Meadowlands in an ice storm.[32]

Now New York was drying up for him and he needed to get away from the drug scene that always tried to lure him back. He decided to make the move.

Cordero invited Antley to his house to say good-bye, and took him to his equipment room, stocked with artifacts from the days when he was king of the track. Antley wanted a souvenir of their time together in New York. "What can you give me that I can keep?" Antley asked him.[33]

"Something that you can use," Cordero said. Antley and Cordero always liked the same size whips and Cordero owned a beautiful collection of different weights. Antley picked one out and used it on special race days from then on.

Cordero had switched over to training, and before Antley left New York, Cordero booked him on his first horse, Puchanito. The horse didn't win but ran in the money. Convincing owners to give their horses to a new trainer was difficult, even for a former racing star. Cordero only had about seven or eight animals in his barn. One day Antley arrived, back from California to ride. "I want to buy you a horse," he told Cordero.

Cordero thought Antley was kidding. The jock handed him an envelope stuffed with cash. "This horse is for sale, go buy it," Antley told him. It was a pretty chestnut colt, a four-year-old named Prince Consort. Antley had worked him in California and saw talent. Cordero was shocked because a thoroughbred was a big gift from anybody. "This is my present for you and your wife," Antley told him. "It's your horse. You don't have to ride me if you don't want. It's all yours." Cordero did ride Antley on Prince Consort at Saratoga, and their victory gave Cordero his first win as a trainer there, where he once ruled the oval. Antley had found a way to repay his mentor.[34]

Out in California, Antley hired the agent Bill "Bear" Barisoff, who had once worked for Willie Shoemaker. Antley and Barisoff met at Santa Anita in the mornings. "Let's go on another stable tour," Barisoff would say, and he took the jock down the shedrows to chat up the trainers while they waited for the vets to finish in the stalls or watched the groomsmen smoothing clay onto ravaged horse legs.[35] Antley was surprised at how few West Coast people he knew and realized breaking in wouldn't be easy. It was like starting from scratch at age twenty-seven. He was no longer the golden boy he had been when he first arrived in the pros. He had broken himself several times over and earned a reputation as a jock who could slide into addiction at any time. Three Hall of Famers—Laffit Pincay Jr., Chris McCarron and Eddie Delahoussaye—rode in California, as well as a strong second tier of jockeys. The number of horses running had diminished in recent years and was now far fewer than the number in New York. That meant all the talent was fighting for a few empty seats.

When Antley was given an opportunity, he didn't hold back. The California riders were shocked by the aggressive techniques he imported from the East Coast. He would ride the other jocks tight when he didn't have to, block them even when he had no hope of winning. His good friend Gary Stevens confronted him after one particularly brutal race. Stevens called Antley every name in the book, which could easily have started a jockey-room brawl. But Antley looked at him and burst into tears. "I'm so sorry," he said, "I'm so sorry."[36]

Broken and put back together again from sheer will, he seemed tortured by the ways he hurt people. "If he would even say something bad or think of something bad," said Fernando Valenzuela, another jock friend, "he would kind of talk to himself and punish himself, and say, 'You know what? I'm not like that. I don't even know what I'm saying.'"[37]

He was excessively generous, buying a computer for Vladimir Cerin because the trainer expressed interest in learning about the Internet; bailing out jockeys who were down on their luck. At one point, Antley kept getting consecutive days, meaning he was repeatedly found guilty of infractions. Mace Siegal booked him in a race with a purse of around forty-seven thousand dollars. Antley won, but then his number was disqualified. He went back to the jocks' room and wrote a check for the amount he would have won if he hadn't been disciplined, $3,400. The loss wasn't their horse's problem, he told the Siegals. It was his. The Siegals had never seen anything like it and handed the check back.[38]

To Antley, everything seemed a torment or a delight, with nothing in between. He could lose himself marveling at tea swirling in a cup, or at an owner's baby dressed in silks to match his own. In the midst of a hard-fought race, amid the grunting and cursing, the other jocks would hear someone singing, "I'm going to wi-in, I'm going to wi-in . . . ." It would be Antley calling out as he surged to first. "See you in St. Lou-ey," he would yell and sail off.[39] MC Hammer booked Antley to ride his horse at the 1992 Derby, and at a party before the event, Antley became so excited trading moves with Hammer, he danced right off the stage.[40] In one post parade, he took on a few liquored-up hecklers who were attacking his friend Chris McCarron for an earlier defeat. Antley told them to bet on him in the next race and leave McCarron alone. When the horses came down the stretch, Antley's mount surged ahead to take the lead. Despite the concentration of the moment, Antley turned to look directly at the group seconds before he hit the wire. "So did you do like I told you?" he shouted.[41]

He fell in love and brought the girl home to meet his family. But in March 1995 they broke up. "It tore everything out of me," he said four years later. "I don't even know if I could see her right now and be able to stand it."[42] After that Antley's attendance at the track grew spotty. Barisoff remembered how Antley had looked at him helplessly at a Santa Anita reception at the beginning of his first California season. He was offered a drink and he stood there, paralyzed by the magnitude of the decision, until he ordered one, then another.[43] Now he had fallen back into drugs, and his new agent, Ron Anderson, tried to get him into rehab. Antley had become interested in day-trading on the Internet as a way to ensure his money was being properly managed. Early each morning, before going to exercise horses at the still-dark track, he traded stocks online and made substantial profits. He told Anderson he didn't want to go into rehab because he didn't want to leave his computer for long. The staff at Grandview, the rehab facility chosen by the track's onsite counseling center, assured him he could bring the computer, so he checked in.[44]

When he got out in early 1997, he went back to Elloree to race at the Trials, where he had gotten his start as a sixteen-year-old. The crowd gave him a standing ovation, and he won the Elloree Cup on board Tied Up, a horse owned by Goree Smith's daughter Caroline. He tied the Trials record time of 46.2 seconds. "From here on out, the Elloree Trials is going to be even bigger," Antley said. "There's no doubt. I've put my word on it. Because I'm going to bring some people in here, and they're going to be bigger than my name. My name's not that big. It's a greatness from Elloree and all that, but I want to do something for the town."[45]

In May 1997, the agent from Antley's New York heyday, Drew Mollica, got fired by jockey Jose Santos because Santos wanted to shake up his business. Mollica now had a wife, two small kids, a mortgage and nothing he could dream up to pay the bills. He was desperate. He had heard Antley's claims to the press that he took a hiatus from racing because he got a little "sour" and went home to attend his great-grandmother's one hundredth birthday, the birth of his sister's first child, and his brother's wedding.[46] But Mollica knew that Antley had gotten into trouble again and then cleaned himself up. Now he was back riding, this time in Louisville.

Mollica hadn't really talked to Antley in eight years. They hadn't exchanged more than cursory greetings at the track since the day Mollica called the stewards and told them he was resigning as Antley's agent, ever since Antley turned in his license all those years ago. But Mollica was flat busted broke again, as he was that day in 1984 when Mel Grossman first put their partnership together. If Antley really was clean again, there was no one Mollica would rather work with. The jockey agent Ron Eubanks set up the meeting in his basement and Mollica flew down.

"Babe," Mollica said to Antley, "I need this job."

Antley looked at Mollica and smiled. He didn't make Mollica ask twice. "Okay, Drewsky," Antley said. He grabbed the agent and gave him a hug and a kiss on the cheek. "I love you. We'll start Thursday, okay?"[47]

Mollica flew back to New York and Antley followed a few days later to ride for the first time there in four years. He moved into his agent's house. He seemed happiest in that setting, surrounded by a family. He rode a full schedule but he still pitched in cleaning, walking the dog, and cooking dinner. He went grocery shopping armed with a bunch of coupons that Mollica's wife, Joy, gave him. He overbought like a survivalist stocking his fallout shelter and handed the unspent coupons back to Joy. "You have to use those, Chris," Joy said.

Antley slipped her a check for five thousand dollars. "Joy, if I'm living in your house, I don't want you ever using coupons again," he said.

Antley loved playing with their kids—a toddler and a three-year-old. Sometimes he baby-sat, playing computer games with the kids for hours. Joy and Drew came back one night and found Antley sitting on the bed reading to the children.

"I hope you didn't smoke in front of the kids," Joy said. Antley had picked up the habit a few years before.

"They don't like my brand," Antley drawled, "so we stopped smoking."

"Look how many comebacks he made with the weight and look how he outrode those other jockeys," Nick Zito said. "He got his old agent Drew Mollica back and I said, 'Yeah, we'll ride him on everything.' So we started riding him, he started beating the heck out of all of those jockeys. Then somebody complained about his weight. I think somebody in the jocks' room. His weight, he was always fighting it. He might have gotten privileges before, who knows. Things leak and the next thing you know, he can't do the weight."[48] Antley started getting pulled off horses because he couldn't stay under the legal allowance of five pounds over.[49]

In Saratoga that summer, Antley rode a fifty-thousand-dollar claimer named Primazena. Walking out to the starting gate, the three-year-old didn't feel right to Antley. He rode her into the inside and was against the rail on the first turn. Then suddenly she collapsed and went into tremors.[50] Antley hit the ground, but he did not walk away this time as he had with Drachma. He burst into tears. Antley held the horse's head in his arms there on the track until the horse went still, dead of heart failure or massive aneurysm.[51] Three days later, Antley begged off a mount, saying he was too sick to ride.

The next month, Antley was scheduled to ride Geri, a star turf horse in the Woodbine Mile in Toronto, but he was unraveling. "I felt that Geri would be one of the best turf runners in a generation . . ." wrote Dave Johnson, at ESPN.com. "When I heard Antley was going to ride him in Canada, I spoke to Mollica, who shocked me by recounting what he had to go through just to get the unmotivated and distracted Antley to the plane at JFK! This was a young man who marched to a different drummer."[52]

Antley went to Toronto and pulled off nine pounds the morning of the race by downing laxatives, taking Lasix pills and sitting for six hours in the hotbox to make the 117 weight.[53] Amazingly, he won, but he had gotten physically weak again.

He went to a bar in Etobicoke after the race and celebrated hard.[54] He decided it was time to return to California. He was sick to death of the East Coast winter. The summer in Saratoga could be magical, but the tracks in New York and New Jersey started to get him down. "He wasn't an Ozone Park kind of guy," Mollica said, referring to the area of Queens that was home to Aqueduct.[55]

Antley asked Mollica if he would agent him on the West Coast, but Mollica was raising a young family and couldn't relocate. "I have too many dark suits to go to California," he told Antley. While he knew they had restored their friendship, it would be a long time before they worked together again.

On October 31, 1997, Antley won a race out at Santa Anita, but then everything was also-rans. The work was drying up. Charlie McCaul, the clerk of scales who weighed him in every day, started giving Antley self-help books, like *Chicken Soup for the Soul*, because he was so worried about the dark mood that had settled over Antley.[56]

At the beginning of November, the stewards at Hollywood Park asked Antley to take a drug test and he refused. The California Horse Racing Board required that his license be taken away for noncompliance with the testing. He told the press that he was not on drugs at the time but "heading in that direction,"[57] and he was taking a break from racing because of health reasons.

Antley moved into a hotel and for six weeks never came out. His agent, Ron Anderson, visited occasionally, but left not long after he arrived. He sent friends who had gone to rehab to try to coax Antley for treatment, but they reported that Antley was too messed up to move.[58] Finally, Anderson decided to drag him out. The tracks in California had a substance counseling program called the Winner's Foundation run by Don Murray. He arranged for a room at Grandview, in case Anderson was successful.

Anderson drove to the hotel and, as he expected, Antley let him in. "Look," Anderson said, "you're going to pack up all your shit here and I'm taking you for some help."

"Why don't you come back in an hour," Antley suggested.

"Chris," Anderson said, "you don't understand. I'm not leaving here without you. You're coming with me. We're going to get you some help. It's all set up."

Antley looked at him. "Okay," he said. He started to shuffle some of his things as if he was getting ready to leave with Anderson. "I have to take a shower," Antley said suddenly. "Why don't you just come back in an hour or two?"

"Chris, you don't understand," Anderson said. "I'm not leaving. I'm staying here until you leave with me."

Antley looked at him wearily. Anderson could see he had worn himself out over those weeks in the hotel. He was due and ready to go. Anderson waited while Antley got in the shower. Then they packed up his stuff and dragged it outside. Murray was in the car waiting and they took Antley to Grandview.

Antley was scheduled to stay eighteen days but ended up holding on at Grandview for six months.[59] He later said that he stared down his monsters and was able to get outside his own little world for the first time in ages. Because he was a patient for so long, he earned broader freedoms than the other clients. When he was not in counseling sessions, he rode his bike and worked out. He decided that the place needed fixing up and he had the money and skills to do it, so he remodeled the bedroom he shared with a roommate and redid two bathrooms. He gave his wide-screen television to the director because the man didn't have a set. He told his mother at one point that maybe he would live in a rehab clinic since he had gone through so much therapy himself, maybe he could help other people.[60]

By June 1998, the staff decided Antley needed to get on with his life, apply to get his riding license back, and be out in the world. That same year, Chris Antley was diagnosed with bipolar disorder, otherwise known as manic depression. Sixty percent of bipolar patients are substance abusers, usually of alcohol, and secondarily of marijuana and cocaine. Studies show, however, that the effects of heavy cocaine use can produce abnormal mood swings that closely resemble bipolar disorder in people who do not have the condition.

Chris Antley left Grandview in June and moved in with Anderson's family in Arcadia, where he seemed happy. When the racing moved down to Del Mar a month later, he shared an apartment there with Anderson. Antley was ready to get back to the track, but no matter what he did now, the weight would not come off. He dieted. He ran. He sweated and downed diuretics and diet pills, but the weight clung to him. He had outgrown the business.

Antley found himself lost in bewilderment.[61] He could get down within eight or ten pounds of riding and then couldn't get any further. In the back of his mind, he knew he was in serious trouble. For years, it had been harder and harder to make weight, but now it was impossible. He rode the stationary bike for twenty-six or twenty-eight miles a day, he starved himself, did physical labor, then ran eight to ten miles a day. Once he so exhausted himself, he crumpled to the ground when he was running, passed out cold.[62] He knew the game was over for him, the dream had vanished into thin air. One day he lost the courage to step on the scale.[63] When he hit 123 pounds, he stopped trying to get back to racing at Del Mar.

He quit the torture, the fasting and sculpting, and the heaviness filled his body, spread like a disease. He felt too ashamed to go to the track. He didn't even want to go outside because people would see how big he was and how he had failed.[64]

Antley got up to 147 pounds before he finally decided to go back to South Carolina to be with his family. It was September 1998, and he left California in mind-numbing, depressive pain. "After watching him struggle with his weight and all," Anderson said, "I wasn't sure that he would ever ride again. I had seen him struggle and seen him go through the peaks and valleys of losing the weight and the discipline. At that point, I was just hoping he would get his life situated, that he could cope with living. When I saw him leave, he was big and he had some money, he had invested well, and I surrendered to the fact that he was never going to ride again. I didn't think it was possible."[65]

Leslie Moss, Chris Antley's sister, called their father, Lester, one Saturday. "Dad," she said, "you better come over to Brian's." When Les got there, Brian and Leslie were sitting on the couch talking to a friend of theirs whom Les didn't recognize. Les said hello to everyone, nodded to the little fat guy at the end of the couch. He turned to Brian. Then he looked back at the stranger.

"Chris?" he said. He only had noticed the trace of something familiar. He couldn't believe that stranger was his boy. His son was so heavy and his eyes were flat and dull.[66]

Antley seemed glad to see him, but he didn't have much to say. He told his father he planned to stay in South Carolina for a while. He had retired from racing for good. He couldn't find his way back to the sport anymore.

Les drove Antley to the house he shared with his wife Annie down the road in Columbia. He had always told the kids, "I don't have much to offer you, but you'll always have a roof over your head and something to eat."

But this was the bleakest of homecomings. Each day, Antley got up, walked to the living room, and sat on the couch to watch TV. "Do you want to go visit your friends in Elloree?" Les asked. "Do you want to go see your grandmother?" Antley said no. He barely spoke. He never left the house. He was a thirty-two-year-old former jockey. A famous drug addict. A fat sucker with big old cheeks, wearing extra-large T-shirts. He was dead inside.[67] In his first hiatuses from racing, his problem was always drugs. Then the depressions hit. But now on top of the other difficulties was the weight. Antley didn't have any idea how to get back from the weight.

Antley slept in the downstairs bedroom. Over the years, Les had collected sports photographs, including pictures of Antley on winning horses, holding up trophies, leaping from his mount into the winner's circle. The walls were papered with these images, and Antley woke in the night and looked at them, vivid in the dimness. He broke into a cold sweat, lying there and staring at all of them. "Dad," he said, "you're killing me with these pictures."[68] One time when he was flipping channels, Antley accidentally saw part of a horse race. He could feel his stomach churn and the bile rise in his throat. He knew he would never ride again. He changed the channel.

Anderson called every week or ten days and talked about everything but the track. He didn't want to make Antley feel bad that he never was going to be on a horse again.

Two weeks went by like that. Three weeks. Five. Antley just stared at the walls, not talking. Les worried about his son's mental health, but he treated Antley like the other kids.[69] He didn't walk around feeling sorry for him or waiting on him. Antley had chores—clean the bathrooms, take care of the kitchen, vacuum, dust. Antley dragged himself through those tasks.

"Start a new business," his father urged him. "Do something else with your life.

"You've accomplished a lot," he told him. "Racing is dangerous." Over his career, Antley had earned about $6 million on the track and showed real talent as a day-trader. "You have all the money you need," his father pointed out. "Open a restaurant." Antley thought about those suggestions. He considered going back to school. His father told him every day what special talents he possessed, how he could do anything he wanted.

One day in October, Antley was in the other room when he again heard a horse race broadcast on television.[70] He could hear the announcer's machine-gun delivery. He went to the door and looked in. He could see the horses streaming along in a line with their necks pumping and their tails streaming behind them like a river was rippling through them. The jocks were driving against each other, bouncing off each other. They were feeling what it was to have a great thoroughbred beneath them, feeling that danger, that peace. They were fighting each other and one of them would know what it was to cross the line with no one in front. They would feel what it was to win, and then be led into the winner's circle and the owners and trainers clapping him on the back. Antley started to cry.

To say I used to do that . . . , he thought, and he felt nothing but sadness, there in the living room of his father's house, back in South Carolina. Just a fat man in a big T-shirt watching the races.

He felt shaken. He didn't care about the money. He would ride every day even if he had to do it for free. If he could get back on a thoroughbred in a race, even if he came up to the quarter pole and dropped dead, he would have lived exactly as he wanted. He would be the happiest SOB that ever lived, a thrilled dying jockey. He was almost embarrassed to love anything so much.

When his father came home that night, Antley told him he had a job again. He knew what he wanted to do.

"What's that?" his father asked.

"I'm going back to racing," Antley said. "I am going to work every day to get back until the day I die. Even if I get old and never get back there again, I still know what my job is supposed to be."[71]

Although Les knew that the effort might not pay off, he was happy that his son finally cared about something again after all those months.

"Dad," Antley said, "I think I can be better than I was."[72]

Antley started seeing a psychiatrist.[73] He put himself on the Atkins diet, which jump-started weight loss by eliminating carbohydrates. Every morning, he woke up before dawn and put on two sweat suits. He picked up his backpack, his yellow Walkman, and tugged his cap down low to his eyes—his Superman cape, as he called it because it made him feel invisible.[74] When his father went off to work, Antley headed out the door. He had developed his own strategy for running long distances. He started slowly, gimping along, shuffling in the dark to get his adrenaline going. Then after two miles, he picked up the pace. He got to a full run and by then, the adrenaline was flowing and he felt he could go forever.[75]

The guys at the Bender Mender auto repair saw him jog by every day. Sometimes he would stop for a little while to talk about the cars he was fixing up—a Mustang and Chevelle from 1968. He stopped by the Wal-Mart to flip through auto magazines to break the monotony of training and he knew everyone probably thought he was a wack-job, bundled in clothes drenched in sweat.[76] He went by the Hazelwood Market in the morning to buy water and he jogged in place in line. Sometimes he went by a few more times during the day to get a Snickers bar or something to drink. At the end of the day, he stopped in again, pouring sweat, to flip through magazines, and then he was still. Bill Cox, the owner, could see the exhaustion on his face.

Connie Trakas, who worked a register there, always saw Antley on the road when she was driving. "Damn, Forrest Gump," she said to him, "do you ever sit down?"[77] He laughed at the new name.

Everybody started calling him Forrest Gump. People at the bookstore, grocery store, the gas station. They all knew him, or at least they noticed him as the town character, old Forrest Gump. In the middle of the day, his sister, Leslie, found him completely exhausted, sprawled in the hammock in her backyard.[78]

Sometimes Antley ran so far he got lost.[79] He was alone pretty much the whole day, but he saw people through those long hours and thought about who they were. He ran so far he crossed out into the farmlands and he saw the kids standing at the edge of their yards, hungry. He saw the people just killing time because they didn't have jobs. The music on his Walkman gave him a soundtrack which made him think of a storyline, a way of seeing these people as part of a bigger narrative, but it was all a sad one. He wanted to get out of there, to have something more for himself.[80] And he ran back to the house, having carried his body through twenty-five or twenty-eight miles on that day alone.

A racing fan wrote a message online to the "Let's Talk Jockeys" forum. "A good friend of mine who plays the jockeys asked me today at the Santa Fe Casino sportsbook where Chris Antley is. He hasn't seen him on any mounts anywhere in a long time. Does anyone know?" Antley himself posted a response the very next day. "Will resume riding in Aqueduct in mid Feb . . . wgt 127 lbs and falling. Needed time away to be myself."

Antley's pace of training went even quicker than he predicted. In the middle of November, on a Tuesday afternoon when the track was dark, he called Ron Anderson at his home in California.

"Listen," Antley said, "I've been working out every day. I got my weight down. I've been running." Anderson could tell Antley was pumped up. He could hear it in his voice. "I'm within range," Antley reported. "I'm watching everything I eat. I really feel good. I'm going to be back and I'm going to ride."[81]

"That's great," Anderson said.

"I'm going to spend the holiday with my family here. I'll be in some-time after that."

Anderson hung up the phone and turned to his wife and kids. "Chris is going to ride again," he said. "I mean, I can feel it."

Five weeks into Antley's training, right around Thanksgiving, he was hitting peak form when his right knee caved in. He couldn't even walk. For four weeks he was back on the couch watching television and waiting to be healed. It was like having a rocket engine on idle for days. He was sure he was going to explode, but in this case it would be an explosion of fat. That period, waiting to recover, was the biggest test for him. If the weight decided to come, he had no means to chase it off. He could only rely on his own willpower not to eat and the mysterious metabolism of his body.

When Antley got to the point where he could at least walk, he bought memberships for himself and Leslie at the Columbia Athletic Club. He wore a stocking cap, T-shirt, and sweat suit, topped by a 1970s full-length aluminum-rubber suit like baseball players wore during the cold months of spring training. He went there at all times of day, as early as 5:30 in the morning. He started slowly, carefully walking on the treadmill. After an hour or so, Leslie left him there and he kept working out on the elliptical trainers and stair-steppers for five or six more hours. He set the cardio machines to the maximum time of thirty minutes, and when they shut down he went running in the streets for half an hour with two bottles of Gatorade in his hands. Then he came back to the club and got back on machines.[82] Coley Brown Jr., the club manager, went to him and asked what he was doing. A guy who ran like that was either very fit physically or unfit mentally. The staff at the club usually tried to stop people from abusing their bodies that way.

"I'm a jockey," Antley told him. "I have to get back to riding for the winter season."

Antley never let the staff know he had been a superstar in his sport. One time, months into his training, he let slip that he once won the Kentucky Derby and no one could believe it. They kept asking him questions about the experience, but he played the accomplishment down. After Christmas, he started running again, sometimes up to twenty miles a day. People who stopped by the club in the morning found him on the treadmill when they came back at night. They asked the fitness director, F. D. Mudd, "Is there something wrong with this guy?"[83] By New Year's Day, his weight was down to 125 pounds.

On January 11, Eugenia sat in her rocking chair looking out the side window as she did every day in Elloree, gazing at the train tracks, the little strip of street, the porches of the nearby houses. She was waiting until it was time to go to Sunday service. She heard the front door open and was suprised to see Brian come in. He went to use the bathroom, then Chris walked in to the living room. "Happy Birthday, Grandma," Antley said. "We're taking you to church."

Eugenia looked out the window and saw a white stretch limousine slithering into the driveway. "Oh, my," she said.[84]

They walked down her front steps, across the frozen lawn. The chauffeur opened the door. There was a foldout side tray inside with three little glasses filled with amber liquid. Antley handed her one.

"Oh, my," she said, "not before church, Chris."

"Come on, Grandma," he said. "It's apple juice. Just drink it."

So she took the little glass and sipped at it.

During the announcements, Antley stood before the congregation of around two hundred people and gave his testimonial. He said when you go to the bottom, the only place you can look is up.[85] He said he was trying to turn his life around. Everyone came up to him afterward and complimented him. Then they went out to the Elloree training center for lunch. His weight was down to 118 and his stepmother, Annie, could tell he was doing well because he started wearing her clothes and jeans.[86]

In late January, Antley moved back into Ron Anderson's house in Arcadia. On February 3, 1999, he went over to Santa Anita for the first time since his layoff in early November 1997. He walked into the jocks' room, and seeing the place again after fifteen months felt as good as winning the Kentucky Derby on Strike the Gold. He was four pounds heavier than most of the other jocks, but he could tell he was the fittest one there, all lean muscle.[87] He opened his locker and his gear was laid out like he had never left. The other jocks stood under the TV watching the racing channel and yelling and cheering, and tears came to Antley's eyes because he was finally back and he had gotten back before the world he loved disappeared. He lived a nightmare in five months—from the lowest low to the highest high. The transformation was profound.[88]

The trainers could see Antley looked good, and it didn't take any time for Anderson to book him on mounts. "He wasn't tough to sell,"

Anderson said. "In our business, he was seen as a star. As soon as people got a look at him, right away we had instant business." When Antley went to bed at night, he started saying to himself, "I did good today." He never felt that way before. His whole perspective on life had changed.[89]

Vladimir Cerin started putting him on horses, and then Bob Baffert gave him a break. Antley saw D. Wayne Lukas outside his barn most days. "We gotta get together," Antley said. "We gotta do something." Lukas nodded. Antley seemed more intense than before and Lukas liked that.[90] After a while he started booking Antley.

On April 3, Michael Whittingham slotted Antley to ride Walk That Walk in the Santa Anita Derby. It was a 70 to 1 long shot, and Antley came in fifth. The next day he called his grandmother to wish her a happy Easter. He told her how glad he was to be back riding. "Your grandmama's prayers have been answered," she told him.[91]

He finished twelfth in the standings for the season which ran from late December through the end of April, winning 23 races on 138 mounts. It was a far lower rate of success than in his heyday because he was scrambling for opportunities to get good mounts.

But Antley was happy. He told Anderson he still harbored one hope that would make the experience perfect. He explained that when he won the Derby in 1991, he had been messed up. "You know," Antley said, "I'd really like to go back, just to experience the day. To feel the place and see the people and everything." He didn't care which horse he rode, but just to be back there and absorb the sensations.[92]

Anderson couldn't do much for Antley at that time. The jock had only been back racing for a short while, and the top jocks who had never taken a hiatus from the sport, who stayed in the game all of those months that Antley was holed up in South Carolina, would get first shot at any horse running. No more than twenty horses would race that first Saturday in May, which meant only twenty jocks would be riding. And the idea that Antley would be one of them was by no means a done deal.

EIGHT

THE BIG GAMBLE

Chuck and I would be gamblers that first of May at Churchill Downs, but we had staked a pretty important wager on ourselves some months earlier. We had met once through a mutual friend, Darcey, the previous October and had gotten to know each other only through letters since Chuck lived in Oxford, Mississippi, and I lived in New York. The letters went back and forth every nine days or so and always ended with questions, as a joke on how quickly we were becoming close and as a useful way to gather information about each other. "Would you ever buy an expensive car? Do you think a cerebral nature ever hinders the joy in life? What woodland creature does Madeleine Albright most remind you of?"

I asked him what his one vanity was. "To say I had only one vanity would be true vanity," he wrote back. "But to look at a situation no matter how chaotic or emotional with detached insight is what I probably most cherish."

Chuck was a master's candidate in the English Department at the University of Mississippi. In 1995 he had quit his job as a stockbroker at an investment bank in Dallas to go serve for two years in the Peace Corps. As fate would have it, he was assigned to the Ukraine as an English teacher. I mention fate because when he suddenly developed acute leukemia, the doctors wrote in his chart, "Ukraine, Chernobyl."

Although he cherished that experience in the Peace Corps more than any other in his life, he looked at the stint as most valuable because it tested his ability to endure suffering. He loved his students there, the family he lived with, and his friends, particularly the hippies. But there were long lonely periods too. He read constantly, mainly Russian writers, particularly his favorite, Dostoevsky, and more specifically *The Brothers Karamazov.*

In one letter, I asked him what the point of fatigue was. "Fatigue exists to slow us down so we can savor life. . . ."

At the time, for whatever reason, I was on the receiving end of deep speeches from cab drivers. One driver had dropped me off at my apartment and asked me how long I had lived in my neighborhood. When I told him I had only moved in that fall, he nodded approvingly and said, "This is a place of new beginnings. It is a sacred place. When I moved to this country, I worked at the newsstand in the subway there and I couldn't believe the kindness of the people." I wrote to Chuck in one letter about another encounter:

Today's deep cab driver speech was about how this country is special and beautiful because it humanizes people. It started as a comment on how the cab driver was not going to ever buy a Christmas tree again because a year ago he bought a beautiful eight-foot tree, and the tree sucked down two vats of water every day and he realized that the tree was almost human. It was asking him: Do you want me to live or do you want me to die? You cut off my roots, but then you give me water? And he felt the tree's struggle through the whole holiday. Then he told me that when he lived in the Dominican Republic, he flew his girlfriend down from the States as a treat. They went into the market and he walked up to a goat seller and said, "I want that one." The goat seller took the animal and killed it on the spot and my driver was proud. But his girlfriend was appalled and asked him, "How can you do that? You think you can just command life and death." So the driver got to thinking and realized he had never hesitated before. It's a controversial view, but he thinks that the way the U.S. handles meat is much better. One dead animal goes to feed many people. They are killed off in isolation, so people don't get jaded to murder and the death is its own thing, not spectacle. (Now his girlfriend is his wife.)

So life-and-death issues were in the air.

Chuck called one night in early December, and when I called him back a few days later, he was hiding out in his house in Oxford, trying to avoid a party next door. He was tired and had a sore throat, for which he had gone to the university infirmary that day. They thought he might have mono. In our long rambling conversation, he talked about how he wanted to be happy and had tried to help other people be happy in the past, but now it was his time to take care of himself too, and I must feel that way as well. This is the time for people like us, he said. And he talked about the pain that makes people act rotten to each other and said jokingly, at one point, "What do you say? Should we solve all the world's problems?"

The next day I got a message on my machine from Darcey. When Chuck had gone back to the infirmary, they sent him to the cancer wing for tests. They thought he had leukemia. A conference call was set up for his parents the next morning. That night, after his tests and the general conclusion that he had acute myelogenous leukemia, he went to Darcey's house for dinner and I called them. "You must be so tired," he said. "I had you up so late talking."

Chuck still had the idea that he could drive himself home to Dallas for treatment, but within a day of his diagnosis a bruise the size and color of an eggplant appeared on his leg and his body went flimsy, so he flew home to his father's house in Dallas and immediately checked into Baylor Hospital.

In the last letter that Chuck wrote to me before he got sick, he had asked me if I had ever fallen in love with a character in literature. When he was in the Ukraine, the characters in books had become his relationships on some level and he wrote a funny, fast-paced story about romancing many of the female protagonists.

I wrote back that I didn't know if he had noticed, but most male characters in fiction are pretty distressing types, so oddly if there were any character that I fell in love with it would be the boyfriend of the protagonist in the cartoonish novel I was writing back in my early twenties. Before I finished the letter, Chuck's diagnosis of leukemia was confirmed, and then I felt an odd sensation because in the novel as I conceived it, that boyfriend character, in a freak incident, is stricken with a rare blood disease.

I was afraid to confess to Chuck that this was the fictional character I had fallen in love with because it would carry both a sense of doom for him and vulnerability for me. But Chuck begged me to answer his question, and when I did he understood why I was rattled. He kept asking, half joking and half serious, as if what I wrote in the manuscript would really mean something, "What happens? Does the guy die?" and I said over and over to him, "It's an unfinished novel, Chuck. I never wrote the ending."

"But you know that part," he insisted.

And I did, but I didn't want to ever say it. I wanted to rewrite the novel. When I looked back at the manuscript a few weeks later, I noticed that when the female narrator returns to her boyfriend's apartment after his death, she finds a copy of *The Brothers Karamazov* tented on his bed.

Chuck decided he would look on the bright side. Leukemia would look great on his resume. He would go through two rounds of chemotherapy and be cured and then he could wear the challenge as a point of pride. *Peace Corps. Leukemia.* He would have tested his will, his endurance, and no employer would refuse him.

He would not act like a hospital patient. He refused the new robe his mother bought and wore T-shirts and shorts; Birkenstocks, not slippers. He had plans to amuse himself and all of us with this illness. He would preempt his hair loss by having his head shaved, and he would ask

Anthony, the orderly whom he liked a lot, to give him different styles as they went—a Bozo the clown or a Mohawk. These would all be documented in photographs for everyone's amusement. By the time this procedure happened, Chuck told me by phone, it wasn't so ha-ha funny anymore. The pictures don't look funny at all. He's sitting shirtless with a towel over his shoulders. Behind him is the window, looped with unlit army-green Christmas lights which look defeated against coming night. Chuck is staring darkly into the mirror above the hospital sink with his head skinned down to baby fuzz.

When I talked to him by phone, the nurse sometimes came in to rig his bags of chemotherapies and let the poisons run through the tube to his veins. Chuck would keep talking but I could hear him getting weaker and all the liveliness killed, pushed down so he wouldn't stir, wouldn't vomit, and sometimes I thought he might die right then when we were on the phone. He would ask me to talk to distract him, so I concocted dream trips to the Temple of the Monkey God in India—the place and sunrise he had described in one of his letters as most beautiful—or hitchhiking in Ireland and the fictional old couple who would pick us up and invite us to their cottage for dinner.

One time he told me as he was fading that the hospital minister had stopped by and asked if he could pray for him. Chuck told the minister if he thought it was a good idea, he should go ahead and do it. The minister prayed. Then he asked Chuck if he had accepted Jesus Christ. Chuck told him he thought they were on good terms or something like that. And then Chuck said to me, his voice slow and gravelly, "I can't give my life's bounty to just one god. I'll give some to Jesus. Some to Buddha . . . some to Mohammed . . ."

"Like an investment portfolio," I kidded him.

He laughed a little. "Yeah," he said dreamily. "But I can't give it to one god. I think it's all of them." And then he drifted off.

"Chuck, you need to hang up the phone," I said quietly.

And he came to for a minute and said, "Good night, sweet girl," and the phone clicked down. Then I cried for a little while because I thought he might not even get through the first round of chemo.

In that first round, he told me that if anything should happen to him, he wanted the poem "Assurances" by Walt Whitman read at his funeral. I didn't have a copy of *Leaves of Grass*, so I went out and got a copy.

"I need no assurances, I am a man who is pre-occupied of his own soul," the poem begins. Then farther down:

> I do not doubt that passionately-wept deaths of young men are provided
>   for, and that the deaths of young women and the deaths of little
>   children are provided for,
> (Did you think Life was so well provided for, and Death, the purport
>   of all Life, is not well provided for?)[1]

I don't pretend to be the first person who ever loved Chuck or the first person Chuck ever loved. We both had loved other people in the past and had failed people as well. But I would say that up to that point, neither of us had ever loved any person as gracefully and thoroughly as we would come to love each other.

Despite the fact that we talked for hours every night and had gotten so close, I felt extremely shy about the idea of actually visiting Chuck. We only had spoken once in person, the rest was the letters and phone calls. But he wanted me and Darcey to visit him, and I was so worried about him, I needed to see how he was firsthand as quickly as possible. I was terrible with hospitals, but fighting against that weakness was the fact that I wanted to be with him, to sleep in his room on the foldout chair as he hoped I would. I kept imagining a solution where I would outfit myself in a head-to-toe astronaut suit made of white pillows and just walk into his room and lie down on the floor next to him and not say a word. I could imagine pulling that off.

When I arrived at the hospital, I didn't shake Chuck's hand or even go close to him. I went to the chair under the window and started asking him basic questions. We watched a movie and then he asked if I wanted to fold out the chair to sleep.

I turned out the overhead lights, but a glow still seeped into the room from the Dallas skyline and from the illumination under the hospital bed. I could hear a soft whir of machines and every now and then, from a room next door or out in the hall a kind of creaking yawn and rattle that reminded me of a boat. I found out a month later, when men came in wearing white suits and passing blocks that looked like electric sanders along one of the walls, that the soft clinking came from a nearby radiation machine. They were checking for spillover into Chuck's room.

After a while I opened my eyes and saw that he was half on his side looking at me, and I understood how lonely it must have been for him over all the nights he was there by himself, after he had shooed his friends and family home to their beds, wondering what was going to become of his life.

The next day, when my friend Darcey was leaving Dallas, I walked her out to get a cab and told her I didn't know if Chuck wanted me to stay that extra night or if I was tiring him and should go home. "Just ask him," she said. "He would tell you if he doesn't want you to stay."

I went back to the room, and when I walked in he reached his hand out like he had been treading water for days. "Where have you been?" he joked. "Sweet girl."

I flew down to see Chuck every few weeks and stayed about a week at a time. Despite the melancholy circumstances, Chuck and I were oddly happy. We were smiling, laughing people alone in the hospital room, interrupted only by the brief appearances of doctors, nurses, friends and relatives. Each person was a new participant to rope into our bedside debates. "Is it a sign of joie de vivre to stick your bare foot out an open car window or a disgraceful lack of couth?" One nurse for it, one against. Stepmother for. Mother for. Best friend Collin against. Pristine hospital nutritionist who held a clipboard and asked only one question several times a week—"Are you liking the juice?" to which Chuck would reply, "I don't really drink it"—against.

Each morning we woke with the arrival of the nurse, announced by the snap of the fluorescent lights into eye-stinging life and a brisk "Good morning," who had come to take Chuck's vital signs.

I would be on the foldout chair in one of Chuck's T-shirts and would pull on a skirt and shoes then go bleary-eyed to the women's bathroom down the hall, because Chuck was shy about all the equipment for sample collection in the bathroom connected to his room. He might be in a hospital bed, losing his eyelashes, rigged to a machine that delivered chemotherapy and all his nutrition, but, he told me, he was courting me all the same. I would get a cup of weak coffee from the machine in the kitchenette, then some milk out of the refrigerator stocked with pudding cups of Jell-O, orange juice, peach slices, and apple sauce. Back in the room, Chuck's breakfast tray would try to make its way into the room, chaperoned by a hospital worker, and Chuck would refuse it emphatically.

Then Doc Adams would arrive.

He would push the door open and raise the flat palm of his hand in wordless hello. He had wisps of gray hair, a gentle ski slope of a belly, and a husky methodical way of talking, with one index finger tapping the air just above his waist when he had a point to make. He had gotten his medical degree back in 1953 and started working at Baylor in 1970. He had delivered babies and treated mothers and children so expertly he had a whole city of fans and a clinic in the hospital named after him.

He didn't know Chuck until Chuck got sick, but he was a close friend of Chuck's uncle for decades. So when Chuck fell ill, the phone lines connected all the worried people and the knowledgeable, and soon Doc Adams knew Chuck Fulgham was staying on the eighth floor of the Rogers Building. Doc Adams was retired now, but he drove to Baylor every morning to deliver the newspaper to Chuck. Doc Adams wasn't just coming to hold Chuck's big toe and blink away tears and ask about the contents of the plastic bags hanging like bats from the metal tree Chuck wheeled everywhere with him. He was there on a mission: to deliver the paper, and depending on how Chuck felt, he could either talk or not. There was no pressure on Chuck to feel chatty and there was a comforting consistency to Doc Adams's appearances. In the chaos of illness, there was the predictable coming and going of one man.

On the last morning of my first stay in Dallas, Doc Adams came in and joked around with us for a while. Then he asked if I would step into the hall. Out there, he told me that he didn't know what was going to happen with Chuck. He looked great now and seemed to be responding well to the chemotherapies. Beneath the cloud of leukemia, Chuck's health was ironically good. His heart rate was strong, his blood pressure perfect, his organs functioning precisely. But, Doc Adams told me, he himself was going through an unusual time. He had several friends and relatives who were extremely sick and he had seen illness throughout his life as a doctor, but he wanted me to know that Chuck and I were his heroes, the way we enjoyed each other regardless of the circumstances.

Chuck taught me the way to stop crying. When you felt the stinging behind your eyes, you clenched your teeth in a frozen smile, then shook your head back and forth fast. The tears receded into whatever nether region had created them.

When Chuck got out of the hospital the first time in mid-January, I went down to Dallas for a week. He met me at the airport with one vivid red anemone and a couple of books he wanted me to read. That week, we had fun like normal happy people, but we weren't normal anymore. One morning, we were leaving a diner when we heard screeching tires and shattering glass. In the middle of the road, two cars had collided. One had a big angry man inside, and in the crumpled Honda compact was a small Hispanic woman. Chuck ran to see if he could help. No one had been hurt, but the woman couldn't stop crying, whether from the shock or fear or just the fact that somehow she was going to have to pay for this problem. She cried and cried, then Chuck leaned down to her, talking to her, and put his arm around her shoulder to console her. He told me later that, before his illness, he never would have comforted a stranger like that.

So Chuck was in the hospital from mid-December to mid-January, then again from early February to early March. The weeks I was there I tried to distract him from the ordeal, and so did his friends and family, but still there were so many hours he had alone. He would push the button to prop the bed as high as it could go, then slowly swing his legs around and sit there for a few minutes on the edge. His shoulders would be collapsed forward and he would rub the back of his bald head, then slip on his Birkenstocks and stand up, slowly unfurling like one of those Macy's parade balloons inflating. He would take hold of the metal post of the machine he wheeled everywhere and guide it over all of the wires, then unplug it and wheel it slowly into the bathroom. When he came out he would go to the sink and look at himself in the fluorescent light and rub the top of his head, and when I was there watching him I could see how tired and fascinated he was with this unexpected misery.

Which was why, when we arrived at the Kentucky Derby on May 1, 1999, we were so happy to be there. And why my dreaming the name of the winning horse, without knowing the competitors ahead of time, seemed so spectacular.

NINE

KENTUCKY DERBY

The Kentucky Derby was hatched in 1875 by Meriwether Lewis Clark Jr., the renegade grandson of William Clark, half of the Lewis and Clark explorer team and governor of Missouri. Meriwether Clark's mother was Abigail Prather Churchill, daughter of one of the finest Louisville families. Clark liked champagne and tailored suits, and on a European pleasure trip developed a fascination with horse racing and the new pari-mutuel machines that had replaced corrupt bookmakers and their proclivity for race fixing at tracks abroad. When Clark returned to Louisville, he began spending his mother's family fortune to build a racetrack, christened the Louisville Jockey Club and Driving Park. (It started being called Churchill Downs about ten years later.) One of the races on opening day was the Derby—a unique competition because it ran three-year-olds; it was rare for horses that young to race at the time—at one mile and a half then, an unusually long competition.

Over the next twenty-four years of Clark's life, his erratic behavior overshadowed his many contributions to racing, which included establishing racing rules and standards. He became so consumed with the track, he divorced his wife and abandoned his three children. His girth increased uncomfortably and he took to settling arguments with gunfire, once exchanging bullets in his office with a horse owner in a dispute over entrance fees. Another time in a Chicago bar, he declared the city's residents to be "thieves and liars," and when the bartender objected, he fetched a gun and threatened him until the bartender apologized. The incident made the news in Chicago and Louisville.[1]

The family soon cut Clark out of all but a small portion of track operations, and the crash of 1893 wiped out his fortune for good. The Churchill family was forced to hand the track over to the Louisville Jockey Club, then headed by the same bookmakers Clark had fought throughout his life. However, even they made their contribution to the famous track, building the white twin steeples, which Churchill Downs became famous for. By the end of his life, Clark had been demoted to working as a steward, wandering track to track with the shifting meets. Driven mad by depression, he killed himself in 1899.

Matt Winn, a forty-nine-year-old handicapper and tailor, took over the track around that time and made Churchill and the Derby flourish through the highs and lows of racing history. The track, he knew, needed to offer spectators total entertainment. He hired John Philip Sousa's band to play in the infield at a cost of five thousand dollars. He shipped airplane parts to the track and had two planes assembled and flown overhead as the races went off. For the Derby of 1911, he commissioned a film crew to record the events leading up to the race and show the movie around the country.[2]

He soon developed a base of support among Louisville's businessmen. The *Courier-Journal* ran an editorial after the 1916 running, stating, "Such a day's sport as that of yesterday for those who went to see the Derby and such a day's business for the turf, cannot be looked upon by reasonable persons as a blot upon the escutcheon of the city or the state. It cannot cause regret that Kentucky was not swept by the anti-racing wave, partly made up of righteous puritanism, but partly of narrow and ignorant fanaticism, which destroyed the turf in a number of states less interested in breeding."[3] That commentary showed the shift of opinion among even the most influential figures, since Robert Worth Bingham, who owned the paper, had led the campaign to close the track in 1905 because he considered it a haven for vice. By 1918, he joined the Churchill Downs' board.

Winn represented the patriotic side of racing. He donated 10 percent of track revenues to the Red Cross when the United States entered World War I. During the national potato shortage of 1918, he planted the infield with the crops and donated the proceeds from their sale to the Red Cross too.

Enthusiasm for horse racing rose and fell with the vagaries of the economy and the popularity of other entertainments. It was said that you could gauge the nation's vitality by checking the handle, the amount of money wagered, on Derby Day to see if people had riches to spend. During the Depression the handle was desperately low. "Racing conditions are worse than I have ever seen them," Winn wrote to a New York racing executive in 1933. "This great sport, which we both love so much has reached a most critical stage and I am fearful of what the future holds."[4]

Winn revived the track once more before he died in 1949, ravaged by his own drinking. "Some of the best men I knew tried to beat that stuff and lost," he would tell his friends, "so be careful and don't let it lick you." He was one of those who succumbed.

Fifty years later, the Derby was still the highlight of the racing scene, the first jewel in the Triple Crown. On April 17, 1999, D. Wayne Lukas booked Chris Antley to ride a horse owned by Bob and Beverly Lewis in a maiden special-weight race at Santa Anita. Antley took Key to Success to the lead early and stayed there until the finish.[5] He carried his saddle to the scale and stepped on. One hundred and eighteen pounds. He was still fine. In the winner's circle, Lukas congratulated him. "I want you to watch the Lexington tomorrow," Lukas told Antley. "I've got a colt getting to the top of his game. I think he can go a mile and a quarter. See what you think, and give me a call. I can't get Bailey, and you might wind up riding that horse in the Derby."[6] Lukas had in fact already asked jockeys Laffit Pincay, Chris McCarron, Mike Smith, and Bailey to ride Charismatic and been turned down.

Antley couldn't believe he was getting a shot to go back to Churchill Downs. He had never heard of the horse Charismatic, but he felt something magical when Lukas asked him to ride.[7]

Lukas cautioned Antley. "I sure don't want you to come unless you feel as strongly about his chances as I do," he said. "If it's just to get in the post parade and say you rode in the Kentucky Derby in '99, I don't want you riding the horse. But if you sincerely feel in your heart that you have a legitimate chance, which I think you do, then I want you to ride the horse. You're my pick." Antley hadn't ridden in a Derby since 1996.

So Antley watched the Lexington Coolmore Stakes. He saw how Bailey kept nudging Charismatic down the backside, but at the stretch, the colt rushed past all the other horses in a demonstration of heart. Charismatic finished first by two lengths and in record time. His final sprint looked like Strike the Gold's move in the 1991 Derby. Antley called his agent, Ron Anderson, and told him to get hold of Lukas. Then he called his father. "I'm going to the Derby, Dad," he said. "And not only am I on a horse in the Derby, I am on a horse with a legitimate chance. It's for Mr. Lukas."

"What's the horse?" Les asked.

"Charismatic."

"I never heard of him," Les said.

"Dad, this horse has my name written all over it," he said. He pointed out that the first six letters of the horse's name included "Chris A." He had read up on Charismatic and liked the horse's story. The colt was washed up in the game and became a claimer, just like Antley. Even Lukas was in a slump. They were three dead entities that needed each other.

"You're lucky just to get a Derby mount," his father said. "Now you think you're going to win?" When they got off the phone, Les went online and checked the early odds. They were 100 to 1. "Yeah, that's a real legitimate horse," Les said to himself. There was no way his boy could triumph.[8]

About ten days later, Antley walked into the Santa Anita jocks' room and went up to Charlie McCaul, the assistant clerk of scales. He told McCaul that the night before he had had a dream in which he saw himself winning the Kentucky Derby on the back of Charismatic.[9]

"Really, *Hormiga*?" McCaul said, calling Antley the Spanish word for Ant. He had never heard a jockey tell about a winning dream before, but he didn't think the vision had special significance since Charismatic was such a long shot.

Antley told Anderson about the dream too. "I've seen the race," he said.[10]

"What?" Anderson asked.

"I've already seen this race."

"How's that?"

"We won," Antley said.

Anderson laughed. "Chris," he said, "do me a favor. This is going to be our little secret." He didn't want Antley to share the story because people would consider Antley's mystical vision too strange.

The reality, according to the experts, was that Bob Baffert would conquer the Kentucky Derby. His General Challenge and the filly Excellent Meeting were the favorites on a split ticket. General Challenge not only triumphed in his five most recent starts, he had beaten the top three-year-old talent that season in the Santa Anita Derby by a full three and a half lengths. His only drawback was his skittish behavior, but the bettors weren't worried. Excellent Meeting won all of her races as a three-year-old and earned the most money of any horse in the Derby with nearly $1.2 million. Baffert was still mulling over the decision whether or not to enter her, though, since she had only run against other fillies, never against the brawnier colts.

Both of those horses were owned by the Mabees, and the couple also had another horse in the race, or at least a horse they foaled. Worldly Manner, a tall dark-chocolate colt, was bought from them the previous

October for $5 million. As a two-year-old, Worldly Manner ran four times for the Mabees—twice in Holland and twice in Denmark. In three of those starts he came in first, the last two times by five lengths each. In late September they were approached by a horse agent asking their price for the beauty. The Mabees thought a ludicrous $5 million was too steep for anyone to buy him away from them. But the anonymous buyer passed word through the agent that the price would be met, and all training of Worldly Manner should cease. A few days later, Worldly Manner was vanned through the gates of his home track, Churchill Downs, under a horse alias. For weeks, no one knew which tycoon had put up that money. Finally word got out that the horse had been purchased by Sheikh Mohammed bin Rashid al-Maktoum and shipped overseas to Dubai to join the sheikh's Godolphin Stables.[11]

The sheikh wanted a Kentucky Derby victory badly, and to prove he could do it his way, by shipping the horses in at the last minute from Dubai. Bob Lewis heard rumor that the sheikh had twenty horses in training for the Kentucky Derby alone. "We are coming after you," the sheikh vowed to the American press. "We will win the Kentucky Derby from Dubai. Because we think our way is the right way."[12] From November to that first Saturday in May, Worldly Manner raced, but only in closed competitions against other Godolphin horses. The times he clocked remained secret.

Only two other horses garnered serious consideration leading up to the Derby. Nick Zito's horse, Stephen Got Even, began attracting interest and would wind up the favorite by the time he got to the gate. Menifee, trained by the thirty-six-year-old Kentucky native Elliot Walden, was fourth with the handicappers at odds of 7 to 1. Menifee was known for his powerful stretch run and consistency, and Hall of Famer Pat Day was onboard for the Derby.

The horse attracting the most attention that week, though, was Valhol—albeit for scandalous reasons. Valhol had run only four races in his life, with odds in his third start of an astounding 107 to 1. (He actually fared better than the handicappers expected by coming in fourth.) When Billy Patin, a thirty-six-year-old Louisiana bayou native with a narrow, doleful face and whisk-broom mustache, got hired to ride him, he considered the opportunity the chance of a lifetime because he had been so down and out. He was still in mourning for his brother K. C., also a jock, who was shot in the chest by an anonymous gunman outside a New Orleans project four years earlier. On April 10, Patin rode Valhol in the Arkansas Derby, a Kentucky Derby prep race, and the horse won by a decisive four and a half lengths. The bettors were astounded. They had sent the horse off at odds of 30 to 1. In the winner's circle, Patin asked Valhol's owner, James Jackson, if he could pluck a few gardenia blossoms from the winner's blanket so he could bring them home to put on his brother's grave in Lafayette.[13]

Not long after the horses left the track that day and Valhol and Patin posed for their picture in the winner's circle, a maintenance worker driving the tractor that raked the track spotted something lying in the dirt. It was a buzzer, a small battery wrapped with wire coils that, when pressed to a horse's neck, could send the animal rocketing across the finish line. The officials had no idea who had used the device, but they reviewed the tapes of the Arkansas Derby, and sure enough, as Patin rode Valhol out in his cooling gallop after the finish line, they saw Patin's fingers uncurl up by the horse's neck and a small black object tumble down the horse's side onto the track. The stewards called an investigation.

The allegation that Patin used a buzzer seemed bizarre for a stakes race at the end of the twentieth century. In the old days, some jockeys kept phonograph needles tucked in their boots so they could stab their horses into a final burst of furious speed at the finish. They kept a supply of nails in their mouths and spat them out after the race. Trainers said that if a jockey was so audacious as to use a buzzer in a race he would have had to have known that the device actually worked on that horse. The horse would have to have trained with a buzzer to make sure the shock caused him to bolt cleanly instead of tossing his rider and leaping for the grandstands. But those tactics had vanished from major competitions with the advent of stewards' cameras. John Passero, the track superintendent at Pimlico, remembered when he was a young man working his way up he occasionally found buzzers in the dirt at the smaller tracks, but that was only after morning workouts.[14] The trainers would school their horses with buzzers so that in the race the rider could flick a whip to the same spot that usually got the jolt, and the horse would perceive the ghost of the buzzer and take off. But in this case, the trainer, Dallas Keen, adamantly denied any knowledge of the scheme.

To make matters more dramatic around the Churchill Downs' stable leading up to the Derby, Valhol and Patin shipped to the track to await the verdict instead of biding their time in Louisiana. Patin seemed the very image of misery. "They all had a rough life," one of Patin's oldest hometown friends, jockey Tracy Hebert, told the press about the Patin family. "Obstacles in their way. Where we come from, and it's a shame to say, it's a hard road. We try to learn, but it's hard. It's not like people don't try to tell us things, but it's still hard."

On April 27, the stewards ruled that the purse money for the Arkansas Derby could be released to Valhol. The horse could stay for the Derby. Patin, though, had to go home. "Here he is, he gets a break and a shot to go to the Derby. That's every jockey's dream," Hebert said. "It's sad to see, it really is."[15] In late May, Patin, the melancholy jockey who wanted his shot to ride the Derby, perhaps too badly, was suspended from racing for five long years.

Reporters stopped by the Lukas barn only sporadically in the week leading up to the race since the trainer wasn't considered a big factor that year. Cat Thief was Lukas's best chance—at 7 to 1 odds—because he had run in the money in all ten starts of his career. He also boasted early speed, which seemed appealing since it could get him out of trouble in the Derby stampede at the starting gate. But Cat Thief hadn't had a win since October, so no one considered him a favorite.

Pat Day rode Cat Thief in the five competitions leading to the Derby but jumped ship to ride Menifee at Churchill, so Lukas booked Mike Smith to replace him. Smith had recently returned to racing after healing a broken back during a nine-month hiatus. Antley and Smith were good friends and when Antley was training and reducing down in Columbia, he saw Smith on television explaining his regimen to build up to condition. His example gave Antley extra incentive to keep to his program too and try to return even sooner than Smith.

According to the Dosage Index—the measure of speed and stamina—Lukas's other horse Charismatic didn't stand a chance in the Derby, since it was theorized that only a horse with a 4.00 or less could go the distance of a mile and a quarter. Charismatic's number was 5.22. Since 1940, only two horses, including Strike the Gold, had broken that pattern to finish first. Lukas, though, had started taking a shine to the horse in the week before the Derby. He repeatedly told reporters how much Charismatic liked the surface at Churchill Downs. He talked about how strong and resilient the horse had proved to be. Charismatic was, like Lukas, a hard worker, who thrived when asked to endure long periods of labor. Bob Lewis began feeling embarrassed by the attention Lukas was paying Charismatic in his interviews and pulled aside Cat Thief's owner, William T. Young, to apologize.[16]

Lukas did allow plenty of room to be wrong about the chestnut colt, however, and keep his reputation intact. The day before the Derby, he explained what a Charismatic victory would mean. "It will say two things," he remarked. "One is that my judge of talent is very faulty, and number two is it might just be the best training job I ever did."

That kind of relaxed commentary was unusual for Lukas and could only be explained by one factor. He had finally been chosen for induction into the Hall of Fame at Saratoga.

He had gotten the word that Tuesday. The selection community was late by about a decade, in Lukas's opinion, but they finally anointed him, and he wasn't going to turn them down. He finally belonged. Everything he owned in this world, every good happiness and pleasure he had, he owed to a horse.

Horses gave you accolades and riches and even relationships—he had met his fourth and current wife, Laura, training quarter horses—but more important, horses put fire in life. That's why he ran them. When you had a horse racing in the afternoon, you didn't want to eat lunch and your stomach turned. You went out with your friends but you couldn't hear what they were saying because you were so ratcheted up about the race.

When the horse went to the gate, you got so damn nervous your knees started to buckle. Gary Player, the professional golfer who had won $14 million over his career playing in tournaments, also owned a Storm Cat offspring. He told Lukas when the horse went into the gate for his maiden race, Player couldn't even spell his last name. He had sunk three-foot putts to win national tournaments and never even got excited, but when his horse walked into his post, Player thought his knees would buckle.[17]

When the horse went down toward the wire, you felt the rush of adrenaline. And when you won, you ran down the stairs and wanted to hug everybody in sight, perfect strangers. And you were happier than at almost any other time in your life.

Among all the racing ecstasies, Lukas believed there was nothing like the Derby. Lukas liked to tell an apocryphal story from one Derby when he tried to get into his box right before the start. Everyone was pushing and crowding, hats and julep glasses smashing together, and he couldn't even stick a leg in. In front of him, he saw another box with an old lady sitting next to an empty chair.

"Is this seat taken?" he asked her.

"No," she said. "That seat belonged to my deceased husband."

"I'm sorry to hear that," Lukas said. "But why, given how many people want to come to this event and this being such a choice seat, why wouldn't you give the ticket to one of your friends?"

"Oh, hell," she said. "They're all at the funeral."

Churchill Downs held a lottery on the Wednesday before the race to decide which slot each horse ran from in the starting gate. When the official picked a numbered pill from a container, the trainer and owner with that number got to select their post position, from inside at the rail to outside at the fence. The lower-numbered slots closest to the inside rail went first because a run from one of those gates ensured the horse would be traveling the shortest distance to victory. More horses had won the Derby from the inside—twelve horses, in fact—than from any other position. The slots out in the auxiliary gate were considered the worst. In one hundred years of Derbys, only three horses had managed to win from a slot outside gate fifteen.

Baffert picked up the six slot in the draw for Excellent Meeting so the filly was a definite to run in the Derby. Eduardo Caramori, the trainer of First American, earned a late pick. Of his limited options, he chose post sixteen. Afterward, reporters asked him why he selected that number, and he explained he had dreamt the night before that the winner would burst out of post sixteen. He hoped the dream would be prophetic and put his horse in line for victory.[18]

Out at Santa Anita, the jocks watched the drawing on the racing channel while they readied to ride. Antley was hoping for a good position, but Charismatic's name got pulled late in the process, and Lukas was forced into slot seventeen with Charismatic. All the guys started laughing. That was about as bad as you could get, a long-shot horse out in Siberia.[19] But Antley felt confident despite the kidding. He went to Vladimir Cerin's barn and told the trainer he wouldn't be able to work horses for him on Sunday as scheduled. He was going to win the Derby, he explained. He would be held up in Louisville doing interviews. "I'm sorry, Vlado," he said. "I think the press conference after the race will make me miss my flight."[20]

Later that day in Louisville, the staff at the barn of Sheikh Mohammed bin Rashid al-Maktoum made a last-minute call to the stewards. The sheikh had shipped two mounts for the Derby from Dubai—Worldly Manner and Aljabr, who were running on a shared ticket. Now the sheikh's trainer, Saeed Bin Suroor noticed Aljabr was limping and had to be pulled. All the horses from post five, where Aljabr was supposed to start, shifted over one place. That meant Caramori's colt, First American, would start from post fifteen, and Charismatic would go off from slot sixteen, the post of Caramori's winning dream.

*   *   *

The day of the Derby dawned with sparkling blue skies and sunshine wiping away any shadows. Beverly Lewis sat in their suite at the Seelbach Hotel watching the early Derby programming on television. She felt something special in the air. Penny Chenery, Secretariat's owner, appeared on a show about her champion from 1973. "Secretariat had great *charisma*," Chenery said.

"Aha, that's it," said Beverly. "Charisma. That's a clue."[21]

Antley arrived on an early flight and went to the Churchill Downs museum to kill time before the race. He bought a good-luck gift, a bar of soap embedded with a plastic horse, for his old friend Mike Smith.[22] He wandered into the museum itself. In the main exhibit hall, visitors plugged a year into a computer, and television monitors showed footage of the Derby selected. Antley listened to the winning jockeys describing their races. He felt a chill and began to cry.[23] Later he told his friend Fernando Valenzuela that the feeling he had that day that he was going to win was the same he got just one other time, when he rode Strike the Gold.

Some hours later, Antley walked into the jockeys' room. Craig Perret was in there preparing to ride Answer Lively, another long shot. Antley went over to him. Fifteen years had passed since Antley first met Perret at Monmouth, when Antley flopped into the jocks' room there as a bug boy. Now Perret was forty-eight, and Antley was a jock trying to make a comeback. Antley hugged his friend and cried. "I can't believe I got a chance back at the Derby," he said.

"Chris," Perret said, "you worked for it. Just keep your head above water."[24]

The Derby grandstand and infield flooded with spectators. At the gates the No Greater Love Ministries, a missionary group from southern Illinois, greeted spectators with a big sign that read, SMILE, JESUS LOVES YOU.[25]

"He goes to where people are hurting the most," one member told a reporter. "At the Derby, people are looking for something to feel, something to give them excitement."

In the clubhouse, Vice President Al Gore and his wife Tipper shook hands with racing fans. He was seeking the presidency in 2000, and politicians liked paying a visit to the Derby because of its sacred place in the hearts of southerners. It was a good omen, Al Gore said, that George Bush had attended the Derby right before he made his 1988 bid for the White House and won.[26] Other presidents attended the big race when in office and out. In 1952, the first time the Derby was broadcast on national television, Lyndon Baines Johnson stood in the grandstand. When Secretary of State Henry Kissinger attended in 1983 he surveyed the crowd which included Jimmy and Rosalynn Carter, George and Barbara Bush, the governor of Kentucky, John Brown, and his wife, Phyllis George Brown, and concluded that he had met more politicians at Churchill Downs than any other place he had ever been.[27]

Back in the jocks' room, Antley joined the riders attending the traditional Derby service led by the track chaplain, Dan Powell. "My prayer for you," Powell said, "is that somehow God will make his presence real to you today as you ride."[28] The clerk of scales, Ronnie Herbstreit, hollered that it was time for weigh-in. Usually the jockeys went to see the clerk of scales whenever they were ready, but on Derby Day the jockeys lined up, with their valets beside them holding their saddles. Antley wore his boots with "ANT" written on the top and the Lewises' green-and-yellow striped silks with small gold bow tie. Before he stepped on the scale, he took his saddle, pad, and Cordero's whip from his valet. He stepped up and the needle swept to 126 pounds, including Antley's 114, and stopped. Antley had lost 22 percent of himself in eight months.[29] For him the achievement was momentous, but it meant Charismatic would be carrying 11 pounds more than he did in the Lexington Stakes.

Antley walked to the paddock and saw Charismatic, with his burnt-orange coat brushed to a high sheen, for the first time. The horse had been chewing on his bit so was frothing slightly, but otherwise looked attentive and strong. Antley told the Roaches approvingly how well behaved and serene the horse seemed. After fourteen races, Charismatic had gotten over his youthful timidity and now could handle the frenzy of the Derby crowd with aplomb.

Two stalls down, Baffert, wearing his lucky suit and tie, was a nervous wreck, having tossed and turned through the early hours of the morning with nightmares about saddling General Challenge amid the paddock commotion. Back at the barn, he had tied the horse's tongue down and put on his blinkers to limit the possibility for mayhem, but the saddling had to take place in front of the crowd. General Challenge wouldn't stand still. Baffert chased him around the paddock, as a groom led him, trying to adjust the girth without setting off a tantrum.

Bob and Beverly Lewis were there in festive Derby dress. She wore a white suit and matching straw hat with a black border, and they gave Antley all their good wishes. Antley turned to Lukas, who had just walked up after escorting Mike Smith to Cat Thief's side. "We'll get it done," Antley said to the trainer, and Lukas liked that positive thinking.[30]

Lukas gave Antley a few points of instruction: At the start, don't even try to drive Charismatic into the first tier from so far outside, he said. He hoped Antley could make his way into the second tier at the start and hold there. Charismatic was the one horse, Lukas thought, who would make a half-mile or five-eighths run, so Antley's cue to unleash Charismatic's power was seeing the buildings on the backside. "When you get to the red-brick kitchen, you lay it down," Lukas said. "You get me in front at the eighth pole. I'll carry you from there."[31]

"I guarantee there has never been better weather," Al Michaels announced at the start of the ABC broadcast. "Welcome to the final Kentucky Derby of the twentieth century." The broadcasters ran through the whole nineteen-horse field and got to Charismatic last. They pointed out that of all the horses in the race, he had run most often—fourteen starts in nine months. A few decades back that would have seemed like a spare resume. Whirlaway raced twenty-three times before winning the 1941 Triple Crown. But since then, some of the best thoroughbreds had been bought and shipped overseas to enter the European or Japanese breeding mix, thus weakening the U.S. stock, and the overuse of medications had made American horses frail. Nowadays the top bred horses ran sparingly. Charismatic was made of tougher stuff, probably the Bali Babe in him coming out, but his endurance didn't impress the ABC handicappers. "Five races ago, you could have bought him for $62,500," Hank Goldberg pointed out on air. "He beat a soft field in his last stakes race. I don't think I support that." He and Al Michaels chuckled and passed Charismatic over.

Up in the steamy announcer's booth, next to Churchill Downs' twin steeples, thirty-six-year-old Luke Kruytbosch prepared to call his first Kentucky Derby. He stared at the list he'd taped to the wall and started running word associations again, as he had ten times a day for the past three days, that would help him link the names of the horses with the jockey's silk colors. Announcing races had started for Kruytbosch as a dare, back at the fairgrounds in Holbrook, Arizona, when he was in college. As a bar trick he used to imitate the announcer, and one day, he was out at the track and someone came around saying they needed a fill-in for the announcer, who was sick. Kruytbosch got a regular gig out of it, although for two years he had anxiety dreams about calling the wrong horse. He started at Churchill one week before the Derby and now he was about to describe America's most important race in real time.[32]

"Riders up," the paddock judge hollered. The grooms led the horses toward the tunnel, and the jocks vaulted onto their horses' backs—first Jerry Bailey in cerulean blue on Worldly Manner, then Gary Stevens on General Challenge, Kent Desormeaux on Excellent Meeting, and on down the line. David Flores, wearing white silks with two red stripes crossing his chest, blessed himself as he fell into line on the back of Prime Timber. The owners, trainers, grooms and hotwalkers took up the rear to follow the riders through the dark tunnel.

Out on the turf course, the University of Alabama marching band, with the white feathers of their hats flickering in the light breeze, played "My Old Kentucky Home." The crowd paused over their mint juleps and sang:

> The young folks roll on the little cabin floor
> All merry, all happy and bright;

By'n by hard times comes a knocking at the door

Then my old Kentucky home, Good-night!

The thoroughbreds with their lead ponies stepped through the tunnel into the blinding sunlight and the crowd screamed. Mike Smith wore white silks with a blue bull's eye on board Cat Thief, and Willie Martinez took his first ride on Valhol, dressed in brilliant blue silks with silver diamonds down the sleeves. There were so many horses, the line strung from one end of the grandstand to the other. Antley stared straight ahead, holding Charismatic's reins loosely as he walked by the horseshoe-shaped winner's circle on the infield used only for the Kentucky Derby victor.

The horses paraded past the final turn in the opposite direction of the race itself, then started cantering toward the backside. They turned and Antley and Charismatic made their way to post sixteen. Behind the starting gate, Dave "Moon Eyes" Shafer took hold of Charismatic's bit and another assistant starter got his flank and led him into his slot. Shafer pulled him in quickly and the other assistant starter shut the padded back gate. Shafer jumped on the pontoon against the wall of Charismatic's slot. The crowd was cheering so loudly Antley could barely hear the starter on the gate loudspeakers. Charismatic seemed to have an attack of his old skittishness and twisted his head nervously, nodding up and down. "Dave, get his ear," the starter yelled into the speaker. Charismatic hadn't settled yet and all the horses were loaded. If Charismatic didn't calm down quickly, all the other horses would start to balk too. Antley sat still, just looking straight ahead trying to infuse Charismatic with his own serenity, as Shafer grabbed Charismatic's ear and quieted him. The starter looked down the line and saw Charismatic's white nose pointing forward. He pressed the button.[33]

The gates swung open. Like all the guys down the line, Shafer lifted his right arm to show he wasn't holding the horse and his left leg so it wouldn't get smacked. Charismatic jumped fast. "Charismatic gets away quickly," the ABC announcer noted.

Adonis and Three Ring, who were against the rail on the inside, collided a few jumps out. Charismatic strode a few paces from the gate without being bothered, but to his left First American was hopping lanes. First American veered right toward him, bumping him on the flank, then ricocheted the other way, slamming into General Challenge. Excellent Meeting with Kent Desormeaux on board got pinched.

The pace was slow leading up to the first turn, so the horses galloped in a herd. Willie Martinez on Valhol was at the front, with Mike Smith on Cat Thief just outside at his neck. Antley urged Charismatic on, coming up on the outside of Stevens in maroon and gold silks on General Challenge at the turn. Prime Timber was on the other side of Stevens, and all three horses were going for an open slot in the middle of the pack. Charismatic and Prime Timber went at the same time and General Challenge got squeezed between them. Stevens's groan drifted on the wind, and they carried him four strides, caught between the horses' flanks. For a few moments, General Challenge's head was in Antley's lap and his wild eye staring up at him, as Stevens tried to rein the horse back, tugging his head to the side.[34]

Antley veered out toward the fence to get away from trouble. Behind him, a pack of five horses raced against each other and the jockeys were screaming. The whole herd slammed sideways as the horses bounced off each other. Antley could hear Gary Stevens, stuck back there in traffic, yell something to him. "Go, little buddy," he said.[35]

Antley had Charismatic in the center of the track and in the middle of the pack from the lead. Coming down the backstretch toward the far turn, Valhol still led the group with Cat Thief a half-stride behind. Charismatic was back in seventh, but out wide. Antley could see the green and white stripes of Corey Nakatani on Desert Hero inside him, racing along at the same pace.

Eugenia Antley knelt in front of her television at her home in Elloree. On top of the set was the glass decoration her beloved grandson had given her with a red rose frozen inside and filaments sparkling around it. She pressed her finger against the screen and traced her grandson's path around the oval, as she had done for every one of his races that she watched.

All the way down the backside, Antley kept nudging Charismatic, running his knuckles down the horse's neck.[36] If they slipped back for even a moment, with the track that tightly packed, they wouldn't just lose one position, they would be two or three further off. They passed the half-mile mark, the magic spot according to Lukas, but Charismatic didn't pick up the pace. His stamina seemed to have disappeared.

Desert Hero dropped back and immediately collided with another horse and was slowed. At the far turn, Charismatic started flagging. His legs began swinging. Antley went to the whip. At least, he thought, he could stay in the race a little longer if he worked the horse hard. He gave Charismatic a few strokes to wake him and then waited to see what the horse would do.

Antley was proud that he had guided Charismatic through all that mayhem to this point in the clear, but now he needed the horse to do his job. Charismatic took over.[37] With Antley hand-riding him, pushing his neck down to keep his stride long, Charismatic galloped past Craig Perret on Answer Lively. Valhol started to fall back. Then Antley passed Valhol too.

Then, strangely, at the top of the stretch, Antley found he had just Cat Thief and that black giant, Worldly Manner, in front of him. Charismatic and Antley were far off from them, about three lengths back, and those horses were neck and neck. Behind Antley a pack of horses jammed up against each other in their last sprint to the finish.

He was inching closer, tightening the space between him and the horses at the lead. By the eighth pole, Antley and Charismatic were right up against Cat Thief's tail; the white silks with the blue bull's-eye right there, close enough to touch. Antley kept grinding with Charismatic, and then he felt the surge. *Is this really happening?* he thought.[38]

*   *   *

Lukas was sitting in W. T. Young's box, hoping that Cat Thief could pull off the race they knew he had in him. When Lukas saw Cat Thief tearing around the final turn, past Worldly Manner, Lukas yelled to Young. "He hit the front!" he hollered. "Here we go!"

"C'mon, Cat Thief!" he started barking. "C'mon. C'mon, Cat Thief!"

Then he saw the horse coming on the outside, the pretty chestnut colt with the chrome on his ankles, the jock with Lewis's colors on his back. Lukas didn't know what to do. Should he jump up and down? Should he just start screaming, throw his program, what? He turned to Laura for a split second. "It's Charismatic! It's going to happen!"[39] he said. The horses stampeded by him and he strained his neck to the right, hoping to see the wire.

At the sixteenth pole, with just a hundred yards to go, Antley ran up against Cat Thief's throat, pounding for home, and Charismatic buoyed him. *A horse pulling ahead at the sixteenth pole?* Antley thought. *This never happened.* The finish line was right there, just six strides away. Antley wasn't whipping Charismatic. He looked to both sides and saw only empty track. He raised his left hand and pointed up— number one, Almighty God, who had made his dream come true, the first victory of the Triple Crown. He couldn't hear the crowd. He felt there was a tunnel around him, closing him off into a separate world that contained him, a warm glow, and this fact: He had won the Kentucky Derby. After all of that hell. The drugs and the rehab, the stone feeling of misery and the self-hatred, the starvation and the running until the bones of his knee shattered. All he could hear was his own thought: This was the hardest dream to make happen, and it was coming true.[40]

Charismatic stretched his neck, digging his hooves as deep as he could into the dirt and speared across the finish line, and Antley felt a sudden rush as Menifee galloped past. If the finish had been even a foot or two farther, he never would have won.

*   *   *

Joy ran through Lukas and he forgot himself for a moment. "He did it! He won it!" he screamed. He squeezed Laura as tightly as he could.

Bob Lewis saw Charismatic flying down the outside, pounding by all the other horses like Grant took Richmond. How could this happen?

"Have you ever seen anything like it in your life!" he yelled. "Unbelievable!" He looked out toward the track and, with his arms in the air, conducted a crescendo of joy that he could hear best of all. "Unbelievable!"

He grabbed Beverly's hand and they marched down to the winner's circle. He could feel Beverly shaking. He began to collect himself for the speech ahead. *My god*, he thought, *how do we rank here among the most selective group who have ever been involved in thoroughbred racing?* After all, they were just common folk.

Out at Hollywood Park, the jockeys clustered around the television started screaming for Antley, pumping their fists in the air. Laffit Pincay felt himself choke up. The guy had been down at the bottom. And now he was winning the greatest race there is or ever could be for a jock.

Tom Roach saw that Robyn started crying when Charismatic made the run out of the final turn. By the time he hit the wire, she was sobbing uncontrollably.

Antley rode Charismatic out of his gallop after the finish line and looked up. He let the reins go loose, put his hands on his knees and dropped his head. On television, the announcer said his name for the first time that day. "Chris Antley making his comeback off his problems in the past," Hank Goldberg remarked. "What a tremendous story he is. How he must feel today."

All the other jocks rode by Antley in the opposite direction, congratulating him. David Flores gave him a high five. Antley shot the thumbs-up to Gary Stevens. Antley patted Charismatic soundly on the neck and blew a kiss to the crowd. A track official came to lead them into the winner's circle and Antley bent down and hugged him.

Charismatic's time for the mile and a quarter was 2:03 1/5. In all 125 times the race had been run, there had been few horses so doubted. Charismatic had the third worst odds of any Kentucky Derby winner. The last winner with odds that long had run fifty-nine years ago. To people who picked the exacta (the first two horses), the trifecta (the first three) and the superfecta (the first four) that meant enormous payouts. The superfecta during Silver Charm's year, for example, paid $350 on a $1 bet. With Charismatic, the superfecta paid $24,015.

Inside the Derby winner's circle, Antley sprang from the saddle with his arms wide above his head, up into the air, and landed on the turf. He saw Bob Lewis and threw his arms around him. Lukas reached out to shake hands with Antley, and the jock leaned over and kissed the back of the trainer's hand.

Governor Paul Patton presented the silver trophy, topped with a horse draped in a ruby-studded shawl. Broadcast over the loudspeakers, Charlsie Cantey from ABC interviewed the Lewises on their win and historically large $886,200 first-place prize, then turned to Antley. How had he been able to make such a quick comeback to get to this place? she asked.

"Wayne asked me to ride," Antley said.

Everyone laughed. "As simple as that?" Cantey asked.

"I said I was open," Antley said. "When this horse arrived, my name was written all over him. The first six letters of his name are Chris A." He looked over at Charismatic's owners. "I want to thank Bob and Beverly Lewis. Nobody deserves it more than them. They've put so much into the game."

Then he turned to the grandstand. "I want to say something to my family and friends back in South Carolina," he said. "They watched me get here to this road. It was the hardest thing I ever did in my life." He hesitated and started choking up. "Miracles were made to come true and it happened today for me," he said. He nodded to the grandstand. "This is the greatest sport there is. It is the sport of kings. I'm proud to be a part of it."

Lukas patted him on the shoulder. He told Cantey how he had misjudged Charismatic more than any horse he ever worked with. He had only seen the horse's talent in the Coolmore Lexington Stakes. "There's a well-known song that goes, 'There's a chance of a lifetime in a lifetime of chance,' " Lukas said. "And we certainly took some chances with him."

Lukas's assistant, Mike Maker, took Charismatic's bridle and started leading the horse back to the barn. A drunk fan stood at the fence watching them. "That horse will never win another race," the guy yelled.

"He doesn't have to," Maker said.

At the Columbia Athletic Club, the phone started ringing. Coley Brown Jr. picked it up. "I've seen that guy," a client said. He had the TV on.

Brown hung up, and the phone rang again. It was another client. "Is that the guy on the treadmill?" she asked.

After the jocks rode back to the finish line and handed their horses off to the trainers, they tried to deal with the shock of the ride they had just endured. Gary Stevens started walking toward the jocks' room, limping down the paddock runway, but his legs cramped so badly he fell to the ground. All the jocks talked about what a brutal race it was. Three Ring got so badly bumped at the start his saddle slid up the horse's crest until John Velasquez was basically riding the horse's neck. When they came around the final turn, the saddle flew against the rail.

Antley stood in front of the reporters at the Derby press conference after the race. "I'm still kind of in awe," he said. "This was a dream, like a new beginning, for me, starting out. . . ." He recalled a conversation he had had with his father at the beginning of the year. "Dad, the Derby's coming soon, wouldn't it be neat if I could ride in it?" he said he had asked his father. He stopped relating the story to the reporters, overcome as he was by emotion, then tried again. "I'm here," he said.[41]

Jim Stone, the New Orleans native who co-owned Menifee, tried to put his best spin on the close second that his horse pulled off. "He ran a winning race," Stone said. "We just had a little bad luck. I'm a marine, for Chrissake. You lose your platoon, you still smile."[42]

A reporter asked Lukas if he had panicked when Menifee came blowing up the stretch in those final strides and almost caught Charismatic before the wire. Antley's finger had been in the air before they crossed the finish line. "If Menifee had caught us," Lukas said, "you'd be seeing that finger in a glass jar of formaldehyde today."[43]

He told reporters that he wasn't sure Charismatic could pull off a Preakness victory two weeks from then. "I think this is a Belmont horse," Lukas said. "He'll run all day."

The reporters started writing their stories. *Charismatic broke from gate sixteen* . . . and then they remembered Eduardo Caramori's dream before the Derby that the winning horse would come from gate sixteen and wrote about the eerie coincidence.

Antley went back to the jocks' room and Perret was still there packing up. Antley hadn't even won a grade-one stakes since 1997 and now he had conquered the Derby. "I can't believe it," he said. Perret gave him a hug.

"Look," Perret said, looking him in the eye, "you know you're a natural. You got yourself a new life. Take advantage of it."

"I will," Antley said.

D. Wayne Lukas went to the barn to close up shop for the day. He looked in at Charismatic. He knew the horse would eat every oat in his pail and look fat again by morning. Tomorrow Lukas would be at the stable at dawn, ready to put his horses through their paces. He had just won the Kentucky Derby but he didn't go to celebrate. Instead, he pulled into the O'Charley's. He ordered chicken tenders and told the waitress, if you can't have it ready in fifteen minutes, just tell me and I'll go.[44]

"What does it feel like to win the Kentucky Derby?" ABC field producer Natalie Jowett asked Antley in an interview the next day.

He fixed her with his electric blue eyes. "I felt the warmest feeling that I ever did," he said. "It was a feeling that if you were scared and running and crying, you went into your mother's arms and she held you. It was that feeling of comfort. And that's the kind of feeling I had three strides before the wire."

The story of that victory rolled on. Angel Cordero Jr. had watched the race from England. "I was proud of him," Cordero said. "I could see it in his face, when they had that close-up of him, he had tears in his eyes. He was looking at the sky. He had accomplished something that *shocked* him. Because he had won the Derby before, but this time it was beating something in his system, which is a disease, and come back on a claiming horse. And it was like a movie story, like a story you make in a movie. But it doesn't happen all the time.

"A thing like that comes once in a blue moon," Cordero said. "Like good horses come once in a blue moon. Good persons come once in a blue moon. That's it. Just a little taste."

TEN

THE DEVIL'S PICTURE BOOKS

In 1996, President Bill Clinton, whose mother Virginia Blythe was mad for the ponies and blackjack tables in Hot Springs, Arkansas, commissioned a study on gambling in the United States. A social fear had emerged that America was being destroyed by the proliferation of casinos and the Clinton report sought to discover how deep the damage went. Word-of-mouth reports indicated that these businesses generated only low-paying and insecure jobs and attracted drug dealing and other crimes. The nation would crumble, observers feared, if the casinos were allowed to proliferate.

That belief, while plausible, reignited a heated debate about gambling that had persisted for millennia. The definition of gambling as not just a pastime but a disease was memorialized in 1980 when the American Psychiatric Association put together its third edition of the *Diagnostic and Statistical Manual of Mental Disorders* and upgraded gambling from compulsive to pathological behavior.[1]

Fourteen years later, scientists started searching for the gambling gene, which they believed would be a variant of D-2 receptor, the genetic code linked to problem drinking and addictive behavior. Gamblers' brain waves were measured to establish the seductive high they received when placing bets, or alternately to register the low level of the gambler's intellectual processes, suggesting that the passion for gambling was simple stupidity.[2] "Based on criteria developed by the American Psychiatric Association," the Clinton report stated, "we estimate that about 2.5 million adults are pathological gamblers, and another 3 million adults should be considered problem gamblers."[3] A problem gambler was defined as anyone who lost one hundred dollars a year or more on lotteries, horses, bingo, casinos or any other game of chance.

But the report also concluded that casinos did not destroy communities as everyone feared. "Per capita rates of bankruptcy, health indicators, and violent crimes are not significantly changed," the researchers wrote about neighborhoods with casinos. "Unemployment rates, welfare outlays, and unemployment insurance in such communities decline by about one-seventh . . . Per capita income stays the same." Still they added, "There is a wide perception among community leaders that indebtedness tends to increase as does youth crime, forgery and credit card theft, domestic violence, child neglect, problem gambling, and alcohol/drug offenses."[4] The report presented no statistics to bear out those fears, only noted the perception.

But what gambling represents to people and the reality of gambling have always been distinctly different. Throughout human history, people's perceptions have shifted wildly. In classical times, gambling was considered divine, more recently it was an amusement exclusively for the upper classes, a test of bravery and daring, and on and on.

We learn in school the concept of continuity—primitive people first recognizing that an eclipse did not snuff out the sun, Columbus daring to test the earth's infinite curve. But the moment humans first embraced the idea of the gamble must have been fascinating too. At some point, anthropologists theorize, humans noticed what seemed the random nature of events and began simple games of guessing, such as how many fingers a person held behind his or her back or on which side a tossed shell would land.

Humans realized that certain events could be corralled by laying the groundwork for order, such as cultivating plants to increase the likelihood of a yield, but many of life's experiences remained in a netherworld of disorder. And perhaps whatever power caused the rain to fall or an animal to get sick and die might dictate through the language of tossed sticks or cubes which person should get a piece of land or a concubine.

The first relics of gambling date from 6000 B.C., when people in Africa, Asia, and North and South America played with gaming sticks. Two thousand years later, Egyptians crafted astragal, flat pieces of ankle bone from sheep or antelope, as the first dice. At that point, there was no distinction between gambling and divination; the fall of the sticks or astragal expressed the precise will of the gods.

In fact, the gods themselves—Greek, Roman, Scandinavian, and Indian—were said to appeal to chance to decide the most crucial issues of creation, thus making chance some kind of ultimate power above and beyond the deities. After Zeus overthrew his father, Cronus, he sat down for a dice game with his brothers, Poseidon and Hades, to decide which of them would become the supreme ruler. Zeus won and ascended to the top of Mount Olympus. In another auspicious gamble, Mercury won one-seventieth of the Moon's glow at a gaming table. With that light, Mercury created five new days, which were added to those previously marked off in the calendar to make 365. The extra days commemorated to the gods' birthdays. In Scandinavian mythology, the land of Norway was created when two kings played dice to set the borders.

The Greeks were said to be addicted to gambling, but the Romans raised the enterprise to excess. Their games provided entertainment and, with their *audax sponsio*, a crucial test of character. The first lotteries are believed to have been invented by Roman emperors as a form of party favor. They doled out prizes to their delighted guests in ever more random ways. Augustus Caesar liked to cover each prize in fabric to disguise its value. Nero upped the stakes by offering concubines and even villas.

Surely the most eccentric lottery practitioner was the emperor Heliogabalus, who ruled for just four chaotic years from A.D. 218 to 222. He offered winnings of dead dogs, flies and ostriches to nobles at his feasts.

Historians like to say that this romance with chance was a sign of ignorance. The Greeks might be sophisticated at describing the universe in geometric terms but their numerical system was unwieldy. Writing and calculating with numbers did not become widespread until the Renaissance. Scholars argue that early societies were therefore more inclined to see the outcome of wagers as divine intervention, sifting the blessed from the cursed because they had no mathematical description of odds. But intellectuals of the fourth century B.C., such as Aristotle and Epicurus, were interested in chance as its own phenomenon, without religious overtones. Aristotle saw the outcome of events to be the result of coincidental cause—the vectors of all people intersecting at moments of randomness.

Cicero, writing in *De Divinatoire* in 44 B.C., thought there was no reason that those events could not be foreseen. "I am aware of no people, however refined and learned or however savage and ignorant," he wrote, "which does not think that signs are given of future events and that certain persons can recognize those signs and foretell events before they occur."[5]

The first debates about gambling as a social issue cropped up in the first millennium. Gambling was the domain of the rich, and lower classes were prevented from playing. The Roman emperor Claudius redesigned his carriage so he could play dice as he traveled, and wrote a book called *How to Win at Dice*, which unfortunately did not survive.[6] On one throw of the dice, Nero famously wagered the equivalent of fifty thousand dollars and yet laborers were discouraged from any minor bet.

In the eleventh century, bishops saw a master plot in the spread of gambling. The clergy failed to evangelize with sufficient gusto because they spent so much time betting, so their superiors tried to shut wagering down. That fight continued for centuries. In Italy and France, priests and monks were not allowed to gamble because they regularly absconded with church funds to continue their games.

The idea that gambling distracted from more serious pursuits persisted for centuries. In 1388, the British king Richard II ruled that servants and laborers could no longer play dice or other betting games. Instead, he proposed, they should hone their archery skills. Up through the mid-seventeenth century, every antigambling law in Britain insisted on that specific replacement activity.[7]

For gambling's critics, dice were bad enough, but the real scourge on mankind were cards. The first cards are said to have been created in China to amuse concubines during their long hours of tedious waiting. Some scholars say cards were originally designed as ghosts of Chinese paper money, others as printed depictions of the images from chess. By the twelfth century, cards arrived in Italy and were known as *naibs*, a word derived from the Arabic term for prophet or predict, because they were used to foretell the future. The four suits represented east, west, north and south, the religious order of the universe. Their use spread through Europe, mainly because explorers like Marco Polo obsessively played card games during their long journeys and infected whole cultures with card fever wherever they landed.

In the late fourteenth century, the symbols on the cards were Christianized. The newly introduced suit of hearts, for example, represented the church. The pack of seventy-eight tarot cards was pared down to just fifty-two. Besides the loss of the knight cards, twenty-two trump cards were abandoned, leaving only the fool, or joker. The editing of the wild cards demonstrated an attempt to tame the chaos of the card system, since the jokers triggered random events in a game.[8] With them gone, a game proceeded according to a clearly defined hierarchy and order.

From that era on, there was a fierce struggle between the masses who loved their cards and religious and political institutions that wanted to quash the interest. Cards were considered dangerous not just because they distracted from other work, but because they mocked the whole idea of paid labor. Fortunes could be moved from one hand to another without anyone working. In England and France in the late fourteenth century, working-class people were only allowed to play cards on the weekends. In the early fifteenth century, factories began manufacturing cards, and St. Bernadine, the patron saint of Italy and advertising, was so horrified by their ubiquity, he coaxed the citizens of Bologna to throw theirs on a bonfire in the marketplace. Britain was so mad for cards by the early 1500s, Henry VIII passed an edict that the working class could only gamble on Christmas.

The first lottery to raise money for a social good was held in Bruges, Belgium, in 1466, to raise funds for the poor. Within a half century, King Francis I opened lottery offices throughout France to generate government money. In 1569, Queen Elizabeth of England worried that the people living in the Cinque Ports on the southeast coast might revolt if she didn't repair their harbors by winter; she launched a lottery with prizes of cash and jewels to fund the project.[9] Eventually Britain relied on lotteries for many public works, such as the British Museum's first collection in 1753 and London's waterlines. In 1793, a special act of Parliament authorized a lottery to fund the building of Westminster Bridge, and more than 125,000 tickets were sold.

Louis XIV brought an almost Roman passion for gambling to the second half of the seventeenth century. His Versailles became known as *ce tripot*, the gambling den, and he opened casinos all over the country.[10] In private games, players placed outrageously extravagant bets in hopes they would become the talk of society. The goal was to show honor through an indifference to wealth; not necessarily, or even ideally, to win. Wealthy parents hired "gaming masters" to teach their children card games and other amusements of chance. A ripple effect of this fad was that it empowered women, who could win their own money gambling.

It wouldn't be too big of a stretch to say America was founded on gambling. Christopher Columbus, who took a chance with his theory of the earth's curvature, played cards on his 1492 voyage to pass the time. A British lottery in 1607 provided the funds to establish the Jamestown Colony, with the ticket purchasers seen as noble patriots.[11] Five years later, James I approved a lottery for English colonists in Virginia, and during the Revolutionary War they used this method to gather military funds. Some $5 million was supposedly spent on the first lottery, and George Washington allegedly bought the first ticket. He also ran a lottery to fund the building of roads westward from Virginia.[12]

In 1655, New Amsterdam, later New York, held a lottery to raise money for the poor, and residents were regularly enticed to take part in national raffles offering Bibles as prizes. In 1722, the Massachusetts courts agreed to let Harvard College hold two fund-raising lotteries, and Columbia and Williams soon followed suit.[13]

Italians invented lotto, a bingo game, in the eighteenth century, and the pastime swept quickly through the United States. Roulette followed not long after. The paddleboats launched in 1811 that plied the waters from New Orleans to Louisville carried legions of professional gamblers hoping to find a rube, and by the end of the nineteenth century, two thousand paddle-wheel steamers were running that route. In the same era, casino owners came up with the ingenius notion of ejecting clocks from their premises to lull gamblers into a feeling that they existed in a kind of seamless eternity of chance.[14]

In the early nineteenth century, gambling's reputation shifted from something that simply wasted time to something socially and essentially evil. Governments feared that people would not pay taxes because they had bankrupted themselves at the gaming tables. In Europe and the upper colonies, cards themselves were viewed as sinister objects. People refused to have a deck in their homes and banned playing on Sundays and holy days. Puritans called cards the Devil's Picture Books. Ships' captains forbade them, and miners could not carry them into pits because they brought bad luck. By 1875, twenty-six states passed laws to abolish lotteries. Louisiana held on for almost two decades, but then such deep corruption was discovered that lotteries were abolished nationally.

In the last quarter of the nineteenth century, gambling became mechanized, standardized. In Welsh Harp at Hendon, London, a greyhound racing enthusiast rigged a mechanized rabbit to lure dogs along an insatiable quest.[15] The Woolley Card company introduced a deck with numbers clearly printed in the corners and standardized backs so that a player with a quick memory could not cheat.[16] In 1865, a French book-maker named M. Pierre Oller invented pari-mutuel betting, which com-bined all the bets on a horse race and divided that total into separate payoffs for a win. Eight years later a New Zealander named Ekberg devised the totalisor—an albatross of a machine that calculated those numbers automatically. With such precision added to the mix, it wasn't long before governments realized they could derive some benefit from the people's passion for playing the horses. The year after Ekberg crafted his machine, the French government began to take a 7 percent cut off the top of all its nation's horse wagering—4 percent to the tracks for expenses and profit, 2 percent to charities, and 1 percent to horse-breeding research. The first coin-operated gambling machines appeared in that era, and the expanding train systems throughout the world meant more working-class people could be ferried to the racetracks.

The first efforts to truly understand the mechanics of chance began in the mid-fifteenth century. As Italy moved into the era of mercantile cap-italism, entrepreneurs became interested in calculating how likely an event was to occur for the purposes of insuring industry: How much could one depend on a particular ship coming into harbor, for example; or what were the chances that fire would take a storage house. In coun-terpoint to that desire for a rational description of coincidence, the most comprehensive work on the divinatory properties of cards was published around that time too—by Francesco Mariolini in Venice—thus contin-uing the battle over whether chance was a mathematical probability or a divine act.

Gerolamo Cardano, an algebraist and avid dice player, created for-mulas to predict mathematically the likelihood of an event occurring in a closed set of options. In 1550, he wrote *Liber de Ludo Alea* (Book on Games of Chance), in which he stated that each face of the die should come up on top once every six throws. This formed the first kernel of a more formal probability theory. Despite the cleanliness of Cardano's logic, he made room for mysticism. He explained that the reason such regularity did not occur in, say, 100 tosses of the dice was because of personal appeals to luck.

The tension between Cardano's brilliant mathematical career and his belief in such interventions as dreams, charms, angels, and palmistry continued throughout his life. In 1570, he was imprisoned for calculating the horoscope of Jesus. A few years later, he was forgiven when the Pope hired him as an official astrologer.[17]

In the seventeenth century, a French mathematician, Blaise Pascal, invented the roulette wheel while on a retreat in a monastery. He never imagined the machine as a game of chance, but a model for testing probabilities. Pascal had begun expressing sophisticated geometric theorems at age twelve and soon was embraced by the most important mathematicians of his time. But at age twenty-seven, he fell ill and believed his sickness to be punishment for his interest in numerical gymnastics. He gave himself to God.[18]

During the ensuing months, he strayed back to the rational arts, inventing the hydraulic press and corresponding with Pierre de Fermat about probability theory. But he felt reprimanded again when the horses pulling his carriage lunged through the parapets of a bridge and fell to their deaths. He would have followed those beasts if the carriage tethers had not broken at the last possible moment. He wrote the fateful story on parchment and carried it in his breast pocket as a reminder of God's dominion over events.

As a rational understanding of gambling developed throughout the seventeenth century, the amusement became less palatable to religious institutions. The Reformed Church saw gambling as directly antagonistic to hard work, and sacrilegious in that bettors would frequently seek God's intervention in a game. This was the first absolute break between gambling and religious beliefs. Up until that time, players almost universally believed that the author of any game of chance was a divine force. In France in 1634, the book *Le Passtempts de la Fortune des Rez*, which explained the supernatural nature of cards, became extremely popular, suggesting that the church's rejection of cards did not necessarily divest them of spiritual meaning, but relegated them to the occult.

Two of the great thinkers of the eighteenth century concurred that what appeared to be chance was merely a plan so grand that mere mortals could not perceive the order or path. In the early 1730s, the English poet Alexander Pope wrote in his *An Essay on Man:*

> All Nature is but Art, unknown to thee;
> All Chance, Direction which thou canst not see;
> All Discord, Harmony not understood.[19]

Voltaire believed that uncertainty was a weakness of our own minds, not a true perception of the state of the world. Writing in the eighteenth century, he declared: "But there is no such thing as chance. Everything is either a test or a punishment, a reward or a precaution."[20]

In 1812, Pierre-Simon de LaPlace, who entered Caen University to study theology in his journey to the priesthood, abandoned that study to investigate mathematics and physics. He published *Analytic Theory of Probabilities*, an assessment of chance that calculated the probability of many random events occurring simultaneously. This was the first effort to create an equation to explain the likelihood of life's adventures tangling together at once.[21]

A gambler must make these sorts of grand calculations with every card played and horse selected, and yet their divinatory achievements wash away with time. The gambler only has his or her triumphant anecdotes to pass along from marveling generation to generation. Like the tales of a momentous night in a Broadway theater many decades ago, the mark of the gambling moment exists only in an old program. For the horse racer, the evidence of the ecstatic victory is the statistic and the photograph of the winner's circle, always identically arranged with the horse and jockey on one side and the cluster of owners, trainers, and kin gathered around the sunlike silver platter given as an award.

Given the fleeting nature of the big gamble, it is meaningful to appreciate for a moment the life of John W. Gates, the patron saint of American gambling, who embodied all the contradictions, hypocrisies, joys and defeats of wagering and yet whose life story got shuffled back into history's deck.

Gates came into his own around the turn of the twentieth century, at a time when the nation harbored a love/hate obsession with gambling. People adored cards and horse races, but burgeoning organizations sought to halt the stampede toward wayward behavior; in 1890, the coalition for Nonconformist Protestant Churches launched the National Anti-Gambling League (NAGL), the first anti-gambling organization in the United States.

And around that time, two men sat at a table in the Grand Pacific Hotel in Chicago, staring intently at two small sugar cubes on a table between them. Both were stout fellows, dressed in Wall Street suits, who often whiled away the last working hours of the day in the bar playing poker. On this day, every now and again, they scratched a mark on a sheet of paper. The sugar cubes had been moistened with water. When a fly descended to lick the sweetness, the men marked the calculations— one thousand dollars for each landing. The man with the winning cube got the difference from the loser.[22]

One of the players was John Drake, the playboy son of the Illinois governor and a financial wizard who advised American companies. The other gamer was John W. Gates, otherwise known to his eternal disdain as Bet a Million Gates. He would have preferred to claim fame for his business achievements, as the man who rose to the heights of the steel industry from a prosy beginning in a small Midwestern hamlet. But his name usually made the papers for his wagering.

At age twenty-one, he had traveled to Texas to preach to the ranchers that their salvation lay in a new material called barbed wire. In the wild western town of San Antonio he devised an ingenious performance to pitch his product. No steer, he told the townspeople, could break through a fence constructed of the new material, and he would stake money on it. He was just a young salesman then, a drummer trying to revolutionize the thinking of a skeptical citizenry in a state where property lines existed in vague memory and cattle was corralled by herders on horseback.

Gates was making thirty dollars a month then, which he invested in fashion—a gray bowler, long black coat and snug checked pants.[23] He added flash with a gold chain and cameo ring. He held his rodeo right in the town plaza. "Gentlemen, bring on your steers," he crowed. "Bring on the cattle on a thousand hills. This is the finest fencing in the world, light as air, stronger than whiskey, cheaper than dirt, all steel and a yard wide. The cattle ain't born that can get through it. Bring on your steers, gentlemen."[24]

Of course, the show was rigged with some of the meanest-looking but sweetest-tempered cattle Gates could find. The animals barely flinched as the herdsmen raced right toward them brandishing fire. But the show convinced the crowd that barbed wire would save their lives. The ranchers ordered so much of the stuff that Gates could barely fill the requests. When the panic of 1873 hit, fencing proved more lucrative than steel since no one could afford the enormous capital to build more railroad lines, but everyone needed this new method of penning their animals.

"The cost of fences nearly equals the national debt," the U.S. Department of Agriculture reported at the time. "It has the same value as all farm animals in the U.S. For every dollar invested in farm animals, a dollar must be invested in fencing."[25]

This barbed-wire revolution had its ill effects. According to Gates's biographers, Lloyd Wendt and Herman Kogan, barbed-wire fencing nearly tore apart Texas with the land disputes it inspired and horses it maimed. "I've had nothing but trouble since I strung my fence," J. L. Vaughan, a Coleman City rancher, complained. "I wish that the man who invented barbed wire had it all wound around him in a ball and the ball rolled straight to hell."[26]

The man who sold Texas on barbed wire did not go to hell, although he withstood a little capitalist purgatory. Gates fought with his employer, Isaac L. Ellwood, for partnership in the barbed-wire business. Ellwood refused him. Gates started his own enterprise, wrangled over patents, and eventually forced Ellwood to team up again. He made a fortune, moved on to Wall Street, and tangled with J. P. Morgan. Through it all, Gates remained one of the great speculators and consolidators in U.S. history.

At the turn of the century nearly everyone was gambling one way or another. "The business of commission houses swelled beyond all precedent," wrote Edmund Clarence Stedman in the midst of the bull market from 1897 to 1902, "and weary clerks toiled to midnight adjusting the accounts of lawyers, grocers, physicians, waiters, clergymen and chorus singers who were learning to acquire wealth without labor. From every lip dropped stories of fortunes gained in a week by this or that lucky stroke. Florists, jewelers, perfumers, restauranteurs, and modistes rejoiced in the collateral prosperity secured them by the boom in stocks."[27]

Through all his business deals and stock trades, Gates never abandoned his love for amusement gambling. He played poker for a hundred dollars a point, and once famously bet on the raindrops racing down a train window on a business trip between Chicago and Pittsburgh. By the end of his journey, Gates had won twenty-two thousand dollars from his friend and partner, Drake. "Good omen," he is said to have intoned.[28]

Gates's biographers hypothesized that gambling, which began for Gates as a teenager hanging around the railyard near his home, was merely the entertainment of a man with little inner life on which to fall back. He prided himself on having read just one book in his life. A brief interest in subsidizing theater productions left him bored.

But he was endlessly fascinated with chance and would frequently note that "Life is a gamble," whether the bettor was the farmer hoping for a season of gentle sun and ample rains or a man setting off on a train ride unsure that he would ever arrive at his destination. The fact that Gates lived into his later years must have seemed the biggest game of chance of them all. His two older brothers died when he was still a child living in Turner's Junction—one brother killed in the Civil War, the other murdered while on a revitalizing trip out West. On that journey, Gilbert Gates befriended a traveling showman named Alexander Jester and invited him on board his covered wagon. When Gilbert turned up dead, Gates's father, Asel, suspected Jester was the killer and spent years trying to track him down. John Gates never gave up the pursuit, and almost thirty years later his investigators located Jester in Oklahoma. Gates brought him to trial. Unfortunately, there was not enough firm evidence against Jester, and he was acquitted at age eighty.[29]

Gilbert's murder transformed Gates's mother, Mary, from a religious woman, the loudest God-praiser in the Methodist Church each Sunday, to a perpetually pious penitent. She had chanted Scripture as she gave birth to Gates, but her faith went still deeper after her older son's murder. She insisted that John, her only living son, throw himself into religion with a fervor equal to her own. For a time, he did. But then one day he was accused of stealing pennies out of the collection basket and was kicked out of Sunday school. His fury at being falsely accused of such a petty theft drove him from the church almost to his last day.[30]

Gambling had been the one thing Gates's father—a taut, severe farmer—most abhorred. As an older man, John Gates would recall his terror when his father caught him in a poker game in the barn. As a Wall Street tycoon, Gates frequently passed on the reprimands to the next generation, lecturing his favorite newspaper boy on the evils of partaking in dice games.

Gates's *audax sponsio* were legendary. He once lost $375,000 on a single day at the track in Saratoga, and in the evening parted with another $150,000 on the card game faro. August Belmont, then head of the Jockey Club, admonished Gates. "Mr. Gates, we wish you would curtail your betting," he wrote in a letter. "Your activities could well result in restrictive legislation. How can we convince anyone the races are honest if you bet such large sums? Why don't you limit your bets to $10,000?"

"Ah, that's not my way of betting," Gates replied. "I can lose $10,000 without being hurt. I think no man should bet unless he's sure he's right. And when he's sure he's right he should be willing to bet every dollar he owns. That's the way I bet. For me there's no fun in betting just a few thousand. I want to lay down enough to hurt the other fellow if he loses, and enough to hurt me if I lose."[31] Gambling was a way to clarify one's beliefs and stake in choosing them.

Before John Gates's life teeters to its final curtain at his funeral in the ballroom of New York's Plaza Hotel, with the Metropolitan Opera Symphony serenading his memory into oblivion, we should pause for a moment in the verdant countryside of Goodwood, England. In the summer of 1900, Gates teamed up with Drake to buy a stable of horses and run them in England. At the time, American tracks were dying because of restrictive laws and the agitation of puritanical groups, so the only real action for horse enthusiasts in the States was overseas. Money was no object to Gates and Drake so they hired the preeminent American horse trainer Enoch Wishard to run the barn and the famous brother jockeys Lester and Johnny Rieff from Indiana to ride the steeds.

One of the most prestigious races in England was the Goodwood Cup, and Gates planned to compete. He originally told the press that he would not be putting money on his own horse, Royal Flush. Instead, he would back the colt Americus. With that, Royal Flush's odds went to forty to one. But Wishard had apparently been working Royal Flush hard, turning the lackadaisical two-year-old into a runner. In time trials two days before the race, the colt clocked great speed. On the sly, Gates bet seventy thousand dollars on Royal Flush, dispersing the money to many bookmakers just before the start time so no one would perceive his change of course and deflate his odds.

Heading to the gate, fourteen-year-old Johnny Rieff, as usual, cradled a cat and stroked its back three times for luck.[32] When he reached his post position, he handed the cat over to an official. The race went off and Royal Flush finished first. Other bettors had gotten wise to the run of last-minute wagering on Royal Flush and followed Gates to the pool, so the odds were pushed down to a less thrilling five and a half to one. And indeed, there was later grumbling about whether or not Wishard strapped his animals with electric belts and fed them doped cocoa.

But over there on the lawn, Gates, who favored diamonds on his suspenders and had just won $600,000, grabbed his wife, Dellora. He took her in his arms and waltzed with her in front of the chilly British crowd who hated the new American invasion. There could be, for John

and Dellora Gates, despite the redundancy of their fortune and the be-
trayals in their personal life, moments of high ecstasy.

In December 1909, just two years before Gates finally succumbed to
the ravages of illness, he was invited to the Methodist Church of South
Texas in Port Arthur to address a conference of ministers. Gates had actually founded the town and was a hero to the people there. The clergy left
it up to Gates to pick the topic, and he chose "The Evils of Gambling."[33]

"Do not gamble," he admonished the congregation. "Don't bet on
horses. Don't play poker, faro, bridge, whist or any other game with the
Devil's pasteboards. Don't speculate in the stock market. Don't shoot
dice. Stock speculation is only a bunco game for the poor man. Riches
are more a curse than a blessing. Good, honest labor is the only way to
achieve real lasting success. Put your money in a farm, and nurse it
legitimately." We have no way of knowing whether Gates experienced a
change of heart in his later years or was simply trying to run up the odds
on gambling for his own personal payout.

What Gates represents depends greatly upon what era you use as a
prism to view him. If his life had begun before the birth of Christ, he
would have been considered a man in regular communication with the
divine. If he had lived during the Roman Empire, he would have been
thought a noble man for his courageous *audax sponsio* wagers. As a visitor
to Versailles, he would have been honored for his indifference to wealth;
during the Enlightenment, he would have seemed "an empty space
within the discourse of reason." In fin de siècle Britain, a man with a
disease caused by the nervous tensions of the modern era.

In his own time, he was regarded as a working-class striver with
neither the emotional nor intellectual resources to amuse himself with
anything but twirling roulette wheels, cards, and the running of beasts.
He was also considered exactly the sort of insatiable speculator who
sucked the wealth out of the nation for his own enjoyment but, in so
doing, financed many forward-thinking industries, and thus set the country on its path to greatness.

If Gates's lifespan had stretched along the timeline to 1928, when
Sigmund Freud penned his essay on gambling as a psychological theater,

Dostoevsky and Parricide, Gates would have learned that his ipso facto Oedipus complex filled him with such guilt that there was nothing for him to do but punish himself with continual losses. Gates frustrated his own impulses to self-flagellation, however, since he ended life with his fortune of $90 million intact.

Out in his San Francisco workshop in 1895, an American mechanic named Charley Fey crafted a coin-operated machine called the Liberty Bell. The player pulled a lever on one side to set a series of wheels spinning, and if the symbols came up in a row, the player won the coins gleaned from previous players. If they lost, the money continued to collect, and Fey set the licenses so he would get one-half of all profits. For a time, the machine entranced the pioneers of the westward migration. After a subsequent phase of disenchantment, they began calling the slot machine the one-arm bandit.

It had been many years since a great thinker weighed in on the issues of chance and luck, but then on December 4, 1926, in a letter to Max Bohr, Albert Einstein, who had looked at the universe from every angle, from the micro to the macro, made his declaration: "I am convinced that He does not play dice."

In 1942, Americans finally learned what seems to be the truth of how the horrific Chicago fire of 1871 ignited. When Louis M. Cohn died at the ripe old age of eighty-nine, one of his friends revealed that Cohn had been one of several neighborhood boys, including the son of the famous Mrs. O'Leary, who regularly played craps in Mrs. O'Leary's hayloft. Mrs. O'Leary hated gambling and chased the boys out whenever she found them there. That particular October night in 1871, she found them gambling, and as she shooed them away, a boy kicked over a lantern. During his long life, Cohn regularly admitted to his role in the conflagration, at least among friends.

After his death *Chicago Tribune* reporter Anthony DeBartolo learned of the confession and looked into the matter. He found the claim credible because of the proximity of Cohn's home to the O'Leary barn and Cohn's age at the time. It was also not beyond reason to believe that nine-year-old James O'Leary might have been running a gambling racket. "James grew up to be Big Jim O'Leary, a notorious gambler and pioneer off-track betting operator," wrote DeBartolo. "In his DuPage County OTB parlor, he took bets on races run at five tracks. His Long Beach, Ind.–based OTB, meanwhile, had barbed wire, armed guards, vicious canines and secret tunnels."[34] Everyone had blamed the cow for almost three-quarters of a century. The cow, as it turned out, was innocent. Gambling, or depending on your perspective—intolerance to gambling—was to blame.

Down in Louisville, Kentucky, the first Gamblers Anonymous was founded in 1948, and within thirteen years there were twenty-three branches in cities across the country.[35] By then, the group estimated that there were two million addicts losing $20 billion a year. "No matter what theory of handicapping may seem most plausible," wrote expert bettor Tom Ainslie in his *Complete Guide to Thoroughbred Racing*, "the handicapper will be attempting to predict the future by interpreting past events of uncertain character and inexact significance. Yet survival at the track will demand predictions of considerable accuracy."[36]

ELEVEN

THE PREAKNESS

Within hours of the Kentucky Derby, the trainers, owners, handicappers, and turf writers began to put Charismatic's fluke victory into context. It was shocking, of course, but in the 125-year history of that race, there had been two other comparably shocking flukes—Donerail in 1913 and Gallahadion in 1940, who ran at staggering odds to win the most coveted prize in American racing. So, the reasoning went, a horse that seemed to have no hope, could, in the right situation, stand a 2 percent chance of winning. It could happen with odds of 50 to 1.

All the excuses for why the favored horses didn't win the Derby came out at the annual Alibi Breakfast where owners and trainers gathered on the Thursday morning before the Preakness. The breakfast held at the Pimlico Race Course in Baltimore, Maryland, has been a tradition since the 1930s. Derby owners and trainers gathered to swap sad stories of why they had been defeated at Churchill and why their horses would surely win the second race of the Triple Crown series the next day. In 1999, everyone used the excuse that the mayhem on the track had slowed their champions down. The horses that should have won—Worldly

Manner or Excellent Meeting or Menifee—had been slammed, pinned, crushed together, making the Derby more like a bar brawl than a contest of speed and stamina. Bob Baffert, in particular, felt humiliated that with a stable full of highly rated mounts he hadn't made it to the winner's circle. His Prime Timber came in fourth, Excellent Meeting fifth, and General Challenge eleventh. "We just don't know how to act," he said. "We're sort of lost souls. We didn't have any luck. There were just too many horses and so much traffic."[1]

Everybody at the breakfast agreed that if the Derby had been orderly, if the horses stayed in their slots until they were far enough ahead to change lanes, if the pace had been quick enough to thin out the competition in the first furlong, then the Lukas claimer never would have won. Charismatic's improbable victory came down to the fact that Antley found a relatively clean path wire to wire. He had what they call in racing a "dream trip."

The Roaches and the Lewises thought that theory was ludicrous. Not only had Charismatic proved he was the best horse, they thought, but his hope in the Preakness was brewed into his very blood. His sire, Summer Squall, won the Preakness in 1990, clocking the second fastest time in the race's history. "He was a five o'clock Saturday afternoon horse," his owner, Cot Campbell, said, referring to the witching hour for the competitions with high purses. "I adored him. If he had been a human being he would have been Spencer Tracy." The horse knew how to run alone and in company. In one race, he managed to worm his way through a pack of stampeding horses so easily he "popped out of the pack like a seed out of a grape," Campbell said.[2]

Angel Cordero Jr., a jockey who had spent some three decades hovering on horses' backs, saw in Charismatic an athlete who had just begun to bloom. "To win the Kentucky Derby, you have to have some ability," Cordero said. "That Charismatic ran as a claimer doesn't shock me because a lot of horses are like people—they're late developers. Some people are assholes when they're young. You don't see them for five, ten years. Then you see them and you expect to see the same asshole, and it's a different person. Horses are the same. We ask and expect a lot from horses young, and when they don't bring it to you, you feel down on them. And then time hits them, and they mature like people."[3]

The trainers other than Lukas didn't believe Charismatic had ripened. They felt sure enough that Charismatic would lose that a record nine who had entered the Derby paid the twenty-thousand-dollar fee to go on to the Preakness. Three new horses—Badge, Patience Game, and Torrid Sand—would join them. Tom Keyser, the racing reporter for the *Baltimore Sun*, described the 1999 Preakness as "the rematch race for settling scores after the Kentucky Derby that didn't settle anything."

In the late nineteenth century, the Pimlico Race Course was one of the most stylish entertainment centers in America, but its fortunes had reversed over one hundred years. The Belvedere neighborhood surrounding Pimlico fell into poverty and violence and now the track was an urban fortress. Guards minded the gates, discouraging anyone from walking the sidewalk from the backside to the grandstand, even in broad daylight.

Pimlico opened on October 25, 1870, making it America's second oldest track after Saratoga. The Maryland governor Oden Bowie, a mustachioed lieutenant in the Mexican War and a visionary builder of the Baltimore-Potomac railroad line, was also a farmer and racing enthusiast. Just after the 1868 racing season at Saratoga he attended a dinner at Saratoga's Union Hotel, hosted by socialite Milton Sanford, who proposed that the men in attendance nominate entrants for a new race. The competition, called the Dinner Party Sweepstakes, would be held in two years at an undetermined location with a nomination fee of one thousand dollars. Representatives of Jerome Park racetrack in New York immediately piped up that they would contribute an extra five thousand dollars to the purse if the race were held at their facility. Not to be outdone, Bowie stood to give a rousing speech on equine virtues, promising fifteen thousand dollars for the purse if the race were held in Maryland and pledging a world-class track for the running. The gathered crowd thrilled at his ambition and daring. Unfortunately, Bowie didn't have a racetrack of that calibre back home.

The people of Maryland loved the ponies, however, so he knew he wouldn't have difficulty raising the funds to build a stately racecourse. The Maryland Jockey Club had started all the way back in 1743 to organize competitions and claimed George Washington as a member. Maryland had only interrupted its racing schedule once in 125 years, around the time of the Revolutionary War, when crowds gathered for the autumn meet of 1775 but were turned away on recommendation of Congress "in consequence of a report upon the state of the country," and everyone "quietly returned to their homes."[4] As soon as the British were vanquished, horses returned to the Maryland starting tapes.

With Bowie's promise to the Saratoga revelers made, he hustled back home to find a suitable venue for the track. He discovered a plowed oval on a high plateau outside Baltimore, well situated to serve not only the racing enthusiasts from Maryland's farm country but the elite of Washington, D.C. An Englishman from the neighborhood of Old Ben Pimlico's tavern in London had hosted some racing on the same spot twenty years earlier, and the course could be embellished for this new grander use. Bowie bought the land, and by 1870 Pimlico Race Course was ready for the first running of the Dinner Party Stakes, as promised.

The yellow clubhouse Bowie built was tiered like a wedding cake and accented with white trim and green shutters. A weather vane with jockey and rider swiveled on the cupola roof. A porch wrapped around the entire second story and spectators with a little luck and long-term reservations could lunch there on Preakness Day for a perfect view of the finish line. Most spectators watched from the lawn, the violet grandstands, or a small mound in the infield, which earned Pimlico the nickname Old Hilltop.

Bowie's term ended in 1872, and a year later, presumably suffering from the diminished stimulation of civilian life he launched the Preakness as the kickoff event for a new spring season. Bowie named the May 23 race after the horse that won the first Dinner Party Stakes. In the weeks leading up to the first Preakness, the Baltimore papers carried front-page articles promoting the race, and a crowd of twelve thousand gathered at the track that steamy afternoon to watch. A horse named Survivor won by ten lengths, the longest winning span in the history of the race right through 1999.

The race continued to be a major event for many years, but then, toward the end of the nineteenth century, Pimlico fell on hard times, largely due to competition from nearby tracks. The Preakness moved to Morris Park, New York, for one year, and then for fifteen years to the Gravesend track in Brooklyn, New York. The Preakness did not return to Pimlico until 1909.

Meanwhile, the horse Preakness raced through his eight-year-old year, then shipped overseas to stand as a stud for the Duke of Hamilton in England. Allegedly he became more ornery as he aged, and the duke grew even more vicious. In a rage one day at the horse's impertinence, the Duke of Hamilton took a gun and shot Preakness dead. As the official Pimlico history notes, not only did Preakness become the namesake of the race that became the second jewel in the American Triple Crown, the horse left another legacy. In response to his death, the English citizenry horrified by such brutality on the part of the supposed "nobleman," rebelled. Their protest led to new laws on the handling of animals that stand in the books to this day.[5]

Many memorable moments unfolded at Pimlico. On October 24, 1877, the House of Representatives adjourned so that all its members could watch a day of races with the nation's superstar horses. In 1938, with the hilltop leveled for viewing, Seabiscuit beat War Admiral on the dirt in their famous match up, and in 1951, the track hosted the first nationally televised horse race.

The ashes of several legendary Maryland residents swirled in the air on the final stretch and finish line—those of the musician Percy L. Barry, trainer Dillon Grey, and jockey Willie Doyle. The Italian auto driver Emmanuele Cedrino met his maker there in 1908 when he attempted to break the speed record for the mile. He shattered the time barrier, taking the course in 0:51, but as he drove in his victory lap, his car spun out of control and he hurtled to his death.[6]

Pimlico lost much of its beauty over the years. The old clubhouse, and with it, the Jockey's Hall of Fame, burned to the ground in 1966 when an errant fireplace ember caught hold in the old wood. Around that time, management built ten brick-and-cement barns on the backside that looked like barracks. Throughout the night, the watchmen could hear the pop of guns going off in the Belvedere neighborhood just over the wall.

Near the track's entrance, the old Pimlico stakes barns which housed the horses for the big races were more friendly, low wooden sheds painted green. Leading up to the Preakness, turf reporters overran those barns. They milled about talking about "the big horse"—the star animal that would grab the world's attention like Secretariat, the messiah of racing, and stop the sport's freefall into obscurity. The reporters would agree on which horse was potentially the big horse, and it was hard to know if they really believed that the horse was that perfect or if they were just hoping to find a hook and story that could carry their reporting for a season. They would concoct their trifectas and wheels around the animal and place bets at the windows in the press box. Then when race day came, they would suddenly see the brilliance and predestiny in whatever horse beat that big horse.

In 1999 the turf reporters were certain that Charismatic was not the big horse. The Derby winner was a fluke and the reporters predicted Menifee would win the Preakness. In the Derby, Menifee had come from far behind, hurling himself from fourteenth—almost eight lengths back—with a quarter of a mile to run, all the way to second at the wire. Menifee had performed impressively in his two-year-old year as well, in stakes races and against some of the same horses he would be facing in this Preakness, such as Cat Thief. His rider was forty-six-year-old Pat Day, a five-time Preakness winner, and his trainer, Elliott Walden, led the competition that spring at Churchill Downs.

Menifee was co-owned by Arthur Hancock III, son of Bull Hancock, whose father in 1910 founded Claiborne, one of the country's greatest breeding farms. In 1972, Bull Hancock died suddenly and his wife Waddell decided to pass the farm on to the next generation; she considered their eldest son, Arthur, too wild to protect their equine legacy, and skipped over him to bequeath the operation to their second son, Seth. Arthur, in a fury, went and started Stone Farm, down the road, and ended up showing talent in the breeding business. Just the year before he had sold a Mr. Prospector colt for $4 million at the Keeneland auctions. Now he had the Preakness favorite.

When the turf reporters were not busy boosting Menifee, they walked the shedrow hoping for a morsel to write up in the day's paper, perhaps a trainer taking a swipe at another trainer. Of all the world's reporting beats, thoroughbred racing was one of the toughest that did not involve sniper fire. In politics, elected officials came and went with their terms and scandals. A reporter could write honestly about their weaknesses without fear of being shut out of all future stories. In baseball, media access to the players for the season was determined by public-relations honchos and not the manager, who just got blasted in the sports pages and was looking for vengeance. But in horse racing, the horses couldn't talk, the jockeys were often men and women of few words, and a reporter would be dealing for decades with the same personalities, such as Charlie Whittingham, Woody Stephens, D. Wayne Lukas, and now Bob Baffert. If you got on their bad side, the chill could dog you your whole career. D. Wayne Lukas was known as the most thin-skinned of them all, but no reporter could afford to skip covering Lukas entirely. Luckily for the journalists, Lukas didn't isolate specific enemies in their midst. He considered each and every one "cockroaches."

Early on Wednesday, May 12, the reporters gathered at Pimlico's stakes barn, to greet Cat Thief and Charismatic who had just vanned in from Baltimore-Washington Airport. Lukas in his bone-colored cowboy hat climbed into the back of the van and came down the plank with a horse. The reporters murmured to each other. Charismatic?[7]

It was Cat Thief. Lukas led him past the reporters and into his stall. Then he went back into the cavern of the van and led Charismatic down to his public.

Charismatic had raced four times over the last forty-three days, but unlike other horses who wasted down to sinew on such a schedule, his flesh was ripe, his flanks rounded with muscle and fat. He was the Gene Kelly to the other horses' Fred Astaire. He bounced a bit as he walked to the barn and, in the gesture that always impressed people as a sign of equine curiosity and personality, turned three times to face the photographers directly. He stood patiently while a groom hosed him down and rubbed him head to hoof with a soapy sponge. Lukas watched the operation through his dark aviator sunglasses, his hands on the hips of his pressed jeans, his white shirt bright in the morning light.

Also on hand were Charismatic's owners. It was Bob Lewis's seventy-fifth birthday, a moment he never thought he would see when he suffered that heart attack some thirty years before. He and Beverly wore matching red windbreakers with "Charismatic" written in white on the front. They stood watching as their Derby winner bathed and grazed in the small patch of grass by the fence. Despite the audible hope among the reporters and the Lewises, Lukas seemed to favor Cat Thief for victory in the Preakness. As Lukas talked to reporters, he focused on him almost exclusively, referring to Charismatic only as "the other horse."

To Chris Antley there was no other horse at that moment. On Wednesday after the Derby, Antley drove up to the Santa Anita parking lot. Stuck in one car visor was a tongue tie from a cheap horse Antley won on when he first came back to racing that winter. In the other visor was a pennant from the Derby. He looked at both of those and knew he wanted to live.[8] Antley walked into the jocks' room, and Laffit Pincay came over and congratulated him on the victory at Churchill the previous Saturday. Antley couldn't believe how gracious Pincay was. Charismatic was, after all, the horse Pincay turned down for the Derby after riding him six times.[9]

Everything in Antley's life seemed to be falling into place. He was strong and light enough to ride these Triple Crown races at 116 pounds. In January, he had launched an e-mail newsletter called the *Ant Man Report*, which gave stock advice to about thirty colleagues at the California tracks. Every morning he got up at 3:00 in the morning to work on the summary for three hours before going to the track. The Derby coverage had drummed up interest and now he had almost a thousand readers. He hoped to start a Web site after the Belmont and eventually charge for his financial advice. "People e-mail me and tell me how much money they made," Antley told a reporter. "I can see them laughing and being happy. I like people being happy."[10]

Antley sat for a parade of interviews in the weeks before the Preakness. "God is in every one of us," he told Ed Fountaine of the *New York Post*. "You just have to find him. Something was growing inside of me without realizing how powerful it was. Before I was blind to see that. I had paranoia about sharing my feelings. I was hiding behind a wall. I don't have to live that way anymore."[11]

"I look back on my career," he said, "and people say, 'Look at his achievements. He won the Derby. He's been the leading rider in America.' But, still, it never put anything in my head: 'He's good.' Maybe I was never able to see what my capabilities are or were."[12]

"You hear people say, 'If I had his talent,' " he told another reporter. "You hear these beginnings of sentences all the time, and I don't want that said anymore. I want to be a new person. I am a new person in this world. I want to enjoy every day, not lie in bed being miserable and thinking, 'What's next?' "[13]

Hamilton Smith asked Antley to ride a horse for him in the allowance race right after the Preakness, and Antley happily agreed. If Antley lost the Preakness, it would be nice to be back where he first won with Smith at Pimlico. If Antley triumphed in the Preakness, Smith said he would get another rider since Antley would be tied up with festivities. They would wait to see what the future held. "A few months ago," Antley told the *Boston Globe*, "if someone told me I could be riding a horse at Pimlico on Preakness Day, any horse in any race on Preakness Day, I would have thought I was the luckiest man in the world."[14]

Antley had ridden in the Preakness five times before, but never finished better than third with Rock Point in 1989. When he went to Pimlico with the Derby winner, Strike the Gold, he came in sixth. This time with Charismatic would be his sixth shot at the Preakness, but this was going to be a charmed six. Antley's birthday was 1-6-66, and he considered six to be auspicious.

To top it off, the Preakness lottery decided Charismatic would break from the sixth post. Not only was that slot lucky for Antley, but it traditionally hosted Preakness winners. Ever since 1909, when track officials began keeping records of post positions, thirteen of eighty-nine winners started in the six slot.

But Pimlico had another traditional advantage that seemed ready to outweigh the power of the six post. In the 1970s and early 1980s, Pimlico had been considered a "dishonest" racetrack, because in a regular day of racing, the winning horses usually broke from an inside position—a bias, in track lingo, that could not simply be explained by the usual advantage for a horse running inside from wire to wire, the shortest distance to the finish. A lawyer named Frank De Francis bought Pimlico and Laurel in the mid 1980s, and demanded that the bias be corrected and the track softened to keep horses from getting injured. He hired fifty-five-year-old John Passero, the son of a former jockey and a man who worked track crews for decades, to fix the problem. Just days into his tenure, Passero received a call while he was up at Laurel that, in the middle of the race at Pimlico, a horse snapped both front legs, making repairs on the track even more urgent.

Passero harrowed the dirt to a quarter of an inch around the entire length of the track to soften the surface. Digging that deep, he knew, would be the beginning of the end for the underlying clay, but the dirt needed to be aerated. After a year or so, the jockeys began to see bits of orange on the track, indicating that the old clay base was breaking up from the rain and heat. Passero pulled up the base and put down limestone screening, then sand, and furrowed the top four inches of dirt to the base, creating a perfect firm cushion that would dry quickly and provide an ideal stage for the pandemonium of race day.

Passero remembered the days when jocks were daredevils, without a thought to their own safety. They were bachelors with many girlfriends and they would ride in the snow if it was a race day. But now, jocks were married with lots of children and wouldn't risk their necks on rough tracks.

But despite all Passero's hard work, in the first six races on the Friday before the Preakness, the winning horses came from posts one, two, one, one, one, and one respectively. On Friday evening, as everyone celebrated the coming day of racing at the Preakness party in Baltimore, Passero climbed on a tractor and harrowed the track, grading from the inside out rather than the outside in. Then he walked the track, checking the angle. Before he left for the night, Passero saw that the track was perfect.

The next day, the Preakness bias inexplicably returned. Of the eight other races on the dirt that day, five before the Preakness were won by a horse running along the rail the whole time. With the track biased for the rail, the inside horses Torrid Sand, Kimberlite Pipe and Cat Thief gained an advantage in the race, and Charismatic would be competing at a disadvantage.

On May 15, the crowds started arriving early that bright morning and by the late afternoon, an astounding 100,311 people had gathered to watch the horses called to post for the Preakness. It was believed to be the largest assemblage for an on-site sports event in Maryland history.[15]

The favorite Menifee's odds were 2 to 1 as the day began. Then came Cat Thief; the Shcikh's $5 million horse, Worldly Manner; and Baffert's filly, Excellent Meeting. Charismatic appeared fifth in the betting order at 9 to 1. Only one other Derby winner had been given worse odds in the history of the Preakness—Dark Star, who went off at 11 to 1 in 1953, and that horse fulfilled predictions, finishing fifth. With his long odds, Charismatic moved into record books as the second most disrespected Derby winner ever. "He may be Charismatic," ABC announcer Al Michaels said as the broadcast went live, "but he doesn't have much charisma with the bettors." ABC handicapper Hank Goldberg described the main contenders in the race and plotted their trip around the oval with diagrams but did not include Charismatic. Only Jim McKay selected the former claimer as the future winner.

The horses at Pimlico usually saddled indoors in a glassed-in paddock on the ground floor of the grandstand. For the Preakness, the trainers saddled on the turf course, so the fans could get a better view of the pageantry. Pimlico had sent Tom Roach a special pass to stand next to

Charismatic during the race preparations and Robyn, Hallie, and Amanda watched from the upper tier of the grandstand, as Tom excitedly waited for their horse.

The grooms and trainers led the Preakness competitors from the stakes barns, past the drunk fans in the infield hollering curses at the animals, past the hurricane fencing separating the track from the Belvedere neighborhood, with the kids and old men pressing against the gate watching. Robyn Roach saw Lukas parading toward the grandstand with the rest of the trainers, then he suddenly separated from the group with his two colts. This was so much like Lukas, taking every special advantage. Robyn figured he didn't want to wear out his horses in the hot sun. He led Cat Thief and Charismatic into the belly of the grandstand. Robyn and the girls turned around and ran down the stairs to the saddling area just as Charismatic and Cat Thief were led in. The room was quiet except for the commands that Lukas, in his pinstriped suit and dark aviator sunglasses, barked out to the horses' grooms. He was all business, but in his jacket pocket, he carried a four-leaf clover that he received from a little girl from Lexington, Kentucky, who believed in the red colt and wanted to pass good fortune on to him.[16]

Antley walked in and greeted the Roaches, whom he had met at the Derby. He went over to Charismatic and patted him, then kissed the horse's nose. Robyn and the girls had seen plenty of jockeys kiss a horse in the winner's circle after the animal won, but never *before* a race. Right then, Robyn and the girls felt in their hearts that Charismatic and Antley were going to win.

In pre-race interviews, Antley talked about wanting to start the horse's big run early, to be in the lead after the final turn. "In many of these Triple Crown races," he told a reporter, "the horses laying 1-2-3 at the three-sixteenths pole finish that way. Today, I considered the three-sixteenths pole to be my wire."[17] Lukas added a few other ideas. He told Antley not to ride the rail. All the other horses would surely try to get inside to exploit the speed bias and if Antley were there too, he risked getting the horse boxed in from the beginning. "I think the horse can run at full speed for four furlongs," Lukas said. Most horses could run two, and a good one three, but Lukas started to believe that Charismatic might have the abilities of a great horse who could pull off a full four.[18]

Joe Kelly, the Pimlico bugler, wearing a red cutaway jacket and black top hat, blasted the call to post. The horses paraded by the grandstands, and the U.S. Naval Academy Men's Glee Club in dress whites sang, "Maryland, My Maryland." Since Antley was the Derby winner, ABC had wired him for sound. "He's warming up great," Antley told Al Michaels. He explained that when he took the horse up the track in the post parade, going against the direction of the race, the horse walked normally, but when Antley turned him around to face toward the finish, Charismatic strained against the bridle, ready to run. His brassy coat gleamed and his silky tail and mane flopped up and down as he walked.

To encompass the race's full mile and three-eighths, the starting gate was set up just past the final turn. The horses would run past the finish line, around the track, and then come down the homestretch again.

Menifee didn't want to go in the gate without tugging. "I want the one backed out and bring him back in," the starter yelled, watching the assistants struggling with the horse.

"Hey, I need a tail here," one assistant hollered.

Another guy ran over to him. "I got you," he said. "I got you."

All the horses seemed agitated. "Easy now," the starter yelled. "Settle down. Easy, daddy." Charismatic and Antley made their way to the gate and post position six. Lucky six. The assistant starters pushed the padded doors closed behind Antley.

Charismatic's head kept bobbing. "Easy, Chris," the starter said. "Easy, whoa."

The last horse loaded and the starter made a sound like a pig call. "Whuh, whuh, whuh." At 5:28 P.M., the gates sprang open and the horses flew toward the rail, each rider trying to wedge his way into that coveted spot on the inside. Antley and Charismatic stayed out about four horses wide. Robbie Albarado on Vicar careened across their path, speeding across six lanes from the ninth slot, headed toward the inside before the horses even got to the first turn. At the front of the pack, Albarado sidled up against Mike Smith on Cat Thief, who was pressed against Shane Sellers on Kimberlite Pipe against the rail. All three horses triggered off each other, setting a wild pace for the pack. In jockey terminology, they were running rank. The three jocks gripped the reins tight to steady the horses and tried to crouch as still as possible to calm them, but the horses accelerated, challenging each other for the lead. The frontrunner's pace pushed to a wild forty miles per hour through the clubhouse turn.[19]

Antley rode about five lengths back, holding Charismatic in tenth. Dirt flew from the stampede of those three horses in front, hitting his goggles, stinging his face. They passed the parking lot on the other side of the chain link and the narrow row houses of Belvedere. Gary Stevens in his red silks on Stephen Got Even was a head up from Antley on the outside, and on the rail, a little in front of Stevens was Pat Day in purple silks on Menifee. Behind Charismatic, with a little breathing room, ran Kent Desormeaux on Excellent Meeting.

At the first half-mile mark, just after the turn going down the backside, the horses had only slowed slightly from the rapid start. They were a full two seconds faster than the half-mile mark at the Derby; the second fastest first fraction in Preakness history.

The pack passed the cement barns on the backside. Coming up to the three-quarter pole, Smith on Cat Thief grabbed the lead, a head up; and Vicar faded back to Kimberlite Pipe's flank in third.

Antley kept the reins tight on Charismatic, still back in tenth, running in the trio between Menifee and Stephen Got Even. Antley knew he had to break out of that box to make his move for the lead. They sped by another parking lot filled with yellow school buses. At the far turn, the speed was still a little more than thirty-eight miles per hour. This was the place Lukas had talked about with Antley, that marked four furlongs to the finish. If Antley hoped to win, to keep the dream going, he had to let Charismatic run his hardest now but the way in front of him was choked by horses. Antley needed to find a path for him to shoot through without getting blocked. Pat Day on Menifee was still up a little on the rail. Stevens chugged away to Antley's right. "G-man," Antley yelled. "G-man, give me a shot. If you don't have any horse, get out of the way."[20]

Stevens could feel Stephen Got Even's gallop loosening beneath him. If Stevens tried to battle Antley, to block him and take the lead himself, Charismatic's power would mow them down. He started to edge away, to give Antley the opening, but then felt Charismatic's flank thump against his horse's neck like two whales colliding. Antley went through the slot, out onto clean track, five horses wide, and he and Charismatic moved ahead.

Charismatic was flying now. He carried Antley past Menifee. Then Charismatic started picking off each of the horses, one by one, like walking down a receiving line. He ran past Valhol, Adonis, Worldly Manner. He had Cat Thief and Kimberlite Pipe running at pace together. *A great horse could run like this for four furlongs.* All these horses were falling back like boats over a waterfall while he alone skimmed untouched by the current. He was running so easy. *But what if Charismatic gave out? What if he could only do this for three? What if he gave out?* Then Mike Smith on Cat Thief and Shane Sellers on Kimberlite Pipe were left behind too. At the top of the stretch, Charismatic pulled his lead further to three lengths, and he kept digging deeper and deeper. Kimberlite Pipe and Cat Thief were chasing him. Antley took a quick look back and saw Menifee coming on too, gaining ground. Charismatic drifted a little further from the rail and Antley whipped him on the right, then went to the left while the crowd screamed at the sight of the red colt now covered in light brown dirt, looking like a ghost horse grinding down the stretch, leaving all of his competitors behind on that Pimlico straightaway. His ears were up, his forelegs tugging him forward with each stride. Antley and Charismatic were closing in on the finish now. They were winning. They were winning.

At the sixteenth pole, just a few strides from the wire, Pat Day on Menifee only had Antley's green and yellow silks in front of him. Day felt Menifee surge, they were lifting off. They were going to catch Charismatic this time before the wire. *This is it,* Day thought. *Menifee's going to do it. We're winning the Preakness.*

Charismatic gave an extra kick and all of his muscle went into his stride. He pulled farther ahead, crossing the wire one and a half lengths ahead of Menifee. Antley flashed the peace sign to show the world what had just happened. He had taken the second point of the Triple Crown. The experts said he and Charismatic couldn't do it, but he believed. He believed in this miracle horse.

Bob Lewis shook with excitement. "That's fantastic," he yelled. "My God. Wow, wow." He and Beverly grabbed each other and hugged hard. Over and over. Next stop, the Belmont. "We're going to New York, New York," Bob Lewis said like a country kid in a 1940s movie. He couldn't believe they had another shot at the Triple Crown and so soon.

Antley let Charismatic run himself out past the clubhouse turn. On the backstretch, he pulled the horse up, and Charismatic raised his head and cocked one ear. His face was clear. There were no signs of stress, even though he had just pulled off one of the most dramatic sprints in Preakness history. Antley couldn't even hear him blowing. It was as if he had been standing in that spot all day, and Antley felt a chill shoot up his spine in recognition that this horse's newfound athleticism was almost mystical.[21]

The ABC broadcast switched over to Antley on the microphone as he rode next to the outrider back to the winner's circle. Antley was speckled with mud, and dirt totally obscured the lower part of Charismatic's blaze. The horses had, in fact, inverted their running order over the mile and three-eighths. The horses galloping 10-8-11-9-12 going into the first turn finished 1-2-3-4-5. Despite the breakneck starting pace, Charismatic's winning time was a modest 1:55.32. Antley told ABC about coming up on Stevens at the three-eighth pole. "He gave me a shot to get out," Antley said. "I want to thank Gary for that."

Charismatic paid $18.80 on a $2 bet to win. The claimer had beaten twelve horses for a chance to compete for the Triple Crown itself. Worldly Manner, the $5 million horse with 5 to 1 odds, came up thirty-six lengths behind Charismatic. "Charismatic beat eighteen horses in the Derby, and that wasn't luck," Baffert said after the race. "Then he made a hell of a move in the Preakness and left everybody. That move broke a lot of hearts, I'll tell you that. After coming out of the claiming race, he looks like a horse who runs like he needs to do it."[22] Antley buried his face in the black-eyed Susans of the victory wreath.

Jim McKay greeted Antley on the Preakness presentation platform. "If you ever fall off again," he whispered in his ear, "I'm going to kill you."[23]

"Jim, I won't," Antley said.

Bob Lewis glowed during his ABC interview. Charlsie Cantey asked him how he felt going for the Triple Crown again. "Charlsie, can you believe it, dear?" he said to her. "If I had a birthday present, this is what I was looking for and it came true." Above the winner's circle, a painter began daubing the Lewises' winning colors onto the weathervane jockey as tradition dictated.

Les Antley and his wife, Annie, joined Chris in the winner's circle. Through his interview with Cantey, Antley pressed down tears. "People are saying smile and everything and be joyous," he said. "I'm trying to take it all in. This is special. This is special."

Lukas watched Antley signing autographs after the race. "It just might be a guy being in the right place at the right time," he said. "Coming off of what he was coming off . . . Now he's on a rocket-ship ride to real prominence.[24]

"The hill gets steeper as you go along," Lukas added, "but I think this horse has the style and the ability to win."[25]

"Think you'll be favored in the Belmont?" someone asked the trainer.[26]

"What difference does it make?" Lukas replied. "Some loyal followers are paying off car payments and getting kids through college with this one." Virginia Ballenger, who served as midwife to Charismatic's birth, won enough in the Derby and Preakness to buy a Wintec riding saddle, the best available.[27]

After the interviews, Antley ran from the winner's circle back to the jocks' room. He changed shirts and jumped down the stairs into the paddock. Hamilton Smith was standing by his horse, looking for a substitute rider to arrive. When Charismatic won the Preakness, the clerk of scales had called Smith to tell him he had to get someone other than Antley to the paddock for the next race pronto. "I told you I would ride for you," Antley said, as he leapt onto the horse. He came in a close second for Smith and was disappointed that he hadn't driven a win home for Smith too.[28]

After the end of the race day, Antley packed up his things in the jocks' room, then walked with Les across the parking lot to their car. Antley stopped and looked his father in the eye. "Thank you, Dad," he said and didn't add anything else.

Les choked up. "To hear those words from your kid," he said later. "You could imagine."[29]

I watched the Preakness at a restaurant bar, sitting next to a stranger who had bet on Charismatic too. A few days after the Derby, Chuck had returned to Texas for a required follow-up biopsy to make sure he was in the clear. I needed to finish some work in New York before we met again a few weeks later in Mississippi. He was going to return to summer school. A couple of days before the Preakness, we argued on the phone and did our best to recover long-distance. We weren't angry any longer, but our talks were stilted. Without telling Chuck, I went to the Off-Track Betting storefront down the street and placed ten dollars on Charismatic to win. That was our horse, after all.

I vividly remember watching on that bar television Charismatic's run at the turn past all the other horses, his gallop that had a little of the puppy dog to it, his legs lofting that muscular body ahead of the pack.

The stranger and I hooted in excitement as Charismatic plowed past the other horses in the final turn. Then Charismatic crossed the wire. I called Chuck on a cell phone and he picked right up.

"Whoo-hoo," he said. "Whoo-hoo."

"We won, Chuck! We won," I said. "How about that Charismatic?"

And he said, "That's my Chary. I knew he would bring my girl back to me." The happiness of the moment flooded over distance and the fight was over. "That's my Chary," Chuck said. "Thank you, Chary."

TWELVE

HANDICAPPING

When Gary Pusillo was just a boy growing up in industrial Carteret, New Jersey, in the 1950s, the neighborhood children would come to him with the wounded animals of that small northeastern city—delivering the fractured bodies of the dogs, squirrels, and sparrows found on the pavement—and Pusillo would try to heal them.[1]

When Pusillo grew up, he studied veterinary medicine at Delaware College in Pennsylvania, then went on for a Ph.D. in nutrition from Iowa State. In his late twenties, he decided he could do a thing or two for racehorses. He went over to the track in Freehold, New Jersey, one day and offered his services to a horse trainer. "Don't mess with my horses," the trainer warned.

But Pusillo insisted he could make the animals run faster. He'd do it for free, he said. If the horses didn't improve, he promised the trainer, he would leave the barn without a dime.

He fed the horses his special feed mixture and they flew like hawks around the track. Soon Pusillo graduated from delivering his feed and medicine by car to hauling it by truck, then by eighteen-wheeler. His salary soared to $400,000 annually. Pusillo worked with various feed companies. Because they were all titans in the market, he figured he fed about 200,000 horses a year. Charismatic was one of the star horses he serviced during that Triple Crown season. Now Pusillo handled not only all those horses, but lions, tigers and bears at zoos around the United States. He calculated that he fed 90 percent of all the nation's tigers.

A few years back, Pusillo became interested in the holistic medicine developed by the rain forest peoples of Latin America. Almost every year, he traveled to Brazil and Argentina to collect curatives and salves for his animals. He became interested in *guadana*, a natural stimulant, with which he treated downer foals, lethargic or sick horses to get them kick-started. He would go barn to barn at the tracks, doing acupuncture and Reiki, an ancient practice of laying hands to release energy centers.

Despite his own unconventional approach, Pusillo felt frustrated by the voodoo and superstition on the track. "If a jockey cut off his arm and won a race, there'd be a lot of one-armed jockeys the next day," he said. When he was just starting out at the Meadowlands, he watched a man drive his truck through the backside with the bed stocked with bottles of blue, green and yellow waters. The trainers would come out of their barns and wave the man down. "Hi, Doc," one would say, "give me the blue one," and the man would sell him a bottle. "Hey, there," another trainer would call, "I'll take a green one." And all of the bottles were filled with sugar water and food coloring. Many of the trainers now sought out a woman who tested their blood and the blood of horses. She swabbed the blood on a slide and peered at it under a microscope, then showed the trainer how both the trainer and his horses had strongyles, worms in their blood. The only way for horse and human to be cured was to take her product at twenty-five dollars a pop. Pusillo watched her give her presentation one time, showing these worms on an overhead projector, and the worms were so large no heart would have been able to handle the strain. If that really was a slide of the trainer's blood, Pusillo thought, the trainer would be dead.

Trainers could be convinced of any mumbo-jumbo that might give them an edge, and they read meaning into everything. Despite his business acumen, Arthur Hancock III, the co-owner of Menifee, harbored his share of superstition. In 1989, he brought Sunday Silence to the Kentucky Derby. As he walked the backstretch at Churchill Downs a couple of days before the race, he found a penny minted in 1982. He considered the discovery a good omen, since he had won the Kentucky Derby that year with a horse that he part owned, Gato Del Sol. Sure enough, a few days later, Sunday Silence won the Derby. They went on to win the Preakness a few weeks later. On the night before the 1989 Belmont, Hancock went to the top of the World Trade Center in New York City to gaze out at the brilliant field of lights below. Two white moths had pressed their dusty wings to the window. Bad omen, Hancock thought. He interpreted the presence of the moths to mean that he would only win the first two legs of the Triple Crown.[2]

Indeed, when the race went off the next day, Sunday Silence did not win that third race. He came in second by eight lengths.

The belief in a greater force came in various forms at the track, but always an intense variation. Twice, Pat Day has heard the audible voice of God. The first was in 1984 when he rode Wild Again in the first Breeders' Cup Classic. That morning, Day, who was headed toward the leading rider title that year, didn't even have a mount for America's most lucrative stakes race. But on the overnight, the listing of the races for the next day with the jockey scheduled for each horse, Day had noticed Wild Again was riderless. The trainer Vincent Timphony had been mulling whether to run the horse in the Classic or the Sprint and enlisted Eddie Maple for the Sprint. When Timphony decided to put his horse in the Classic, he ran into problems because Maple was already committed to another horse on the card.[3]

As soon as Day saw the opening, he sprinted to find Timphony. He collided with him at the door. The exchange was momentously brief.

"Could you?" asked Day.

"Would you?" Timphony replied.

At the start, Wild Again ran at pace, but Gate Dancer and Slew O' Gold battled him down the line. In the last quarter, Slew O' Gold kept charging up against Wild Again's flank. At the finish, Day thought he had won but Gate Dancer was right there with him. The stewards called an inquiry.

For minutes, Day's number sat at the top of the finishers on the electronic tote board but could be pulled down any minute by the ruling of the officials. Despite the $1.35 million hanging in the balance, Day felt completely at peace. God, he said, was the furthest thing from his mind.

Then the results became official: Pat Day had won the Breeders' Cup. With the crowd roaring and the glamour of the moment sinking in, Day took off his helmet and began lifting it in the air to wave at the crowd. Suddenly a voice—no more sonorous or authoritative than a human voice—spoke to him.

It's not them, it's Me, the voice told Day.

Of course, Day thought. He dropped the helmet to his lap ashamed. Then he thought again. He raised the helmet to salute the heavens.

The second time God spoke to him, Day rode a horse past the finish line, thinking he was slightly shaky.

Get off, the voice said. Day dropped the reins and jumped onto the soft dirt, as the horse took a step, crashed against the metal inside rail, and died of a heart attack. If Day had stayed in the saddle, he would have wound up dead or maimed.

Those two moments that God spoke to Day came not long after he was born again. At the end of 1982, Day learned he was the nation's leading rider, and on hearing the news, started a celebration that lasted two weeks. He was, at the time, seriously addicted to drugs and alcohol and the revelry was just a slightly amplified version of his regular life. When he finally emerged from his fog after the binge, he realized he wasn't happy, hadn't been happy, could not acquire happiness no matter how well he rode. He began searching. He even sat cross-legged before an Indian guru trying to find his inner self.

At the end of 1983, he was again the nation's leading rider but the accomplishment felt even more anticlimactic. He flew from Colorado to Miami to ride at Gulfstream Park and checked into his hotel room. He switched on the TV for background noise and Jimmy Swaggart was on. Day didn't like the sound of it, so he turned the television off. He fell into a deep, seemingly long sleep. When he awoke he felt he was no longer alone in the room. He turned the TV back on, not sure whether he wanted to break the mood or because the Lord directed him to do so, and found Swaggart in the middle of the altar call. The congregation stood and walked forward to renounce their old ways, accepting Jesus as their savior. Day fell on his knees and began to weep.

"They say when you die, your whole life passes before your eyes," Day said. "I was dying to my old self. I could see the number of times that I had gotten right up to the brink of destruction. And it was almost as if God would reach down and gently nudge me back. I could see how his hand had been upon me my entire life."

From that moment, Pat Day, superstar jockey, dedicated himself to Jesus Christ. He had a cross embroidered on the collar of his riding turtleneck and the back of his riding pants. He quit using drugs entirely. He stopped drinking. His only fleeting setback was when he had half a beer after the 1985 Kentucky Derby, a momentary whim that left him with a splitting headache and two days of nausea.

I became interested in how people at the racetrack negotiated the meaning of their lives since life at the track was like life on the outside, only more extreme. The horse people went through the highs and lows like everybody else but with steeper sine waves. Most riders got into the sport because horses brought them ecstasy or filled an emptiness that was extreme. When Jorge "Chop Chop" Chavez was a boy, he lived in the streets of Lima, Peru. He moved out of his house at age eight, to escape crowded conditions and cruelty. He slept in cars that he washed during the day for food money and collected coins that had dropped behind the seats. Amazingly, although he was on his own, he went to school every day and even started college.[4]

The bettors didn't care what Chop Chop's life had been. They just liked how he won with regularity. But the horses gave Chavez something more than money. He tried to describe the sensation of getting on a horse the first time at the track when he was a street kid of sixteen. "It felt like I was flying," he recalled, a smile flickering over his sober face.

Horses often functioned as a medium for love between people in a setting that could often be tough. I remember the world-weary jockey Roger Velez, with his wide mouth and twig legs, in the crowded Churchill Downs paddock, where the horses were being saddled and the bettors assessing them before the race, straining to look over the shoulders of all the press people and owners. It was before the start of the Kentucky Derby in 2000, and Velez was searching for his elderly boss, Harold Rose. Two months earlier, Hal Rose and his horse, Hal's Hope, caught the attention of the national racing press as a sweet human-interest story unfolding in the Florida Derby, a qualifying stakes race for the Kentucky Derby. The more important storyline was a love triangle between Velez, Rose, and Hal's Hope.

The reason Hal Rose attracted media interest is that he was a rarity in the high-stakes horse-racing world. Most of the big-time trainers are in the primes of their lives. They begin learning their business as kids, starting in quarter-horse racing or apprenticing with another trainer. Their barns are stocked with high-priced horseflesh. But Hal Rose was a frail eighty-eight-year-old who started training after he retired from the publishing business in his mid-sixties. He worked out of Calder Race Course, a quaint, respectable, but decidedly second-tier track in Miami, running a bunch of claimers. In 1984, he discovered a star, Rexson's Hope, who became a graded stakes winner and a Derby runner, albeit one that came in tenth. That was a brief flash of glamour. Still, Hal Rose showed up at the track every morning at dawn for no reward greater than love of the sport.

In 1997, that horse's daughter, Mia's Hope, gave birth and the foal's name, Hal's Hope, said it all: Hal Rose's audacious bid for glory late in life.

In August 1999, Hal Rose underwent quadruple bypass surgery, which was supposed to keep him laid up at the hospital for eight weeks. In three weeks, he was back at the barn because, he said, he had a contender waiting for him.

What was it about horses that kept him going all those years? I asked him.

"They enthralled me," he said slowly.[5] He stood about five-foot five-inches, a man with delicate hands and the sweet, slightly pinched face of a dried apple doll in wire-rimmed glasses. He wore a cap with a snap brim, a windbreaker and khakis; pale clothes that made him appear bleached by the sun over many years on the backside. He didn't seem to enjoy his newfound press attention, barely responding to questions, but he occasionally laughed or lingered over a reply, which suggested a mind busier than his answers. He had moved his whole family to Florida after his retirement in pursuit of his track dreams, and his beloved wife, Elsie, supported him wholeheartedly, even writing several books tightly packed with the racing statistics of all their colts and fillies. Hal Rose's son said his father had a mind quicker with numbers than the totalisor, which electronically calculated the odds at the track, and obviously his mother shared that affection for a reality that could be plotted in data points.

Roger Velez was a rising star in the late 1970s. But when success came every day, he grew cocky, started drinking, and before he knew it, was an alcoholic. By 1989, he wasn't fit to ride and found a part-time job at a florist. One day when jogging, he suffered a minor stroke. Plagued by his drinking problem and condemned to hobbling around with a cane, he received horrific news. His live-in girlfriend was diagnosed with cancer. On her deathbed, she made him promise to quit drinking and go back to riding.

After her death, he worked to stay sober and gradually rebuilt his career. His personal life improved when, in the early 1990s, he married Patty, a bright-eyed blonde-haired optimist who worked at a beauty parlor. Professionally, Velez still couldn't convince trainers to put him on their mounts. He booked only two or three horses a week and went home crying to Patty every day. Hal Rose was the only trainer to really take a chance on Velez. He saw how much Velez wanted the new beginning and offered to hire him for a few races. "He seemed sincere," Rose explained.

Hal's Hope never knew a rider other than Velez. He was there for every race and every morning exercise. Even at the Bluegrass Stakes, one of the last prep races leading to the Kentucky Derby, Velez took the reins and hotwalked the horse. Velez held Hal's Hope's nose and kissed him, the black colt with the red bridle, who when brushed for race day gleamed like oil ("He looks like Black Beauty," one middle-aged woman whispered with girlish awe in the paddock at Keeneland).

After Velez and Hal's Hope won the Florida Derby together, Velez watched the tape at home and wept. "I guess that's when it hit me. For me to overcome all I did and then to get another chance in life . . . it's glorious." And the person who gave him that chance was Hal Rose, whom Velez visited every day in the hospital when Rose was recuperating from his quadruple bypass.

So it wasn't surprising in the paddock at the Kentucky Derby that Roger Velez became so frantic, peering over the shoulders of all those press people and owners and friends of the owners, yelling to his devoted wife Patty (so devoted that she even watched him sleep through the night to ensure that nothing disturbed his pre-Derby rest), "Where's Papa Rose? Where's Papa Rose?"

Elsie Rose and Patty Velez pointed off above Roger's head to a looming presence entering the paddock with a groom. "There's Hal's Hope," they said.

Roger Velez shook his head. "I don't care about the horse," he said, still scanning the crowd. "Where's Papa?" Rose arrived a few minutes later and the two men embraced.

Roger Velez didn't care about the horse, he said in that moment of anxiety, he cared about Papa, which was exactly what Hal Rose's daughter pointed out the next morning to the old man after Hal's Hope finished a dismal sixteenth. Rose and his son and daughter and their spouses gathered in the early hours of morning to slather the horse's banged-up shins with gray clay and wrap them in sheepskin and pink binding painted with pepper sauce so the horse wouldn't chew them away. Roger Velez was already hotwalking Hal's Hope. Hardly any other jockey would show up to see a losing horse that early in the morning, if they even came by at all. "He does it for you," she said to her father.

And Hal Rose gazed through his glasses at Velez and his beloved horse, who seemed to be declaring through his performance that the last hope of an old man was slipping away, and said precisely, "I know."

The riders dealt with all the extremes of winning and losing, wealth and injury, youthful promise and death, in quick succession. Some became analytical, but many became superstitious, religious, or alcoholic.

Sometimes the horse world, the one place that brought riders happiness, turned darker than anything they could have imagined. One veterinarian told a story encompassing the brutality of the business. Back in the early '80s, he worked undercover for the New Jersey Organized Crime Bureau to bust a killing farm in Monmouth County, New Jersey. Horse owners sent their ailing or unimpressive horses there with the understanding that the animals would "accidentally" die during their stay, and the owners could collect the insurance money. The biggest times for killing would be during thunderstorms, when a variety of grisly deaths could be blamed on skittish horses. The horse-farm workers would break lightbulbs hanging over the stalls so when the horses whinnied up and hit their noses against the exposed wiring they would be electrocuted. Stable hands stuffed oats down the horses' throats and then tied plastic bags over their heads to suffocate them. Sometimes they wrestled the choking horses to the ground to make it look like the animals died of internal injuries. They took the animals to the fields and shot them with arrows, then pulled the weapon out. They ran a fence post through the wound to make it look like the horse accidentally impaled itself.

The culprits were indicted and many sent off to prison, and the veterinarian was relocated to Idaho for several years for his family's safety. Even there, he was tracked down by some of the farm's unindicted associates, and they threatened to kidnap his children, and kill him. He brought in the state police and more criminals were locked up. Some twelve years after the trials ended, he finally felt relatively safe but still packed a gun when he traveled to the states he considered most dangerous.

The horse world often wasn't what little girls dreamed it was. But then when it grew darkest, a lot of the horse people turned to religion to bring them back to the original sweetness of their awe for the animals.

Belmont, where that last point of the Triple Crown took place, was not only the track that fans saw from the grandstand, but in essence a 430-acre town on the backside. Almost 500 men lived in dormitories there, a number that crept toward a thousand in season. At most tracks, the grooms and hotwalkers moved into cheap nearby apartments. At a salary of $175 per week, hotwalkers didn't have many alternatives, so Belmont's free dormitories were in some ways a godsend. They were also primitive: Men often slept three per room, sometimes on the floor. The men who lived and worked under these conditions often drank themselves numb or punched out their frustrations in brawls.

Reverend Jim Watson was assigned to sort out those untranslated emotions. He seemed severe when I first encountered him in his cramped, cluttered office on the Belmont backside, staring out of thick plastic-framed glasses, his dark, graying hair parted to the side like a schoolboy's. His skin had a moonlike glow. Watson barely acknowledged me at first, shuffling papers on his desk, looking for something. Finally he stood, grasping the handle of the front door, ready to leave.

"I have to take someone to the emergency room," he told me. "Would you like to come along for the ride?"

As it turned out, Jim Watson was a good man at the beginning of a typical day. The person he needed to ferry to the hospital was a hotwalker who had let an ingrown toenail fester for months and now needed surgery. The hotwalker didn't speak English and wasn't sure if he had health insurance, so Watson drove him in a tired maroon van to the emergency room and filled out his paperwork and listed himself as next of kin, then came back to pick him up at the end of the day. Watson spoke to him respectfully in Spanish and reassured him. This was his job, to make the men (and it was mostly men) working on the backside feel they were important.

"Everything back here revolves around the horse," Watson told me. "The men are constantly reminded that the horse is most important."

The hotwalkers and grooms rise at 5:30 to get to the barns and pull the feed tubs, water buckets, and hay racks, then brush the horses, tend their ailments and escort them to the oval. The horses can cost millions of dollars, and potentially can win many millions more on the racetrack. The hotwalkers are considered disposable. By the end of 1999, Charismatic's winnings were worth about 224 years of a hotwalker's worklife.

That's why Watson ate at the cafeteria off the recreation hall and not down the way at the Morningline, where the food was better. "There is a plaque on the door there that says 'Owners, Trainers, Officials, Jockeys, and Jockeys Agents Only,' " Watson explained. "There's a takeout window where the grooms and hotwalkers can get something if they want to. I know they're not really enforcing that rule but I made a commitment the day that sign went up that I'm not going to frequent that place. That's discrimination. It's illegal. This is the only place in the world where they could get by with it. And as long as that sign is up, I'm drinking my coffee here."[6]

Watson and his colleague, the activities director Nick Caras, estimated that 90 percent of the workers at Belmont were from Mexico—primarily from Zamora, and the rural areas around Mexico City and Oaxaca—with another 4 percent from South America. They were strangers in a strange land, working a job that kept them perpetually isolated from the larger American population. Watson acted as translator. One man had brought his wife and three daughters from Guatemala and was getting rooked on rent for a basement apartment. These guys were often asked to pay six hundred dollars a month *per room* for an apartment off the track with a shared kitchen and bath. So Watson put in a call to the landlord to haggle a better deal.

Watson conducted weekly religious services using a Bible with a photo of a paddock on the cover and a special title: *God's Conditioning Book: A Guidebook for Running the Race of Life*. But his job was more than the usual spiritual ministrations; mainly to campaign for health insurance, organize ESL and GED classes, and register the workers' kids for public school. He scrolled down the security report every night to see who got in trouble and stopped by their barn to see them about substance-abuse counseling.

Watson had started out with the ambition to be a veterinarian. But as a sophomore in college, he got the calling to the ministry, and a few years later a summons from a chaplain friend who said a track in Baton Rouge needed help. From then on, it was a constant call from track to track until he ended up in Belmont thirteen years ago. Thirty-six of the tracks had chaplains. "When I first met Watson and learned that he was to be the chaplain in New York," Pat Day recalled, "I said, 'They're going to chew him up and spit him out.' He just walked so softly, he'll never cut it. But he's a man of God who walks the walk."

Watson wanted to emulate the life of Jesus and there was plenty of opportunity for self-sacrifice at Belmont. He had experienced moments of intense spiritual crisis on the job. One groom in his thirties kicked drinking and drugs after a long struggle, was sober for six hopeful months, then was hit by a car and killed when biking to an AA meeting. Watson had a hard time reconciling that tragedy with his beliefs, but his faith was strengthened when he saw the people on the backside, who had so little, taking care of each other—gathering donations for surgeries or a family member's funeral.

Religion is pervasive at the track. In the jockeys' room at Churchill Downs just an hour before the first running of the 2000 Kentucky Derby, the track's resident minister, Dan Powell, announced he wanted to start the devotional services before the 2000 Guineas race at Newmarket. "Do you want me to keep the TV on?" the minister asked.

The horsemen said he could go ahead and turn it off. They leaned forward and bowed their heads.

"It's a very special day at Churchill Downs," the minister intoned. "But there is more at stake in life than gambling. . . . We should not think of throwing our life away on a cheap win," Minister Powell went on. "Our lives are eternal."

He invited the horsemen to offer special prayers. "Yes, Bobby?"

"There is a girl we know. . . ."

Pedro from the Florida backside had suffered a stroke.

"There are a lot of horses in this race," one valet began.

"Yes, we pray for the safety of the horses and jockeys," the minister replied.

"Almost everyone is traveling. . . ." Jerry Bailey offered. The minister offered a prayer for them too.

Someone else's sister-in-law had cancer.

"Lord, please make the jockeys' arms strong and their bodies too. Give them wisdom as they ride their mounts," the minister said, and the horsemen answered, "Amen."

Many of the track workers found their sense of a divine force in the excellence of the horses, and the most otherworldly moment on the track surely was Secretariat's race at Belmont on June 9, 1973. The morning of the competition, his jockey, Ron Turcotte, greeted a worried Lucien Laurin at the trainer's barn at Belmont. Laurin told Turcotte he had dreamed the night before that the jockey fell off Secretariat as they left the gates at the Belmont's start.

"That's not a dream, it's a nightmare," Turcotte said. "Of all the things to tell me. What a time to tell me."[7] Of course, the dream was wrong. Secretariat won by thirty-one lengths.

That image of Secretariat dashing to glory at Belmont for the third point of the Triple Crown rarely fails to make me cry, nor did it fail to choke up tougher observers. Secretariat runs head-to-head with Sham for a half mile, then pulls in front, sails along without the whip or nearby competition, stretches his lead from seven lengths to twenty lengths. The red chestnut colt outfitted in the now-famous blue-and-white checkerboard satin blinders pulls farther and farther away from the pack as if jockey Ron Turcotte had told him to run while the rest of the horses merely cantered. And with each step, Secretariat springs from the dirt and lands twenty-nine and a half feet farther along, on and on until thirty-one lengths unfurl behind him like a red carpet.

Angel Cordero Jr., who rode My Gallant that day at Belmont, remembered talking to Braulio Baeza on board Twice A Prince in the middle of the race as they watched Secretariat fly away. When horses get tired, Cordero said, they tend to look smaller, they fold in on themselves. Cordero recalled yelling to Baeza, "Look, Baeza, he's getting tired. He's getting tired. I think we can get him." And Baeza just gazed ahead.

"I thought he looked small because he was tired," Cordero explained. "Actually, it was because I'd never seen a horse so far away."[8]

In the footage of that race, as Secretariat canters back after breaking the speed record in the Belmont, as he had shattered the best times in the other two Triple Crown races, he is not frothing at the mouth or sweating between his flanks. Enveloped in the steep roar of the Belmont crowd, he looks ready to run on.

It seems amazing that this horse's speed is independent of competitive incentive. Secretariat cannot see or hear other horses nearby. And he doesn't run because of fear. Turcotte never uses the whip, but Secretariat soars into a whole other dimension that seems to imply that this horse, like some rare and remarkable humans, is doing its absolute best not in relation to others, but in relation to its own potential, and by unleashing that potential on a scale so far from the ordinary this creature pulls back the veil on the divine.

It is said that the key attribute of a great racehorse is its large and strong heart—literally. The ease of its circulation determines how well it will run in those final furlongs. Secretariat had an enormous heart— three times the normal size—and I accept that as a biological and not metaphoric fact.

But the other biological fact is that horses prefer not to stray too far in front of or behind the pack since this would theoretically expose them to predators. Accordingly, a horse that is not whipped should have no natural inclination to run far ahead, but there he was, his enormous heart and easy running rhythm creating the lead that defied even survival instinct.

I came to believe for a time that you win when you need to win, and America needed a win during the days of Watergate and Vietnam. Secretariat gave it to them and the horse world, and the world beyond the horse world repaid him in the only way it could but a horse would never understand, by putting him on the cover of *Time*, *Newsweek* and *Sports Illustrated* simultaneously, by remembering him for decades to come.

"What did you think when you saw Secretariat at the Belmont?" I asked Reverend Jim Watson.

"It's just such an awesome performance," he said. "You can't watch that thirty-one-length victory without realizing you're seeing something almost supernatural. That record still stands. Most of his records still stand. You get to the Belmont and see him crossing the finish line and the next horse is coming around the curve. . . ."

"I can't look at that scene with Secretariat at the Belmont though," Watson continued, "without knowing that two years later, Ron Turcotte is in a wheelchair, paralyzed from the waist down." Ron Turcotte had fallen July 13, 1978, in an accident at Belmont. "He has to wake up every day," Watson continued, "and say, This is what I was and this is what I am now."

Chris Antley came to be known during his later years in New York and California as a superstitious man. He would see signs in numbers, like his lucky number six, and in the conjunction of letters, like "Chris A" and the first letters of Charismatic. "He was never the kind of guy who could boast about himself," said Mike Smith. "So he had to explain it as coming from someplace else. He couldn't say, I'm the greatest rider out there. He had to say, I'm in slot six, I'm going to get lucky."

I was interested many months after the 1999 Triple Crown season to find an old Internet posting by a man named Larry Wood from the backwoods of northwest Florida. "The Internet is the domain of Satan, the ruler of the world," Wood wrote online, "but it is also a powerful means of communication." He was willing to dally in that world to free those people "doomed to spend eternity in the Lake of Fire unless someone reaches them with the gospel." He had worked at NASA for twenty-five years. "I was on the team that built the Launch Processing System for the Space Shuttle. . . . Upon completion of the system, I transferred with it to the Shuttle Engineering Directorate to prepare application software for Shuttle processing." He had applied that same obsessive, analytical mind to searching for larger meaning in life events.

On his site, called "Current Events, Divine Viewpoint of History," he wrote a posting with the headline *Charismatic Wins Preakness*.

"The horse ran from post position #6, the number for man and for the humanity of Christ in Hypostatic Union," he explained. "The jockey was Chris Antley, age 33, who made a comeback by accepting the authority of God in his life and recovering from problems with drugs and alcohol reversionism. He was originally placed in post position #17 (reversionism) in the Derby before the scratch put him in #16 (sanctification). He said there was one reason for winning the Derby: God. He said that God gave him the horse to win. Kentucky represents the womb, and does indeed, demonstrate that breeding is the beginning of a winner." The author went on to talk about the meaning of the Preakness being held in Maryland, "the land of the Virgin Mary."[10]

"The victory of Charismatic in the Kentucky Derby and the Preakness is a tribute to the grace of God," Wood continued. "The story of how the trainer made decisions like a coach that led to victory, and how the jockey, Chris Antley, a former champion, overcame the world by obeying God will make one of the great stories in the history of horse racing, especially if the Triple Crown is won. The last Triple Crown win was in 1978, the year that means sexual abuse. The Lord Jesus Christ controls history, even horse races. In spite of the gambling and drunkenness associated with the sport, the Lord integrates it into His Plan and fights to maintain justice compatible with His Integrity."

What were the chances of the long-shot Charismatic winning the first two legs of the Triple Crown? That a thirty-year-old Texan contracted leukemia? That a random dream would lead to a bet for a happy moment in life? The odds could be calculated in the first two cases, at least.

And everything was theoretically calculable. Probability theory said that if you threw a die, each side would come up the same number of times. This was the sort of certainty that drove Dostoevsky mad at the gaming tables of Wiesbaden. "Already on twenty or so occasions," the depleted Dostoevsky wrote, "I have observed as I approached the gaming table that if one plays coolly, calmly, and with calculation, it is quite impossible to lose! . . . It is blind chance pitted against my calculation."

If the die kept coming up six, then it was bound to stop soon and come up twos because it had used up its sixes. Probability theory predicted that of course each side of a die would come up the same number of times. But that order didn't hold true for a hundred or a thousand tosses. The problem was that human beings didn't know the scale. How many tosses? In all the tosses of a die from all the toddler hands reaching for a board game and wrinkled palms slumped over an Atlantic City casino table, on the fall of all the astragals and gold cubes, from the hands of John Gates, our nation's greatest gambler, and the Roman soldiers casting lots for the executed prisoner's cloak, if you added up all those tosses and kept counting until there were no more hands to throw the die, until time had run out, then the theory of probability dictated there was a certainty that human beings could depend on: Each side of the die would come up the same number of times. If you could count that high.

THIRTEEN

THE BELMONT

A few days before the Belmont, staff reporter Michael Madden wrote in the *Boston Globe*: "Charismatic, a colt nobody wanted, is ridden by Antley, a jockey everybody doubted. That either could be a mere mile and a half from winning the Triple Crown would be astounding; that the two of them together are so close to racing immortality would be a figment, a fantasy, a fantastic improbability . . . except that it is real."[1]

The American Triple Crown is not just difficult to win. At times over the history of racing in the United States, experts came to believe the feat was impossible. Maybe in earlier eras, when bloodlines were sturdier, a horse could rally through the three races in five short weeks and hold off all challengers. But in the modern era, experts feared that inbreeding had made the thoroughbred too delicate. Too many drugs pumped into the horses made them weak. There had been long cold spells without a Triple Crown winner—as from 1948 to 1973, when Secretariat finally won the three races. After Affirmed won the Triple Crown in 1978, the horse-racing world waited for its next star. Waited for another decade and was still waiting. Six horses had reached the brink since—with wins in the Derby and Preakness—then faltered: Spectacular Bid, Pleasant Colony, Alysheba, Sunday Silence, Silver Charm, and Real Quiet.

The American Triple Crown wasn't initially conceived of as a unit. The Belmont came first in 1867, the Preakness six years later, and the Kentucky Derby two years after that. The first known mention of the term "Triple Crown" appeared in the pages of the *New York Times* on June 8, 1930, when journalist Bryan Field wrote about Gallant Fox "completing his Triple Crown," after the horse won all three.[2] Omaha pulled off the same feat in 1935, and then the papers started using the term more regularly. When Sir Barton swept all three races in 1919, no one thought of the competitions as a unit, so he became the first Triple Crown winner only in retrospect.

The three victories are difficult to achieve not only because of the short resting period between races—the British Triple Crown, in contrast, spans five months—but because of their unique features. The Derby requires not just athleticism and stamina, but also real luck. Horses pack the field because every thoroughbred owner dreams of possessing that blanket of roses. A horse needs an opportunity, a moment to run clear of the stampede at the start.

Just two weeks later, the Triple Crown hopeful goes to the Preakness. Two weeks is an unbelievably brief time for a horse to be ready for new competition. Most trainers like to wait four to six weeks between races. On top of that, the Pimlico track is just one and a quarter miles. A horse needs running technique to negotiate the tight turns at fast speeds.

If the horse manages to secure victory in both the Derby and Preakness, it must be ready for the Belmont just three weeks later. The interminable Belmont. One and a half long miles with those sweeping turns, as wide as the Outer Banks of North Carolina, as gradual in their curve as the planetary orbits, and a last stretch, so daunting, as Bob Baffert pointed out, a horse must get to the final turn, look to the finish and say, "Whoa, are you serious?"[3]

The Triple Crown is, as Jim McKay, the ABC announcer who saw thirty-eight years of sports thrills and agonies, the hardest athletic achievement. Leading up to the 1999 Belmont, officials had been discussing perhaps rejiggering the schedule or order since they had been waiting twenty-one years for a new victor. But that kind of talk had come and gone so many times before.

The Belmont Stakes was named for August Belmont, an unparalleled horse enthusiast and pioneer of finance in New York City. He was a German Jewish immigrant who arrived in America at age twenty-one, having catapulted "from sweeping floors in the Rothschild bank [in Europe] to representing the firm in the Papal Courts," as turf writer Edward Bowen summarized in his biography.[4] In the United States, Belmont continued life as a banker and played a pivotal role in the history of the country when, during the Civil War, he convinced European businessmen to finance Lincoln's military efforts. Belmont himself underwrote an entire Union regiment.[5] Small and stocky, with gray whiskers accenting each cheek like a check mark, he was not traditionally handsome, but the women of New York found him dangerously beguiling.[6]

Belmont's main contributions to racing came after the war. The sport had halted during the conflict while most horses went to battle themselves. But at the war's conclusion, entrepreneurs tried to resuscitate racing and transform it into a real business. Belmont opened Nursery Stud on Long Island, then leased land in Kentucky for breeding to boost the depleted stock. In 1866, the year after the Civil War's conclusion, Belmont's friend Leonard W. Jerome opened an eponymous track in the Fordham section of the Bronx. Belmont became the first president of Jerome Park with a membership of thirteen hundred people.

Jerome named one of the track's contests for his friend. In the Belmont Stakes, the horses would go one mile and five furlongs along a course that started as a straightaway, then looped into a kidney shape. The purse was $2,150, of which the winner received $1,850 and the second finisher took home $300 and a "beautiful saddle made by Merry of London, England."[7] The filly Ruthless secured first prize at the first running on June 19, 1867. Only one other filly—Tanya in 1905—would win in the 130 iterations of the race through June 1999.

Twenty years after the first Belmont, the New York municipal government took over Jerome Park to dig a reservoir on the property, and the race moved to Morris Park for a few years. August Belmont II, Belmont's second eldest son, made a fortune building much of the New York subway system, and in tribute to his father constructed Belmont Park, a world-class track out on Long Island. The gates opened in 1905, and from then on, the Belmont Stakes was run at Belmont Park.

The younger Belmont followed his father's passion. He teamed with William Collins Whitney, the other builder of the New York subway system, to bring Saratoga Springs back from decay. As head of the American Jockey Club from 1895 to his death in 1924, he fought against the Reformists who tried to kill the sport. The year after the Agnew-Perkins Bill passed in 1911, Belmont stood up at a meeting of 125 sportsmen at the Waldorf Hotel and passionately argued that racing should continue to keep the country ready for war. Misguided people, he pointed out, were standing in the way of safety and amusement. "The entire system of stake and cup races on the turf," he said, "is framed to prove and test out the three great qualities I have held up to you as cardinal and valuable: Endurance, early maturity, and courage." In 1913, he finally won an easement of the liability laws against track operators and racing in New York recommenced, but by then, so many tracks in the state had grown over with weeds and so much enthusiasm was lost, only Jamaica, Aqueduct, Belmont and Saratoga reopened.

In 1917, with World War I ripping Europe apart, Belmont II sought a commission with the U.S. forces overseas to express his patriotism even at the age of sixty-five. He was posted to Spain, gathering supplies for the American Expeditionary Forces.[8] By 1918, he was so consumed with his efforts, he was forced to sell his yearlings at home in America. Among those gangly colts and fillies was Man o' War, who would mature to be the greatest thoroughbred in modern history. Belmont held the yearling out of the auction lot until the last possible moment, but then decided he must part with Man o' War too. He watched the horse's rise to greatness from the sidelines.[9]

Belmont died in 1924, and his remaining horses were sold. Two men partnered to purchase the lot: New York governor W. Averell Harriman, and George Herbert Walker, grandfather of the forty-first United States president, George Herbert Walker Bush, and great-grandfather of the forty-third president, George Walker Bush.

D. Wayne Lukas knew the press liked to play up the relationship of horse and jockey in the Triple Crown races, but the truth was, it was the trainer who got up every morning and worked with the animal, a relationship that usually went on for years. It was the trainer who sweated when the feed bills weren't paid or injuries laid up the horse. And now Lukas stood ready in the same year he entered the Hall of Fame, to claim the Triple Crown, a feat last achieved by the Cuban-born trainer Laz Barrera in 1978 with Affirmed. "Our industry is full of fairy tales and romance and stuff," Lukas told *USA Today*, "and this is no exception."

Lukas's original plan was to ship Charismatic and Cat Thief by van to the Belmont on the Sunday after the Preakness. But a few days before that race, he decided the horses would go to Churchill first—win or lose. Lukas had run seven horses in the Belmont, starting in 1980. The three times he won—in three consecutive years, with Tabasco Cat in 1994, then Thunder Gulch, and finally Editor's Note—he hadn't shipped them to New York to get ready. He trained them for the mile and a half at Churchill. That was the lucky formula for teaching a horse to run that distance of a mile and a half, a length the horse would run just once in its life. And Lukas felt Charismatic was even more likely to win the Belmont than the three horses he had won with in the past.

Lukas flew to Churchill on a private plane with Cat Thief and Charismatic and sent his assistants ahead on a commercial flight. After a seventh-place finish in the Preakness, he decided there was no point in taking Cat Thief back to Belmont. Lukas focused on Charismatic. For three days, Charismatic rested, then Lukas breezed him. For the rest of that week, Charismatic did whatever he wanted—ran hard, took a light gallop. Lukas told the exercise rider to let the horse set the pace. But the second and third weeks, Charismatic went under Lukas's regime again. Three days before the Belmont, Lukas flew the horse up to New York and waited to see what they had. If Lukas won the Belmont, he would gain glory and his part of the $600,000 winner's purse. But he would also earn 10 percent of the $5 million VISA Triple Crown match prize, ensuring he would be able to pay his feed bill. He figured he was that far behind.[10]

Unfortunately for Lukas the Belmont was a rider's race. For the Derby and Preakness, you could study the history of the other horses and calculate what they might do. You could instruct your rider to position his or her horse accordingly. But by the time the horses hit the Belmont, all the participants had seen each other run before, usually head-to-head. Menifee, Stephen Got Even, and Adonis would be coming from the Derby and Preakness. Patience Game would return from the Preakness alone. Lemon Drop Kid, who finished ninth in the Derby but skipped the Preakness, would also be back. The riders and trainers were strategizing now and, in the collision of plans and schemes, the outcome was up for grabs. A trainer couldn't dictate much in the Belmont.

He could ponder all day, when should Antley unleash Charismatic's powerful four furlongs in that twelve-furlong race—at the start to clear ahead of the pack? The problem was if he gunned the horse early he risked tiring him before the competition kicked in. He could run the horse hard up the backstretch to get a good position for the final turn, or he could save his kick for the final sprint, to try a cannonball move past the other horses. But if he held Charismatic back at the start, the animal could lose hope and refuse even to try at the end. Lukas wouldn't have much say, just a few words uttered in the paddock and whatever he could bark out into oblivion amidst the howling of the crowd. Antley had the control. For Lukas, a man who orchestrated even the pattern with which his shedrow was raked, the prospect was painful.

He had to trust Antley would do the right thing and believe his horse was the best. One Belmont eve, back in the mid-1990s, Lukas sat down and watched all the Belmont races available on tape. Among them was the race in 1973 when Secretariat went to the front at the start and ran at the lead to the finish. Lukas watched the tapes and studied every move, and when it was over, he had his big tip. "It's a hell of an idea to have Secretariat as your horse," he thought.[11]

The pressure was on Chris Antley. "I want so badly to do it for America," he told reporters. "If I can put the cherry on top and win the Triple Crown, it can unite so many people who are not in the sport and they find an enthusiasm or a goal in life, that anything can be achieved in life if you put your heart into it."

Back in California after the Preakness, he saw Laffit Pincay again. "Laffit," Antley said, "you were on him most of the time. . . ." Pincay didn't seem to harbor any jealousy. He smiled.

"Congratulations," Pincay said. "Keep it up. One more."

The support continued in widening circles. Jay Livingston at the Bender Mender said if he had to, he would shut down the business that Saturday to watch his buddy win the Belmont. The people at the Columbia Athletic Club were throwing a get-together around the television. His mother Shelly even decided to make the trip to New York. She usually refused to cast so much as a glance at his races because they made her too nervous, and instead would sit drinking Tequila shooters while someone else gave her the play-by-play. But she would come to this one, along with the whole family.

Antley had become a celebrity of sorts—not for what he had achieved but for the expectations of what was possible. It was a notoriety built on hopes, not congratulations, but the interest was wide-ranging. The National Thoroughbred Racing Association for the first time invited Antley to participate in the Jockey Championship at Lone Star Park in Dallas at the end of June. Vice President Al Gore and his wife, Tipper, asked Antley to visit the White House after the Belmont, win or lose. Tipper had put a two-dollar bet on Charismatic at the Derby, and she liked the story of Antley's comeback from drugs and weight issues.

For Antley, the most exciting honor of those piling up on his desk was an invitation to ring the opening bell at the New York Stock Exchange on the Friday before the Belmont.[12] He liked being recognized for his trading acumen and wanted to meet CNBC's anchor for financial news Maria Bartiromo.

In the three weeks between the races, Antley's phone rang constantly and Anderson hired a girl to answer his e-mail. The jock did twenty interviews a day. He corresponded online with the Roach family: "And you see . . . I get blessed every day now . . . touched by people who have felt a special feeling from only being of self," he wrote four days after the Preakness, "it feels so good to love again. . . . God has given me a life back now. . . . and that is my dream of health. . . . thank you again. . . ."

Twelve-year-old Hallie Roach wrote back, "I truly believe that you and Charismatic were meant to go down in history and I pray that you will."

And he replied. "Hallie . . . I believe too!! And I want him to enjoy the rest of his 3 week vacation . . . , as peacefull as so well deserves!!!!! For we shall meet again . . . so very soon . . . God has Blessed. . . . I await our third leg of a dream . . . so pleasing . . . to be in . . . ! Your Friend Chris. . . ."

The owners too were the perfect casting for the fantasy. "They're always happy," he told a reporter about the Lewises. "They're always shoulder-length apart. If he turns to the left, she turns to the left behind him. They're about as true people as you would ever know."[13]

"I want to savor all three weeks," Antley said. "I get to live in a dream for a little longer."[14]

"I'm willing to accept failure for not being able to achieve something this big," he told another interviewer. "If somebody could get inside my body and be as happy as me now, they'd be the happiest person in the world."[15]

"I've already won the Triple Crown," Antley told the *Boston Globe*, just days before the Belmont. "I mean, you think about a gift. Charismatic is a gift."[16]

The handicappers finally jumped on the Charismatic bandwagon making the colt the favorite in the Belmont at 2 to 1 odds. Menifee won second choice at 7 to 2 odds. The handicappers figured if Menifee could get a cleaner trip in the Belmont, he could grab the purse, since he'd moved from tenth at the top of the stretch to second at the wire in the Derby and kicked from seventh at the far turn to second in the Preakness.

Baffert was, however, a significant problem again. His comings and goings were getting to be irritating for his rival Lukas. Baffert had thrown three horses at the Derby—Excellent Meeting, General Challenge, and Prime Timber—and threatened to run his filly Silverbulletday that first day in May too. Then at the last minute he scratched the filly and put her in the Kentucky Oaks, where she demolished the competition. Then in the Preakness, Baffert brooded over whether or not to run Silverbulletday, only to again scratch her late in the game and send her to beat the other fillies in the Black-Eyed Susan. A disconsolate Baffert announced after the Preakness that he was "getting off the bus" of the 1999 Triple Crown races for good.

But for good didn't last long. Ten days later, ten days before the Belmont, Baffert announced he changed his mind. If he could win a good post position for Silverbulletday in the drawing for the race, she would run. She had never competed against colts before, and Tanya had been the last filly to win the Belmont back in 1905,[17] but with Silverbulletday's impressive showing that spring, the oddsmakers gave her 4 to 1 odds. Baffert told the press he was only sending Silverbulletday to the starting line to keep Charismatic from winning the Eclipse Horse of the Year Award. He wanted one of his thoroughbreds, Real Quiet, Silver Charm, or Silverbulletday to get that prize.[18] He hoped Charismatic would look Silverbulletday in the eye and "fall in love with her," he said, chasing the filly until his strength gave out and she romped to victory.

Bob Lewis was publicly annoyed by Baffert's spoiler strategy and announced he would bet Baffert $100,000 that his Charismatic would beat Silverbulletday. Baffert turned down the offer. "Only if he'll lend me the money," he said. "I don't have $100,000 to bet, unless I borrow it."

Lukas was furious. He canceled a Tuesday teleconference with reporters because he despised what he considered double treatment. If the situations had been reversed, he said, "The cockroaches would have come right out of the woodwork."[19]

At 6:00 A.M. on June 2, Lukas readied to drive Charismatic to the Louisville airport. The sky was black and thunder rumbled on the horizon. Rain poured down and lightning sizzled across the sky, illuminating the world over and over in weird blue. Lukas could barely see the road in front of them as they drove. At the airport, they led Charismatic onto the plane, and Silverbulletday boarded too. For an hour they sat on the tarmac until the storm broke slightly. Then they took off, rising above the tumult. Charismatic, as gentle as he was as a yearling, stayed calm through the whole ordeal.

On Saturday, June 5, under a crescent moon, Lukas's groom led Charismatic out of his Belmont stall, his metal shoes clapping across Man o' War Boulevard to the track. Lukas was up on his pony and one of his exercise riders, Joanne McNamara, rode on the champion's back. They were only taking Charismatic for a walk but he wanted to run. This was the longest interval he had rested between races since early March and, only two days before, Lukas had vitamized him for the first time that spring. He was almost overenergized. The day before the Belmont, Lukas made the unusual decision of galloping Charismatic one mile and three quarters, a quarter mile longer than the race itself.[20] Most horses would only do an easy mile the day before the race. When Charismatic came back to the barn he had broken a sweat.[21] Now on the morning of the race, Charismatic stamped his foot in the dirt, and McNamara held him back to save that fire for twelve more hours.

At the barn, behind a police barricade, Charismatic bathed and ate oats and sweet feed. Antley came by at 6:00, since he had been awake since 3:00. He had arrived on Tuesday night at 11:30 and stayed up doing laundry. For the next two nights he only got a total of two hours' sleep. He lost his wallet on Wednesday night, then caught a cold Thursday and canceled all his interviews except for a visit to Ronald McDonald house to spend time with kids being treated for cancer. The reporters had asked so many times, "What does it feel like?" he had almost stopped being able to process the experience.[22] But he suspected he was happy. "What's the name of that movie," he said to a reporter as he stood, watching the horse, *As Good As It Gets?* If I could experience the ultimate, this would be it. This would be heaven."[23]

At quarter to nine, the Lewises arrived to have their picture taken with Lukas and the horse. "We're going to try to get one of these at 5:28 p.m.," Lukas said, referring to the winner's circle photo that would take place for one lucky horse that evening.[24] A few hours later, Charismatic ate again and lay down on the hay and dozed.

At 8:30 in the morning, the crowds started arriving. Elsewhere in New York, the Yankees were playing the Mets, and the Knicks were going head-to-head with the Pacers in the Eastern Conference Finals. Those events should have reduced the crowds, but people swarmed in—a record 85,818 of them—filling the grandstands, the lawn by the rail at the final turn, the clubhouse and the paddock. ABC's Al Michaels noted, "One definition of the word charismatic is the ability to inspire followers with devotion and enthusiasm. This horse has done nothing of the sort until today." The throngs filling the tiers confirmed that the name was finally fitting.

Now all the experts liked the red colt. "I think it's time to get on Charismatic's bandwagon," ABC handicapper Hank Goldberg declared. Jim McKay, who had been the sole on-air personality to pick Charismatic for the Preakness, seconded the selection. "Charismatic will catch the filly and win the Triple Crown," he declared.

Charismatic was clearly a different horse than the past stars of the Triple Crown. He had won only one stakes race going into the Derby, while Secretariat, by comparison, had won seven stakes races and Affirmed had eight. But, like his great grandsire Secretariat, Charismatic thrived on competition. Even Penny Chenery saw her Secretariat coming through in Charismatic as the weeks ticked by and hoped he would win.

The Belmont would be Charismatic's fifth race in sixty-three days. His baby fat had melted away and he seemed smarter, more mentally mature. Although Charismatic hadn't won as many stakes races leading to the Triple Crown, he routed more competitors in the big races themselves than the superhorses of the past. He beat eighteen horses in the Derby—more than Secretariat, Seattle Slew, or Affirmed—and more horses in the Preakness. In the Belmont, he was up against a dozen horses, compared to four each for Secretariat and Affirmed, and seven for Seattle Slew. This race wouldn't just be a formality for Charismatic to prove his excellence. He would have to fight for victory.

Chuck and I were supposed to be at Belmont that day to cheer Charismatic's Triple Crown. But on May 24, Chuck called me in New York to tell me he had relapsed and would need a bone-marrow transplant. I flew down to be with him a few days later.

Chuck seemed determined to be the ideal patient for this third round of treatment because he knew it was his last chance. If cherry tomatoes and soy milk might assist the recovery, as various nutritionists/alchemists claimed, he would eat forty tomatoes a day and prune a head of broccoli down to its stalk. He would go for a massage for relaxation because this was said to boost the immune system, but not too deep because this, it was said, could set off faster cell replication. He would get sleep, fresh air, the anthology of spirited stories from cancer survivors, and the antibacterial shampoo that would keep him appropriately sterilized as his hair fell out again. He would vaguely believe the nurses in charge of his bone-marrow orientation when they told him that the fourth floor of the Collins building was considered the "Baylor spa" because of all the luxuries—a treadmill, VCRs, a menu dictated by your own tastes. He wouldn't let that hope fade that there really might be something nicer at Collins than there was in the Roberts building, where he had received his chemotherapy treatments, when really the only nicer thing at Collins were two phenomenal nurses and a couple of reasonable ones. The rest of Collins was mouth sores, rashes, peeling fingernails, nosebleeds, sheets covered in a thatching of lost hair, tubes feeding into the catheter punched into his chest, neupogen shots into his emaciated thigh, diarrhea, searing neurological pain that could not be numbed by drugs and that left him shaking and huddled on his bed, his feet plunged into buckets of ice water, and him vomiting a chemotherapy bile so toxic that on one occasion I was not even allowed into the room to comfort him because the nurse insisted that just breathing the fumes would be too dangerous. And to put this in even more pathetic perspective, I waited in the hall outside his room torn between horror that I could not be in there to help him and anxiety that if I pushed too hard to get in, I might be ruining his surprise for me because it was my birthday (for Valentine's Day he had gotten his room strung with decorations). This time, Chuck had in fact been vomiting. When I finally was allowed in, he presented me with a gift and card that read: "Dear Biz, Happy Birthday. . . . Don't worry, things will work out fine. They have to . . . Chuck."

All the horrors of Collins seemed to most overwhelm Chuck at 4:00 in the morning when the nurse switched on the fluorescent overhead lights and roused him from fitful sleep after his chemotherapy. He would stagger with his metal stand of tubing and saline bags to the shower, where he would wash the lotion and chemical sweat from his raging skin, then collapse into a wheelchair, a towel over his bald head to combat the chill, and be taken down to radiation, where he would vomit again on the machine as it tried to kill nearly every cell in his body. At those times, when the nurse came to get him, his eyes showed that he was absolutely convinced Baylor didn't have a spa, and he would hoist one exhausted hand in the air for a joking good-bye wave and croak, "See you soon, sweetie."

But Chuck and I went to watch the Belmont at Lone Star Park before all that, when the pain and worry seemed extreme but were only gauged at three out of a possible one hundred. In those early days of June, Chuck still was most concerned with boosting his immune system, getting financial issues ironed out at the hospital, enjoying life as much as he possibly could with a weakening body, and capping off the miraculous saga of Charismatic with a Triple Crown win.

Waiting with him on the aluminum bench at Lone Star for the screen to reveal the horses on their way to the gate, I visualized all possible outcomes of the race simultaneously. There was Charismatic's stupendous victory with the New York crowd cheering via satellite, the Texans whooping toward the screen, and Chuck and I hugging the

breath out of each other. All of our friends and family would be screaming in front of small screens all over the country. Then in another version, there was the close finish, and, of course, there was the possibility
of defeat, with nothing left for us but a bewildered moment of indecision
about when to leave the track and how to avoid talking about the whole
sorry thing with the friends and family who had snapped their televisions
off right after the other winner crossed the wire.

On that Belmont Day, it did not occur to me to wish for victory or
pray or engage in any of the other internal rituals that imply direct par-
ticipation. Instead, I was obsessively curious as to whether this would be
a happy ending or a sad one, and I was fully geared to read meaning
onto a broader spectrum of events if Charismatic should win. In the
realm of my original dream, I had always felt that the qualifier I offered
my guide at the art show—"Not enough charisma to be in a museum or
art gallery"—had suggested that the horse would not make it into the
history books by achieving a Triple Crown victory. But, of course, I also
thought many times how I had no idea what my dream meant or how it
could be interpreted or what dreams were exactly.

At the stakes barn, Charismatic's groom and an assistant trainer, Mike
Maker, took hold of Charismatic's bridle and led him out of the shedrow,
past the police barricades. The security guards fell in line behind them
and they started the walk toward the long race, the longest race any
thoroughbred would run in his life. The reporters tromped behind and
cameramen raced ahead, lumbering with their equipment to get a shot
of the champion. More and more people fell into the parade.

They got to the paddock and walked into stall four for saddling.
Sparrows flew back and forth in the eaves, and the crowd filled every
space by the fences in front and behind.

Antley was in the locker room, warming up, doing splits and hur-
dler's stretches. His middle and ring fingers on his right hand were taped
for protection against the pull of the reins since he was still so fresh back
in racing he hadn't developed calluses.

The clerk of scales called the riders for weigh-in, and they went one at a time. Pat Day climbed on and the clerk noted the weight, then Antley stepped up and his valet handed him his saddle and cloth. "He needs a pound," the clerk said, and they went to get a lead pad to tuck in the saddle.

Antley walked out to the paddock where the late-afternoon summer sun cast dark, precise shadows on the grass. The glow glinted off everyone's hair and shoulders. Lukas, wearing a charcoal pinstriped suit and yellow tie, instructed Antley he wanted Charismatic three to four lengths behind Silverbulletday, closer than he held to the leader in the previous two classics. Behind them, Charismatic kept bobbing his head, anxious to run.

Some minutes later, Silverbulletday arrived from the backside barn, a nine-minute walk away. She had been housed there instead of the stakes barn to keep her away from the commotion.

Sam Grossman blew the call to post and the grooms led the horses onto the walking ring. Antley leapt onto Charismatic's back and they went once round the paddock, while people cheered. They walked into the dark tunnel, toward the brilliant sunlight out on the track, under the red, white and blue bunting that looped down from the grandstand. Someone in the crowd held up a sign that said only, "Wow."

In the post parade, Antley was checking systems, like a pilot before flying a plane. The Broadway actress Linda Eder sang "New York, New York," while the horses walked by. After they passed, a maintenance worker drove the starting gate onto the course right in front of the grandstand. The horses galloped past the final turn, warming up. They would run one full tour of the oval to make the mile and a half.

The starter Robert Duncan had told his men ahead of time to make sure they made eye contact with him for instruction in those last minutes since they wouldn't be able to hear each other over the roar of the crowd. Duncan turned on the magnetic power that held the gates closed so the horses could load in. When, at the start, he pressed the button, the power would be killed and the gates would fly open.

The horses started approaching the gate to load in. The crowd thundered. First Teletable with Jose Velazquez in his yellow silks went in against the rail, then Vision and Verse with Heberto Castillo Jr., in a purple shirt and pink sash. Silverbulletday loaded with Jerry Bailey in ruby with yellow sleeves. Chris Antley urged Charismatic forward and the assistant starters grabbed his bridle and guided him into the slot, pushing the doors closed behind him against the tension of the springs.

Behind them Lemon Drop Kid balked and tugged his head back against the pull of the assistant starter.

The crowd was so loud, the vibrations coursed through the starters, the jockeys, the horses, like the first tremors of an earthquake. Duncan could feel the very air molecules shaking. When the starters came for Menifee, the colt tried to back up and the men grabbed him and pushed him in.

"Two out," the assistant starter yelled from the end of the gate, screaming as loud as he could. Duncan on the other end could only see the man's lips moving.

Shane Sellers in bright red silks loaded in on Stephen Got Even.

"One out," the assistant starter bellowed and again Duncan could only see his face straining to yell above the noise.

Best of Luck went into his slot, closest to the grandstand. "You got 'em," the assistant starter screamed down to Duncan.

Duncan took a step toward the button. He pressed his lips against the microphone to get as much volume as possible. "Let's get tied on," he yelled. The riders could barely make out what he said. The cheering got louder until all the horses and riders were being shaken like maraca beads.

Duncan reached his hand toward the black button. And even in that roar, there was one instant that seemed like silence, with the horses and riders still and facing forward in their ordered rows. Duncan pressed the button, and the gates slammed back into their clips with the noise of a dozen car crashes. The horn blasted. Duncan saw the start as he always did, in slow motion, each second fractured into minutes. Down the line, all the horses lunged forward in a colossal swell with the kaleidoscope of racing silks flashing at once, and Duncan felt his heart and breath stop as it had every time he let that tidal wave loose over thirty years.

Charismatic's weight was perfectly distributed, head low, and he pushed off on his back legs, his forehoofs getting a clean footing but not too hard so he overshot the front and knuckled forward. He kicked forward in perfect rhythm and Antley felt that colossal surge beneath him as they skimmed out of the slot, not brushing either side, and ran a few strides with Charismatic setting the pace so he could get his bearings. He moved in toward the rail but with a little breathing room. Silverbulletday glided up too on their left. Antley had Bailey's ruby silks right there next to him and the filly set the pace with Charismatic following along.

Antley could hear Castillo on Vision and Verse one length back, and glimpse Menifee and Stephen Got Even just behind Castillo as they hit the first quarter. They were packed tight. The pace was more humane than the Preakness but still almost 38 miles per hour—significantly faster than the pace Bob Baffert had hoped for at the start, which meant in the grandstands, Baffert was officially worried.[25]

Turning up the backside, Antley drove hard on Silverbulletday's neck at the front of the pack. They were running at record time. The fraction was 47⅗ seconds at the half mile, which was significantly quicker than the Triple Crown winners Affirmed and Seattle Slew had paced themselves. And still Charismatic and that filly Silverbulletday battled to get their necks out in front of the other. Antley could feel Charismatic was overexcited. He tried to keep the rein tight in his hand, keep the bit tugging firm in the horse's mouth, tried to crouch as still as possible. They passed the clubhouse turn and came down the backstretch, out where the noise of the crowd sounded miles away. The yards were slipping away as the seconds ticked by. Which horse suddenly was going to blast into the lead? When would the neck and neck pace give way, with one horse way out front, clearly winning? They galloped like the same breath was going through them at once.

Silverbulletday's jockey, Jerry Bailey, could see to his side now that Charismatic was running rank, out of his pace, chasing the filly.[26] He saw Antley trying to hold Charismatic back, but Antley couldn't restrain him.

The horse wouldn't give up the pace, and a jockey couldn't just stand up and go water-skiing on him. Sellers on Stephen Got Even was a half length behind them both.

At the mile mark, the horses timed at 1:36, which meant the first mile was about thirty-seven miles per hour. Silverbulletday faded slightly and Antley started stalking up. Stephen Got Even was a head behind him. This was it. The four-furlong mark. This was when Charismatic always hit his hot pace, and Silverbulletday had already fallen off. Antley had a slight lead. They were going to do it. They were going to win the Triple Crown.

Now that Silverbulletday was left somewhere behind them on the track, Charismatic seemed comfortable. He showed no sign of straining. The pack, however, seemed to be tiring. Antley and Charismatic took the final turn still at the lead, and they galloped into the force of the wind and against the wall of sound from the screaming crowd. Charismatic's ears were up now and he seemed alert, sprinting down the final stretch. They had run the distance of the Kentucky Derby but had a full quarter-mile to go. Four horses came to the front alongside Charismatic, galloping in a line—Menifee, Lemon Drop Kid, Stephen Got Even, and Pineaff.

Then Menifee fell off the pace, and it was only Antley up against Sellers on Stephen Got Even. The wind was in their faces and the crowd shrieking. Stephen Got Even put more muscle into his stride at the quarter-mile mark and edged up on Charismatic. There was no way Antley could let that horse pass them now. They only had a quarter of a mile to go and they were out in front.

Antley went to the whip. He called on Charismatic and the horse quickened.

But then in a stride, the horse's power wicked away, like the air had been let out of him. Why was he slowing? Antley couldn't tell.

He saw the streak of Sellers's bright red silks on Stephen Got Even flying into the lead.

Just before the eighth pole, out of nowhere, Santos in his checker-board silks on Lemon Drop Kid drove up on Charismatic's right. Stephen Got Even gave out, and Lemon Drop Kid took the lead. Antley was in second, and they were passing the eighth pole. Vision and Verse came on the rail. There was hardly any distance left in this race but Antley just watched Santos on Lemon Drop Kid slipping ahead.

Santos had a length and a half on Antley. Antley wasn't whipping Charismatic anymore. He wasn't touching the horse. He just had his hands up on Charismatic's withers and was riding him. Riding him however the horse wanted to be ridden, however the horse wanted to run, and Castillo in the purple silks on Vision and Verse was there at his head. With just those few strides left, Antley was hoping to hold on, to hang on for third. He didn't whip Charismatic anymore. He let the colt run how he wanted, and with the finish just strides before them, Charismatic dipped down. He gave out like a tire blowing beneath him and Antley could feel the pain,[27] could feel that sharp ache somewhere in the horse's lower front legs. He could feel the horse's effort, how he had run as hard as he possibly could and it wasn't enough, not enough to win the Triple Crown, not enough to keep pace with Silverbulletday and hold on and be able to keep all those other horses from hitting the wire first. And it wasn't his fault. There was something going on that talent and will couldn't touch. There was something bigger that didn't care about talent or will. Antley and Charismatic hit the wire third, one and a half lengths behind the winner, the six horse, Lemon Drop Kid.

Most people at Belmont that day only remembered the silence. Everyone was on their feet in the way they always are for the last seconds of a horse race as the jocks whip away down the homestretch and the crowd screams for their betting pick. But this time, no one was so disinterested as to be sitting for the finish because these were the last seconds of the Belmont, the last of the Triple Crown, the last moment to get a good look at a twenty-one-year cold streak being broken, the best chance to get a first view of racing's new hero, the last of the millennium. Just past the wire, about 150 yards past, Antley punched his feet forward against the stirrups as hard as he could, leaning all his weight past the saddle, and Charismatic stopped short. Antley jumped off Charismatic's back and fell to the ground with the reins in his hand and one leg splayed out awkwardly, like a tossed novice rider, like a doll fallen on the floor. Then he crawled through the dirt to the horse and quickly ran his hands down both front legs searching for the injury. He lifted up the left front leg and braced it against his body.

The spectators stayed standing as they had for the finish, with their heads angled just past the finish line, watching in dumb horror as Chris Antley struggled against the weight of Charismatic. The red colt nodded his head over and over. Then people started crying.

ABC had wired Bob Lewis for sound and he had a camera in his face. He couldn't hear what was going on and couldn't see the finish. He had seen Charismatic take the lead at the turn but then lost his view of the stretch. People next to him started telling him that a horse was hurt. Beverly turned to her daughter in the row behind. Perhaps she could see. "Who broke down?" she asked.

"Charismatic," her daughter said.

Beverly climbed on her seat to get a view but the cameras were in the way. Bob took her by the hand and they left their box, went down the escalator to the paddock and watched the instant replay on the monitor.

Bob watched as the cameras fixed on the scene unfolding on the track. He had seen horses break down before, watched them wobbling around on their injured leg until they had to be euthanized. It was an awful thing to witness.

But Antley had ahold of the horse. He didn't seem concerned about his own safety, did not try to jump clear. He had the horse's leg with its white chrome sock in hand and he fell down and continued to hold that leg, and he got back up again and kept hold of the leg. If Antley had not held the leg in that position, Bob Lewis believed the horse would have thrashed and the fracture could very well have punctured the skin. And in that case, there would have been no question. The veterinarians would have had to put the horse down.

Les Antley was also wired for sound. He knew Charismatic hadn't won. Then he looked down and saw the ambulance.

In the jocks' room, the riders had watched the race, clustered under the monitors. In the first furlongs, they were surprised Antley was out at the lead with Silverbulletday since most horses couldn't run at pace for a mile and a half, but Charismatic seemed to be galloping comfortably. Then turning for home, Antley and Charismatic looked like they were going to win easily. When Antley pulled the horse up, the jockeys kept watching silently. Some of them teared up. People outside racing never understood. When you felt a horse bobble beneath you, there was no worse feeling in the world.

I was standing at Lone Star, and it was silent there too. After a moment, I could hear a few Texans crying in different sections of the bleachers. Chuck still held his plastic cup of beer in one hand and put the other around me so he could pull me in to sob against his shoulder. He stared at the Jumbotron with his jaw working. It was so hot.

Antley tried to unbuckle Charismatic's girth and get the saddle off. A groom ran up and helped. When he slipped the belt off Charismatic's belly, the horse started shaking. The veterinarian ran out onto the track and he took over from Antley and more grooms sprinted across the dirt toward Charismatic. Antley knelt in front of the horse. The white ambulance pulled up, and the grooms took off Charismatic's bridle and petted his nose while the vet put an inflatable cast on his leg until they could get him to his stall. Antley stood up and stroked Charismatic's head. Lukas had arrived and he put his arm around Antley and said something and Antley was crying. Hallie Roach ran out to him and they sobbed together.

The ABC reporter Charlsie Cantey stopped Antley as he made his way back toward the tunnel. She said the horse seemed in distress toward the end.

"Yeah, he was," said Antley. "He broke down just after the wire." His voiced cracked. "You know," he said. "It's just a sad thing when these things happen." Tears began running down his face. "Um, he gave us a lot," Antley said. "He gave America a lot."

"He gave you a lot, Chris," Cantey said, "and he gave us all a lot. He's going to be safe. He's going to wind up fine."

"He will," Antley said, nodding. "I think he's going to be okay."

"But it's a bitter end to a huge dream," Cantey added.

"Yes, it is," Antley said. "These things come. If God wanted us to win and be there today, it would have happened. But you know, the game goes on. Charismatic is going to be okay, I think. I'm just a little upset right now."

"I know you are and well you should be," she said. "But you know what? You and Charismatic were a wonderful, wonderful comeback team. He came back from a lot and you came back from so much and both of you gave us a wonderful, wonderful ride. And we're proud of both of you."

"Thank you, Charlsie," he said.

"Keep it up," she said.

"I will."

Antley walked toward the tunnel and the reporters surrounded him. His mother came to him and rubbed his back. "Horses are in shock when something like this happens," Antley said. "They can't feel any pain yet. Sometimes, they'll want to go up in the air."[28]

He saw Amy LoPresti, who first trained Charismatic as a yearling when he was just running for the fun of it. "I'm so sorry," Antley kept telling her. "I'm so sorry. I wish there was something more I could have done."

Antley made his way through the crowd and photographers pushed against him, batting each other with their lenses. One of them tried to stick a leg between him and his mother, to wedge her out of the shot. "Excuse me, but I think you're going wrong," she said.

The reporters had so many questions. "Right now," Antley told the *Houston Chronicle*, "I'm just thinking about the horse, and the Lewises, and Wayne. It's just devastating."

He had lost. The horse was hurt. The hope had vanished, and there was something else wrong. His lucky number turned out to be a lucky number, but it wasn't his lucky number. He got back to the jocks' room and his father made his way toward him. "Dad," Antley said. "Number six won it."[29]

His father shook his head. "I don't care about that," he said. "I came to see you." He grabbed his son and hugged him. The journalists kept asking Antley questions. "He gave everything he had and ran as hard as he could," Antley told the *Atlanta Constitution*, "but he couldn't give the people what they wanted."

Back at stall seventeen, Lukas, Laura, Jeff, Joanne McNamara and a few other friends and workers stood around waiting for the verdict on whether Charismatic would be all right. Lukas had taken off his suit jacket and his face was grim but he kept telling everyone the horse would be fine. This was the fifth time a Lukas colt had ended his career in a Triple Crown event. The media cockroaches were sure to go after him.

Dr. Jim Hunt and Dr. Larry Bramlage x-rayed the break. Lukas showed the Lewises the pictures. There were two fractures. "It's unsure when it happened," Dr. Bramlage told the *St. Louis Dispatch*, "but it could've been just before the wire. The way it happened means it cracked, and they went on before he pulled up."

Charismatic had fractured the condylar bone, near the ankle outside of the main cannon bone, shearing it vertically. He also fractured his sesamoid, the ankle bone. There was no swelling or bleeding, but on the X ray you could see the fragments of bone floating in the leg. One shard jutted out toward the skin but hadn't pierced it. Charismatic had probably run on three legs from the eighth or sixteenth pole.

They gave the horse tranquilizers and anti-inflammatory medicine and fit him with a tighter cast to get him through the night until surgery the next morning. "This may have happened in different strides," Lukas told reporters, "because there are two different fractures. He does seem pretty comfortable now."[30]

"What we ask as an industry of a three-year-old horse is unbelievable," Lewis told a reporter. "This horse just ran his heart out." Chris Antley walked up and Lewis put his hand on Antley's shoulder. "I'm proud of you," Lewis said. "You did all you could possibly do."

"The veterinarian was very complimentary toward Chris," Lukas told reporters on the scene. "She said she's only seen that twice before in her life when somebody jumped off. He immediately made sure he didn't put any weight [on the leg]. That probably kept it from separating."[31] Charismatic turned to the hay ball hanging near his stall door and started eating.

Charismatic would have three screws inserted into the cannon bone and the fragments picked out of the ankle.[32] Despite the fact that Charismatic now seemed comfortable and safe, real danger lay ahead. In 1975, the great filly Ruffian competed in a challenge race against the best colt of the time, Foolish Pleasure. Ruffian had built a fan base with American girls who saw in her a champion of their gender. The "Great Match Race" was like Bobby Riggs versus Billy Jean King and was broadcast live on CBS from Belmont. Coming down the backstretch, suddenly there was a crack, a snap so loud the spectators and television microphones could pick it up from the backside. Ruffian smashed against the rail. She was sedated, a cast put on her leg, and rushed to surgery. But after the veterinarians operated on her shattered sesamoids, she came out of her anaesthesia and struggled, trying to stand. She was so badly hurt in the attempt, she would never be able to live her natural life, even with surgery. "Put her down," her owner, Stuart Janney, said.[33] And she died on July 5, while all over America little girls sobbed in their beds.

"We don't want another Ruffian deal, we want him to be calm for his surgery," said Dr. Stephen Selway, Lukas's veterinarian. "He really shattered the sesamoid. It's like a jigsaw puzzle where all the pieces have the ends rubbed off. But if we can get everything to fall into place, the procedure shouldn't take more than two hours. My main objective is to get the fetlock joint aligned exactly. If we can do that, we should have a fairly sound horse with a happy life ahead of him." Charismatic would never race again, but they hoped to fix him up well enough that he could stand as stud.

Chuck and I drove, so sad, barely talking, to a bar in Dallas's Deep Elum neighborhood and watched the Knicks with a bunch of loud talkers clustered around us. We agreed that it helped when Larry Johnson shot a four-point basket with less than six seconds to go to defeat the Pacers by one point. We needed someone we cared about to win.

The Lewises worried about their horse, but they had planned a party at the Garden City Hotel. All the friends they brought in for this Belmont and all the people they needed to thank would be there. They asked Chris Antley if he would come. His presence would mean a lot to them, they said. So he left the barn to join them.[34] He told everyone at the party that the horse would be okay. He danced with the Roach daughters and sat talking to ABC field producer Natalie Jowett and his brother, Brian.

As the party wound down, people started drifting to the downstairs bar. Several people remember Antley ordering a drink from the bartender, then another one.

Two days later, Andrew Beyer of the *Washington Post* wrote a column about the race in which he asked, "Would Charismatic have won the Belmont Stakes if jockey Chris Antley had ridden him more patiently?" He faulted Antley for racing head-to-head with Silverbulletday. "Charismatic was a tough competitor, but he was able to become a star only because his rival three-year-olds were so undistinguished," wrote Beyer on June 7. He went on:

> Menifee, the runner-up in the Derby and the Preakness and a flop in
> the Belmont, has won a single stakes race in his career. Lemon Drop
> Kid hadn't won a stakes this year. Vision and Verse's greatest claim to

fame was a victory in the Illinois Derby. The winning times in the Triple Crown races confirm the impression that the three-year-old crop of 1999 is a below-average bunch.

If Charismatic had been born two years earlier, and had competed against Silver Charm, Free House and the rest of the class of '97, he wouldn't have finished first, second or third in any of the Triple Crown races. And if Charismatic had stayed healthy to run against the nation's top older horses later in the year, he would have found himself over-matched. If he were like the other Lukas-trained horses who have won Triple Crown races, his career would have ended not with a bang but a whimper.

Racing fans don't need to weep for Charismatic. He was never going to do anything that topped the dramas of his victories in the Kentucky Derby and the Preakness, and he departs the sport as a be-loved, tragic hero.[35]

Early that Monday morning, the day the *Washington Post* piece appeared, Ron Anderson waited at the Hay-Adams Hotel, all mahogany paneling and patterned carpets across from the White House, for the Ant Man to come in on the red-eye from Los Angeles. Antley had flown back to California to ride a few horses on Sunday. When he walked into the Hollywood Park paddock, everyone cheered for him and he was sur-prised. Then he saw the horse waiting for him in its stall, a red chestnut with white markings on his nose, and Antley felt like he was staring at the ghost of Charismatic.

In Washington, Anderson kept looking at the official schedule. Meet with the vice president and Tipper Gore. Have an audience with the president and first lady. Antley would take part in a forum on depression, hosted by Mrs. Gore. Ron Anderson had talked to Tipper's secretary three times arranging the details and finally said to her, "By the way, would you mind if I came?" and the secretary said they would love to have him. Anderson, for one, had never gotten to rub elbows with people like this, and now it was the whole day at the White House.

Good Morning America got word of Antley's invitation and rented the adjacent room at the Hay-Adams so they could interview him before-hand. They were right over there, on the other side of the wall, buzzing around, setting up lights.

Anderson noticed it was past 6:00, the time Antley's flight should have landed, so he called the jock's cell phone. The automated message picked up. He tried again later. Still no answer. He started calling California, tried phoning his own house now a little frantically.

Antley picked up. He said he'd missed the flight and wouldn't be able to get to D.C. He said he had forgotten his ID and couldn't get on the plane. He didn't apologize. He didn't sound upset.

As soon as Anderson hung up the phone, he knew he would have to go next door and knock. He would have to tell the camera crew with their hot lights and silver panels and cables and wires, and the producer, who like all morning producers was probably friendly and hopped up on coffee. He would have to hear them tell New York, who would probably have fits about the last-minute problem. And he would have to call the vice president's office, and those secretaries would print an amended schedule that made the names Chris Antley and Ron Anderson vanish without a trace, and Mrs. Gore's people would do the same as soon as Anderson called them and told them: Chris Antley missed his flight and won't be able to attend.

Anderson would tell them the information he needed to tell them, but not the awful truth that he now knew.

FOURTEEN

THE LONGEST ODDS

It's kind of hard to explain now why I contacted Chris Antley in June, weeks after his Belmont loss. Chuck was being ravaged by the chemo and radiation treatments, headed toward the actual day of his bone-marrow transplant, and I noticed that Antley would be riding out at Lone Star Park in a special jockeys' race. After watching Chuck endure almost two and a half months in the hospital over a six-month period, I felt desperate to amuse him, distract him in some way. In the first rounds of treatment, he felt well enough to enjoy music, watch movies, or take a short walk around the hall. But with the chemotherapy and radiation combined, he could, with effort, build up to watching the basketball play-offs at night. He would force himself to get on the treadmill occasionally. The best I could do to break his monotony was add a new poster to his walls every few days and stick stars in constellations on the walls while he slept so he would wake to something a little different.

So what seems like an odd contact was made in desperation. I thought it would be great for Chuck if the star athlete whom we had rooted for so intensely made one of those hospital bedside visits. I thought it would give Chuck something to think about afterward.

About a week before the race, I called Lone Star Park, and was referred to Ron Anderson. He told me to write Antley an e-mail, making the request. I told, in short form, the story of the dream and how happy we had been at the Derby when he had won, and so had we. All I knew about Antley at the time was that he was around our age, had been down and out, made a comeback, cradled Charismatic's leg, and had cried.

Right up until the day before the race at Lone Star, I hadn't gotten a response and wrestled with the idea of whether to push the whole thing by making another call. Maybe it was a stupid idea. Maybe Chuck would hate having a stranger in the room when he was so sick. Maybe Antley would be a bad guy. But I thought too, if one phone call could make Chuck happy I would be stupid not to make it.

Anderson immediately knew what the call was about. "Chris just needs directions," he said.

Antley was scheduled to arrive at 9:00 the next morning. Chuck vomited almost continually through that night. No ice was cold enough to numb the pain in his feet. He flashed in and out of delirium. "Hello, Granddad?" he said, participating in a one-way phone call complete with pauses for the replies. "Doing good, doing good. How's Norma?"

I kept fearing I had done something truly awful by setting up this meeting with Antley. When the jockey arrived, I would have to tell him to go away. I would feel guilty, but that was how things went sometimes. When dawn finally came, Chuck faded in and out of consciousness. As the clock's hands moved toward nine, I sat next to him on the bed. "Chuck," I said, "if you feel up to it, you might want to stay awake for a few minutes."

He held my hand and smiled. "Why? What's happening?"

I said, "There's something coming for you."

"From you?"

"Yes."

"In the mail?" he asked. "What is it?"

I heard some talking in the hall and through the slats of the louvered blind I could see a pair of smallish hands washing up at the sink in the nurse's station. There was some more talk from the hall. Then, the nurse, Trish, swung open the door.

"Chuck," she said, with a question in her voice, "there's a professional jockey here to see you . . . ?"

"Chris Antley?" Chuck laughed, his eyes still half open and not even looking at the doorway yet. Antley walked in, tan and fit, with clear blue eyes. He went up to Chuck and grasped his hand and pulled a chair to the bed.

Chuck, as it turned out, had dozens of questions about racing and specific people in the business, and Antley answered them all. He would look at Chuck and talk and smile, then turn to me, and tears would be welling in his eyes.

He told us the Lewises had given him a breeding share in Charismatic and that he was going to ride the colt's offspring to the Triple Crown in three years. And he described how, after the ambulance ferried Charismatic off the track on Belmont Day, he had walked toward the grandstands and the jocks' room. He heard the crowd clapping and cheering. He turned around to look behind him to see where the winner was absorbing this applause, but there was no one there. He realized the crowd was cheering for him and he couldn't believe it.

He told us about an injury he once sustained when a horse trampled him and he had to shoot his swollen forearm with cortisone to ride in the next race. "Hey, Chuck," he said, in a tone that implied they had been friends all their lives. "No fear, man. No fear." And he gave a closed fist gesture of power, and Chuck laughed and did it back and said, "Okay, Chris."

He stayed almost an hour, and then the woman who drove him there from the track said they had to get going. Chuck thanked him profusely, and Antley said that he had gotten the e-mail, with the dream and all, and liked those kinds of things. He said the race had seemed so much bigger than just a race, like a movie, like a magic thing, you couldn't believe how it affected so many people.

When he walked out, we could hear the nurses talking to him and laughing. Trish came into Chuck's room later and asked why a professional jockey had visited, so we told her the story. She told us that after Antley left, he came back to the nurse's station because he had forgotten his cell phone. He seemed really happy and said to them, "You take care of Chuck. Chuck's going to be okay."

He said to them, "I'm the miracle man, and I'm going to make sure he's okay."

I called Antley's agent later to see where we could send thank-you flowers and Anderson told me the visit had been important to Antley. He had been so depressed after the Belmont, but seeing Chuck's struggle made him ashamed for thinking he had it rough. He had just agreed to do the Special Olympics because he wanted to help people. He told Anderson to ask me to send updates on Chuck's health and to get an address where he could mail some signed pictures.

But in the next weeks, Chuck had a hard stretch accepting the new bone marrow. The graft-versus-host disease caused fiery rashes and nausea and excruciating pain in his feet. On the fourth of July, a fill-in nurse set the valve on a transfusion of platelets too high, clogging his blood, and his pulse raced at sprinting speed for almost five hours. The doctors had to put him on oxygen to feed the effort of his heart.

When he finally left the hospital, I went to join my family on vacation and found out before seven in the morning the first day that a close friend from New York had died in an accident, so I flew back to the city for the funeral, then returned to Dallas. In those first days back, Chuck started experiencing stabbing back pain caused by an infection. His pulse would be so high I could see his ankles rippling. The doctors gave him antibiotics but discovered that the infection was lodged in his heart catheter, so every time the hospital gave him transfusions of platelets and red blood cells he was flushed with a potentially fatal bacteria.

So we were back in the hospital and, in the night, I dreamed that my friend from New York died. I woke sobbing and found that I was lying on the foldout chair, and then I realized that my friend from New York's death was not a nightmare but an evil reality, and then it came to me that not only was my friend from New York's death real, but reality also included the fact that I was in the hospital with my beloved Chuck, who was teetering precariously on the edge of life himself. Chuck woke to my sobs and said, "Sweetie, sweetie, come here," and I lay down on the bed with him, with my head on his chest, but carefully so I did not hurt him by pressing on his heart catheter.

I did not call Antley to update him because I did not think this progression of events was the sort of miracle Antley was looking for.

There's a rotten theory given credence in health trade paperbacks that optimistic people, patients who refuse to give up, beat their illnesses and live miraculous trophy years. For some reason, thinking that you can imbue dice with lucky powers is considered a mental snap but thinking you can control cell replication through willpower is credible. It used to torture Chuck that perhaps he wasn't regarding the whole event with suitable spirit.

One day a nurse told us a story about a curmudgeonly patient she treated in the chemo ward who told her he looked forward to dying. He was such an awful patient, she worried he was trying to speed along his demise. She asked him, didn't he feel he had anything to live for? He said no. She asked him, what about family, friends, career, beauty in nature? He hated all of it, he said. He had absolutely nothing to live for. His decline continued until the nurse was sure he would die the next day. Then suddenly he rebounded. He walked out of the hospital one day and never returned. Had he suddenly found a reason to live? No. He despised every breath, he wished he would die, but he didn't. That story ought to be told to every fatally ill person who is not only dying, but is made to feel guilty for it.

Chuck was released again and began to build some strength over the next weeks, but he wasn't rebounding as he had in the past. He suspected he had relapsed in the middle of September. I had moved into his father's house by then, and he would come to see me in the morning and tell me how he had woken several times in the night drenched with sweat and changed T-shirts. "I think it's the blanket on that bed," he said.

"Yeah," I assured him. "I used to get night sweats all the time. It's nothing. Just nerves."

A few small red spots appeared on the palms of his hands. He stroked the skin. "Do you think that looks like petechia?" he asked, a sign of low platelet counts. "You know," he said, "it's probably just something I did opening that bottle of wine the other night."

We drove to the hospital for another biopsy and after they performed the test, he lay down in one of the rooms and I sat beside him. The nurse came in and said that in the preliminary examination under the microscope, there was an abnormal cell. It didn't look good. If he had relapsed, Chuck was out of chances. Chuck lay stretched out over the length of that table with his arms crossed behind his head. I started crying. He told the nurse he was grateful for all they had done for him during the treatment and he didn't hold anything against them. He knew it was hard for them and they had been really sweet.

Then the doctor came in and said it didn't look like a blast cell, after all. Chuck probably had an infection. He hadn't relapsed and they would treat it with antibiotics. We went home exhausted.

The next day we went back for Chuck's transfusion, and in the waiting room surrounded by other patients in various stages of treatment, the nurse came and sat down next to us. She said in fact Chuck had relapsed. The blast cells were 50 percent of his marrow. He looked around blankly at all the people who had just heard his death sentence and asked if we could go in the back.

In the examination room, the doctor and nurse told Chuck he could try for a second bone-marrow transplant but the odds of success were something like 12 percent that he could live for two years. They would treat him with the same chemotherapies he had been given the last time, but they wouldn't be able to use the radiation too because his body couldn't take it. Without treatment, they said, Chuck had three to six weeks to live.

Chuck didn't want to die in the hospital with his mouth tasting like metal. The nurses on the outpatient ward concurred. "Oh, Chuck," they would say softly, with their hands on his arm. "You must be so tired. I know I wouldn't do two transplants."

His family and friends called frantically around the country trying to find a hospital that had a treatment that might save him, and he would say, you do what you can, but I can't spend my last days like that. Still, you could see hope breathe through his face when Sloan-Kettering, for example, told me they thought there was a protocol Chuck would fit into, and they would check which one. Then you could see the hope in him exhale the next day when I came back from the pay phone in the outpatient lobby and reported they had been very sad when they told me, "I'm sorry, we have nothing for your friend Chuck." He was already too close to death.

Doc Adams offered to go talk to the doctors in charge of Chuck's treatment to see how his prognosis looked from a medical perspective. I remember glancing out the window of the Fulghams' house one afternoon and seeing Doc Adams making his way up the walk, slightly stooped and looking as sad as an older man could look, his eyes cast down, his steps coming slowly one after the other, and his face slack under a lovely Texas sky. He and Chuck sat in the living room and talked, and when they finished, Doc Adams came to say good-bye, and Chuck clapped him on the shoulder. "Thanks, Doctor Adams," he said, but they both looked tired. Later on, Chuck told us the doctor treating Chuck had told Doc Adams that Chuck's chances of survival after a second bone-marrow treatment were 6 percent. The doctor had doubled the odds when talking to us civilians.

In those last weeks, every few days I would drive Chuck to the outpatient clinic for transfusions of platelets to keep him from bleeding to death. He sat in the passenger seat sipping water that he always carried with him to moisten his drying mouth, and he was so thin and tender, so fragile, he could have been a baby at the beginning of his life and not a thirty-year-old man at the end. It seemed he always started discussing the hardest subjects on the drive. "Now, sweetie," he would say. "Tell me what you're going to do in the first few weeks after I die. I want to be sure you have a plan," or "If the pain gets too much at the end, you're going to have to help me get out. Will you?" I would let the car stray over the dotted line on the two-lane curving road in Highland Park, almost scraping a BMW or Mercedes to the right or almost jumping the median and careening across the road into the park that ambled alongside, through the rhododendron, over the manicured banks, and pushing down the lily pads into the depths of Turtle Creek, but unfortunately, Turtle Creek would not be deep enough.

"Hey, there," Chuck would coo to the nurses at the clinic's front desk. "How you doing? I think I'm only going to be needing platelets today." He would engage in this smooth-talking bargain with his own death. He did not want to have to wait for the tests to come back on his own morning blood sample, then bide his time for the pouch of replacement blood to be ordered and delivered, then watch while the transfusion dripped into his veins. On the daily printout, we tracked the losing battle. On September 1, he had 137 platelets. Twenty-eight days later, 10 showed up bold and underlined to signal emergency. A transfusion brought him up to 23 for the next day, but then back down to 12 on October 4, and 9 three days later. He could not hold on to the platelets, which burned off in 106-degree fevers almost every night.

All the sad people sat around us at the clinic, the older women with dyed red hair and pocketbooks in their laps talking about how they could go to the Sonny's after the transfusion, and the gaunt forty-year-old men in worn jeans who stalked outside every now and again to get a smoke or take the toddler for a little run down the hall and otherwise sat worried and reticent, thumbing the *People* magazine from three months prior and saying from time to time to their wives, who still wore lots of makeup in brave and beautiful defiance of the chemo pumping into their veins, "How are you feeling?" And then there was John, who was in his midtwenties with hair growing back in what I remember to be stylish blond tufts and a goatee, whom Chuck befriended and whom Chuck worried about in and out of the hospital. He died on one of the days Chuck was worrying about him, but the nurses didn't tell Chuck that bad news until they knew Chuck was dying too.

Chuck's friends in the Ukraine pooled their funds to make a long-distance call. We have found help for you, they told him, there is a doctor in Moldavia (or was it Moravia?) who does a hot-water treatment for you in your veins. You should plan to go see him.

Chuck would thank them profusely, speaking Ukrainian. He had called many of them when he first found out he would be dying and asked me to stay with him as he told them, the sibilant language on his tongue, trying so hard to be tender with the tragic news, it sounded as if between each syllable he was giving a comforting, hush, hush, hush.

He received cards and letters from all over the world—friends, relatives, coworkers, students, teachers, all telling him in one last gasp how they felt about him. Some people wrote him poems that seemed oddly elegiac when he was lying right there in shorts and a T-shirt from the club where he once worked the door, planning whether he wanted a burger from Jack's, a childhood haunt that he eternally loved.

He was known for giving great advice and now, with the hot beam of mortality on him, people asked for insights as if he were an oracle.

A sweet young couple sat on the edge of the bed and asked if he had any suggestions on how to raise their child.

"What did you say?" I asked.

"I said, 'I don't know. I never had kids,' " he replied, laughing and bewildered.

And in this amazing time that most people would love to be allowed before their death, but few could handle with such grace, the praise and recollections and tears kept coming, like high-stakes yearbook entries, and I went to see him between visitors and he looked stunned. He said, "It's too much. I can't even hear what people are saying anymore. I can't absorb it." But he did, for us.

The day Chuck died, the hospice nurse came to check on him. He still had the heart rate of an athlete at rest. She said his pulse was strong. She thought, if we really felt he might need it occasionally, maybe it was time for him to consider getting a cane.

*   *   *

What is it that distinguishes us from animals? Perhaps it is our insecurities, our fear that we are not lovable or being loved. "When I was small, I felt and knew that I was a good person," Chuck told me late in a night bisected by insomnia about a week before he died. "Then as things went on, I lost that sense. But you know everything about me, you know all my secrets, and you loved me unconditionally, and I feel that way again—the way I did as a kid, that I'm right with the world." He had tears running down his cheeks, but his voice never cracked. He had done the same for me.

After his death, I felt I could see the way people are desiccated for lack of love, how they would change if they received an infusion, how if you look at everyone in the world at any time as if they were the subject of a casual snapshot placed in an album, tacked on a wall, cherished by someone who knows that person or knew them and loved them, you would rather die than treat them cheaply.

Nature always seemed like the best place to perceive some greater meaning in the world, but it started looking like just chaos to me. I did still feel something divine in the love between people, which from time to time flared up pure and steady as the flame of a Bunsen burner, and one of the places I could sometimes watch it or feel it was at the racetrack, which in a way seemed paradoxical because the track was filled from stable to starting gate with loners.

One day in the spring, after Chuck's death, I went to Claiborne Farm in Paris, Kentucky—one of the greatest breeding farms in the world and the resting place of Secretariat, Mr. Prospector, and Swale—to see if someone would show me around. A man at the front gate buzzed me in, but told me rather curtly that I would only be able to look at the stallion barn. Someone, he said, would meet me near the door.

A big-framed man named Charlie offered to show me the studs and the little horse cemetery behind the main office. Swale was there, often said to be the first racehorse to be buried whole. People used to inter just a racehorse's head, heart and hooves to represent the most important parts of a thoroughbred, but Swale was so well loved, he earned the dignity of entering the earth in his entirety. After Charlie showed me the cemetery, we went to see Unbridled in his paddock. A younger guy walked down, leading the horse. Charlie introduced him as Greg Roberts, and Charlie told him that I was writing a book and wanted to learn a little more about breeding farms. He asked Greg if he would take me around, and the guy scowled and said something about lunch. Unbridled kept pulling on his bit and showing his teeth and Greg yanked at the lead to settle him. The studs get a little mean in breeding season, Greg said, and walked him into the barn.

I was getting into my car to go, when Greg walked up. Okay, he said, I'll take you around for a quick tour. He got in the front seat.

He directed me to drive up the hill toward the foals' paddocks, and he told me about how Swale got his name as a yearling. The farm had a "lightning list" of all the horses to be brought in during a storm because they were so valuable, but one time a thunderstorm hit the farm that was so severe the workers gathered all the horses to go inside, but they couldn't find that one colt. The next morning they found him curled in a swale on the hill.

Greg took me to the old cemetery at the back of the farm where the great teasers were buried. He told me about the weaning process, when the yearlings are separated from their mothers so they can learn to race and the mares prepare to breed again.

"Is that upsetting for the horses?" I asked.

"Yes," he said.

"How do you know?"

"Well, when the foals stand all day at the fence screaming and the mothers can't stop pacing the rail you get some idea."

He told me about the old racehorse Easy Goer, who one day was brought out of his paddock to be shown to a tour group and dropped dead on the spot. And he described how the guys in the stallion barn cried the day they were forced to put the great stallion Mr. Prospector down and how each of those guys still remembered the exact time to the minute.

After we drove around, under the sycamores tall as city buildings and by the practice track painted a friendly yellow and surrounded by dandelions in seed, Greg asked if I would do him a favor and drive him into town to watch a race on TV at the bar.

I said that was fine. At the bar, we talked a little bit then he leaned back. "So," he said, "I've got a good story for your book."

"What is it?" I asked.

"It's about leukemia and horse racing," he said. He took a picture out of his wallet of a young girl, maybe fifteen. "This is Amanda," he said. She was being treated at a hospital in his Ohio hometown. He had read in the local Kentucky paper about how she once lived around Paris, Kentucky, and loved horses, so when he was up visiting his family in Ohio, he went to the hospital and dropped off pictures and a bridle for her. She loved the gifts, and they started corresponding. He wanted to figure out something more he could do for her, to make her happy while she was going through all that treatment.

I told him then, "I have a story about leukemia and horse racing too."

I dropped Greg back at the barn about an hour later. He asked me, if one of the Claiborne mares went into labor that night, would I want to see a foal being born. I said yes. He said wear old clothes.

The barn looked lovely, so dark with just a yellow glow fanning out from the three stalls of the mares who appeared ready. Greg and I sat on a hay bale and talked about the moon, a few days from ripeness, and whether its fullness had an effect on the pace of birthing, because three foals in one night was certainly a lucky coincidence for me, just there that one day. We studied the logbooks to see if this were a regular lunar phenomenon, but no tendency seemed clear. The moon chart, the horse equivalent of a horoscope, indicated that "bowels" would be most important that day, and indeed one of the newborn foals ended up with a vicious gastrointestinal disease in his first months.

The office was about a hundred feet from the barn, and that's where James and Gravy sat watching TV. They were two white-haired men who probably didn't chat much but had seen it all in the foaling world. The birth log stored in the desk drawer listed the expected date of delivery, the kind of horse, and occasionally, written above or below the listing, the words "nice foal"—or occasionally the shorthand for tragedy, "foal put down" or "mare put down." Above the door hung framed photos of a dozen or so clean-cut men who made their marks at Claiborne. It was such a strange business—managed with militaristic precision but buffeted by the mayhem of nature, detached in its volume of births but sentimental in the way both men proudly draped their arms around new foals in a collection of stray snapshots.

In the dark stalls, the neighboring mares would only be able to see the light between the cracks of the wallboards and hear the constant restless swish of straw as the mare in labor paced the perimeter. Evening Primrose embodied the very ember of pain that night. She stalked, rubbing her flanks against the walls. Sweat ran down her neck and across her chest, along the crooked paths of veins that laced under her full belly and waxy teats. Every now and then she stopped in the center of the stall and lifted one hoof slowly, like someone raising an index finger to make a point. Then she put it down, like the idea had vanished and there was nothing to do but scrape her hoof lightly on the ground. At other moments, she circled to the stall door and pressed one eye and a flaring nostril to the crack, as if she were on a quest for sympathy, but in reality probably gauging our distance from her sanctuary since horses in the wild tend to give birth in dark isolation for safety.

James and Gravy came to check the horses. They talked about the coyote spotted at the far end of the farm. Gravy took a flashlight into the hayloft to see if the raccoons were still making a home there. The mare lay down and then struggled to her feet again. That was the sign. James and Gravy went around the corner, got into their coveralls and pulled on long, latex gloves. Gravy grabbed a twitch, the leather loop attached to a long pole, and then the men entered the stall. Gravy caught Evening Primrose's halter. He slipped her nose and lip in the twitch and the brown hide and pink flesh bulged out like a dying party balloon. The horse was obviously in pain, showing the whites of her eyes. Jim stepped behind her flanks and snipped open her vagina with a small pair of silver scissors. It had been stitched up eleven months before to keep out bacteria, as soon as she first showed signs of pregnancy.

Fluid gushed out and then a white bubble inflated from between her flanks. She began pacing again. James stopped her. He reached a hand into her vaginal cavity to feel for the foal. Its nose was straight, he told us. He had me reach in too. I think I can safely say that when you push your hand into a mare's vagina for the first time, your powers of detection are not exactly fine-tuned, but I did feel the firm snout about eight inches in.

I stepped back. Slowly the front hooves of the foal emerged, crossed like chopsticks and lifeless, looking almost ridiculous sticking from her. She lay down again. Gravy and James attached wires with handles on the end to the foal's legs. When she pushed, they pulled. They asked me to take one of the handles. With each pull, the mare's body gurgled as its warm innards released the foal. The nose appeared, then the head. James and Gravy grabbed the foal's body and leaned their weight backward to get more power. Then the foal slid out on a wave of fluid and blood.

"It's a colt," one of them said. The colt's eyes were open. One of the men brushed the liquid off his nose so he could breathe. The colt lay behind Evening Primrose, who rested on her side breathing heavily. He kept lifting his head and laying it down on the straw drizzled with watery blood.

Less than six months before, I had sat on the side of Chuck's bed and watched him die, watched that weird blue shadow sweep over his face as if cast by a low-flying plane. I watched the skin of his face pull taut like the fabric in an embroidery hoop, and leave him nothing but a cooling body. And now, six months later, I watched an animal emerge through the wormhole of its mother's body into this world. I would like to say that I felt a celestial symphony of meaning at those exact moments, but in fact, the moments of transition seemed fascinating but strangely flat. It was the times before and the times after that made my heart pound and my body shake with the enormity of it. What Chuck meant to me before and the agony that followed his departure was what rocked me. The profundity of the mare's pain as she silently pawed the air, and then the colt a few days later, scampering by her side like a sea unicorn, bounding and playing.

But in the precise moment when that colt was born, I was struck only by his bewilderment. In his clumsy movements and bobbing head he seemed not to be the golden gift of Poseidon, noble and assured, but instead, with his legs folded under him—as useless as a person's arms after they have fallen asleep beneath a heavy head in the night—he seemed to embody the baffled sentiment, "I'm a horse?"

Evening Primrose got up again and pawed hard now at the ground by her colt.

"You stupid," Greg said, pushing her away from the colt's fragile, supine body. She paced the stall, trailing the white membrane, with its streaks of blood and dangling ruby sac, like a sheet after the ancient wedding night.

Evening Primrose licked the colt's flanks to encourage him to stand, and he, in turn, licked the stall wall. He made a few flailing attempts to prop himself on his legs like stilts, like tent poles, and then crumpled in the corner, banging his head against the wall. Each time he tried, a tremor shook his small body.

Yet, within twenty minutes he was standing. Within thirty, he was nursing. The second mare gave birth to a filly almost simultaneously to Evening Primrose, and the third mare stood in her stall crunching hay between her teeth, biding her time.

I saw Greg again at the end of the 2000 Kentucky Derby. We went over to the barn where his friend worked as an assistant trainer and walked through the shedrow, stopping at each horse stall. He petted the horses' noses and put his cheek up against their necks and they let him do it immediately, without jerking away. Then we went outside, down the road, with the track just past the fence to our right. The infield was littered with plastic cups and paper plates. Although the sky had started to go pink with sunset, the evening still simmered in the long orange rays of Derby Day. I felt the sweat that had basted my skin through the long hours, the dust, the weariness from trundling along since dawn.

A pale, shirtless man came running toward the fence from the track side and rolled over the rail, throwing his immense, sunburnt belly forward like a medicine ball. He hit the ground, got up and ran a few more plodding steps. A policeman vaulted the fence just after him, threw himself on the man and brought him down with a mighty thud in the dust in front of us.

"That's good," Greg said, stepping around the man, who was now being punched, cussed, and handcuffed. "You've got the whole Derby experience."

Greg told me he wanted to send me some things that might help my research, and he was putting in something he wanted me to have because it would mean more to me than it did to him. He had already told me that he had watched the 1999 Kentucky Derby, from the backside. When the race was over, he and his friends sprinted across to the winner's circle and jumped in right next to the Lewises and Charismatic.

The package arrived a few days later. He sent me stories on great racehorses, some old programs. I leafed through the clips, then came to an envelope bulging a bit. Inside was something wrapped in a paper napkin. I unfolded the napkin and found a dried rose. Greg had plucked it from Charismatic's winning shawl on that Derby Day and now was giving it to me.

The last day of Chuck's life, I was putting lotion on his feet because it was the only thing I could think to do that might make him feel vaguely good. He started waving them side to side. "What are you doing?" I asked, afraid I was hurting him.

"I'm flirtin' with you," he said huskily.

All of a sudden, I had a perspective on the whole situation that seemed to take in the universe at once. The romance and passion had all been a beautiful trick, a way of throwing Chuck and me together into the deepest leagues of intimacy when we both needed it most. "You know, Chuck," I said, "you're my best friend . . . the best friend I ever had." And I had known him such a short time, one full year almost to the day.

FIFTEEN

FALLING OFF

In September 2000, I tried the numbers I had for Antley from that visit he made to the Dallas hospital fifteen months earlier. I wanted to get his insights on horse racing because along the research trail, people kept referring me back to Antley. Trainers told me he was one of the smartest jockeys they ever met. Track workers volunteered that he was the nicest guy in racing. But when I tried to reach him, he had disappeared into a fortress. The e-mail I sent him was returned because of an inoperable address. His agent's cell phone number now belonged to someone else. I finally reached the agent through another number but he sounded sad. "He's a great kid, but I don't know how to reach him," he said. "If I e-mailed him, I probably would never hear from him. He's all confused. I stopped working with him four months ago, and then he stopped riding."

Another former agent just sighed. "Howard Hughes would have been easier to find," he said. I explained how I met Antley a year before. "I've known him for a long time," the agent said. "Don't put hearts on him."

In January, Antley gave an interview to the *Kentucky Derby 2000* magazine. "I beat myself last year," he said. "Now I want to direct my energy outside. Get off of self. It's time to do something in my sport with people—learning and teaching. I'm tired of fighting me. I want to set an example." But then Antley vanished from public view. The superstar jock had gone stealth again.

How much Antley tormented himself after the Belmont was a subject of speculation among his friends. "When it was over," Craig Perret said, "you ever know something in your heart? He was standing there crying . . . I knew he was on a disaster. It was just too much for him."

Antley's main drug counselor at the Smithers Institute, Dr. Allan Lans, who worked with other athletes like Dwight Gooden and Darryl Strawberry, also thought Belmont had taken a toll, exacerbating a bad situation. Lans said that he and Antley mainly talked about the jockey's addiction itself, not about its possible roots. He knew that Antley had a tough childhood, although not the worst the doctor had heard of. There was no trauma so severe in Antley's personal history that it couldn't be overcome, Lans thought. He didn't think the jockey was born manic depressive but that Antley had exacerbated his mood swings through the years with starvation and narcotics. Still, Lans believed he could detect a factor in Antley's basic makeup that led him to trouble. "This is a guy, when we talk about his communication with horses," Lans said, "this happens with someone who is really in tune with what he's feeling. There's not a lot of difference between his actions, feelings and thoughts. That personality is unique and rare, and it's also someone who is very vulnerable. It's emotionally very advanced, but also not too smart. To allow yourself to be exposed that way is dangerous. The bad guys could move in. But that's also what the animals sensed in him and why he could communicate in a very rich way, more than the rest of us really can."

I asked him about Antley's superstitions, his thinking that the number six had meaning for him. Lans said that was all harmless superstition, just childish thinking. I talked about Antley's telling his father that number six had won the Belmont, and Lans looked saddened. "I just remember thinking, with that race, how it ended, somehow it was . . ." He rubbed his hangdog face with his hand. "I had this almost spooky feeling that it was over for Chris. His response . . . I thought, You can't survive in this world like *that*. Anyone who feels that . . . The track's a place for big boys. Big, nasty people. You know how there's no crying in baseball?" Lans shook his head. "And I thought, Chris decided that the only way to deal with this was just to die."

After Antley returned to California, his jockey friend Fernando Valenzuela used to tease him about the Belmont. "Boy, you just did it so dramatically," Valenzuela said. "You know, you won everybody's hearts. Mr. Wonderful. Mr. Nice Guy."

And Antley laughed. "Shut up," he said.

One of Antley's jockey friends told me a story how one night Antley called his agent from his car phone as he was speeding down the freeway.

I'm being followed, the jockey told his agent. Pushing something like ninety miles an hour, he couldn't shake a black SUV riding on his bumper.

Try to get a license-plate number, the agent advised him.

Antley slammed his car into a 180-degree spin and let the tailer fly by. He caught the numbers and rattled them off. When they called the plate into a buddy at the police department, the vehicle came up FBI. It was not clear what part of that story actually happened, but Antley's friends passed it along and debated between their cynical and awestruck selves: Were Antley's conspiracies and predictions truth, a delusion caused by some chemical brew in his brain, the after-tremors of years of drug use, or a kind of soothsaying.

"There was a fate thing going on in his mind that was deeper than most people have," said Don Murray, who ran the Winner's Foundation, the drug counseling program at the Santa Anita track. "He would almost laugh at you about his predictions and stuff. He'd say, 'Someday you'll understand.' You wondered about it because how does a guy make one million dollars a year off of day-trading. He must know something I don't know, because I didn't do it.

"I think he had a sense that something bad was going to happen,"

Murray added. "But that could be from depression and alcohol. When you're drinking too much, a feeling of doom hangs over you."

When Antley told his friend Gary Stevens one day in November 2000 that "they" were going to get him and there was nothing Antley or anybody else could do, Stevens didn't know whether this was a symptom of manic depression or something else.

Who's they? Stevens asked.

But Antley only smiled and shook his head. He seemed peaceful, as if he had accepted the situation. The whole thing, Antley said, would be clear in a few weeks. Antley told his mother a few years earlier that he would die on the track, but that didn't end up being one of his accurate predictions.

One day in late November, Antley took down the picture of Laffit Pincay on the day he broke Willie Shoemaker's win record. It had hung on his living room wall, across from a panel of mirrors that he despised. In their reflection, he saw how he was gaining weight day by day. Where the photograph of the legendary jockey had been, Antley drew a crucifix. The wall was being rebuilt, and at that point was just plasterboard being readied for painting, so no one thought the temporary artwork was too strange. Antley had liked to draw as a kid, after all.

Several people remembered seeing the depiction of Jesus on the cross, but no one could later agree what Antley had written beneath the scene. Gary Stevens thought the words were "Jesus, Please Save Me." Don Murray remembered them as, "God Loves," and didn't pay too much mind. Alcoholics, he said, tend to get highly emotional when they're drinking and do such things. No one would be able to verify what Antley was trying to communicate in those last days because a week before he died, his real estate agent, Cathy Park, asked Andy the handyman to paint the drawing over. Antley wanted to get a smaller place up in Sierra Madre, now that he was living alone. Park was showing the house to prospective buyers and that kind of artistic expression could kill a sale. By the time Antley died on December 2, 2000, facedown in his hallway, blood pooled around his head, the wall was a fresh white.

Antley was barefoot, in a blood-spattered T-shirt and khaki pants, and there was more blood low on the walls near him and on the floor. It had soaked the rug beneath him and was trailed in pawprints near his body. He had a large hematoma high on his forehead and a puncture wound near the scalp. His forearms and feet were covered in bruises and his knuckles were scraped. A cluster of crumpled tissue lay near his head, as if he had tried to staunch one of the wounds.

Part of the glass coffee table in the living room was dusted with a powder that looked like methamphetamine, but otherwise the house was orderly, except for the bedroom. The door had been torn from its hinges and was leaning against the hallway wall. Blood speckled the door frame and the floor just inside the entrance. The sheets were tugged off the bed. By the front door, at some distance from where Antley was found, the first police officer on the scene discovered a few drops of blood.

The detective and firefighter called to the scene that night filled out their reports as "homicide." The coroner's investigator there concurred. He reported, "This is a homicide. The decedent has suffered blunt force trauma to the head. He has defensive bruises and abrasions to the arms. There are obvious signs of struggle throughout the home." Commander Mary Schander of the Pasadena Police Department arrived to handle questions as reporters got word that one of America's top jockeys had met his end. She told the journalists assembled that Antley had died of "massive head trauma," and passed out a press release echoing the same.

The morning after Antley's body was found, his neighbor across the street, Jerry Holt, walked over to clean up the mess that the media left on the curb outside his dead friend's house. Instead of regular trash, he found envelopes of marked blood evidence that the detectives had left behind. Holt got in his car and drove them down to the police department.

Every day Chris Antley went to work, tens of thousands of people made predictions through bets on whether he would do well or not. The night Chris Antley died, the handicappers in the police, fire, and coroners departments as well as many of his friends and family bet that his thirty-four-year-old life had ended in murder. While the official investigation got under way, Antley's friends and family started piecing together their own understanding of what his life had been from that Belmont day in June 1999 up until December 2000, looking for clues as to how he died.

Just before the 1999 Derby, Antley made an offer on a $1.2 million house through his real estate agent Cathy Park. The place was a large single-story home on a quiet cul de sac in San Rafael, a leafy neighborhood that was a quick commute from the Santa Anita track in Arcadia. He had four bedrooms now so he invited his brother, Brian, and half-brother, Richie, to move from South Carolina to stay with him. Park promised to set them up in their own construction business, Antley Brothers' Building Service.

The house had an office, three fireplaces, a big library and a pool. Most of the backyard was taken up by a lake with a painted blue bottom that was a back hole of a neighboring golf course. Antley said it reminded him of home. A bridge connected Antley's yard to a small island, and his brothers and Park bought him a sailor hat and called him Gilligan. To add to Antley's little paradise, his neighbor Jim Herzfeld gave him a stray dog, and the jockey named him Summer.

Antley had been hard hit by the experience of Belmont, but there were signs he still looked optimistically on life. He proudly told Valenzuela that ABC's *20/20* was coming to do a profile on him. Natalie Jowett, the ABC field producer on the Triple Crown series, had fallen for Antley. When he walked into the studio for an interview the day after his Derby win, she remembered being surprised at how good-looking he was. Then, when he answered her questions, he didn't try to deny the problems he had struggled with, and she fell for him right there. By her own admission, she relentlessly pursued him. She had dated Mark McGwire, the St. Louis Cardinal who had become the home run king in 1998, a few times. Antley's friends said he was proud that she had been romantically linked to someone famous before and now she had a crush on him.

Jowett wrote Antley daily e-mails, called regularly and sent letters. In August, she told him he should take part in the Special Olympics, which she was covering. "He loved those little kids at the Special Olympics," Cathy Park recalled. "He came back covered with pins they traded."

Antley now had a home, a romance, and a potentially lucrative side career with his stock-market reports. Around five thousand people received the *Ant Man Report* every day and he made more than $1 million investing in the stock market in one year. Antley still had that magic touch with horses too. The trainer Vladimir Cerin and his wife, Kellie, couldn't fathom what was wrong with one of their horses, Diablo's Express. The colt would go into a trance and look as if he might collapse on the track. The Cerins put the horse through extensive cardiac evaluations but couldn't find anything wrong. That summer of 1999, Kellie Cerin and Antley were sitting outside their barn when Diablo came back from a gallop. He started shaking and his eyes rolled back in his head. Antley walked over to the horse and wrapped his arms around Diablo's neck. "It's all right, buddy, you're okay," he said. He kept talking into the horse's ear. Diablo sighed and stopped shaking. Eventually the colt went on to win purses.

But Antley started unraveling professionally. "Things got worse," Ron Anderson said. "Chris seemed to get very depressed after the Triple Crown situation. I went through this with Gary Stevens too when he rode Silver Charm. I think in their own little way they felt like they were going to rescue the business, because we really needed some sort of hero. We *still* need a Triple Crown winner. Chris and Gary thought that they could rescue the business on their own shoulders. And when it didn't work out, they both went through a depressing time.

"I worked with Chris until the end of the year," Anderson continued. "By that point, he was a complete mess. He was heavy, he wasn't paying attention, he wasn't coming out to work. He used the excuse that he needed time to keep reducing, but that wasn't the problem."

Cerin said Antley thought that 2000 would bring the Second Coming. He studied the Bible and started quoting Scripture. He said when he was weight lifting he sometimes could rise up above the room and look down.

The day after the Breeders' Cup, Antley stopped riding. He didn't go near the track for almost seven weeks, because the knee injury from the autumn of 1998 had acted up again. He tried at the end of January to exercise horses, but it was too painful. On the morning of January 29, 2000, he underwent arthroscopic knee surgery. He told his friends he would be back at the track by the end of the next month.

But Antley's loved ones and associates were leaving him. Jerry Bailey had called Anderson to see if he would move East to represent him. Anderson had waited through January for Antley to get back. His other client, Gary Stevens, needed a break from the tight U.S. weight restrictions and left for England to reinvigorate his career. With one jockey disabled and the other out of the country, Anderson felt he had no choice but to go to Bailey. Anderson told Antley he was leaving. They would have to find Antley a new agent. "At that point, Chris copped an attitude that I'd given up the ship or whatever," Anderson said. "Believe me, I didn't give up nothing. Nobody could have done what I did."

Antley went back on February 25 to work horses and then got mounts for races. Charlie McCaul, the clerk of scales at Santa Anita, recalled his getting more depressed as the meet went on. Every day, he dreaded asking Antley to weigh in because the needle crept up and Antley didn't seem to know what to do. Too heavy to get the good horses and distracted by his depression, Antley's racing statistics sunk lower. Jim Herzfeld, Antley's next-door neighbor, said the jockey told him he wanted to quit. The whole ordeal was getting to be too hard, not being able to eat what he wanted he said, and he couldn't do it any longer.

On March 19, Antley rode Commendable, a star horse trained by Lukas and owned by the Lewises, in the San Felipe at Santa Anita. The horse was listed as carrying 116 pounds, but Antley couldn't make weight and the horse carried two more pounds than he was supposed to—just inside the legal limit but a disadvantage for the horse. Antley and Commendable led for the first six furlongs, then finished fourth.

Chris Antley's final race was on board a three-year-old filly in a six-furlong maiden special-weight race that same day. A six-furlong race, and the horse was aptly named Sixshooter. Six and six. Antley crossed the finish line in second. He dismounted Sixshooter and never got on another thoroughbred again.

Antley called the stewards at Santa Anita on March 22 and told them to take him off his mounts, and the next day he said he wouldn't be riding anymore. He asked to be taken off the card because he had emotional issues and weight problems.[1] Vladimir Cerin had penciled Antley in to ride Archer City Slew in the $600,000 Spiral Stakes that Saturday. When he heard the news, he erased Antley's name and wrote in another jockey.

"I don't know when he'll come back," Antley's new agent, John DeSantis, told the press. "He'll keep working horses in the meantime. He'll be back as soon as he's ready. He was one of the best when he was active, and he'll be one of the best when he gets back."[2]

Natalie Jowett said Antley told her he started using meth after a breakup a number of years back. It was around that time, when he lived in Monrovia, California, that he liked to pass a bug detector over the light sockets to show his friend, the jockey Fernando Valenzuela, how his every move was being monitored. "If you put it on all the other light sockets it doesn't beep," Antley said, "and all my light sockets beep. Somebody is listening to my every move."

"Boy, that's scary, man," Valenzuela said. In later years, he tried joking Antley out of his paranoia. "You know, this is not *The Truman Show*," he teased him.

"Oh, you think it's funny," Antley said.

In late 1999, Valenzuela ran into Antley when he was leaving a supermarket near the Del Mar track. He hadn't seen his friend in many months.

"Don't even come close to me," Antley said. "If you don't want to get in trouble, don't follow me, don't come near me, because they're out there." Valenzuela got in his car and drove away.

During the early 2000 Santa Anita meet, another jock found Antley sitting in the steam room. "Monitors float," Antley told the jock.

The other jockey didn't respond.

"I've lost a lot of money in the stock market," Antley went on. "I threw my computer in the swimming pool. It sank to the bottom. Then I threw the monitor in the pool. Monitors float."[3]

Jowett went to visit Antley in March 2000 and on April 6, she returned to see him again. She said he was bewitching at that time. Every morning, she woke to find fresh roses by the bed. In the night, he would wake her and take her by the hand to show her a beautiful bird or small animal that had lighted in the backyard momentarily. They would lie in bed and he told her his past troubles and they held each other and cried.

Six days after she arrived, she was making spaghetti sauce while Antley worked on something at the table. He wrapped his arms around her. She offered him a taste of the sauce.

"Will you marry me?" he whispered in her ear. She was completely surprised, but immediately told him yes. She thought how exciting it would be to be Mrs. Chris Antley, like the way Marcia Brady daydreamed of being Mrs. Bobby Sherman. He held out a ring he had just made of a twisted paper clip and purple crystal. Her intended husband was such a romantic, she thought. She told him she would marry him if they could have the ceremony before she went back to New York. Later when people asked Antley how he knew that he and Jowett should be together for the rest of their lives, he joked that it was the sauce that convinced him.

Gary Stevens remembered Antley's truck pulling into his driveway one afternoon, and them getting out, happy and in love. "I need a best man," Antley said. Stevens couldn't figure out what his friend was talking about and then he realized Antley meant for his own wedding. Jowett and Antley told him they were getting married the next day in Las Vegas. Stevens couldn't go because he had a potential Derby horse to exercise and worried that if he took a day off he would lose the mount.

Antley called his father that night. "Dad, you're coming to Las Vegas tomorrow," he said.

"Oh, boy, this is going to be a good gambling trip."

"No, it's not a gambling trip," Antley said. "I'm getting married."

"Whoa," Les said. He had no idea that Antley and Jowett were even close, but he knew Jowett from when she interviewed the family during the 1999 Triple Crown season. "Okay, we'll be there," Les assured his son. He considered the announcement good news.

Jowett asked the trainer Bob Baffert, whom she had become friends with during her reporting, if he would come. "I've got to see this," Baffert thought. He asked Jowett if she knew what she was doing. Antley has a lot of problems, he told her, and he didn't want to see her messing up her life. But Jowett told Baffert that she loved Antley and had faith she could help him.

The wedding took place on April 12 at the Little White Chapel, where Michael Jordan got married. When Antley arrived for the ceremony, Baffert started teasing him about his weight. "Turn the other way," Baffert said. "I'm afraid your buttons will pop off and hit me in the eye."[4]

For a little while, Jowett and Antley were happy. Jowett said he painted hearts and flowers on the living room wall. "I don't need drugs anymore," he told Jowett. "You're my drug."[5] Jowett, they discovered, was pregnant with a baby due nine months after their wedding in January. The newlyweds went back East to meet each other's families. Antley took Jowett to the Elloree Training Center and described how exciting it was when, in late March, the whole place was filled with cars and spectators for the Trials.

Antley's brothers moved back to South Carolina by the late spring and Jowett wanted Antley to relocate to New York. He was planning to get back to riding at Del Mar in late July, though, so they continued to live apart. Jowett visited sometimes, but the house seemed empty.

Antley decided to try to get back to riding weight without checking the scale for two weeks. He endured the arduous regime of starvation, running, and sweat box, then on the appointed day, he stepped on the scale and the number hadn't changed at all. He was 135 pounds.

Don Murray would go by the house to visit, but the gate was shut tight. Antley's neighbor Herzfeld recalled seeing Antley pacing around his pool for hours with a wireless phone plugged into his ear, supposedly fashioning lucrative trades. Then he disappeared for days. Herzfeld pounded on the door, but no one answered. To Herzfeld, the worst sign of trouble was when he saw Summer wandering the streets. Antley had always cared about that dog more than anything.[6]

In the late afternoon of July 26, as Del Mar opened for racing, Chris Antley got in his Jeep Grand Cherokee and drove through the center of Pasadena. He stopped for a red light on his way back toward home, saw a cop next to him and flipped him off. The traffic light changed and the cop started driving away, but he noticed that Antley hadn't moved. A few seconds later, Antley started driving, but he was swerving, almost hitting the cars parked along the curb. He picked up speed and wove in and out of traffic, driving back toward the center of town, toward the police station. He turned and went the wrong way down a one-way street but the cop didn't follow him. By the time the cop circled around to the other side, Antley had been stopped by police officers just blocks from the station.

"I'm drunk. I'm drunk. I'm very drunk," Antley said. "I've had a lot of vodka."[7]

"How much?" an officer asked.

"A whole bottle," Antley said. "I'm very drunk."

They asked Antley to stand on one leg, and the jockey fell over. His alcohol level was three times the legal limit. He told the officers that he had slept for three hours and started to drink at home as soon as he woke up. He said he wasn't taking any medication or drugs and didn't have physical or mental disabilities. The cops let him off easy. He was told to pay for drunk-driving classes, which would begin in August.

Something had set Antley off that day. Cathy Park said he was angry, but would not say why. "He was starting to feel nervous about being a dad and worried about whether he would be a good father," Jowett later told the papers after his death. "We talked about how this child was definitely wanted."[8] They talked about what Antley wanted to name the baby and he said something southern, like Billy Bob, or maybe better, the baby could be named Six.

Around that time, he told Jowett that he thought the doctors who operated on his knee back in February had inserted a chip to track him. He believed there was a larger conspiracy to watch his every move and that Jowett herself had been sent as an agent from ABC to find out more.

A few weeks later, Antley ran into a guy he knew from rehab at Grandview. Tim Tyler was a tall, twenty-four-year-old preppie, the scion of a prestigious Pasadena family. He had a twenty-one-year-old wife and a young baby and apparently no consistent job. He moved into Antley's house for a few weeks and claimed he was helping with the construction. Every time Park found him there, she would kick him out. Tyler and his wife swore to Park that they never did drugs.

In late September, Jowett became frustrated because she was calling Antley from New York but could never reach him. She telephoned the Pasadena police and asked them to check on her husband. They found Tyler and Antley sitting in the living room. Antley told the officers that he wasn't picking up the phone because he was mad at his wife. His pupils were dilated.

"Did you use dope recently?" one officer asked Antley.[9]

"Yes. Last night," Antley said, then admitted it was just hours before. "Tyler brought a bag of meth and we were both doing it."

When the cops asked if he had more in the house, he led them to the kitchen, opened a drawer and took out a baggie with off-white powder in it and another baggie of pot.

They asked if Tyler lived at the house, and Antley said he had just met Tyler when he was trying to buy dope and invited Tyler back. He said Tyler was now living in his back room without his consent.

In the back room, the officers found equipment that could be used to make meth. "Is this yours?" the detectives asked Tyler.

"That is not mine," he said. "I can't get in trouble. I'm on probation."

Antley was arrested for possession of a controlled substance and marijuana, and Tyler for being present where a controlled substance was being used. Later the D.A. decided to drop the charges against Antley because the evidence was recovered during a regular check on welfare. The charges against Tyler stuck and he was scheduled to go to court in late October for a hearing but he never showed up and a warrant was issued.

*   *   *

Fernando Valenzuela heard that Antley was having troubles and started stopping by. One time, Jowett was there. Valenzuela went golfing with Antley, who said he had scarcely been out of the house in almost a year. Another time, Valenzuela stopped by and Antley seemed more optimistic. He had just gone running, and told Valenzuela he planned to get back in shape and be racing by the first of the year. About a week later, in early October, Valenzuela came again to take Antley golfing and the house was empty. "Where's Natalie?" Valenzuela asked.

"She went back to New York," Antley told him. Valenzuela got the picture that the relationship was rocky and didn't ask again. He told Antley, "Maybe you should go back to Carolina and go running through the town like you did before you won the Derby. That was the best I'd ever seen you."

"You know, you're right," Antley said and laughed.

Antley's friends saw his drug problems worsening over the next weeks and tried two interventions. Jowett flew in for one of them, and pleaded that he get help for the sake of the baby but Antley politely refused help. At one of the interventions, Park said if he didn't like it at the hospital, then he could go home. "I'm already home," he said, and they didn't know how to answer. The intervention fell apart.

A few days later, Jowett took a more forceful approach. She called 911 and told the police to come pick up Antley, that he had threatened her life. She telephoned Park and told her what she was doing and Park hurried over. The dog, Summer, had joined Antley in the patrol car and Park went to fetch her. "Don't worry," Park said to him. "They're not taking you to jail. You're just going to Las Encinitas." Antley was upset that he would be sent to a psychiatric hospital. The next day Jowett returned to New York and never saw her husband again.

Antley's mother called him in the hospital. "Mama," he said, "if they don't let me out by noon, I'm leaving."

"Chris, if you need to be in there to let loose," she said, "then you need to stay."

"You don't understand, Mama. You don't know what's really going on."

"I just don't want to see you die, honey," she told him. "I want one more chance to be with you and I am scared."

Antley was held for the required seventy-two hours and released. He told Park his doctor advised him to get marriage counseling. All of his friends believed that Jowett hadn't been threatened but had called the cops as a way of assuring Antley would go for treatment.

Michelle Antley wrote an eleven-page letter to her son in early November telling him that he should be sure not to carry guilt in life that he had no control over. Her theory was that his guilt came from leaving home young when he was in essence the man of the family, for having an argument with his father when he was a kid. "Feeling responsible just eats you up," she said. "Say it happened, and go on. Tomorrow is tomorrow."

After Antley got out of Las Encinitas, he spent most of his time on the Internet or watching TV. Park's doctor prescribed medication to stabilize him until Park could get him more consistent help, perhaps get him to go back to South Carolina. The drugs made him lethargic though. He would sleep most of the day. She brought him buckets of golf balls. When his brothers lived at the house he liked to stand by the bedroom window on the far side of the pool and hit them to the island, but he wasn't so interested in this anymore. Now he just sat by the lake and stared.

He fired his gardener because his friends said he was overpaying, and the place started getting disheveled. Dead leaves blew across the yard behind the gate. Antley's mood grew similarly desolate. He said the books left behind by the previous tenant in the library were telling him what was going to happen in his life.

Back in the summer, Antley liked playing with an electronic dartboard that Park bought him. One day, toward the end, she noticed the dartboard had been ripped apart and the metal frame nailed to a tree. She asked Antley what had happened, and he told her Tyler had taken it apart and put it there. Tyler would be in and out of the house, camping out in the back room under construction. A 7-Up logo that Antley drew on the mirror in the living room disappeared and Park noticed Antley was drawing circles within circles, like a maze. Park thought maybe he had been trying to draw the dartboard and had just gotten lost in the design.

Antley seemed to have stopped doing drugs, but he still was drinking. Park talked to him one night in November about cutting back. "Everything's fine," he said, "everything's normal."

Park lost her temper. She grabbed him by the arm. "This is not normal," she said, pointing to a bottle, "this is not normal." He looked scared.

She walked out of the house and he paged her when she was driving home. "I swear to God, I just threw it down the sink," he said. "I swear, I swear. Let's eat."

She could tell he was already drunk. "I'll call you tomorrow," she said.

In the middle of November, Gary and Nikki Stevens went by the house. Gary figured he might be able to urge Antley to get more help since he hadn't been at the other interventions and would be a new voice pleading the same case. "You can't help me," Antley told Stevens. "I can't help me. They are after me. Things will be clearer in a few weeks."[10] Antley and Stevens said good-bye to each other in tears.

"He had mentioned a few times that something bad was going to happen," said Valenzuela, "and personally what I can't ever get out of my mind is one day, my wife and I went to visit him, and we started playing with the little dog, Summer. We loved that dog so much, and Chris is watching us and he goes in his room and brings out notebook paper with a little will written out. He says, 'When I die, I want my dog to go to Monica and Fernando.' And I read this, and I threw it back at him. I said, 'I don't want to hear this.' I said, 'You're not going nowhere. I don't want your dog. Man, I don't want to see these types of letters.'

" 'You think I'm messing around,' Antley said. 'It's really going to happen. You just watch.'

"I will never forget that," said Valenzuela. "That's kind of scary."

Valenzuela didn't want to speculate on what had happened to Antley, didn't want to think who might have hurt him. "One of the things that I keep on thinking was how depressed he was about life and I kept wondering why he was so depressed," Valenzuela said. "This is a man who was the most talked about person maybe in the world a year ago."

Les Antley called the house every day checking on his son, but he hadn't gotten a call back in months. He spoke daily with Park who had become his caretaker, trying to figure out what to do. At one point Park and Jowett considered telling Antley he had to go back to South Carolina because his grandmother was sick, but they decided that would be too cruel.

In late November, Antley decided he had had enough of Tyler. He told him to leave the house and never come back. They got into a heated argument in the street and a neighbor and the postal carrier saw Tyler taking swings at Antley with a golf club.[11] Antley just walked back inside the gates. On the last Thursday of November, Tyler was again at the house.

At 1:30 on Saturday, December 2, Park stopped by on her way back from lunch with friends. She and her daughter had food left over and thought Antley might like it. When Park got there, Tyler's truck was parked in the carport and he was standing at the back, trying to pry open a pristine silver toolbox with a crowbar.

What are you doing? Park asked. She always kicked Tyler out when she found him there.

Tyler said his wife had taken the keys to the box and he needed to get it open. Through the crack he had wedged up, Park could make out a leather edge, like the side of a briefcase.

Yeah, you probably stole it, Park remembered taunting him.

No, Cathy, I didn't, he said.

She told him he had better leave since Antley didn't want him around.

She walked past him to the front door and turned the knob. The door was locked. She knocked and didn't get an answer. She walked to the guest bedroom window and called out to Antley and he appeared. He didn't want to open the door, he said, because Tyler was outside and he wanted to be left alone. She told him she would leave the food on the wall near the door if he wanted it. He seemed subdued but sober. He told her he had been sleeping, and she said he should keep napping now. Brian would be coming in later, not on the 2:00 flight as they had thought because he had missed it, but on the 10:00 P.M., and she would bring him by when he arrived.

Each day for the past week, Park had heralded Brian's visit. But each day, Brian's plans changed, so Antley had begun to scoff, "He ain't coming."

"I swear, he's coming today," she assured him.

Antley didn't know that Brian was coming not just to visit but to whisk him back to South Carolina for the holidays and hopefully for a period of sober living. Out in Columbia, South Carolina, Brian would board a plane empty-handed, so sure was he that the trip would just be an overnight expedition.

Park tried each of the doors on all sides of the house and found them locked. "Brian's coming," Park warned Tyler for the umpteenth time that week. "And he won't let you around here." She thought Tyler must think Brian was some kind of god, from the way she talked.

Around 2:00 P.M., the mail woman worked her way along the cul de sac of Rosita Lane. She saw Tyler standing near the back of his truck and handed Antley's letters to him. At around 9:00 P.M., Jerry Holt, the neighbor across the street, who had turned in early, heard tires screeching away into the night. He looked out, but couldn't see anything. He thought the noise sounded like Tyler's truck.

When Park arrived back at the house with Brian, Antley didn't answer the door. The lights were out. Park used her key to get in and that's when they found his body.

Just hours after the police pronounced Antley dead at the scene, they arrested Tyler a mile from Antley's home on outstanding warrants for drug charges. For an hour of questioning, they didn't tell him Antley had been found dead. Tyler kept asking, "Is everything all right?" They told him Antley had been killed and he said, "Oh, God, no. . . ."[12]

That same night, the police took Park to a house near Antley's house and asked her to identify Tyler's truck. "Yes, that's it," she said.

About two weeks later, Gary Stevens walked back into the jocks' room at Hollywood Park after the seventh race and found a red envelope lying on the bench in front of his locker. He opened it and found a Christmas card and three photographs showing him crossing the finish line in the 1995 Kentucky Derby on the winning horse Thunder Gulch trained by D. Wayne Lukas. Timber Country had been expected by the handicappers to win, but Stevens had pulled off a victory on the 24 to 1 horse and some people grumbled that the race was fixed. An inquiry found nothing to substantiate the allegations.

Inside the red envelope, a handwritten note told Stevens to be at a pay phone outside the Elite Western Motel in Arcadia at 9:00 the next morning. If he were late, the note said, horse racing authorities and the FBI would be contacted. Stevens immediately thought of Antley's death and called security.

At the appointed time, Stevens stood outside the Elite Motel wearing wires given to him by the Arcadia Police Department. The phone rang. "Hello?" Stevens said.

"Hello, Gary?" The caller had a heavy New York accent.

"Yeah," Stevens said cautiously.

"How are you doin'?"

"I'm a little concerned on what's going on here," Stevens said. He could feel the sweat pouring down his body.

"We aren't trying to extort or anything," the caller told him. "We just want what is rightfully ours."

"Who's we? Who is we?" Stevens asked. "I don't understand what's going on coming with the pictures and stuff." He looked around to see if he could make out anyone watching him. "That was five years ago. They had video patrol films and everything. The stewards looked into it and they found nothing. So that's why I'm a little lost now five years later."

"We've got more on you and Pat than just those pictures," the caller said.

"What? What's that? What's Pat got to do with this?"

"We lost two hundred dimes on that race and we just want it back from you and Pat," the caller said. Back in 1995, rumors of a fix centered on a high five Gary Stevens exchanged with Pat Day just after the finish. People suggested that Stevens had handed off a buzzer—that would be the only way to explain the upset victory—but none of the accusations turned out to be true.

"Okay," Stevens said. He looked around. He wondered if someone was going to shoot him while he talked on the phone.

"Be at this phone. At two-thirty p.m. tomorrow."

"Okay. Two-thirty?"

"Or we will release the tapes."

By the next phone call, not only was Stevens wired but the Inglewood police, called in to assist, had tapped the line. This time Stevens asked for proof before he paid the caller the $200,000, and the caller told him to be back at the phone in forty-five minutes.

The trace showed that the guy was calling from a payphone in Encino. Forty-five minutes later, Stevens talked to him again and said he would pay the money when he saw proof that the caller had goods on him. The caller told him to be back at the phone in an hour to receive instructions for the exchange. That call traced to a cell phone in the Alhambra section of Los Angeles, but the police couldn't get the precise number.

An hour later, the caller told him to go to Baby Joe's restaurant in Pasadena, and he would find a videotape under the trash can out back. Stevens was told to leave the money in a bag at the same spot.

Several hours later, the police watched a white man walk to the Dumpster, drop a brown paper bag on the ground beside it and kick it underneath. The police tailed him and arrested him. He claimed to have blacked out and said he didn't remember dropping off the bag. A little while later, an undercover detective dropped a bag at the Dumpster with a note supposedly written by Stevens apologizing for not leaving the money and explaining the bank was closed. The note said Stevens needed another conversation to set up a new drop.

Fifteen minutes later, two young white men drove up in a green Honda, grabbed the bag, and sped off. A surveillance team followed them but lost them on the 210 freeway when the Honda accelerated to 110 miles per hour. The license plate traced back to a young man named Adam Frankel, who lived at a residence owned by Al Frankel, a man who owned race horses as late as 1995 and was arrested in September 1999 with his son Mark Frankel for illegal gambling and bookmaking.

Gary Stevens told the police he had met Al Frankel once back in 1995 but didn't remember much about him.

At 10:00 A.M. the next day, when Adam Frankel walked out of his house, undercover cops arrested him. In a bizarre twist, around 3:30 that afternoon, the Los Angeles Police received a call from his brother Mark Frankel. He told the cops that his mother had noticed a suspicious person sitting in a car outside her residence. Mark said he was worried because he was involved in an incident with a videotape and a jockey Gary Stevens and that he had been alarmed to see his brother kidnapped that morning.

The cops arranged for Mark Frankel to come to the station and report the kidnapping, but he called a little while later and said he was scared to come into that area because he might be kidnapped as well. The cops had meanwhile gone to his mother's house and detained her. Since Mark Frankel couldn't get his mother on the phone, he now thought his mother might be kidnapped too. He said that three weeks earlier, a jockey had been killed and he felt the same people were after him. He thought it might be the Mafia.

Mark Frankel eventually was coaxed to the police station and arrested. Al Frankel arrived at the station on December 27 and said he knew nothing about his sons' recent activities prior to getting a call from their mother telling him they had been arrested. In the end, Adam said he had only driven his brother from place to place without knowledge of the overall scheme. But when he was arrested, he had a handgun in his possession, which he said his brother had asked him to bring with him, so he was charged with that. He was given probation. Mark was convicted of extortion and placed under house arrest for a time.

In late January, Stevens received another extortion note at the jocks' room, this one written in Spanish, but no follow-up ever arrived, and the new threat just passed into the swirl of life at the track.

On January 11, 2001, nearly six weeks after Antley's death, the Los Angeles County Coroner's Office issued a press release stating its final verdict. Antley, the brief statement said, died of multiple drug intoxication. The case was closed. The final report would not be available for another two weeks or so, but the coroner's spokesperson, Scott Carrier, assured a reporter that although there was no alcohol in Antley's system, the level of drugs was "incredibly high." Carrier explained that the wounds were self-inflicted. In a drug haze, Antley had wandered through his house and fallen.

In a way, this was the awful verdict that Antley's friends preferred to hear. They would rather think Antley died accidentally by his own hand than that he had been murdered. But many questions remained. Why, his friends wondered, had drops of blood been found near the front door at some distance from Antley's body? And why had the detectives failed to conduct DNA tests on all of the blood found at the scene to be sure that it was all Antley's? Why, Park wondered, had there been a bloody shoe print near the body of the barefoot Antley? The coroner said that the wounds were all self-inflicted, but where in the house did Antley crack his head and give himself the lacerations? Why were the wounds on his arms so excessive and how could he bang them up so much himself on the inside flesh? How could he injure his chest and receive a deep soft-tissue hemorrhage to his back? Why was the door off its hinges? How did the mail get in the bedroom and who was drinking the vodka found open there if Antley had no alcohol in his system? Where was the ring with the extra set of keys to Antley's Jeep and house?

On top of that, Antley had always been careful to keep his drug use out of sight of his good friends and family because he knew they would not approve. Why would he take what the coroner's office was calling "incredibly high" amounts of drugs when he knew that his brother and Park would be returning to the house in a couple of hours?

Evening had just descended on Pasadena the night the press release was issued when Antley's neighbors on Rosita Lane heard a commotion at the jockey's house. The police sent over a helicopter and ground patrol and found Tim Tyler and a buddy, Jeffrey Jones, inside the locked gate and the carport. They were in the process of taking a body-surfing kneeboard and lawn trimmer. The detectives discovered that the hasps for the doors to both storage rooms had been removed from the wall, and that tools were piled together, as if in preparation for taking them away.

Jowett got the news of the break-in while she was in the delivery room in New York. That same evening of January 11, which was also Eugenia Antley's birthday, Jowett gave birth to Chris Antley's daughter. Jowett named her Violet Grace Antley.

At the beginning of February, the coroner's final report was released. Besides describing in detail the wounds apparent to the detectives who first arrived on the scene—including the head lacerations with "abundant acute hemorrhage" and bruises on the arms and feet—the coroner described chest contusions, a deep soft-tissue hemorrhage in the back, and cuts in the mouth and on the tongue.

The coroner had found four drops of blood along the walkway to the back door. Inside one of the bedrooms, he found many pill containers, as well as thirty-five green gel capsules scattered on the rug. Those pills tested as Clobenzorex, a weight-loss drug not sold in the United States, but believed to come from Mexico.

That drug, which turns into an amphetamine in the body, was found in Antley's system, as well as methamphetamine. They also found carbamazepine, an epilepsy drug used to treat bipolar disorder; the antidepressant Paxil; propranolol, for hypertension, migraine or arrhythmia;

Xanax, for anxiety; and Viagra. He had no alcohol in his system. The coroner, Dr. Louis Peña, found no skull fractures or deeper wounds that would in themselves be life-threatening. That's why the cause of death had been ruled drug intoxication.

To Antley's friends, the report left too many unanswered questions.

Scott Carrier, the spokesperson for the coroner's office, refused to respond, saying the report stood for itself. He would not allow Dr. Peña to be available for interviews, citing department policy. Commander Mary Shander of the Pasadena Police Department said that with the coroner's conclusions, the detectives considered the case closed. They never crafted a scenario to explain the last hours of Antley's life—including where or how he was injured in the drug-induced haze.

At the January 26 hearing for Tyler's breaking-and-entering charge, the crime was downgraded to trespassing through the work of a powerful local lawyer. The judge didn't notice Tyler was on probation and gave him a sentence of a few months in rehab. Detective Pete Hettema answered a few questions about the Antley case outside the courtroom when pressed. He said the door had been damaged by someone other than Tyler or Antley in a fight a few weeks before the jockey's death and a witness had seen him remove it the day before he died. Later, a witness said that it was Jowett who damaged the door. He said there was no shoe print, just paw prints.

What about the toolbox Tyler had in the truck, what was inside?

Books, Hettema replied. All kinds of books. That was what Tyler had come to deliver that day, the detective explained. Tyler and Antley had that kind of relationship where they would hand books back and forth.

What was the book?

The detective hadn't written down the title, but at first he thought it was a spiritual book. Perhaps an anthology of poetry and short stories with a spiritual theme. Antley's friends later said they never saw Tyler and Antley exchanging books.

Hettema said several times that he was continuing to investigate who provided Antley with the drugs, but a few weeks later, Commander Shander sternly denied that the department would extend any part of the investigation. "Detective Hettema was mistaken," she said. "He violated department policy by answering any questions. The case is closed."[13]

What could have been the cause of Antley's death, if not drug toxicity? Antley's friends wondered. Dr. Steven B. Karsh, the assistant medical examiner in San Francisco and a specialist in amphetamine abuse and cardiac pathology who authored *A Brief History of Cocaine*, explained that a drug toxicity death basically means that a coroner had not found another cause of death and that drugs were present. But even in an amphetamine-related toxicity, he said, one would expect to find some effects on the organs. "The biggest thing you would look for is an enlargement of the heart," he said. He asked to hear the description of the heart in the autopsy report. The heart was no heavier than that expected for a healthy man of Antley's height and weight, and showed no significant trauma.

Antley had a number of drugs in his system, he said, but the drug concentration levels in the heart blood where the coroner took the readings were unimpressive as evidence of a drug toxicity death. "Concentrations in the heart blood are invalid, particularly for drugs like methamphetamine. In any given instant most of the blood in your body is in your lungs. The arteries that take the blood from the lungs back into the left side of the heart are very thin-walled and after death the amphetamine just zips right across into the heart, so you do everything you can not to use left-heart blood [when sampling for drug levels]. The femoral reading is probably pretty valid and that's consistent with use, that's all you can say. It's not extraordinarily high. It's more than secondhand smoke, but it's a very bad practice to try to make anything out of a blood concentration.

"There's a position paper of the National Association of Medical Examiners coming out shortly," he continued, "and one of the things it endorses, and pretty much all pathologists agree to is, blood concentrations are really good for telling you that a drug was used. That's it. You can't time anything, you can't relate it to toxicity. Now if you had really good changes in the heart, which you don't, then you'd say, that's probably from methamphetamine. Usually the meth deaths we're used to have big hearts.

"I don't think you have an apparent cause of death," Karsh said. "I think you are more likely to have polypharmacy than head trauma. But there is not much heart disease, so I think if you want answers you're not going to get them from the postmortem, but from the scene itself."

What else could Antley have died from? Karsh speculated a person could die if someone lay over his chest, but you would usually, but not always, see some petechia on the lungs, and Antley's were clear. An article in the *New England Journal of Medicine* describes sudden fatal cardiac arrest incidents when athletes suffered blunt impact to the chest during sports activities, and those incidents have occurred off the field too. The autopsies then show no sign of damage to the heart either. But those incidents are rare.

Antley's friends had often feared that he would die from his drug use, but in the wake of the contradictions and unexplained questions of the coroner's report they had unsettled feelings that something more happened at the time of his death. They wished that if Chris Antley had such a strong sense of his own impending death, that he had told them more of what he could see.

You could examine the forensic pathology for years, look at it from all sides, and still not solve the mystery in full. A human could live with far more drugs in their system and they could die from a much smaller dose. You could die and, when they opened up your corpse, all your organs could look perfect. But somewhere along the line, you had to deal with the fact that the scientific why of death was an afterthought and the reality was that a life had ended. A man would never be seen again by his family. He had lived his life to its conclusion, and now his friends could look at its larger meaning.

"I think Chris Antley was born with a generous heart to start with," Don Murray of the Winner's Foundation said slowly, his legs up on the desk in his office next to the Santa Anita racetrack. "When Chris Antley was born, he was a perfect little person. He was really a good little person. I can't picture him being anything else. He was just a nice little boy and very competitive and he fell in love with horses. And he developed that. . . .

"There wasn't a selfish gene in his body and as successful as he was, money wasn't extremely important to him. The thrill of making it was— whether day-trading or winning horse races. The results of the money were pleasurable, but he didn't idolize it." Murray paused. "And he had some spiritual beliefs that were strong." He pointed out a signed photograph Antley had given him, thanking him for his help and crediting God for his recovery.

Murray brought his legs down and leaned forward. "Perhaps he was overwhelmed by demons . . . whatever they are. I've had demons, you know. You sit in an apartment with nothing but a beautiful bay out in front of you and thousands of pleasure boats and the light's twinkling on the bay and you're sitting there crying and you don't know why. . . . There's something *wrong*. But that's because alcohol's a depressant, and if you're depressed anyway, then you got a serious problem."

Dr. Allan Lans of Smithers talked about Antley's fatalism. "I think the feelings of hopelessness that overcome people sometimes have a predictive quality," he said. "But it doesn't have to end that way. He's writing the script that he wants to follow. What is all this talk about dying? Why does he think about the eighth-pole and dying? It's already in his mind. It's like mapping things so that's what has to happen."

"It's very sad," Antley's agent, Ron Anderson, said. "Believe me, there's lots of people that I've met in my life, and especially in our business, which is kind of dog-eat-dog, something like this would happen to somebody and you'd say, 'Who really cares?' but he definitely wasn't like that. He was loved by a lot of people."

When I talked to Anderson, he was mourning another friend he lost in June 2000. The California trainer Eddie Gregson went to his office after saddling horses at Santa Anita one day and shot himself in the head. "The one thing that I can look back and say with him and Eddie Gregson," Anderson continued, "is I'm not really sure that they loved themselves. They were very critical of themselves. They were never able to look in the mirror and say, you know, 'I'm okay.' "

I asked Anderson what he thought was at the root of Antley's insecurity. "Well, I think his appearance and his weight, not being able to lick that issue," Anderson said. "Probably the fact that he could never establish some sort of a relationship. You know, probably if he had a woman like Natalie that could have gotten hold of him years ago and kind of baby-sat him along, or babied him along, he might have been much better off.

"But, you know . . ." Anderson said, "it wasn't in the cards."

SIXTEEN

THE WIRE

A few miles out from Elloree, South Carolina, the first yellow and green ribbons appeared, hugging each dark telephone pole along the straightaway of Main Street, marking the route to a town in mourning. The ribbons were the same colors as the silks Chris Antley wore when he came within a colt's cracked sesamoid of winning the Triple Crown, and they looked uncommonly bright against the dreary December day, the frozen cotton fields and gray sky with rain coming down from time to time.

There were so many black, shiny limousines in front of the First Baptist church—brick with small white pillars—the event looked like a premiere. It was the same church where Eugenia Antley sang in the choir every Sunday and her grandson testified about his second chance in life on her birthday almost two years before. The pews were packed with well-dressed neighbors who looked like they knew the importance of small earrings and lint brushes and who murmured to each other about Antley with the plain intimacy of people who had known a guy since he was writing book reports. Poinsettia plants ringed the sacristy in celebration of Christmas, but there were also red roses heaping the coffin just in front of the altar to represent the victory of the Kentucky Derby.

Weeks later, a track person who knew Chris Antley from the glory days in New Jersey would comment about the service with an astonished shake of his head, "They certainly were loving Baby Jesus." And they were. Clay Weeks, a forester who left the woods for the seminary and now worked as an intern at the church, spoke quietly and plaintively about the longing in all hearts that can only be soothed by Christ. Antley's uncle told about how, one Christmas ago, he and his wife sat their nephew down to discuss their concerns about what his life had become. They asked him, "Have you ever taken Christ Jesus to be your savior?"

To which Antley replied, fixing them with his blue-eyed gaze, "Yes, I have."

"That is some comfort," his uncle now told the congregation.

Then Reverend C. Clark McCrary III stood to read a statement from Natalie Jowett, who sat up front, probably the tallest person in the room. Her long dark skirt and black sweater stretched over her pregnant belly because she was still a full month from delivery. "My Beloved," McCrary intoned, in his booming baritone, "the time and space between us has unraveled, and now I'm rushed to the end of this road where our journey together ends . . . for now. You told me many times that every day is a battle against self. Well, my love, I pray that your battle is over. . . . How many times did I whisper in your ear that if I could take your pain away and feel it for you, I gladly would? If you are now dancing in the angels' arms, which I believe you are, then the torment of my heart is well worth the bargain.

"My beautiful husband, I want to thank you for all the gifts you brought to my life: Your smile and your strong hands, your loving words and your laughter, your amazing family who will always be a part of me. Your tears which let me see inside your heart. And for the greatest gift any husband could give his wife—our child, who will always be the most beautiful and pure part of the life we shared together . . . I know she will always have her own angel watching over her."

McCrary told the congregation that Natalie wanted to share some music with them as well. He cued someone in the choir loft. The sound system crackled and then the voice of pop artist Sarah McLachlan sang "Angel." That song made most of the women in the church cry. I cried at the end when I saw Les Antley stagger against a pew for a moment as he left the service, blinded by his tears and grief.

So many cars joined the trip to the grave that the cortege looked like a traffic jam on that flat road. I've never witnessed a pretty funeral day and this was no exception, with the sky sulking above us, the scraps of cotton tangled at the base of the brown stalks like trash caught in a chain-link fence. The cars stopped along one of the frozen fields, past the sign that read HAY FOR SALE. The telephone wires were zinging in the wind and across from the small, low walled cemetery a rooster crowed again and again, although it was probably around 3:00 in the afternoon. A sign facing toward Antley's final resting place still held the ghost of fading paint that read FOR SALE, and then beneath it in plastic letters: PNUTS, CORN, OATS AND WHEAT.

Antley was buried about thirty feet from a fat cypress tree that loomed up out of the cemetery. Reverend McCrary later told me the graveyard was used in a film called *Wild Hearts Can't Be Broken*, about a young girl who rides horses in a circus and becomes blinded. The old-man trainer with a heart of gold who befriends her is laid to rest there. A card on one of the wreaths at Antley's grave said: "From the town of Elloree," and Goree Smith had said from the pulpit how Antley always shared his joys and successes with his town and made them feel special. *People* magazine sent a wreath to express their condolences. The jockey had ridden 19,723 races, won 3,480 times and accumulated $92,261,894 in purse money for owners over the length of his life. I paid my respects for a minute by Antley's grave, like he had paid his respects at Chuck's hospital bed, then I trudged back to the cars with everyone else.

A few days earlier Natalie asked Clay Weeks, "What will I tell Violet about her daddy?" But she had already answered the question herself. She told the *Times and Democrat* on December 9, "Chris definitely wasn't perfect. He had his struggles. But I think the important thing to remember is that even at Chris's lowest point, he would never, ever, ever hurt anybody else. He really cared about people. He cared about other people much more than he cared about himself."

"I really believe in my heart," Craig Perret, his jockey mentor, said, "as long as I've known him: He was great when he had nothing. I think he could deal with that. I just don't think he could deal with the fame, the money . . . and the power. He was a *great* country kid. For his ability, he could do anything in the world on a horse.

"But he got to where he wanted to do it in a cocky way," Perret said. "Instead of a nice positive way, carrying himself as the right kind of guy, he got lost. He was still a nice person, but his aggressiveness got kind of confusing with his personality. It started being where he was arguing with his friends. That was never Chris. And that was the addiction, I guess, coming. Or his demons. I don't know."

Perret sounded tired. "I love him today as I loved him the day he died. And I showed up there in Elloree," said Perret, "and it was a great loss. It was a great loss. Because I'll tell you, he was a true and true natural."

As I tried to piece together what happened that Triple Crown season of the last millennium, I wanted to talk to the jockey Jose Santos, to find out, almost two years later, what that devastating race at Belmont looked like from the happy side, from the perspective of the victor on board Lemon Drop Kid. Santos had been a 29 to 1 shot and won in the fastest Belmont time in five years—2 minutes and 27.88 seconds. Belmont was his home track, since he lived in Garden City, only a mile away, so the victory was extra sweet.

Many people I interviewed had said that, in a way, Antley won the Belmont too, because no one remembered who actually came in first, whereas Antley's dramatic moment cradling the horse's leg lived on. The track record books, of course, remembered who won, and in videotape of the race, in the moment of Charismatic's injury, the thirty-eight-year-old Santos appeared almost sinister in victory, captured on camera blithely high-fiving the jockey who came in second as they rode past the wire and left the shattered Charismatic and crying Antley behind them.

"I was just watching the tape of the Belmont today with my son," Santos said in his soft Spanish accent as we sat down to talk at Gulfstream Park in Miami, Florida. "We were laughing," he added, "and at the same time kind of upset, laughing because he falls down past the wire, butt-first. . . ." He trailed off.

"I had a beautiful trip, a perfect trip," he went on, describing the race. "Around the three-eighth pole I knew I had it. I saw my brother-in-law, Heberto Castillo, in front of me on Vision and Verse so I came around and opened a length in front and then I saw the shadow. He was coming back to me. The wire got to me before my brother-in-law's horse. It was exciting. Very exciting."

"What did you think as you hit the wire?" I asked.

"It was the highlight of my career," he said, smiling sweetly. "I was thinking of my mom. She's not here but she would be real happy."

I asked him if he was aware of Charismatic's injury before the spectators were. He said he remembered meeting up with the outrider by the quarter pole and hearing over the radio that one of the horses was down. He looked back and saw Charismatic standing there, and then Antley's colors.

I asked him if he knew Antley well. "Yeah," he said, "I rented his house from him in California when I first got out there." They were friends, he told me. On the Thursday before the Belmont, they had dinner together at the Garden City Hotel and Antley was confident of victory with Charismatic. Santos teased him by telling the maitre d' to bet on Lemon Drop Kid instead, and they all laughed. Antley was drinking water that night.

But Santos said he never saw Antley again once the race was over. After winning the Belmont Stakes, Santos went right back onto the track for the last race of the day, then met reporters at the press conference. By the time he got to the jocks' room, Antley was gone. They weren't the types to call each other. They were more likely to spend time together if they ran into each other, and their paths didn't cross from June 1999 until Antley's death in December 2000.

Santos went on to talk about his career, how he started riding as a teenager in Chile because his father was a jock and trainer. Santos came to America in 1984 to try his luck as a jock, and two years later met his favorite horse, the horse that would change his life, Manila. He won the $2 million Breeders' Cup Turf on him and that made all the trainers look at Santos differently, like he might have the stuff to bring home big purses, and they started giving him better mounts.

I asked Santos if, when he was growing up, his family taught him about racing's dark side. "The dark side of the business is you get injured," Santos said. He pulled up the right sleeve of his shirt to show two thick grisly scars running from wrist to elbow with what looked like the fossil of sutures.

"Who gave you that?" I asked.

He looked down at the wound and pushed his sleeve back to his wrist again. "Chris Antley," he said and smiled slightly.

Santos told me the accident happened on July 13, 1992, when they were riding at Belmont. Santos was laying third on In a Walk and Antley was in front on Skinnydipper. They were both riding against the rail. Jean Cruguet, who drove Seattle Slew to the Triple Crown in 1977, was laying second on the outside. They were turning for home, when all of a sudden Antley moved his horse off the fence like he was driving to an outer lane. Santos saw his opportunity and let In a Walk's bit drop, and the horse took off like a rocket, up that slot against the rail.

Cruguet realized that Santos was about to get a perfect shot at the front, so he yelled to Antley, "Watch out for the rail."

Antley didn't turn around. He ran his horse right back against the rail without checking who was there yet, something jockeys never do to each other. "I flew in the air," said Santos. "Three horses fell down that day and one of the horses fell on my right side. I broke fourteen bones. Shattered my arm, broke my pelvis, my foot, my eye.

"I was very lucky," he added.

He remembered flying through the air, screaming his last words. "Fuck you, Cruguet . . . !" Then Santos hit his head hard and rolled. He didn't remember the horse falling on him.

From the officials' point of view, Antley didn't do anything wrong and they maintained Antley's third-place finish, but Santos held Antley half responsible for the collision. After that accident, Santos didn't hear about Antley for months, and he thought the jock had dropped out of racing—maybe because he felt bad, maybe because he was dealing with drug problems at the time.

Later, I checked to see if Antley had stopped riding, but he actually went to Saratoga for the season. Santos never heard from Antley the whole time he was recovering in the hospital, but Cruguet showed up at his bedside one day. He told Santos he was sorry, and Santos accepted the apology. From then on, the Frenchman came to the hospital almost every day.

Santos spent nine months recuperating, then went down to Florida to ride. In the spring, he flew back to Belmont for the season. One day, he saw Antley sitting in the hotbox, and Santos told all the guys who were reducing to leave them alone in there. He needed to speak to Antley one-on-one.

"So we had a nice talk," Santos recalled. "He started crying and saying he was very sorry and he was having problems, emotional problems and stuff like that. I know him very well—he was never going to confront me. So I went and confronted him."

I asked him if it seemed like that awful accident weighed on Antley's mind during the intervening months.

"No," said Santos.

"Then why did you think he was such a good guy?" I asked.

Santos thought a moment. "When you are in the drug abuse," he said, "you are a different person. But overall, he really have a real good heart, that guy."

Santos went on to explain that, when he first started riding in Chile with his father, he lived such a straight existence, he wouldn't even drink a coca cola. Then he went to ride in Colombia and became a coke addict for five or six years. The drug was so easy to get, on any street corner. When he was using, Santos lost his ability to ride and his career fell apart. Then he moved to the United States.

The day his plane landed in Miami, he set his right foot on the ground and said to himself, "I quit." Those first three months, all alone in a new country, tested his will to the limit, he told me. Sometimes, he felt he needed the drug, so he would force himself to stay in his room, saying over and over to himself, "Don't go and get it. Don't go and get it." And seventeen years later, he still hadn't gone to get it. Now he had a wife and six kids, had won dozens of riding awards and $139 million in purses over his career.

I asked him what he thought about when he first heard that Chris Antley died.

"I cried," said Santos. "I cried.

"I rode with him when we was at the Meadowlands," he added. That was shorthand for the glory days when Santos was a new immigrant getting a fresh chance at life and Chris Antley had just arrived in New Jersey, a brilliant teenager from little Elloree, South Carolina, enjoying the first taste of the sport he loved. Santos tried to explain to me, someone outside the track, what kind of bond that shared ecstasy could forge. "We was winning the races together," he offered.

All the meaning of that time was in the valences, the overlapping leaves of that Triple Crown season. When Chris Antley died, I got a call from Tom Roach, who remembered that we had spoken briefly about Antley when I was down visiting his farm. "We need you to find out what happened to our friend," he said. "We've got horses so we can't do it ourselves. We've got to be here every day. But it was the happiest time of our lives and it ended in tragedy and we want to know why." I thought about how Roach had gotten the gift of that happy season right after he brushed up against death himself the autumn before, and how his oldest daughter was there with them to enjoy it before she went off to school. I thought about the Lewises, who had twice in two years come up to the brink of winning the Triple Crown and had it snatched away, but whose perspective on life was so optimistic they had seen both upsets as a blessing. Then just a few months after the Belmont, Bob Lewis underwent bypass surgery, but in his desire to be like his father in most ways—except by echoing his father's defeatism—he let his trainers buy twenty-one more racehorses for him while he was still recuperating in the hospital, a hopeful gesture if ever there was one because it implied so many races ahead.

And I thought about the secret kindnesses that lurk on the edge of tragic events. Michelle Antley told me of two moments at the Belmont that meant a lot to her. One was about a little boy, about eight years old, named Evan Nader, whom she met in the paddock that day. He was going on to his mother about how much he idolized Chris Antley and loved his tall boots, and the boy reminded Shelly so much of Chris himself at that age that she introduced herself. Then the kid tagged along with her all the way through Charismatic's breakdown, at which point he murmured, staring out at his hero awash in tears, "He needs a hug really bad. He's so sad." So Shelly grabbed his hand and led him through the crowds, back to the jocks' room and there she stopped her son and said, "Chris, this little boy says you need a hug." Her son balked, groaning, "Mama," but then leaned over and accepted the embrace and said, "You're right, Mama. I did need that hug." Some reporters asked if the boy was any relation to Antley and when Shelly said no, the reporters lost interest in writing about the incident. "Does it not count what kind of person that little boy is?" she said. Actually I found one reporter, Pat Forde, who did think it was important what that little boy was and wrote up the encounter .

And Shelly's other story was how, well after the race ended, she was sitting in the jocks' room and the clerk of scales approached her. "I hate to bother you, Mom Ant," he said, "but the little fellow that did win will not talk to any of the newspapers until you say it's okay."

"What do you mean, he won't talk to them?" she asked. "He's the winner, regardless. There has to be a winner. He would be it."

The clerk of scales hesitated. "Well then you need to go over there and tell him," he said, "because he will not talk to the first reporter until you say it's okay."

I told her that what made Santos's compassion—refusing to trumpet his victory until the Antleys were beyond their upset—more impressive was that he hadn't even mentioned it when I spoke with him. "See,"

Shelly said, as if she had been waiting for this vindication a long time. "A lot of that goes on among people who are really deep friends and they don't realize how connected they are. It's all connections."

And if you wanted to look at connections, you could certainly see them. Antley died in awful circumstances, but in the last years of his life he managed a few redemptive acts. He told Anderson when he first got back to racing at the beginning of 1999 that he wanted to go once more to the Derby so he could really experience it with a clear mind. And he had done that, and won. And then even in defeat at the Belmont, he showed the kindest part of himself, his compassion for the horse, making almost a perfect repair of one of the worst moments of his life in the late 1980s, when he let Drachma, the horse at Saratoga, flail away to her death down the homestretch. The circumstance had come up again—a horse injured on the track—and this time Antley got it right. Not long after, his life was over.

Six months after Antley's death, D. Wayne Lukas faced the 2001 Kentucky Derby without a horse strong enough to run in the race. After twenty years of entering competitors to run for the roses, Lukas finally had to sit one out. He was talking to a reporter around that time about the other Derby hopefuls, when suddenly he blurted out that he wished he never kept Antley on the horse after the Preakness in 1999. He wanted to change jockeys and should have, he said. Antley "wasn't focused," Lukas complained. Lukas raged that Antley should have been at the barn sleeping with the horse every night to show his commitment to the Triple Crown.

"He was talking to the press outside the barn after the race," Lukas told a reporter. "Charismatic was standing there in his stall, and we didn't know if he would live or die. Now, if you cared about the horse, don't you think you'd walk the twenty feet to see him? I know I would. But he just got back into his limousine and drove away. I never heard from him after that, and he never rode another race for me again."[1]

But the truth was that one of the reasons Antley hadn't come by Lukas's New York barn again was because he had to jet out to California the night of the Belmont and ride Lukas's horse Magicalmysterycat in, appropriately enough, the Cinderella Stakes the next day. The trainer watched on television from New York as Antley won the $74,550 race for him. And that day, Lukas was so high on Antley, he said the jockey had ridden Charismatic appropriately. "He got there awfully easy," Lukas said about Antley's place neck and neck with Silverbulletday at the beginning of the Belmont. "I told Chris, 'Don't give up what comes easy. We found ourselves on the lead. Why take back five, six, seven lengths and try to make it up later?' "

Then when Antley first returned from knee surgery in February 2000, he rode Lukas's horse Dance Master in the Baldwin Stakes. One of Antley's last races was on board a top Lukas horse, Commendable, also owned by the Lewises, who later went on to win the 2000 Belmont. Antley told the press in early June that he owed Lukas even more than the opportunity to ride Charismatic. He was sorry he hadn't sent Lukas a thank-you note yet, since "Wayne was the guy who introduced [Natalie and me]."

It was a year later that Lukas blew out a storm of fury for a couple of months and then refused to talk further about the 1999 Triple Crown.

"You've got your Black Beauty story," he said to me, refusing to meet for an interview he had previously agreed to.

I told him I knew racing was a difficult life and wanted to talk to him about that aspect as much as anything. "It's a lot harder when you're on drugs," he said and ended the talk.

All around the racetrack, jockeys, jockey agents, and other trainers said D. Wayne Lukas wasn't going to get away with what he said about Chris Antley. To go after a jock after he was dead and couldn't defend himself, was the lowest you could get in the horse-racing world. And it was mystifying to the other jockeys since Lukas had praised Antley up and down at the time. Antley had expertly ridden Charismatic, a claimer, into victories that no one could imagine, they said, and then the horse broke down. Many of the jockeys had gotten their own heads taken off by Lukas over the years. That was negotiable because they were alive to stand up for themselves, but to go after one of their own, who was gone?

I asked Bob Lewis for his view on the tirade. "I can't understand Wayne Lukas saying those things now," Bob Lewis said. "He is his own worst enemy. If you have no respect for the dead, then why say anything. . . . It is beyond my comprehension. We knew Chris as not only an outstanding individual professionally but socially we had an opportunity to go through the New York Stock Exchange with Chris, an outstanding experience. We asked Chris to come to our Belmont party and he spoke very eloquently and emotionally about his love for the horse that night. If he was rushing off from the stable it was to satisfy Beverly and I and our activity."

I asked Dr. Lans what he made of the outburst, and he said it wasn't worth dignifying. He said Antley and Lukas's relationship had been difficult going back a dozen years. The trainers wanted Antley for his ride, but they hated his troubles. "I think a lot of people were enraged at Chris," Lans said. "Even I could tell his talent was special. But very often those are the athletes who fall—Dwight Gooden, Darryl Strawberry. People who have something above everyone else."

That thing, Lans said, was magic. "They used to say about Caruso, if he took care of his voice, he would be a great singer. They said about Babe Ruth, he would have been a great ballplayer if he took care of himself. But what these people give us is something beyond. It's not harnessable." He said it was hard for people to keep themselves whole when they had such talent. "First of all, they are more mystified by the gift than we are," he said, "because they have no idea what they did to deserve this gift. And it takes them away. It also makes them vulnerable. It interferes with maturity because of the adulation . . . and it's a magnet for trouble. There's always someone wanting a piece of it and they're angry and cynical and so full of hate they want to bring this down. There are people with hidden agendas. They are self-serving. Maybe they are in the position that they can't allow some beautiful thing to live. There were always those kids who would tear up the flowers."

It was ridiculous to suggest Antley didn't care about the horse, Dr. Lans said. A person needs some center that gets them through the ups and downs of life, and that was the center of Antley. "Horses," Lans said. "He had this extraordinary thing, this gift of communication, where he felt at home and peaceful and understood by and understanding of horses. He knew their limitations. They are beasts, after all, but somehow that was right for him. He could trust them."

Did Chris Antley ever apologize for taking his friends through the worry? I asked Drew Mollica. "Numerous times and never," said Mollica. "His idea of apologizing was kissing my cheek and taking me back. He was never going to walk in and say, 'Boy, was I a jerk.' He was very complicated. . . . I truly believe he was devoted to the Lord, and at the same time he could be mercenary. He could reduce me to tears and make me want to kill him and at the same time know I would throw myself in front of a train for him.

"He had deep insecurities about a lot of things. He had a hard life as a kid, a split home. I'm not qualified to say it was his childhood, but something was obviously troubling him. He never got his *quan* straight. It wasn't for lack of love," Mollica said. "We all tried in different ways and none of us knew what was right or wrong. Everything failed and nothing worked and the end result is that he's in that poor lonely place on the side of the road in Elloree, South Carolina. And it's a horrible end to what could have been a storybook career."

There were a few theories about what was haunting Antley, but Mollica sighed. "Look, by all accounts I should be a serial killer," he said. "And some shrink will say, 'Oh, poor Drew, he's just denying his feelings.' Excuse this, but, 'Blow me.' I'm a little tired of it. We all fail, but I won't use it. Tony Robbins did say one thing. He said, 'The past does not equal the future.' I said it to Chris and I say it to myself. It's the mantra I live by.

"My mother, if it wasn't for my father, would have been a bag lady. I came home and found her setting the house on fire. I found her attempting suicide seventeen times. She was in and out of Bergen Pines and Greystone, and anything you ever saw in *One Flew Over the Cuckoo's Nest*, I lived. That's how I was raised. I locked the door of my room because my father said you never know when she's going to try and plunge a knife in your chest. That was nine years old. I don't tell you that to make you feel sorry for me. I share it with you only to say that

I am just sick and tired of all this psychology bullshit. You know Nike's got the best slogan, Just do it. You go to the shrink and you say, 'My mother hit me so I hit my kids.' That's bullshit. Or, 'My mother hugged me every day, that's why I'm so soft.' That's bullshit. Any argument you want to make, they'll coddle you. You give them two hundred dollars an hour and they'll tell you anything you want. You want to go on Prozac, they'll put you on Prozac. It's bullshit.

"I dressed myself. I clothed myself. I fed myself. I was on my own since the time I was eight years old. Everything I got—this house in Garden City, kids that I raised—I earned by myself with no help. That's not to say I don't help you, I'll help everybody. I understand the weak, the downtrodden.

"I was the most popular kid in high school, I was the student-council president. I went to Rutgers University on my own, I made the dean's list eleven semesters and, yeah, maybe I underachieved in this life, you know. But I'm not only a jock's agent, I'm on WFAN radio one night a week, I do television four nights a week, I've done a lot of things. But by all accounts, I'm supposed to be in Creedmore, smoking Camels and drinking black coffee. You know, and I'm *not*. So to use a vulgarity, Fuck them. I am nobody's statistic."

Mollica told me I could use what he had just said if I wanted, and I said I did. It was the most optimistic thing I had heard in a long time.

At the end of 1999, with a lot of hemming and hawing, the turf writers voted Charismatic horse of the year and instated him in the Hall of Fame. Many writers argued that he hadn't deserved the title because he didn't win enough races but the fans in their midst overrode the naysayers.

A year later, I went to see him where he stood as stud at the Lane's End Farm in Versailles, Kentucky. Charismatic had proved prolific— booked for some fifty mares that spring of 2000, he impregnated almost all of them and had another fifty added to his dance card before summer rolled around. When I walked into his barn, the guides stood chatting in the hallway, so his stall area was empty except for the horses. His coat gleamed red caramel against the bright white of his chrome ankles and his injury was undetectable. After his surgery he had been confined to his stall for a full three months, and everyone who worked with him was stunned at his patience. How does a horse in top condition, a long runner for that matter, go from the peak form to utter stillness? They had never seen anything like it. In another Lane's End barn, Charismatic's father, Summer Squall, still stood as stud. On the organized tour of the farm, the guide stopped in front of him and Summer Squall gazed at her quietly. He raised his right front hoof and the tourists laughed lightly. Then he reached his small head forward and licked a round peppermint from the tour guide's outstretched hand.

Whenever I interviewed people about Charismatic they would talk about what a great name that was for a horse. It was a strange name for the foal of Bali Babe and Summer Squall because it broke so from tradition. But it was the inspiration that hit Beverly Lewis around three in the morning when she was christening their new colt. When I looked at the Kentucky Derby program, there was no other name that would have fit quite as well into a moment so magical as that fluke win. I looked for a name that would have conveyed as much effervescence, or that could have leapt out to me from my dream as the possible winner, and the story could have gone a whole other way. But what was Kimberlite Pipe or Cat Thief to me?

I knew the general religious implication of the name Charismatic—the preachers who spoke in tongues, the ecstasy of the Haidewich nuns. But I looked the word up in the dictionary for true lexographic accuracy over a year after the 1999 Kentucky Derby.

"charismatic – Of or pertaining to a charism

"charism [Gk. *charisma* gift] Theol. A special divine or spiritual gift; a special divine endowment conferred upon a believer as an evidence of the experience of divine grace and fitting him for the life, work, or office to which he was called; a grace, as a miraculously given power of healing, or of speaking with tongues, or of prophesying, etc., attributed to some of the early Christians."

Chris Antley had once said to a reporter, "You talk about a gift. Charismatic is a gift," so he had known that definition from the start.

I dreamed the word *charisma* and Antley dreamed his Derby victory days before it occurred. Curious, I called Eduardo Caramori, the trainer from the 1999 Kentucky Derby who told reporters that he dreamed the winning horse would come out of slot sixteen. That was why, at the post position draw, Caramori picked that post position. Then the horse from Dubai was scratched and all the horses shifted over, and Caramori's First American moved to slot fifteen and Charismatic took sixteen. When Charismatic won, all the reporters gave Caramori mystical credit for dreaming the victor.

In his broken English, Caramori said the whole incident never happened. "No," he said, laughing. "I have to say anything." He told me that the reporters came up to him to get his spin on the post-position draw. "Sixteen horse is too bad," Caramori said. "We trainers talk good b.s. and we thought we had a shot in the race. I was kind of disappointed with the post position. I said, 'I have a dream: sweet sixteen.' I made some kind of joke."

In the first spring after Antley died, I went to his hometown to see the Elloree Trials, the horse race where he started. I had set up interviews with his father and grandmother and Goree Smith. Since his mother had been described by ABC Sports as "marching to the beat of a different drummer," I decided to interview her at another time. When I arrived that night in the neighboring town, I left my bags at a Days Inn that looked out toward the parking lot and a Piggly Wiggly. I picked a place to eat off the Internet and when I arrived, the dining room was full so I was sent to eat in the bar. The bartender was overwhelmed and kept apologizing for the wait in taking my order. That stretched on for over an hour, but since I had nowhere to go, I stayed where I was, and the people at the next tables started talking about how long they had waited.

The bartender seemed distracted and overwhelmed, but then she would wink in a friendly way and sweep by again, "It will be just another minute, sweetie," she said. I might have gotten annoyed, but I couldn't muster anything like it. When I finally ate and the check came, I looked at the top and saw the name: "Michelle A." I asked her if she knew anything about the Elloree Trials, and she said, "I sure do." And then I told her I had come to interview Chris Antley's father and grandmother, and she said, "I sure am glad to meet you. I am Chris's mother." She squeezed my hand and told me to come see her at the fish store where she was working the next day because we had a lot of things to talk about.

Early in his life, Chris Antley found something he loved, but sometimes what you love breaks your heart. You have to figure out which way you want to gamble on these things.

"Oh, God, he's feeling responsible again," his mother said she thought when she saw him crying at the Belmont. "Because he was. Because he knows there are issues that he chooses to not be a part of that's part of the game. And one of the issues is racing the horses too young. It's a big issue. He mentioned that at the party after the Belmont. Oh, yes he did. So he's feeling responsible again for hurting this horse. For money. For gain. For profit."

I asked her why she thought her son was so distraught in general. "I think a lot of it is my fault," she told me. "I know. Because I brought him up to believe the things that I wanted to happen: If you be good to people, they'll be good to you. If you share, they'll share. You never start a fight, but don't back out. You never instigate. Be kind and gentle. Think of someone else's feelings first. And guess what?" she said. "The world doesn't work the way a mother would have it. He took everything to heart and every time somebody would screw him over . . .

"I enforced things. I made him believe them. I always wanted them to see the other side of the picture. Brian's thing was, 'You always make excuses for everybody, Mom. That's why I'm so bad, because you made excuses for me.' I said, 'Brian, you were perfect. I'm sorry. It's not my fault you were taken up with the world.' "

She said she could never get Chris off of feeling like he had let the world down. "You can't be responsible for the rest of the world," she said. "It's not your cross to bear. I think he felt at times that he wasn't doing enough to change the world in a better way. Either by actions or, 'Oh, god, I goofed.' He would say, 'Mom, it's just terrible the way people put us in a certain position and if we falter, we falter all the way down, not just a rung, and they watch you constantly like they have you on a pedestal, and you can never make wrong decisions because you are nine times as wrong as they would be if they ever did it.' I was like, 'Uh, haven't you done that to me?' "

The next day, the fields around the Elloree Training Center were filled with cars and American flags were taped onto the fence posts. There were T-shirt stands and food booths selling hot dogs and fried chicken. In one area, men reeled a floppy cloth rabbit across the bumpy ground to race pairings of bird dogs on a track bounded by hay bales. In another section, a mammoth bison sat sunning himself, while young children walked warily by. At professional tracks, all the jockeys are basically the same size and the horses well mannered. But at the Trials, the jockeys came in various versions of lightweight—stocky but short as a fireplug, or tall and thin as shepherds' hooks. The horses got riled from time to time, trotting in the paddock when they should be walking, bumping against each other while the grooms tugged hard on the bridles.

Les Antley wore a baseball cap and smoked cigarettes while we talked up on the porch of the office where Goree Smith had first spotted Antley cycling up the drive. He loved his son, but he confessed he didn't know details of his life. He said he himself had been depressed, angry and confused since his son's death, but he didn't know whether he should question the police reports "Did you see Lester at the funeral?" Mollica had asked me. "Lester didn't have a chance to be an asset to Chris in that environment. Lester was a good man from rural South Carolina. Chris became, in our business, the Michael Jordan."

I asked Les what his goal had been for his own life. "I just wanted to make it to retirement, get the kids a good education," he said. "That was my goal, just to work and provide for my family. I didn't have the ambitions Chris had—to be a millionaire—because I knew it wasn't going to happen."

Antley's brother, Brian, was standing with his father when I arrived. Later, I ran into him watching the races. He had taken his shirt off in the heat. Tattooed on his bicep was the date of Chris Antley's birth and the date of his death, and then twining down vines the words "We Buried Thee, Ant Man." Brian had gotten the tattoo the day after he found his brother's corpse. He talked about how hard it was to arrive just hours after Chris's final breaths, how angry he had been. But then he said you could look at it as good too. If he had found someone hurting his brother, or delivering drugs . . . "If I had gotten there two hours earlier, I could have killed someone," he said. "Because I would have lived my life right there."

Brian said when he went through drug problems himself, his older brother had leaned on him like a father to stop. But then when Brian tried to reverse the situation and rein Chris in, he got nowhere. "You can't teach a genius to be smart," he said. His brother thought since he could handle everything else, he could handle drugs too. Brian told me that what his brother needed and what everybody needed was "small-town information," where everybody knows what everybody else is doing. If you have a problem, everyone is watching out for you.

He asked me what I thought about his brother, and I told him that in fact I had met his brother back in 1999. He said he knew. He said Antley told him at the time about going to Chuck's hospital room. That's why Brian was waiting with his father when I walked up. He wanted to see if his brother's assessment of me was correct.

He gave me a few of Antley's comments. Then he told me his brother said that my request for him to visit came from our hearts, and his going to the hospital had been from the heart too. Later, he said that his brother always wanted to bring people their dreams. He could tell what people wanted and he would try to do what he could, to be that for people. Clearly the worst was when he lost the Belmont. He failed to finish the perfect storyline so many people hoped for.

The Elloree Trials announcer stood on the viewing platform, which looked like a small beach house stuck on high stilts. Garlands of flowers and green and yellow ribbon decorated the rails. The white-haired announcer hailed the confederate flags hoisted high on makeshift poles around the field and draped over truck windows. Then the Reverend Ray Anderson offered the prayer, "Remember the tragedies of this community of the past few months. Remember your child who took our hearts with him to the heights of this sport."

Then it was time for the Miss Elloree Trials contest for the high school girls. Bob Hickman, a solid older man wearing a white hat, stood on the platform, rumbling through the introductions. In two visits, Elloree had already become a small town to me. There was Dora Shirer, of the family who owned the pond where Antley fished as a boy. Jean "Laurin" Weeks was the daughter of Clay Weeks, who spoke at Antley's funeral. One by one, the girls walked out, in sleeveless shifts or skirt and blouse—nothing provocative, but the image of sweet, pretty, Southern teens. The lists of interests and accomplishments Hickman read over the microphone seemed like a war between teen frivolity and world-worn wisdom. Robin Powers, who won the crown the year before, listed her hobbies as "shagging, snow skiing, and putting together scrapbooks." But her life philosophy suggested tough times already behind her. "Whenever it feels like the whole world goes out," she listed as her guiding wisdom, "a friend comes in." Amanda Courtney Strock, running in 2001, listed her hobbies as "horseback riding, talking on the phone, watching TV, spending time with friends and playing with animals," but her philosophy was, "It is better to be hated for what you are than loved for what you are not—Andre Gide." She won.

At the end of the day, Smith held a race named for Antley.

Coming back from Elloree, I walked out of the airplane passageway into the New York waiting area. On the floor was an abandoned playing card, a joker illustrated with a horse's head. I picked up the wild card and put it in my pocket for luck. I read once that a multimillion-dollar lottery winner admitted to a reporter that he kept buying tickets not just from habit, but from real hope. "It'd be nice to get one more win,"[2] he said. And I guess that's the sentiment I came to have.

I returned to New York about a month after Chuck's death, in late 1999, and hadn't settled in for two weeks when I got a call from someone telling me that another friend had died too. That night I met another friend at a bar with a poured concrete floor and blue lighting with everyone dressed up and talking about their purses, and it all seemed so foreign. I got into a cab to return home to my apartment and started crying. I couldn't stop, all the way down Seventh Avenue, down to the north edge of the World Trade Center and over to my home. When I went to pay the driver, he said, "Miss, may I ask you a question?"

"Sure," I said.

He said, "Why are you crying?"

I told him, and the cab driver told me that he had lost his father fifteen days before, and he wasn't sure he would see his mother again, but I had to stop crying. He said that it was hard on the souls of the people who are gone when you cry so much. Their souls become hard. I had to pray instead, he said, or do something for someone, give money to a man on the street, that kind of thing. I told him I was trying and that I would try to pray for his father, and he said he would pray for the man I had loved.

I sympathize with the hard-core horse gamblers I met at the track, these guys who gather at dawn each day to gauge the length of the thoroughbreds' pasterns, the stretch of their necks, to see if their build is right to win. They study the fractional times of the horse's recent races and its Beyer speed rating the last time out, its breeding, the track conditions on the days of its wins and the days of its losses. The handicappers are always computing, crunching the numbers to see if they can detect a rhyme or a reason, some pattern to which horse bursts across the finish line first and who follows too many lengths behind. Who will close in the money and in what order. They want to win to have the money for gas, or hookers, or a car for their wife, to feel they are special—especially lucky. But they also want to find the equation that proves that they are not just people whiling away whole days, perhaps whiling whole lifetimes watching animals run around a circle, circling an oval track with hungry people on their backs. Sometimes they hit big and at the betting window, the teller slips their ticket through the machine and the payout glows in green numbers, and it feels like a gift, like grace, like a big present just for them.

ENDNOTES

CHAPTER TWO

1. Desmond Morris, *Horsewatching* (New York: Crown Publishers, Inc., 1988), p. 136.
2. Gerda Reith, *The Age of Chance: Gambling in Western Culture* (London and New York: Routledge, 1999), p. 46.
3. http://www.imh.org/imh/kyhlp11b.html, the International Museum of the Horse.
4. Roger Longrigg, *The History of Horse Racing* (London and Basingstoke: Macmillan London Limited, 1972), p. 9; Iliad xv.625sq.
5. Longrigg, p. 37.
6. Edward L. Bowen, *Man o' War: Thoroughbred Legends* (Lexington: Eclipse Press, 2000), p. 42.
7. http://www.derbypost.com/history2.html.
8. Ibid.
9. Ibid.
10. Interview with Tom Roach, November 3, 2000.
11. Woody Stephens, *Guess I'm Lucky: My Life in Horseracing* (Garden City, N.Y.: Doubleday & Co., 1985), p. 22.

12. Glenye Cain, "Birth of a Classic Winner," Daily Racing Form—Belmont Stakes 131 Coverage, http://www.drf2000.com/home/hdp_cent/bs2.html.
13. Bill Christine, "From Claim to Fame; Until Recently, Charismatic Never Looked Like a Triple Crown Winner," *Los Angeles Times*, June 2, 1999, p. 1.
14. Glenye Cain, "Birth of a Classic Winner."
15. Interview with Robyn Roach, November 3, 2000.
16. Ruth Slack Leadership Scholarship Program, http://www.midway.edu/alumni_affairs/ruth_slack_roachleadership.htm.
17. Larry Bortstein, "Prime Timber Runs with Only 3 Shoes," *Orange County Register*, April 5, 1999.
18. Equine Line Product 14B—Charismatic; https://www.equineline.com/eqlreports/12079092.htm.
19. Interview with Bucky Sallee.
20. Bill Christine, "Lukas Is Rising to Occasion," *Los Angeles Times*, May 17, 1999, p. 5.
21. Interview with Tom Roach.
22. Bill Christine, "From Claim to Fame."
23. Jay Privman, "Colt Who Could Be King," Daily Racing Form—Belmont Stakes 131 Coverage, http://www.drf2000.com/home/hdp_cent/bs2.html.

CHAPTER THREE

1. "Elloree Training Center," the 39th Annual Elloree Trials special issue, *The Times and Democrat*, Orangeburg, South Carolina, March 23, 2001, p. 18.
2. Thirty-Seventh Running of the Elloree Trials program, March 20, 1999, "The History of Elloree Trials."
3. Interview with Michelle Antley, March 23, 2001.
4. Lenny Shulman, "Back on a Tear," *Kentucky Derby Souvenir Magazine*, May 6, 2000, p. 30.
5. Bill Pennington, "Antley's Wild Ride Reaches Violent End," *New York Times*, December 17, 2000, Sports, p. 1.
6. Ibid.
7. ABC 1999 Preakness coverage.

8. Interview with Lester Antley, March 24, 2001.

9. Interview with Michelle Antley.

10. "Antley Says He's 'Happiest Person in the World,' " *Sunday Tennessean,* May 30, 1999, http://www.tennessean.com/sii/99/05/30/antley30.shtml.

11. Jane Carson, "Small 'Package' Asset to Jockey," *Times and Democrat,* March 13, 1983.

12. Interview with Brian Antley, March 24, 2001.

13. Interview with Franklin Smith, March 23, 2001.

14. Unofficial Chris Antley Page, http://www.ptinet.net/~cowgirl/chris. htm, and interviews with Franklin Smith, Hamilton Smith, on March 23, 2001, and Brian Antley.

15. Shuman, "Back on a Tear," p. 30.

16. Edward Hotaling, *The Great Black Jockeys, the Lives and Times of the Men Who Dominated America's First National Sport,* Forum (Rocklin, Calif.: Prima Publishing, 1999), p. 330.

17. Greg Melikov, "The Ant Man," *Horseracing,* Suite 101.com, June 29, 1999.

18. Interview with Lester Antley.

19. Interview with Hamilton Smith.

20. Interview with Lou Rosenthal, September 5, 2001.

21. Tom Canavan, "Riders Get the Costly Word," AP A.M. cycle, November 21, 1985.

22. Gregory Gordon, UPI, April 20, 1981.

23. Steven Crist, "Racing-Fix Inquiry: Board Lacks Clout to Halt Corruption," *New York Times,* June 28, 1981, sec. 5, p. 6.

24. *Monmouth Park: 1985 Thoroughbred Facts Book,* May 24–August 31, p. 11.

25. Interviews with Sam Boulmetis, July 20, 2001, and Craig Perret, June 25, 2001.

26. Interview with Hamilton Smith.

27. Tom Canavan, AP A.M. cycle, November 21, 1985.

28. "Horse Racing Roundup," UPI, July 30, 1984.

29. *Monmouth Park: 1985 Thoroughbred Facts Book,* p. 11.

CHAPTER FOUR

1. Geoffrey Willis, "Santa Anita, the Great Race Place," *Roadsigns* (Route 66 Newsletter), vol. 5, num. 1, http://wemweb.com/chr66a/roadsign/ vol_5/v5num4.html.

2. Commission of Wartime Relocation and Internment of Civilians 1997: 139, quoted on "Life in the Centers," http://www.du.edu/~anballar/Life_in_the_Centers.html.

3. "Bob and Beverly Lewis, True Ducks with a Passion for Life and Horse Racing," University of Oregon News, http://giving.uoregon.edu/highlights/news/lewis.htmllewis.html.

4. Interview with Bob Lewis, October 17, 2000.

5. Ibid.

6. Jon Saraceno, "Charismatic's Owners Riding High on Life," *USA Today*, Arlington, May 12, 1999, 03C.

7. Ibid.

8. Gerda Reith, *The Age of Chance: Gambling in Western Culture* (London and New York: Routledge, 1999), p. 73.

9. Bob Baffert and Steve Hasking, *Dirt Road to the Derby* (Hong Kong, Lexington: The Blood-Horse, Inc., 1999), p. 124.

10. Ibid., p. 28.

11. Steve Wulf, "Hi Ho Silver Charm," *Time*, June 9, 1997, p. 72.

12. Baffert and Hasking, *Dirt Road to the Derby*, p. 34.

13. Interview with Bob and Beverly Lewis.

14. *Thoroughbred Champions, Top 100 Racehorses of the 20th Century* (Lexington: The Blood-Horse, Inc.), p. 10.

15. Edward L. Bowen, *Man o' War: Thoroughbred Legends* (Lexington: Eclipse Press, 2000), p. 112.

16. Ibid., p. 113.

17. Ibid., p. 139.

18. Ibid., p. 120.

19. Bill Christine, "From Claim to Fame; Until Recently, Charismatic Never Looked Like a Triple Crown Winner," *Los Angeles Times*, June 2, 1999, p. 1.

20. Interview with Bob and Beverly Lewis.

21. Bob Fortus, "Charisma Charisma Helps Lukas Make Point," *Times-Picayune*, New Orleans, May 2, 1999, C1.

22. Jon Saraceno, "Charismatic's Owners Riding High on Life," 03C.

CHAPTER FIVE

1. Steven Crist, "Big Chance for a Hot Jockey," *New York Times*, September 1, 1984, sec. 1, p. 15, col. 1.

2. Interview with Craig Perret.

3. Interview with Nick Zito, June 15, 2001.

4. Interview with Sam Boulmetis.

5. Interview with Joe Rocco, June 19, 2001.

6. Interview with Lou Rosenthal, September 5, 2001.

7. Pohla Smith, "Horse Racing: Puckish Antley Loved, Troubled," Post-Gazette.com, Sports, December 9, 2000. http://www.post-gazette.com/sports/notebooks/20001209smith.asp.

8. Interview with Angel Cordero Jr., March 16, 2001.

9. Ira Berkow, "Horse Racing: The Rides and Falls of an Emperor Named Cordero," *New York Times*, Late Edition, February 24, 1992, sec. C, p. 1.

10. Interview with Gary Stevens, January 26, 2001.

11. This idea that Antley had a special knack for the way a race would unfold came from many people, including Angel Cordero Jr., Vladimir Cerin, Ron Anderson, and Drew Mollica.

12. Susan Finley, "Chris Antley at the Crossroads," *The Thoroughbred Record*, April 1989, p. 353.

13. Interview with Dominick Bologna, January 23, 2001.

14. Jim Cornelius, "Supreme Court Bars Drug-Test Challenge," *The (Bergen) Record*, December 2, 1986, p. C13.

15. Bob Raimonto, "Antley Closing on 500 Winners," *The (Bergen) Record*, November 26, 1985, p. C08.

16. Neil Milbert, "His Off-Track Streak Just as Noteworthy," *Chicago Tribune*, April 25, 1989, Sports p. 4.

17. Andrew Beyer, "Cocaine Rides Antley," *Washington Post*, September 28, 1989, B1

18. Pohla Smith, "Commentary; Inside Track," UPI, July 24, 1986.

19. Beyer, "Cocaine Rides Antley," B1.

20. Interview with Drew Mollica, December 12, 2000.

21. Jim Cornelius, "Antley Fails Breath Test, Pays," *The (Bergen) Record*, October 22, 1986, p. C09.

22. Milbert, "His Off-Track Streak."

23. Steven Crist, "Horse Racing," *New York Times*, August 16, 1987, sec. 5, p. 4.

24. UPI, Sports News, September 2, 1987, BC Cycle.

25. "Antley: Record 9 Winners," *The (Bergen) Record*, November 2, 1987, p. D14.

26. Bill Christine, "Horse Racing," *Los Angeles Times*, November 5, 1987, Sports, p. 6.

27. Smith, "Horse Racing: Puckish Antley Loved, Troubled."

28. Mike Farrell, "By Night and Day, Antley Finds Winner's Circle Often," *The (Bergen) Record*, November 17, 1987, p. C07.

29. Steven Crist, "Antley Surrenders His Jockey License," *New York Times*, September 28, 1989, sec. D, p. 24.

30. Finley, "Chris Antley at the Crossroads," p. 356.

31. Tom Pedulla, "Antley High on Horsepower: Celebrated Jockey Seizes Reins to Battle Addiction," *USA Today*, May 14, 1999, 01C.

32. Ibid.

33. Paul Moran, "Antley Takes Himself Down," *Newsday*, September 28, 1989, Sports, p. 151.

34. Paul Moran, "Jockey Draws Fire for Leaving Horse," *The (Bergen) Record*, August 24, 1988, p. E09. I also interviewed Bruce Johnstone on December 5, 2001.

35. Interview with Jose Santos, March 9, 2001.

36. Finley, "Chris Antley at the Crossroads," p. 356.

37. Interview with Craig Perret.

38. Curtis L. Barrett, Ph.D., and Don C. Clippinger, *Winners! The Story of Alcohol and Drug-Abuse Programs in the Horse Racing Industry* (Highstown, N.J.: Daily Racing Form Press, 1997).

39. Milbert, "His Off-Track Streak."

40. Finley, "Chris Antley at the Crossroads," p. 357.

41. Milbert, "His Off-Track Streak."

42. Andrew Beyer, "Cocaine Use Puts Antley at Crossroads of Career," *Washington Post*, March 18, 1989, p. D8.

43. Ibid.

44. Beyer, "Cocaine Rides Antley."

45. Beyer, "Cocaine Use Puts Antley at Crossroads of Career."

46. Milbert, "His Off-Track Streak."

47. Steven Crist, "Antley Surrenders His Jockey License."

48. Milbert, "His Off-Track Streak."

49. Interview with Drew Mollica.

50. Crist, "Antley Surrenders His Jockey License."

51. Beyer, "Cocaine Rides Antley."

52. Steven Crist, "Antley Receives Ban from Belmont," *New York Times*, September 25, 1989, sec. C, p. 3, col. 5.

53. Crist, "Antley Surrenders His Jockey License."
54. Moran, "Antley Takes Himself Down."
55. Ibid.
56. Beyer, "Cocaine Rides Antley."

CHAPTER SIX

1. William Nack, "While the Rest of the World Sleeps," *Sports Illustrated*, May 6, 1985, p. 74.
2. Provided by D. Wayne Lukas, December 2001.
3. Chuck Culpepper, "Lukas Started Out Life as an Outsider," jdnews. com, June 5, 1999, http://www.jdnews.com/stories/1999/00/05.
4. Carol Flake, "The Intensity Factor," *The New Yorker*, December 26, 1988, p. 44.
5. Ibid.
6. Joe Drape, "Lukas Makes Himself Seen and Heard Once Again," *New York Times*, May 30, 1999, sec. 8, p. 1.
7. Robert Summers, "Confident Lukas Says This Is the One," *Buffalo News*, May 16, 1999, p. D10.
8. "The Domestication of Equus cabullus," http://members.nbci.com/_ XMXM/margret/history.html.
9. The story of the horse's being foolishly disciplined comes from a speech D. Wayne Lukas delivered on October 30, 1999, to the American Quarterhorse Racing Conference in Anaheim, California. I found these stories to be the best examples of Lukas's manner of speech, interests, and values that I came across in my research and tried to keep them as close to the original as I could. Used with permission of the *American Quarter Horse Racing Journal*.
10. Flake, "The Intensity Factor," p. 37.
11. Culpepper, "Lukas Started Out Life as an Outsider."
12. Owen Canfield, "Gold Key Fits Central's Lukas to a Tee," *The Hartford Courant*, February 18, 1992, Sports, p. C.
13. "Lukas Inducted Into Racing Hall," *Buffalo News*, August 10, 1999, p. B6.
14. Tim Reynolds, "Among the Immortals," *Times-Union*, Albany, August 10, 1999, p. C1.
15. Drape, "Lukas Makes Himself Seen."
16. Ibid.

17. Flake, "The Intensity Factor," p. 43.

18. Interview with Cot Campbell, May 3, 2000.

19. Nack, "While the Rest of the World Sleeps," p. 84.

20. Canfield, "Gold Key Fits Central's Lukas."

21. Ibid.

22. Nack, "While the Rest of the World Sleeps," p. 78.

23. D. Wayne Lukas, speech to the American Quarterhorse Racing Conference, October 30, 1999.

24. Nack, "While the Rest of the World Sleeps," p. 78.

25. Flake, "The Intensity Factor," p. 54.

26. Canfield, "Gold Key Fits Central's Lukas."

27. Nack, "While the Rest of the World Sleeps," p. 79.

28. Flake, "The Intensity Factor," p. 56.

29. Ibid.

30. Culpepper, "Lukas Started Out Life as an Outsider."

31. Nack, "While the Rest of the World Sleeps," p. 82.

32. Culpepper, "Lukas Started Out Life as an Outsider."

33. Nack, "While the Rest of the World Sleeps," p. 82.

34. Flake, "The Intensity Factor," p. 44.

35. D. Wayne Lukas, speech to the American Quarterhorse Racing Conference, October 30, 1999.

36. Flake, "While the Rest of the World Sleeps," p. 56.

37. Drape, "Lukas Makes Himself Seen."

38. Ibid.

39. Flake, "The Intensity Factor," p. 62.

40. Ibid., p. 63.

41. Ibid., p. 65.

42. Robert Henwood, "Death on a Sunday," *Blood-Horse Weekly*, December 4, 1982.

43. Joe Bagan, *Lukas at Auction* (Denver: Sachs-Lawlor, Co., 1989), p. 45.

44. Interview with Tom and Robyn Roach.

45. Flake, "The Intensity Factor," p. 66.

46. D. Wayne Lukas, speech to the American Quarterhorse Racing Conference, October 30, 1999.

47. Ann Hagedorn Auerbach, *Wild Ride: The Rise and Tragic Fall of Calumet Farm, Inc.* (New York: Henry Holt, 1994), p. 303.

48. Drape, "Lukas Makes Himself Seen."

49. Ibid.

50. Jay Hovdey, "Journey to the Winner's Circle," *Reader's Digest* 146 (May 1995), pp. 86–91.

51. Drape, "Lukas Makes Himself Seen."

52. Alan Truex, "Trainer of the '90s; Hard-working and Proud, Lukas Reigns Supreme," *Houston Chronicle*, May 14, 1999, p. 5.

53. Flake, "The Intensity Factor," p. 44.

54. Bob Baffert and Steve Hasking, *Dirt Road to the Derby* (Hong Kong, Lexington: The Blood-Horse, Inc., 1999), p. 79.

55. Ibid., p. 76.

56. Ibid., p. 30.

57. Ibid., p. 123.

58. Ibid., p. 32.

59. Bill Christine, "Honor Won't Leave Lukas Speechless," *Los Angeles Times*, April 28, 1999, p. 1.

60. Baffert and Hasking, *Dirt Road to the Derby*, p. 32.

61. Bill Christine, "Charismatic May End up with Last Laugh," *The Tennessean*, June 3, 1999, http://www.tennessean.com/sii/99/06/03/horsey03.shtml.

62. Interview with Vladimir Cerin, October 18, 2000.

63. "Sports: Jockey Wins in Paris Debut," http://www.sptimes.com/Sports/122898/Jockey_wins_in_paris_.html.

64. Interview with Amy LoPresti, August 21, 2001.

65. Bee Sports Staff and News Services, "Bell Slams Home Easy Victory for Sac City," *Sacramento Bee*, January 9, 1999, p. D2.

66. Alan Truex, "Kentucky Derby/Charismatic Beats Long Odds/30–1 Pick Holds off Menifee as Lukas Wins for Fourth Time," *Houston Chronicle*, May 2, 1999, p. 1.

67. ABC 1999 Preakness coverage.

68. Tom Pedulla, "On the Threshold of Greatness Charismatic, Antley Can Write Amazing Conclusion to Fairy Tale," *USA Today*, May 17, 1999, p. 03C.

69. Christine, "Charismatic May End up with Last Laugh."

70. Ibid.

71. Mickey Herskowitz, "Few Could Have Prophesied This Charismatic Movement," *Houston Chronicle*, May 3, 1999, p. 11.

72. "Kentucky Derby: Call to the Derby Post Weekly Reports," February 23, 1999, http://www.derbypost.com/Archive/Reports/1999reports2.html.

73. Truex, "Kentucky Derby/Charismatic Beats Long Odds."
74. "Weekend Motorcross Events at Arco," *Sacramento Bee*, February 25, 1999, Sports, p. E8.
75. Bill Finley, "Baffert Hold on Kentucky Derby Gets Loose," *New York Daily News*, April 2, 1999, Sports, p. 102.
76. Christine, "Charismatic May End up with Last Laugh."
77. Ibid.
78. Ed Fountaine, "Bluegrass and Wood Looking Like Winners," *New York Post*, April 1, 1999, p. 106.
79. "Prime Timber Scores High," *St. Petersburg Times*, April 5, 1999, p. 5C.
80. Herskowitz, "Few Could Have Prophesied."
81. Billy Reed, "Best Usually Shine Even in Big Field," *Lexington Herald-Leader*, http://www.kentuckyconnect.com/heraldleader/news/050499/kyhoofs/hoofs/hoofsdocs/04reed.htm.

CHAPTER SEVEN

1. "Cambridgeshire England Geneology-Ancestors-Frederick ARCHER," *Newmarket Journal*, November 13, 1886, http://www.rootsweb.com/~engam/FrederickArcher.htm.
2. Horse Racing Information Online, Direct Racing Ltd., www.directracing.com/cgi-bin/ads/ads/.cgi.
3. Interview with Laffit Pincay, January 5, 2002.
4. Susan Finley, "Chris Antley at the Crossroads," *The Thoroughbred Record*, April 1989, p. 358.
5. "Horse Racing; Returning to Track, Antley Wins Three," *New York Times*, Late Edition, Sunday, March 18, 1990, sec. 8, p. 5.
6. Paul Moran, "Cordero Ages Frantically Not Gracefully," *Los Angeles Times*, August 11, 1991, p. 7.
7. "Horse Racing; Suspension for Cordero," *New York Times*, Late Edition-Final, September 11, 1990, sec. D, p. 22.
8. Steven Crist, "Breeder's Cup: Racing's Darkest Day, A Belmont Disaster; Go For Wand and Mr. Nickerson Dead," *New York Times*, October 28, 1990, sec. 8, p. 1.
9. Interview with Lester Antley, March 24, 2001.
10. Interview with Angel Cordero Jr., March 16, 2001.
11. Interview with Nick Zito, June 15, 2001.
12. Interview with Lester Antley.

13. Lenny Shulman, "Back on a Tear," *Kentucky Derby Souvenir Magazine*, May 6, 2000, p. 31.

14. George Vecsey, "Sport of the Times; Young Angel Strikes Gold in the Derby," *New York Times*, May 5, 1991, sec. 8, p. 1.

15. Interview with Nick Zito.

16. Billy Reed, "Zito Should Get Best, Pick Day over Antley," *Herald-Leader*, April 23, 1991.

17. The account of how Strike the Gold moved in the Derby comes substantially from Antley's direct quotations in "Back on a Tear," starting on p. 32. Angel Cordero Jr. also confirmed the description of this race in his interview. The progress of the other horses primarily comes from a review of the 1991 ABC Preakness coverage and the description in the charts for the race.

18. Ray Buck, "Wide Strike Good as Gold in Derby Win," *Houston Post*, May 5, 1991, B1.

19. Vinnie Perrone, " 'I Didn't Want to Put It Down,' Says Antley of Arm Raised in Triumph," *Washington Post*, May 5, 1991, p. B12.

20. Buck, "Wide Strike Good as Gold."

21. Shulman, "Back on a Tear," p. 31.

22. Ron Indrisano, "Striking Peace Pact Brophy May Sell 'Gold' Interest," *Boston Globe*, October 5, 1991, p. 38.

23. Paul Moran, "Cordero Ages Frantically Not Gracefully."

24. Ira Berkow, "Horse Racing: The Rides and Falls of an Emperor Named Cordero," *New York Times*, Late Edition, February 24, 1992, sec. C, p. 1.

25. Ibid.

26. Ibid.

27. Interview with Angelo Cordero Jr.

28. Thomas Grant Jr., "Hometown Hero," the 39th Annual Elloree Trials special section, *The Times and Democrat*, Orangeburg, South Carolina, March 23, 2001, p. 2.

29. Joe Drape, "Horse Racing: An Addict with One Weapon: Hope," *New York Times*, May 15, 1999, sec. D, p. 1, col. 3.

30. Ibid.

31. Bill Christine, "Thoroughbred Racing: Antley Hopes Move Revives Riding Career," *Los Angeles Times*, January 13, 1994, p. 9.

32. Interview with Ron Anderson, February 2, 2001.

33. Interview with Angel Cordero Jr.

34. Ibid.

35. Christine, "Thoroughbred Racing: Antley Hopes Move Revives Riding Career."

36. Interview with Gary Stevens.

37. Interview with Fernando Valenzuela, January 8, 2001.

38. Interview with Mace Siegal.

39. Interviews with Vladimir Cerin and Fernando Valenzuela.

40. Pohla Smith, "Horse Racing: Puckish Antley Loved, Troubled," Post-Gazette.com, Sports, December 9, 2000, http://www.post-gazette.com/sports/notebooks/20001209smith.asp.

41. Interview with Vladimir Cerin.

42. "Antley Says He's 'Happiest Person in the World,'" *Sunday Tennessean*, May 30, 1999, http://www.tennessean.com/sii/99/05/30/antley30.shtml.

43. Interview with Bill Barisoff, June 19, 2001.

44. Interview with Don Murray, January 11, 2001.

45. Grant, "Hometown Hero."

46. Joseph Durso, "Aboard Gentlemen, Stevens Wins Pimlico," *New York Times*, Late Edition, May 11, 1997, sec. 8, p. 11.

47. Interview with Drew Mollica, December 12, 2000.

48. Interview with Nick Zito.

49. Bill Finley, "Antley Battles Bulge," *New York Daily News*, January 8, 1999, Sports, p. 96; and Bill Finley, "Driving One Hard Bargain," *New York Daily News*, July 3, 1997, Sports, p. 118.

50. Elizabeth Benjamin, "Requiem for an Equine Athlete," *Times-Union*, Albany, August 9, 1997, p. B1.

51. Interview with Drew Mollica.

52. Dave Johnson, ESPN.com, December 10, 2000, http://espn.go.com/horse/2000/1207/929395.html.

53. Bill Christine, "A Weight Is Lifted," *Los Angeles Times*, May 12, 1999, p. 1.

54. Ron Longley, "A Harsh Weighting Game Losing Pounds Wreaks Havoc on Jockey's Health," *The Toronto Sun*, Sports, p. 111.

55. Interview with Drew Mollica.

56. Interview with Charlie McCaul.

57. Drape, "Horse Racing: An Addict with One Weapon."

58. Interview with Ron Anderson.

59. William Gildea, "The Ride of His Life; Charismatic Jockey Antley Rebounds from Personal Problems," *Washington Post*, June 3, 1999, p. D01.

60. The description of Antley's time at Grandview came from interviews with Michelle Antley, Ron Anderson, Don Murray, and Cathy Park.

61. Jack Wilkinson, "Belmont Stakes: Ride of His Life," *Atlanta Constitution*, June 2, 1999, p. E1.

62. Interview with Kellie Cerin, December 28, 2000.

63. Interview with Ron Anderson.

64. Bill Nack, "Comeback Kid," *Sports Illustrated*, May 10, 1999, p. 40.

65. Interview with Ron Anderson.

66. Interview with Lester Antley.

67. "A Triple Crown Threat Is on Right Track with Stocks," *Gambling Magazine*, http://www.gamblingmagazine.com/articles/23/23-65.htm.

68. Wilkinson, "Belmont Stakes: Ride of His Life."

69. Ibid.

70. Ibid.

71. Bob Fortus, "Antley Wins Battle of Bulge, Then Derby Jockey Shows Determination in His Bid to Return to Riding," *Times-Picayune*, New Orleans, May 2, 1999, p. C5.

72. Tom Pedulla, "Antley High on Horsepower: Celebrated Jockey Seizes Reins to Battle Addiction," *USA Today*, May 14, 1999, p. 01C.

73. "Antley Says He's 'Happiest Person in the World,' " http://www.tennessean.com/sii/99/05/30/antley30.shtml.

74. Shulman, "Back on a Tear," p. 34.

75. Shannon Conner, "Antley Gets Redemption; Lukas Gets His 4th Win," *St. Louis Post-Dispatch*, May 2, 1999, p. F1.

76. Shulman, "Back on a Tear," p. 34.

77. Wilkinson, "Belmont Stakes: Ride of His Life."

78. Ibid.

79. Ibid.

80. Shulman, "Back on a Tear," p. 34.

81. Interview with Ron Anderson.

82. Interview with Coley Brown Jr., August 21, 2001.

83. Wilkinson, "Belmont Stakes: Ride of His Life."

84. Interview with Eugenia Antley, March 23, 2001.

85. Interview with Reverend C. Clark McCrary, December 14, 2000.

86. Wilkinson, "Belmont Stakes: Ride of His Life."

87. Shulman, "Back on a Tear," p. 34.

88. Gildea, "The Ride of His Life."

89. ABC 1999 Preakness coverage.

90. Bob Fortus, "Antley Wins Battle of Bulge," p. C5.
91. Bob Mieszerski, "Sentimental Journey; Charismatic's Jockey Chris Ant-ley Went Home to South Carolina to Lose Weight and Regain His Appetite for Racing," *Los Angeles Times*, June 1, 1999, p. 1.
92. Interview with Ron Anderson.

CHAPTER EIGHT

1. Walt Whitman, *Leaves of Grass* (New York: Bantam, 1983), p. 356.

CHAPTER NINE

1. Call to the Derby Post: Horse Racing in Kentucky, Churchill Downs/Kentucky Derby History, Part III, The Legacy of Matt Winn, http://www.derbypost.com/churchill3.html.
2. Ibid.
3. Ibid.
4. Ibid.
5. Santa Anita Park, April 17th, Race 4, Equibase, ChartPlus.
6. Alan Truex, "Kentucky Derby/Charismatic Beats Long Odds/30-1 Pick Holds off Menifee as Lukas Wins for Fourth Time," *Houston Chronicle*, May 2, 1999, p. 1.
7. Tom Pedulla, "On the Threshold of Greatness Charismatic, Antley Can Write Amazing Conclusion to Fairy Tale," *USA Today*, May 17, 1999, p. 03C.
8. William Gildea, "The Ride of His Life; Charismatic Jockey Antley Rebounds from Personal Problems," *Washington Post*, June 3, 1999, p. D01.
9. Interview with Charlie McCaul.
10. Interview with Ron Anderson, February 2, 2001.
11. ABC 1999 Kentucky Derby coverage.
12. Interview with Sheikh Mohammed at Kentucky Derby 2000.
13. Marty McGee, "More Tough Times for Patin," Daily Racing Form, April 18, 1999, p. 8.
14. Interview with John Passero, August 18, 2001.
15. McGee, "More Tough Times for Patin."
16. Bill Christine, "A Weight Is Lifted," *Los Angeles Times*, May 12, 1999, p. 1.

17. D. Wayne Lukas, speech to the American Quarterhorse Racing Conference, October 30, 1999.

18. "Right Dream, Right Post, Wrong Trainer," *Lexington Herald-Leader*, Associated Press, May 4, 1999, http://www.kentuckyconnect.com/heraldleader/news/050499/kyhoofs/derbydocs/04first_american.

19. Interview with Charlie McCaul.

20. Interview with Vladimir Cerin.

21. Mark Story, "Luck, Drag Race Land Lewises Win," *Lexington Herald-Leader*, May 2, 1999, http://www.kentuckyconnect.com/heraldleader/news/050299/kyhoofs/derbydocs/02aaowner.htm.

22. Interview with Mike Smith, September 5, 2001.

23. Interview with Fernando Valenzuela.

24. Interview with Craig Perret.

25. *Lexington Herald-Leader*, May 2, 1999, p. AA7.

26. Ibid.

27. *Louisville Courier-Journal*, May 8, 1983.

28. *Lexington Herald-Leader*, May 2, 1999, p. AA7.

29. Chuck Culpepper, "Believe It, Antley Wins Again," *Lexington Herald-Leader*, May 2, 1999, http://www.kentuckyconnect.com/heraldleader/news/050299/kyhoofs/derbydocs/02aajockey.html.

30. Tom Pedulla, "Return Is Bigger Win to Antley," *USA Today*, May 3, 1999, p. 07C.

31. Bob Fortus, "Charisma Charisma Helps Lukas Make Point," *Times-Picayune*, May 2, 1999, p. C1.

32. Interview with Luke Kruytbosch, May 4, 2000.

33. Interview with starting judge, Roger Nagle, June 6, 2001.

34. ABC 1999 Preakness coverage.

35. "Antley Says He's 'Happiest Person in the World,'" *Sunday Tennessean*, May 30, 1999, http://www.tennessean.com/sii/99/05/30/antley30.shtml.

36. Lenny Shulman, "Back on a Tear," *Kentucky Derby Souvenir Magazine*, May 6, 2000, p. 36.

37. ABC 1999 Preakness coverage.

38. Bill Nack, "Comeback Kid," *Sports Illustrated*, May 10, 1999, p. 40.

39. Nack, "Comeback Kid."

40. Shulman, "Back on a Tear," pp. 28, 36.

41. Chuck Culpepper, "Believe It, Antley Wins Again."

42. Fortus, "Charisma Charisma Helps Lukas Make Point."

43. Christine, "A Weight Is Lifted."
44. Chuck Culpepper, "Big Field Better, Lukas Says; Baffert Disagrees," *Lexington Herald-Leader*, May 3, 1999, http://www.kentuckyconnect.com/heraldleader/news/050399/kyhoofs/derbydocs/03derbynotes.

CHAPTER TEN

1. Gerda Reith, *The Age of Chance: Gambling in Western Culture* (London and New York: Routledge, 1999), p. 7.
2. Ibid.
3. "Gambling Impact and Behavior Study," Report to the National Gambling Impact Study Commission, submitted by National Opinion Research Center at the University of Chicago, Gemini Research, the Lewin Group, Christiansen/Cummings Association, April 1, 1999, p. viii.
4. Ibid., p. x.
5. Reith, *The Age of Chance*, p. 15.
6. Howard Eves, *Great Moments in Mathematics After 1650*, Dolciani Mathematical Expositions (United States: The Mathematical Association of America, 1983) vol. 7, p. 3.
7. J. Philip Jones, *Gambling Yesterday and Today* (Great Britain: W. J. Holman Limited Dawlish, 1973), p. 21.
8. Reith, *The Age of Chance*, p. 60.
9. Jones, *Gambling Yesterday and Today*, p. 130.
10. Reith, *The Age of Chance*, p. 65.
11. Jones, *Gambling Yesterday and Today*, p. 139.
12. Sanford J. Mock, "Playing the Lottery with Washington," *Manuscripts* 1998 50(1): 5–13.
13. Frederick W. Preston, Bo J. Bernhard, Robert E. Hunter, Shannon L. Bybee, "Gambling as Stigmatized Behavior: Regional Relabeling and the Law," *Annals of the American Academy of Political and Social Science*, March 1998, vol. 556, p. 186.
14. Reith, *The Art of Chance*, p. 142.
15. Jones, *Gambling Yesterday and Today*, p. 92.
16. Reith, *The Age of Chance*, p. 75.
17. Morris Kline, *Mathematical Thought from Ancient to Modern Times* (New York: Oxford University Press, 1972).
18. Eves, *Great Moments in Mathematics*, pp. 4–5.
19. Alexander Pope, "Essay on Man," Epistle i, line 289.

20. Reith, *The Art of Chance*, p. 29.
21. Kline, *Mathematical Thought*, p. 495.
22. Lloyd Wendt and Herman Kogan, *Bet a Million! The Story of John W. Gates* (Indianapolis and New York: The Bobbs-Merrill Co., 1948), p. 134.
23. Robert Irving Warshaw, *Bet-a-Million Gates: The Story of a Plunger* (New York: Greenberg Publisher Inc., 1932), p. 32.
24. Ibid., p. 22.
25. Wendt and Kogan, *Bet a Million!*, p. 50.
26. Ibid.
27. Warshaw, *Bet-a-Million Gates*, p. 184.
28. Ibid., p. 43.
29. Ibid., p. 60.
30. Wendt and Kogan, *Bet a Million!*, p. 18.
31. Ibid., p. 243.
32. Ibid., p. 179.
33. Ibid., p. 302.
34. Anthony DeBartolo, "Who Caused the Great Chicago Fire of 1871? Mrs. O'Leary's Cow? Or Louis M. Cohn?" Hyde Park Media, http://www.hydeparkmedia.com/cohn.html.
35. Jones, *Gambling Yesterday and Today*, p. 179.
36. Tom Ainslie, *Ainslie's Complete Guide to Thoroughbred Racing* (New York: Simon & Schuster), p. 45.

CHAPTER ELEVEN

1. Bob Fortus, "Charisma Helps Lukas Make Point," *Times-Picayune*, New Orleans, May 2, 1999, C1.
2. "Dogwood Stable: An Interview with Cot Campbell," http://www.dogwoodstable.com/cot_campbell.html.
3. Interview with Angel Cordero Jr.
4. *2000 Media Guide*, Laurel Park, Pimlico Race Course, p. 7.
5. Ibid., p. 62.
6. Ibid., p. 8.
7. William Gildea, "The Trainer with Charisma; Wayne Lukas Readies Surprise Derby-Winner Charismatic for Preakness," *Washington Post*, May 14, 1999, p. D01.
8. Joe Drape, "Horse Racing: An Addict with One Weapon: Hope," *New York Times*, May 15, 1999, sec. D, p. 1, col. 3.

9. Michael Madden, "Antley: Long Shot Has Come In," *Boston Globe*, June 3, 1999, p. C7.

10. "Antley Says He's 'Happiest Person in the World,' " *Sunday Tennessean*, May 30, 1999, http://www.tennessean.com/sii/99/05/30/antley30.shtml.

11. Ed Fountaine, "Derby Champ Battled Inner Demons," *New York Post*, December 4, 2000.

12. Tom Pedulla, "Antley High on Horsepower: Celebrated Jockey Seizes Reins to Battle Addiction," *USA Today*, May 14, 1999, p. 01C.

13. Ibid.

14. Madden, "Antley: Long Shot Has Come In."

15. Joe Drape, "A Race for the Riders," *New York Times*, June 5, 1999, p. 5.

16. ABC 1999 Preakness coverage.

17. Bill Christine, "Now He's Doubly Charismatic," *Los Angeles Times*, May 16, 1999, p. 1.

18. Joe Drape, "A Race for the Riders."

19. Interview with Gary Stevens; ABC 1999 Preakness coverage; *Boston Globe*; *USA Today*; Andrew Beyer, "It's Another Charismatic Display; Horse Needs Belmont for Triple Crown," *Washington Post*, May 16, 1999, p. D01; Christine, "Now He's Doubly Charismatic."

20. Joe Drape, "A Race for the Riders."

21. Madden, "Antley: Long Shot Has Come In."

22. Bill Christine, "From Claim to Fame; Until Recently, Charismatic Never Looked Like a Triple Crown Winner," *Los Angeles Times*, June 2, 1999, p. 1.

23. ABC 1999 Preakness coverage.

24. William Gildea, "The Ride of His Life; Charismatic Jockey Antley Rebounds from Personal Problems," *Washington Post*, June 3, 1999, p. D01.

25. Beyer, "It's Another Charismatic Display."

26. Bill Christine, "Now He's Doubly Charismatic," p. 1.

27. Interview with Virginia Ballenger, June 22, 2001.

28. Interview with Hamilton Smith.

29. Jack Wilkinson, "Belmont Stakes: Ride of His Life," *Atlanta Constitution*, June 2, 1999, p. E1.

CHAPTER TWELVE

1. Interview with Gary Pusillo, July 30, 2001.
2. Bill Christine, "Signs from Above," *Los Angeles Times*, May 15, 1999, p. 1.
3. Interview with Pat Day, June 7, 2000.
4. Interview with Jorge Chavez, May 10, 2001.
5. Interview with Roger Velez and Hal Rose, May 7, 2000.
6. Interview with Jim Watson, June 5, 2000.
7. "Secretariat Turns Nightmare into Perfect Finish," *The Sporting News*, May 30, 1998.
8. Interview with Angel Cordero Jr.
9. Interview with Mike Smith.
10. Larry Wood posting, "Charismatic Wins Preakness," Current Events, Divine Viewpoint of History 5-14-99 thru 5-15-99, http://members.nbci.com/_XMCM/wood11/history/19990514.htm.

CHAPTER THIRTEEN

1. Michael Madden, "Antley: Long Shot Has Come In," *Boston Globe*, June 3, 1999, p. C7.
2. 2000 Media Guide, Laurel Park, Pimlico Race Course, p. 8.
3. Joe Drape, "Strategies Vary When It Comes to the Belmont," *New York Times*, sec. D, p. 8, col. 1.
4. Edward L. Bowen, *Man o' War: Thoroughbred Legends* (Lexington: Eclipse Press, 2000), p. 16.
5. Ibid., p 19.
6. Ibid., p. 15.
7. 2001 NYRA Yearbook & Media Guide, Aqueduct, Belmont Park, Saratoga, p. B32.
8. Edward L. Bowen, *Man o' War*, p. 18.
9. Ibid.
10. Robert J. Summers, "Confident Lukas Says This Is the One," *Buffalo News*, May 16, 1999, p. D10.
11. Joe Drape, "A Race for the Riders," *New York Times*, June 5, 1999, p. 5.
12. Interviews with Ron Anderson and Don Murray.
13. Steve Hummer, "Likable Lewises Have Horse Sense," *Atlanta Journal-*

Constitution, June 4, 1999, Sports, p. 7E.

14. Beth Harris, "Thrill of Chasing Triple Crown Completes Antley Comeback," Associated Press, May 29, 1999.
15. "Antley Says He's 'Happiest Person in the World,'" *Sunday Tennessean*, May 30, 1999, http://www.tennessean.com/sii/99/05/30/antley30.shtml.
16. Madden, "Antley: Long Shot Has Come In."
17. Joe Durso, "Charismatic Is Fully Prepared in His Bid for Triple Crown," *New York Times*, June 5, 1999, p. 1.
18. Skip Bayless, "Charismatic's Ruin? Scent of a Lady," *Chicago Tribune*, June 6, 1999, Sports, p. 1.
19. Jay Privman, "A Tale of Two Trainers and One Triple Crown," Daily Racing Form-Belmont Stakes 131 Coverage, http://www.drf2000.com/home/hdp_cent/bs2.html.
20. Durso, "Charismatic Is Fully Prepared."
21. Ibid.
22. Antley's *New York Post* diary, June 2 through June 4, 1999.
23. "Charismatic: From Dawn to Darkness," jdnews.com, http://www.jdnews.com/stories/1999/00/00.
24. Joe Drape, "Horse Racing: For Charismatic's Camp, an Afternoon of Pain and Shock," *New York Times*, June 6, 1999, sec. 8, p. 9, col. 1.
25. Drape, "A Race for the Riders."
26. Bayless, "Charismatic's Ruin?"
27. Shannon Conner, "Charismatic Breaks Two Bones Injury Ends Career as Triple Crown Bid Falls Short," *St. Louis-Dispatch*, June 6, 1999, p. F1.
28. Bob Fortus, "Team Charismatic Worried About Injured Horse," *Times-Picayune*, June 6, 1999, p. C4.
29. Mickey Herskowitz, "Broken Leg Compounds Charismatic's Misery," *Houston Chronicle*, June 6, 1999, p. 1.
30. St. Louis Dispatch, Rob Longley, "Belmont Ends in Tears," *Toronto Sun*, http://www.canoe.ca/Belmont/jun6_bel.html.
31. Pat Forde, "Antley May Have Saved Charismatic's Life," *Louisville Courier-Journal*, June 6, 1999, http://www.tennessean.com/sii/99/06/06/life06.shtml.
32. Interview with Bob and Beverly Lewis.
33. *Thoroughbred Champions, Top 100 Racehorses of the 20th Century* (Lexington: The Blood-Horse, Inc.), p. 119.
34. Interview with Bob and Beverly Lewis.

35. Andrew Beyer, "A Heartbreaker But Not a Triple Crown Talent," Daily Racing Form—Belmont Stakes 131 Coverage, http://www.drf2000.com/home/hdp_cent/bs2.html.

CHAPTER FIFTEEN

1. Interview with Charlie McCaul.
2. Bill Christine, "Horse Racing; Antley Seeking a 'Weigh' Back," *Los Angeles Times*, March 24, 2000, D10.
3. Dave Johnson, ESPN.com, http:/espn.go.com/horse/s/2000/1207/929395.
4. Interview with Bob Baffert, December 28, 2000.
5. David Leon Moore, "A Jockey's Final, Violent Ride," *USA Today*, December 19, 2000.
6. David S. Jackson, "Death and the Horseman," *Time*, December 18, 2000.
7. Pasadena Police, DUI Evaluation & Arrest Report, July 26, 2000.
8. Bill Pennington, "Antley's Wild Ride Reaches Violent End," *New York Times*, December 17, 2000, Sports, p. 4.
9. Pasadena Police Department, Crime Report, September 28, 2000.
10. Bill Pennington, "Antley's Wild Ride Reaches Violent End," p. 1.
11. Interview with John Henna and "Preliminary Findings of the Death of Chris Antley," Luper and Associates, January 19, 2001.
12. Interview with Detective Pete Hettema, January 26, 2001.
13. Interview with Commander Mary Shander, February 28, 2001.

CHAPTER SIXTEEN

1. Ed Fountaine, "Lukas Laments Not Giving Antley the Boot," *New York Post*, June 9, 2001, http://www.nypost.com/06092001/sports/41393.htm.
2. Gerda Reith, *The Age of Chance: Gambling in Western Culture* (London and New York: Routledge, 1999), p. 150.

INDEX